The Art of
Studio Gainax

ALSO BY DANI CAVALLARO
AND FROM McFARLAND

*Anime Intersections:
Tradition and Innovation in Theme and Technique* (2007)

The Animé Art of Hayao Miyazaki (2006)

*The Cinema of Mamoru Oshii:
Fantasy, Technology and Politics* (2006)

The Art of Studio Gainax

Experimentation, Style and Innovation at the Leading Edge of Anime

DANI CAVALLARO

McFarland & Company, Inc., Publishers
Jefferson, North Carolina, and London

LIBRARY OF CONGRESS CATALOGUING-IN-PUBLICATION DATA

Cavallaro, Dani.
The art of Studio Gainax : experimentation, style and innovation at the leading edge of anime / Dani Cavallaro.
p. cm.
Includes bibliographical references and index.

ISBN 978-0-7864-3376-6
softcover : 50# alkaline paper ∞

1. GAINAX (Firm)   2. Animated films — Japan — History and criticism.   I. Title.
NC1766.J32G353   2009   791.43'340952 — dc22   2008038235

British Library cataloguing data are available

©2009 Dani Cavallaro. All rights reserved

No part of this book may be reproduced or transmitted in any form or by any means, electronic or mechanical, including photocopying or recording, or by any information storage and retrieval system, without permission in writing from the publisher.

On the cover: Poster art for the 1995-1996 television series *Neon Genesis Evangelion* (ADV Films/Photofest)

Manufactured in the United States of America

*McFarland & Company, Inc., Publishers
Box 611, Jefferson, North Carolina 28640
www.mcfarlandpub.com*

To Paddy,
with platinum gratitude

Table of Contents

PREFACE 1

1. A Brief History of Studio Gainax 5
2. *Royal Space Force: The Wings of Honneamise* (1987) 20
3. *Gunbuster* (1988) 26
4. *Nadia: The Secret of Blue Water* (1990–1991) 40
5. *Otaku no Video* (1991) 53
6. *Neon Genesis Evangelion* I — The TV Series (1995–1996) 59
7. *Neon Genesis Evangelion* II — The Movies (1997; 2007–2008) . . . 78
8. *His and Her Circumstances* (1998–1999) 111
9. *FLCL* (2000) 123
10. *Mahoromatic — Automatic Maiden* (2001–2002) 141
11. *Magical Shopping Arcade Abenobashi* (2002) 154
12. *This Ugly Yet Beautiful World* (2004) 160
13. The *Diebuster* Saga (2004–2006) 178
14. The Anime Magic of Studio Gainax 201

FILMOGRAPHY 205

APPENDIX: ANIME PRODUCTIONS WITH
STUDIO GAINAX MEMBERS 213

CHAPTER NOTES 217

BIBLIOGRAPHY 223

INDEX 227

We like to think we live in daylight,
but half the world is always dark;
and fantasy, like poetry,
speaks the language of the night

      — Ursula K. Le Guin
      World Magazine
      21 November 1979

Preface

This book is the product of a deeply ingrained interest in the animated medium in general, and in the art of anime in particular, incrementally refined over time by research into the output of diverse directors and studios within the field. Its objective is to document the prismatic achievement of one of the most adventurous and widely esteemed anime companies currently on the scene — Studio Gainax.

Although Gainax's immense popularity is a factor that could in itself justify the devotion of a monographic study to its members and to their diverse creations, what is more intriguing still is the studio's unique approach to animation. Formal experimentation, genre-straddling, self-reflexivity, unpredictable plot twists, a gourmet palate for stylishness, proverbially controversial endings and a singularly iconoclastic worldview are among the major components of Gainax's individual cachet. These aspects of its work, moreover, have emerged from the studio's temerarious engagement with all of the principal anime genres. This has served to establish its reputation as a veritable groundbreaking presence in domains as diverse as space opera, steampunk, apocalyptic narrative, psychological drama, slapstick comedy, modern romance and mockumentary work on the vagaries of anime fandom. In each chapter, attention will be drawn to the various ways in which the studio has engaged in the pursuit of pioneering styles and plotlines, with a focus on experimental gestures peculiar to individual productions.

In assessing the present relevance of a study of Gainax's anime, it is vital to emphasize that the company has recently found itself at the receiving end of a considerable amount of critical attention. This scenario is attributable to several factors, the most notable among them including:

- the recent U.S. releases on DVD of the studio's seminal OVA *Gunbuster* (1988), of the sequel *Gunbuster 2* (2004–2006) and of its twentieth-anniversary production *This Ugly Yet Beautiful World* (2004);
- the re-release in stunningly enhanced formats in both the U.S. and the U.K. of the *Evangelion* saga (1995–1997);
- the airing of an entirely novel TV series titled *Making Breakthrough Gurren Lagann* (2007) that promises to reinvent established anime genres and thus consolidate the company's fame as a boldly experimentative enterprise;
- the ongoing production and release of four more brandnew *Evangelion*-related features which bear witness to undying interest in the franchise.

The last named deserves special notice in the context of this book. Indeed, while *Evangelion* has consistently held a focal position in the domain of anime fandom (not least thanks to the steady turnout of ancillary goods over the years), news of those imminent releases has fuelled current levels of interest in the franchise within not merely the anime sector but also the realm of animation at large.

In seeking to provide a critical analysis of a kind that has not yet materialized in the realm of Anglophone anime scholarship, the book does not presume to cover every single Gainax production. Given the company's extraordinarily prolific performance, doing so would sacrifice depth for quantity. It seeks instead to provide detailed evaluations of an appropriately chosen gamut of titles, selected for the following reasons:

- they exemplify the studio's cumulative aesthetics and approach to anime;
- they illustrate individual directors' and artists' distinctive signatures;
- they represent some of the studio's most original contributions to the anime universe in both thematic and technical terms;
- they rank among the most popular Gainax productions in the West and are therefore likely to be of interest to prospective readers of this book.

The Gainax works to be explored in detail in the ensuing chapters include:

- *Royal Space Force: The Wings of Honneamise* (feature film; dir. Hiroyuki Yamaga, 1987)
- *Gunbuster* (OVA series; dir. Hideaki Anno, 1988)
- *Nadia: The Secret of Blue Water* (TV series; dir. Hideaki Anno, 1990–1991)
- *Otaku no Video* (OVA series; dir. Takeshi Mori, 1991)
- *Neon Genesis Evangelion* (TV series; chief dir. Hideaki Anno, 1995–1996)
- *Neon Genesis Evangelion: Death & Rebirth* (feature film; dirs. Hideaki Anno, Masayuki [*Death*], Kazuya Tsurumaki [*Rebirth*], 1997)
- *Neon Genesis Evangelion: The End of Evangelion* (feature film; dir. Hideaki Anno, 1997)
- *Rebuild of Evangelion* (feature films x 4; dirs. Hideaki Anno and Kazuya Tsurumaki, 2007–2008)
- *His and Her Circumstances* (TV series; chief dir. Hideaki Anno, 1998–1999)
- *FLCL* (OVA series; dir. Kazuya Tsurumaki, 2000)
- *Mahoromatic—Automatic Maiden* (TV series; dir. Hiroyuki Yamaga, 2001–2002)
- *Magical Shopping Arcade Abenobashi* (TV series; dir. Hiroyuki Yamaga, 2002)
- *This Ugly Yet Beautiful World* (TV series; dir. Shouji Saeki, 2004)
- *Gunbuster 2* (OVA series; dir. Kazuya Tsurumaki, 2004–2006)
- *Gunbuster vs. Diebuster: Aim for the Top Gattai Movie* (feature films x 2; dir. Kazuya Tsurumaki, 2006)

Where relevant, the book will also engage in some in-depth assessment of related Gainax works, including *Petite Princess Yucie* (TV series; dir. Masahiko Otsuka, 2002–2003), *The Melody of Oblivion* (TV series; dirs. Atsushi Takeyama and Hiroshi Nishikiori, 2004) and *Making Breakthrough Gurren Lagann* (TV series; dir. Hiroyuki Imaishi, 2007). *Petite Princess Yucie* offers a variation on the age-related theme at the heart of *Mahoromatic—Automatic Maiden*, transposing it into the realms of magic and legend, whilst also mirroring some of the emotional conflicts explored in *This Ugly Yet Beautiful World*. In their deployment of epic, mythological and *mecha* formulae, both *The Melody of Oblivion* and *Making Breakthrough Gurren Lagann* echo at once large-scale productions such as *Neon Genesis Evangelion* and works of more modest proportions such as *Mahoromatic* and *This Ugly Yet Beautiful World*. (A comprehensive list of anime works to which various Gainax members have contributed to date, including in relatively marginal capacities, is provided in the appendix).

Moreover, this study does not aim to deal with the studio's protean output as a circumscribed phenomenon. In fact, while aiming to do justice to Gainax's incontestable uniqueness at both the thematic and the technical levels, it also intends to contextualize assiduously the company's accomplishments through cross-reference to other anime features, TV series and OVAs. All of the secondary visual sources directly cited in the main body of the book and/or the chapter notes are listed in the fourth segment of the filmography alongside additional titles viewed for the purpose of background research. This approach will help the reader situate the works examined here in relation to broader stylistic and generic trends within the world of anime in its entire compass. Concomitantly, the discussion will tease out the distinctive elements that make the studio seemingly compliant with dominant trends, on one plane, and yet flamboyantly subversive thereof, on another. It is hoped that this book will thus constitute an appealing volume not only for inveterate Studio Gainax enthusiasts but also for anime fans and scholars across the board.

Chapter 1: A Brief History of Studio Gainax outlines the most salient aspects of the studio's trajectory from its salad days to the present as both an artistic cenacle and a commercial venture. It then assesses Gainax's distinctive aesthetic vision, with an emphasis on its preference for markedly deconstructive strategies. The chapter closes with a discussion of the studio's unique integration of hand-drawn visuals, computer-generated images and textual elements drawn from the various writing systems present in the Japanese language.

Chapters 2 through 13 examine in depth the titles listed above, endeavoring to highlight the specific contribution made by each production to the progressive evolution of the company's mission. Chapter 2: *Royal Space Force: The Wings of Honneamise* focuses on Gainax's engagement with the discourse of space opera and attendant commitment to a massive exercise in worldbuilding. Chapter 3: *Gunbuster* explores the studio's first foray into experimental sci-fi with an emphasis on its inspired amalgamation of disparate generic formulae drawn form mecha anime, sports comedy, high school drama and *shoujo* anime. In Chapter 4: *Nadia: The Secret of Blue Water*, the focus is on Gainax's appropriation of the visual rhetoric of steampunk and infusion thereof with both cosmic and personal conflicts of genuinely epic proportions. The studio's penchant for self-deprecating parody is thrown into relief in Chapter 5: *Otaku no Video* through a close analysis of the pseudo-documentaries used by Gainax to satirize the joys and vicissitudes of fetishistic fandom. Chapter 6: *Neon Genesis Evangelion I—TV Series* and Chapter 7: *Neon Genesis Evangelion II—The Movies* constitute this study's core by exploring in detail the cluster of works through which Gainax has asserted its stature in the cinematographical arena by radically reimagining not merely several established genres (e.g., the postapocalyptic saga, the Bildungsroman, the psychological thriller) but also the art of anime as a whole.

Chapter 8: *His and Her Circumstances* delves further into the studio's experimentative thrust through a focus on the series' synthesis of romantic comedy and serious drama, abetted by sparkly graphic gestures that consistently foreground the stylistic peculiarities inherent in the anime-making process itself. The thought-provoking integration of formulaic motifs, on the one hand, and original tropes, on the other, is likewise shown to be pivotal to the OVA series discussed in Chapter 9: *FLCL*. This stands out as a true gem of surrealist anime combining weighty science fiction and zany farce. In Chapter 10: *Mahoromatic—Automatic Maiden*, emphasis is placed on Gainax's knack of imparting a seemingly blithe *shoujo* comedy exuding cuteness and fan service with harrowing elements redolent of tragic drama at its purest. In the series addressed in Chapter 11: *Magical Shopping Arcade Abenobashi*, Gainax's appetite for intertextual pastiche reaches its zenith. The show leaves virtually no popular genre unscathed in its irreverent, yet warm-hearted, exposure of the codes and conventions of war movies, film noir, martial arts adventures, fairy tales and role-playing games (among several others). The show examined in Chapter 12: *This Ugly Yet Beautiful World* also sets out as an innocently lighthearted adventure but rapidly consolidates *Mahoromatic*'s legacy, adding considerable substance to the earlier show's dark dimension by bringing into play cosmic forces of unfathomable complexity. Chapter 13, on *Gunbuster 2* and *Gunbuster vs. Diebuster: Aim for the Top Gattai Movie*, focuses on Gainax's highly imaginative approach to the concept of "sequel," highlighting both continuities and disjunctures between the seminal 1988 OVA and its recent successor at the levels of both theme and technique. The chapter also considers the composite feature integrating key scenes and characters from *Gunbuster* and *Gunbuster 2, Gunbuster vs. Diebuster,* as a unique application to cinematic structure of the *mecha* technique known as "*gattai*," namely, the combination of two or more elements to form one formidable construct.

Chapter 14: The Anime Magic of Studio Gainax offers a panoramic recapitulation of Gainax's impact on the anime galaxy, with a focus on the studio's aesthetic and ethical priorities. In so doing, the chapter also endeavors to underscore this book's pedagogical usefulness. As shown in detail in the course of Chapter 1, Gainax's corpus is sustained by the consistent deployment of three complementary tools: manually executed visuals, CGI and characters drawn from diverse writing systems. In inviting the reader to consider how these pictorial discourses interplay and contribute to the generation of cinematic meaning, the current study seeks to assist prospective teachers and students in the analysis not only of Gainax's works but also of the broader patterns of perception and cognition underpinning the simultaneous processing of visual and textual information. Detailed filmographical and bibliographical data supplement the discussion.

CHAPTER 1

A Brief History of Studio Gainax

>Question: *What was the longest you ever stayed at the office without going home?*
>Hideaki Anno: *I dunno ... a few years?*
>Question: *What's your favourite anime quote?*
>Anno: *Umm...*
>Question: *Fill in the blank: "Gainax, ___ forever!"*
>Anno: *Gainax, there's no such thing as forever!"*
>— The Restoration

While Hayao Miyazaki has been hailed as the "Disney of the East," and both Production I.G and Madhouse Studios have been commended for their innovative interventions in the field of computer-assisted animation, the anime studio behind some of the most cherished and challenging productions of the past two decades is unquestionably Studio Gainax. The company's fan base has been steadily expanding over the years, not solely on home turf but also in the West and particularly in the United States, occasionally attracting more attention there than in Japan.

With characteristic consistency, Gainax's productions initially present themselves as innocent additions to classic genres and incrementally morph into darkly thoughtful explorations of the human condition featuring some of the most convoluted personalities ever committed to film — animated or otherwise. What these explorations ultimately amount to, regardless of the levels of drama or jocularity evinced by specific films, is a passionate desire to fathom an inveterate two-pronged conundrum that any artist — indeed, any person — can be required to confront, namely, what it means to be human and to live as a human in relation to both oneself and others.

"Anime as quest" therefore seems an apposite description of the company's aesthetic mission. The phrase alludes both to Gainax's ongoing search for innovative forms, generic blends, experimental techniques and intertextual tapestries and to its pursuit of ingenious narrative molds capable of dramatizing the characters' own voyages of self-discovery. In savoring the studio's productions over time, one gradually realizes that these two levels of Gainax's "quest" are inextricably interwoven. Indeed, both the studio's artists and the personae that populate its stories are engaged in a courageous and open-ended journey toward self-knowledge as the precondition of both ethical integrity and creative strength. To take the two complementary titles of the closing episode of the *Evangelion* TV series, namely, "The beast that shouted 'I' at the heart of the world" and "Take care of yourself," it could be suggested that the former points to the inchoate self frantically struggling toward self-knowledge, whereas the latter constitutes an invitation to look inside oneself and accept what one sees despite its possible unsavouriness.

Spectators committed to a thorough investigation of Gainax's productions are likewise drawn into an exploratory journey and, ideally, enabled to augment their own self-understanding. This is because the works pertinaciously discourage us from merely absorbing their images as passive receivers and ask us instead to participate actively in the process of their making. They indeed exhibit all the salient features of the type of text described by Roland Barthes as "writerly" (*scriptable*). Such a text is not "replete" with meanings leading to unequivocally discernible interpretations but rather traversed by multiple and even conflicting messages whose "goal is to make the reader no longer a consumer but a producer of the text" (Barthes 1974, p. 4). Whereas the "readerly" (*lisible*) text presents itself as a closed and finished "product," the "writerly text is ourselves writing, before the infinite play of the world is ... plasticized by some singular system (Ideology, Genius, Criticism) which reduces the plurality of entrances, the opening of networks, the infinity of languages" (p. 5). Contributing actively to the text's production turns interpretation from "a parasitical act" into a "form of work" (p. 10).

Thus, whilst this book is committed to a thorough academic evaluation of Gainax's oeuvre, it also seeks to do justice to its tantalizing openness and invitation to participate in its coming into being. To do so, it endeavors to engage dynamically with the films' visual and verbal signs, acknowledging their plurality and resistance to monolithic readings, and thus elaborating its own "form of work." Working *in tandem with* the studio's animations rather than acting *upon* them from a standpoint of critical mastery, the book thereby hopes to assist their coming to life in the guise of a parallel discourse that amounts to an animating act in its own right. According to Barthes, the writerly text combines numerous codes, each of which represents "one of the voices out of which the text is woven," and none of which can ultimately claim incontrovertible precedence over the others. Even when one particular code appears dominant, one should never forget that "Alongside each utterance, one might say that off-stage voices can be heard" (p. 21). Critical evaluations that relinquish the prerogative of mastery, of the type here proffered, could be said to play the part of one of those off-stage voices and hence to write not so much *about* a text as *alongside* it.

◆ ◆ ◆

A florid vein of information regarding the company's history is provided by *The Notenki Memoirs: Studio Gainax and the Men Who Created Evangelion* (originally published in Japan in 2002 and in its English version in 2005), the work of the Gainax general manager and producer Yasuhiro Takeda. The book focuses on the pre–*Evangelion* days and thus offers precious insights into the studio's foundational moments and budding sense of its aesthetic mission. Above all, it foregrounds Gainax's identity as a fan-based organization; namely, a company not only designed *for* anime lovers but also run *by* such a breed. This key feature of the studio's makeup has characterized it from inception, as borne out by the sheer passion with which its prospective founders devoted themselves wholeheartedly to the exploration of anime conventions (especially in the area of science fiction), the creation of clubs and discussion groups and, gradually, the formulation of distinctive styles of their own.

The actual company found its embryonic inception in 1981, when a group of university students with virtually no prior experience in the art of animation, including Takami Akai, Hiroyuki Yamaga, Toshio Okada and Hideaki Anno, boldly decided to create a five-minute animated short for presentation as the opening piece at the 20th annual Japan National

Sci-Fi Convention, a.k.a. *Daicon 3*, held in Osaka. (This was the third convention of this kind to be held in Osaka and derives its name from the combination of "dai," an alternative pronunciation of the "o" in "Osaka," and "con," the abbreviation for "convention.") Takeda, a cofounder of the Confederation of Kansai Student Sci-Fi Clubs (1977), was one of the principal event organizers.

It was as an organizer that Takeda met Anno and Yamaga in 1980. As he explains, at the time he "had very little interest in anime," and when he asked Anno, who, like Yamaga, had recently entered the Osaka University of Arts, what "kind of stuff" he could do, he "wasn't expecting anything spectacular." Takeda's expectations would, however, be presently contradicted: "he whipped out a pad of accounting paper and started drawing. After a bit, he held the pad up and flipped the pages rapidly. A Powered Suit ran across the paper." This would later provide the basis for the principal *mecha* that featured in the *Daicon 3* opening piece. "It's hard enough drawing a *single* Powered Suit with all the lines and complex shapes," Takeda continues, "but here he was animating one right in front of us.... That settled it—we were doing an anime for the opening film" (Takeda, p. 48). For Anno, this was a highly challenging prospect since he had never attempted a cel anime before, having only experimented with paper animation requiring just some drawings and an 8mm camera.

Yamaga has likewise emphasized the crucial part played by *Daicon 3* in Gainax's embryonic stages: "The very first thing that got my friends and [me] together was this convention.... At those conventions of course there were tons of sci-fi novel fans, but I wasn't anything like that at all.... It's certainly not always the case that people [get into this industry] because they've watched sci-fi works and say 'I'm going to do that!'" (quoted in "[inside] Gainax," p. 8). Therefore, not only were Gainax's prospective founders amateurs but they were also, by and large, relatively casual bystanders in the realm of sci-fi fandom, namely, the subcultural sector almost coterminous with anime fandom in general in those days.

Being unacquainted with the protocol of professional production, the people involved did not divide the project up into several stages but tended instead to handle it as a holistic entity without any sharply identifiable direction, engaging in ongoing discussions and collective decisions. Their dominant drive, ultimately, was to have some *fun* with the creative opportunities at their disposal, and accordingly to identify the area wherein those could be optimized. While this modus operandi may appear haphazard today, it undeniably constitutes, in nascent form, the foundation for what would later become Gainax's exuberantly improvisational and staunchly collaborative approach to the art of animation.

Though technically rudimentary, the piece exhibited at *Daicon 3* was highly ambitious and exhibited *in nuce* some of the qualities to be found in later and considerably more accomplished works. Specifically, in bringing into play a thoughtfully orchestrated ensemble of poignant visual symbols and a wide range of intertextual allusions, the short could be said to anticipate vividly Gainax's predilection for multilayered scenarios and self-reflexive imagery. The subject matter itself bears witness to the creators' ardent commitment to the celebration of imagination and creativity, and to their attendant faith in animation's ability to abet that goal with greater vigor than any other medium. The piece revolves around a little girl fighting a plethora of monstrous and *mecha* creatures based on visual sources from numerous sci-fi shows (such as *Star Trek*, *Star Wars*, *Godzilla*, *Ultraman* and *Space Battleship Yamato*). The heroine's telescoped exploits culminate in her arrival in a desert, where she pours water over a desiccated white radish ("*daikon*" in Japanese: please note the pun on "*daicon*"). The vegetable, miraculously regenerated by the girl's gesture, is symbolically representative of the triumph of the creative drive over the stultifying forces epitomized by the protagonist's many foes. It rewards her by metamorphosing into a massive spaceship and welcoming her aboard—

thereby also upholding the lusty appetite for awesome sci-fi imagery destined to become one of Gainax's major attributes.

Daicon 3 represents an epochal landmark not only in the evolution of what would come to be regarded as one of the most visionary anime studios of all times but also in the history of animation at large. Indeed, it single-handedly redefined the notion of "convention," paving the way for today's ever-blossoming events of that ilk. Daicon 3 also contributed vitally to the germinal sector of ancillary merchandise. At a time when the thought of even accommodating "a commercial booth at a sci-fi convention" seemed audacious, Takeda and his mates not only exhibited and sold anime-based models but also offered visitors a space where they could play "a Star Trek simulation game on PCs," which was in turn flagged by "staff members dressed up in Star Trek garb." The "official goods" included "tiny mascot figures" and "Powered Suits made of polyresin. We weren't calling them 'garage kits' yet, but that's pretty much what they were" (Takeda, p. 57). Before long, Okada would develop this operation into the pioneering garage-kit venture General Products, inaugurated in 1982.

Nowadays, we are so familiar with the concept of tie-ins and spin-offs aimed at fans that the magnitude of Okada's enterprise might go unheeded. In the early 1980s, however, there were only a few outfits selling merchandise based on sci-fi films (particularly in Japan) and those based in Osaka, Takeda explains, "all went out of business within a few months.... Back then, most sci-fi shops sold imported goods from foreign films, but General Products innovated by focusing mainly on its own original products" ("Glossary of Terms: 59. Sci-Fi Specialty Shop"). Yamaga corroborates the originality of the ludic enterprise undertaken by the group: "At the time, toy stores didn't really carry things like spaceships and stuff from anime, sci-fi films or whatnot. There were some cheap things for kids, but absolutely nothing for hardcore fans. What we did was build them ourselves from the prototypes on up and sell them" (quoted in "[inside] Gainax," p. 8). Furthermore, the venture's steady expansion eventually inspired Takeda and his associates to set up Wonder Festival, something "like a flea market for garage kits" ("Glossary of Terms: 90. Wonder Festival") that would bring together pros and amateurs granting both sectors equal promotion opportunities. (The eminently collaborative spirit that would later become one of Gainax's most distinctive features can again be sensed in its inceptive guise.) The event, hosted by the Tokyo Trade Center, was a huge success and kept growing unwaveringly in the course of its subsequent biannual occurrences.

Convinced that getting jobs that would not be creatively challenging at the end of college would be "a huge waste," Yamaga, Takeda and their mates soon realized that setting up their own company was the most palatable option (quoted in "[inside] Gainax," p. 8). In 1982, accordingly, the independent movie production group "Daicon Film" was established in preparation for the 22nd annual Japan National Sci-Fi Convention, a.k.a. *Daicon 4*, to be held in Osaka the following year. Having made a handsome profit from the sale of copies of the *Daicon 3* opening animation, the group could now turn those earnings into capital for films to be screened at the convention. Three movies were accordingly produced:

- *Kaiketsu Notenki* ("Superhero Notenki," 1982), a live-action spoof of hero-centered shows lacking a designated director and starring Takeda himself in the lead role (the film gained Takeda the nickname that he carries to this day and the title of his book appropriately includes);
- *Aikoku Sentai Dainippon* ("Patriotic Rangers of the Great Nation of Japan," 1982), a parody of the *sentai* ("fighting squad") TV shows created by the animation giant Toei, directed by Akai and greatly admired for its convincing explosions;

- *Kaettekita Ultraman* ("The Return of Ultraman," 1983), an ambitious *tokusatsu* ("special effects") movie directed by Anno and praised to this day for its complex script, sophisticated storyline and realistic SFX.

For the opening animation of *Daicon 4*, held in 1983, the group aimed even higher than they had two years earlier, this time producing a technically brilliant five-minute clip to which audiences responded with undiluted enthusiasm. Opening with a recapitulation of the first short, the new piece then proceeds to present the female protagonist in her fully grown-up version and garbed in a Playboy-style bunny costume, with an even more varied range of figures from countless sci-fi and fantasy texts to confront (including Darth Vader, Aslan and Spider-Man). *Daicon 4* marked a groundbreaking moment in the history of anime fandom, attracting 4,000 visitors (*Daicon 3* had accommodated 1,500), integrating an astounding number of staged events, and resolutely emplacing manga and anime within the domain of science fiction as legitimate art forms.

The creators drew great inspiration from the positive reception met by their experimental work at *Daicon 4* and went on to plan a large-scale production initially titled *Royal Space Force*. Yamada wrote a short story and formed what would later become Studio Gainax to produce a four-minute short based upon that narrative, in the hope of thus obtaining adequate funding for a feature-length adaptation. The animation giant Bandai agreed to sponsor the project, approving a budget of over 8 million yen (about $3.3 million) — an unprecedented plan in anime history. (Daicon Film's last project, incidentally, was *Yamata no Orochi no Gyakushu* ["Eight-Headed Giant Serpent's Counterattack"], an epic satire of the *tokusatsu daikaijuu* [special effects/giant monster] genre released in 1985.)

Studio Gainax officially came into being on 24 December 1984. (Fans intrigued by the tongue-in-cheek use of Christian imagery in *Evangelion* may find that date an amusing coincidence.) The initial capital was provided by General Products and amounted to around 2 million yen (approximately $8,500 in 1984). The studio's cofounders included the aforementioned Akai, Anno, Okada, Takeda and Yamaga, as well as Yoshiyuki Sadamoto and Shinji Higuchi. Other regular creators associated with the company over time have been Kazuya Tsurumaki, You Yoshinari, Hiroyuki Imaishi and Tadashi Hiramatsu. The animators chose the denomination "Gainax" to court good fortune: as explained in a special feature devoted to the company's twentieth birthday published in *Newtype USA* in September 2004, "'*Gaina*' means 'huge' in the local dialect of Yonago in Tottori, Japan, which happens to be Gainax's founding member Takami Akai's hometown. The letter 'x' was added just because it sounded cool, but no one knows exactly what it's supposed to mean" ("Gainax turns 20!" p. 39). According to Takeda, the "x" has the effect of making the studio's name "look more like 'the name of an anime robot' (I know, I know ... that's a pretty silly reason)." Commenting further on the company's appellation, Takeda has also, with characteristically self-mocking humor, observed: "I recently learned that in the Aichi dialect the word *gaina* means 'rowdy' or 'loose cannon'! Rather funny, because that's not too far from the mark, either..." (Takeda, p. 91).

The new studio immediately moved on to produce *Royal Space Force* (subsequently renamed *Royal Space Force: The Wings of Honneamise*, 1987), one of the most stylistically adventurous and thematically thought-provoking epic tales of all times. It is on this foundation, at once both modest and audacious, that the studio went on to produce the intrepid and widely acclaimed titles that this study examines. Shortly after the release of *Honneamise*, it became clear that General Products was beginning to flounder and that this was due essentially to the store's geographical location. Takeda realized that if he "continued doing business in Osaka," he "would eventually hit a brick wall. Working in the character business meant getting approval from licensors. And all the licensors were in Tokyo.... After much agonizing, I finally decided to move General Products operations to Tokyo" (pp. 98–99). From the early stages of *Honneamise*'s production, Gainax itself had been located at Takadababa in Shinjuku, one of Tokyo's twenty-three wards renowned for its entertainment, business and shopping amenities. General Products would eventually close down for good in February 1992, having radically transformed both the cultural status and the economic amplitude of the model industry.

In spite of *Honneamise*'s epoch-making caliber, Yamaga has endearingly downplayed the work's significance, stressing that its impact on the history of anime never entailed that "that was the be-all and end-all of our existence.... I wanted to make it so much better than we did, to tell you the truth." Additionally, Gainax's very future was something that at the time neither Yamaga nor his associates could afford to take for granted: "Everyone had been saying we should stop [running the company]. I mean, it was a pain to keep it going, and the basic idea was if you could just land that first job and make that first move, then your career would be pretty much in the bag, so after that, who needs a company, right?" In fact, *Gunbuster* (1988) and *Nadia: The Secret of Blue Water* (1990–1991) kept Gainax going past expectations. It was from the company's game division, however, that the bulk of Gainax's revenue ensued. The staff member chiefly responsible for emplacing game production as a pivotal activity was Takai. According to Yamaga, Akai just bought a computer one day and enthusiastically proposed "Let's do games! If we do games, we can make money.... at that time with Japanese computer games, the art was done by the programmers, so it totally sucked." With the benefit of background training in the fine arts, Akai was able to create game-oriented visuals of unprecedented aesthetic appeal. The lush graphics incorporated in the game *Princess Maker* (1991), which forms the basis of the TV series *Puchi Puri Yuchie*, not only made it a big hit in the sector but also influenced deeply the output of other production companies.

Throughout the first decade of its existence, the studio operated on the principle of "doing it one project at a time," not least because enlisting the support of sponsors was a veritably herculean task. This continued to be the case until Gainax achieved unquestioned prominence thanks to the phenomenal success enjoyed by *Neon Genesis Evangelion* (the first production to bring financial gains for the company). The scenario changed rapidly after that crucial turning-point in the studio's evolution: "Even if you bring the project plans to their door in person," Yamaga explains, "all you have to say is 'I'm from Gainax, and I brought some plans with me,' and they'll meet you, whereas usually you wouldn't be able to make it past the front entrance" (quoted in "[inside] Gainax," p. 8).

It could hardly be denied, therefore, that Gainax stands out not only as a studio whose impact on the anime industry is nothing short of momentous but also as a conspicuous example of a studio run by unconventional management. Confirming Yamaga's account of the studio's initial approach to production, Lawrence Eng has noted: "In a company as freewheeling as Gainax, job titles have traditionally not meant very much. People just did whatever was necessary to keep the company going and to finish whatever projects were going on. (Oftentimes, poor management led to projects not being completed)" (Eng 2005). Worse still, as the review of *Notenki* published by the fansite *Gainax Pages* states, "Due to his [Takeda's] complete ignorance of the rudimentary basics of accounting and tax law, Gainax was convicted of massive tax evasion in the wake of *Evangelion* and its company President, Sawamura, carted off to jail" ("*Gainax Pages* reviews: *The Notenki Memoirs* by Yasuhiro Takeda").

It is therefore crucial to steer clear of facile idealizations of Gainax's policies as something of a latter-day incarnation of a cottage-industry philosophy. At the same time, however, it would be downright callous to dismiss the importance of the company's organizational procedures as an attractive, albeit risky, alternative to the profit-driven ethos frequently adhered to by contemporaneous cinematic ventures. As Yamaga notes, there eventually came a point when both he and his collaborators began to acknowledge the advantages of a suitably systematic approach to production: "It's a matter of taking on work, defining the goals and checking to see if they're being fulfilled.... I guess normal people do it from the start." Nevertheless, this pragmatic shift has never entailed relinquishing altogether the studio's proverbially experimentative suppleness: "If we get too uptight about things, we'll end up losing what's made us so great up to now. I think we're much more flexible than other companies" (quoted in "[inside] Gainax," p. 8). Unorthodox business strategies have remained integral to Gainax's unique charisma and creative verve throughout the company's history, and ignoring them would be tantamount to neglecting a significant component of its now legendary standing.

◆ ◆ ◆

A resonantly apposite description of Gainax's vision and corresponding output can be found in Richard Williams's memorable assessment of the elemental factors that draw animators to their art:

> Why animate? Everyone knows it's a lot of hard work doing all those drawings and positions. So what's the hook? Why do it?
> Answer: Our work is taking place in *time*. We've taken our "stills" and leapt into another dimension.
> Drawings that *walk*: seeing a series of images we've made spring to life and start walking around is already fascinating.
> Drawings that walk and *talk*: seeing a series of our drawings talking is a very startling experience.
> Drawings that walk and talk and *think*: seeing a series of images we've done actually go through a thinking process — and appear to be thinking — is the real aphrodisiac. Plus creating something that is unique, which has never been done before is endlessly fascinating [Williams, p. 11].

It would be hard to deny that an unrelenting desire to access alternate dimensions, the retention of an almost childlike ability to be fascinated and startled by the fresh perspectives that those dimensions open up, and, most vitally, a capacity to derive sheer pleasure from the creative act constitute Gainax's most axial and inveterate traits. No reality brought into existence by the animator's pencil ever crystallizes into a conclusive plateau of meaning: in fact, it represents first and foremost a springboard to an indefinite series of other parallel universes. Simultaneously, no stylistic formula ever asserts itself as a dogma to be mechanically and unthinkingly replicated, its function actually being to encourage ongoing experimentation with alternative formulae. Even as one particular world is constructed, or one particular ground plan is adhered to, the studio's images acquire the vibrant aura of aliveness they characteristically emit from a concurrent apprehension of the myriad *other* worlds or ground plans that might have been pursued instead.

The caption accompanying the passage from Williams's seminal text cited above pithily sums up this proposition: "Animation pencil — use both ends." These words, it is worth noting, elliptically echo Jacques Derrida's description of the deconstructive gesture as a matter of writing with *both hands*— by which he meant that in advocating any view or belief, one must never ignore the concurrent plausibility of at least one alternative position. In providing an interpretation of a given text, Derrida is indeed always aware of the possibility of an entirely different interpretation (traces of which may make themselves felt even if they are not developed). Thus, any one text is in fact a double reality: "Two texts, two hands, two visions, two ways of listening. Together simultaneously and separately" (Derrida, pp. 75–76).

Gainax's take on the art of animation echoes this approach in its tendency to both embrace and to disrupt the conventions of established genres in the same act. The studio's deconstructive interventions consist, quite in accordance with the Derridian model, of exposing the internal contradictions undermining from within the putative solidity of those genres. An eloquent example of this tendency is supplied by Gainax's transgressive redefinition of the *mecha* (giant robot) genre: supposedly a glorification of virile heroism, this hugely popular branch of anime is actually predicated upon the premise that colossal armors are rendered necessary by societal or cosmic vulnerabilities. Even if the story is cumulatively or climactically presented as one of strength, its fabric remains at all times lacerated by insecurity and doubt. This is clearly attested to by productions as diverse as Yoshiyuki Tomino's TV series *Mobile Suit Gundam* (1979) and its multifarious offshoots; Mamoru Oshii's features *Patlabor 1: The Mobile Police* (1989) and its sequel *Patlabor 2: The Movie* (1993); and the TV series *Bubblegum Crisis—Tokyo 2040* (dir. Hiroki Hayashi, 1998). Gainax takes this idea to its ultimate conclusions by overtly emphasizing the weaknesses of the cultures and individuals who depend on *mecha* for their survival, as well as the idiosyncrasies of the mechanical or cybernetic creatures themselves. What if, the animators boldly posit, the *mecha* heroes/heroines are actually tormented and abused adolescents and the mammoth biomechanoids they are enjoined to pilot are bestial entities with dark drives of their own?

The *shoujo* (young girl) genre of anime, putatively devoted to the celebration of a quintessentially "feminine" ideal encapsulated by the term *yasashii* (meek, kind, generous, sensitive), is likewise subverted. The *shoujo* is conventionally intended to uphold *yasashii* values by charting a budding female protagonist's psychosexual development with varyingly overt reference to romantic entanglements. Yet, not all is well in *shoujo*land (any more than in Alice's Wonderland or in Dorothy's Oz, for that matter) since those values are insistently challenged by the callous imperatives of dominant structures of power that frequently threaten to swamp them altogether. Hayao Miyazaki's *Laputa: Castle in the Sky* (1986) is undoubtedly one of the best-known instances of this trend. Gainax's forays into the *shoujo* typology openly capitalize on the aporia at its heart by ushering in heroines whose ostensible *yasashii* virtues are not merely defied by the status quo but actually shown to be unreliable—to represent just *one* side (and not necessarily the guiding one) of multifold personalities with a propensity for very non-*yasashii* concessions to selfishness, intolerance and even crudeness.

The *moe* genre, customarily based on a neat distribution of gender roles that clearly polarizes the object of desire and its worshipper, is also called into question by Gainax productions seemingly located in that category. The animators are acutely aware that *moe* is not just an expression of time-honored chivalric tenets (peppered with innocent snippets of "fan service") that should be left doxastically unexamined but an ideologically biased form that both accommodates and legitimizes unsavory expressions of fetishistic scopophilia. Accordingly, they seek to expose the genre's internal ambivalence by introducing characters that do not unproblematically incarnate clear-cut subject positions but actually harbor unresolved contradictions that render them alternately desirable and odious.

While echoing Derrida, Gainax's output also encapsulates, in this respect, the aesthetic vision advocated by the early twentieth-century Portuguese author Fernando Pessoa. In his *Book of Disquiet*, in particular, Pessoa states: "I've discovered that I'm always attentive to, and always thinking about two things at the same time.... [T]he two realities that hold my attention are equally vivid.... This, perhaps, is what constitutes my tragedy, and what makes it comic" (quoted in Sontag). As explained in some detail later in this discussion, Gainax's directors assiduously integrate both hand-drawn visuals and computer-generated images with snippets of text based on the various writing systems encompassed by the Japanese language.

Therefore, if on the thematic level the studio's artists arguably write with two hands by both adopting and transgressing established conventions in a single movement, on the technical plane they could be said to bring into play not just two but *three* hands.

The studio's commitment to formal experimentation has been consistently matched by a commodious openness to a variety of tools and techniques. It would be quite preposterous to proffer a definition of *the* Gainax style, as this would be inevitably conducive to sweeping generalizations and hence obfuscate the exhilarating diversity of approaches exhibited by its members and productions. A few recurring elements could, however, be safely extrapolated from that wide-ranging spectrum of distinctive stylistic signatures.

Characterization

All of the studio's works rely on depth of characterization to draw audiences into the disconcerting realities they explore; hence, they supply richly evocative galleries of characters that are painstakingly grounded in the atmosphere of the worlds they inhabit. The grounding rule applies with great consistency regardless of whether the character in question is an alien princess (the eponymous heroine in *Nadia*), a combat android (*Mahoromatic*'s protagonist), an interstellar evolutionary force (Hikari in *This Ugly Yet Beautiful World*), a reticent hero (Shinji in *Evangelion*, Naota in *FLCL*) or, quite simply, a school kid struggling with the mysteries of growing up (Yukino and her mates in *His and Her Circumstances*, Sasshi and Arumi in *Magical Shopping Arcade Abenobashi*).

Most importantly, even when Gainax's elaborately constructed alternate worlds showcase eccentric menageries of both earthy and fantastic creatures, the studio's methods of characterization tenaciously remind us that those worlds are at base very much like our own — unfamiliar as they may seem — insofar as they are populated by beings with markedly human emotions exuding the feel of a universal human drama. Even the peripheral accessories that come to be associated with the characters serve to underscore their humanity by avoiding quirky looks as an end in themselves and using catchy but recognizable iconographic points of reference. This is no less true of *mecha* such as the Gunbuster, *Evangelion*'s biomechanoids or the Dix-Neuf from *Gunbuster 2* than of the literally human personae. Emotions are conveyed by recourse to both overt stylization and realistic shading depending on the action's particular context. For example, in depicting the mien of a blushing character, the artists at times adopt overtly schematic purple-pink lines, whereas at others they favor a diffuse glow convincingly showing how the light is hitting the face from a specific source. The two visual moods correspond to distinct levels of engagement with the cause of embarrassment, shame or guilt on the character's part. This kind of ruse makes Gainax's personae psychologically convincing without having to pander to the tenets of classic realism, which would be quite incongruous with their status as animated actors in general and anime creations in particular.

Characterization is assiduously kept within the contexts of specific productions and of their particular look and feel, occasionally resorting to realistic physiognomies for touches of style rather than in pursuit of photographic authenticity. Ironically, these subtle nods to realism are more successful than strictly documentary representations in conveying credible personalities. Depth of characterization is often abetted by the most economical means imaginable: for instance, by communicating a character's emotional state through the jarring of the chromatic and textural properties of his or her field of vision. In these frames, the constructed nature of the medium is triumphantly thrown into relief. The strategies employed include the sudden flattening of a plastic mass to a 2D cut-out; the flooding of the screen with abstract patterns that appear to have been achieved by random ink-dripping or crosshatching; the desaturation of palettes and related lighting effects.

Backgrounds

Gainax's entire opus eloquently attests to the proposition that backgrounds play a vital role in drawing the audience into the situation being portrayed — irrespective of whether they capture scenes of space-operatic grandeur (as exemplified by *Honneamise*, *Gunbuster*, *Nadia* and *Mahoromatic*) or a prosaic moment of everyday life (as paradigmatically demonstrated by *His and Her Circumstances* and *FLCL*). Playing imaginatively with depth and perspective, often varying color saturation values according to an object's distance from or proximity to the camera, the backgrounds enable viewers to feel truly immersed in the scene. Geometric perspective is not necessarily invoked in order to convey a convincing impression of depth: for Gainax, as for most anime artists generally, the retention of an element of flatness is actually crucial to the perpetuation of an aesthetic legacy rooted in 2D graphics. Aerial perspective is, therefore, prioritized instead. For instance, in the representation of far-off objects, distance may be evoked by interposing layers of haziness between those entities and the foreground that serve to suggest their distance from the viewer's vantage point. The further away they are meant to be, the greater degree of atmospheric "noise" is introduced, the overall illusion being one of incremental distance. The relatively rare but genuinely memorable moments in *Evangelion* devoted to the contemplation of Nature's beauty deploy this strategy to maximum effect.

No less impactful, especially in the rendition of distinctively urban backgrounds, is the alternation between photorealistic scenarios and allusively stylized settings. It is not uncommon, for example, for the screen to switch from meticulously rendered street scenes replete with the familiar markers of town architecture and props (ubiquitous pylons and power cables stand out as Gainax's major landmarks across productions as diverse as *Evangelion*, *His and Her Circumstances* and *FLCL*), and soft-hued watercolors of ethereal gentleness intended to take the focus ways from the setting and draw attention instead to a character's affective intercourse with his or her environment. (*His and Her Circumstances* and *Mahoromatic* offer some particularly notable illustrations of the latter modality.)

Lighting and Coloration

The studio's animators are profoundly aware of the cardinal role played by lighting in creating or breaking the dramatic impact of a shot, sequence or entire film. Since its adoption of digital programs, in particular, Gainax has tirelessly experimented with lighting effects accomplished through deft variations in the stacking and blending of layers. Lighting effects are faithfully accompanied by chromatic gradations, insofar as particular portions of any fictional world depicted are characterized by specific color schemes. The interplay of light and color is thus enthroned as a vital aspect of the overall presentation. The bucolic episodes in *Mahoromatic* and *This Ugly Yet Beautiful World* attest most emphatically to this pictorial proclivity.

In addition, light and color are methodically integrated with the natural or architectural structure of any given scene. For example, harmonious blends of shimmering pastel colors and perplexing juxtapositions of accentuated highlights achieve their singular impact in conjunction with structures that likewise connote a sense of balance or else a sense of discomfort at the level of the scene's physical environment. Gently sloping landscapes and curvilinear compositions typically aim for the former; tangled urbanscapes replete with crisscrossing lines, for the latter. Although these contrasts are not solely indigenous to Gainax territory, what is unique to the studio's handling of their dramatic force is a penchant for swift, yet seamless, transitions from one locale — and attendant atmosphere — to a discordant one. This tendency can be detected across the company's whole outturn, from the juxtaposition of claustrophobically intricate grids and sublimely open vistas offered by *Wings of Honneamise*, to the clash of spectacularly supernatural scenarios and cozy domestic interiors presented in *This Ugly Yet Beautiful World*.

Both characters and settings gain depth from the consistent adoption of an iterative, coral-reef approach. Drawing designs much the same way as a sculptor would deal with clay, Gainax's artists allow their initially rough sketches to grow incrementally, through the incorporation of new elements into the mix according to rhythms dictated by the drawings themselves no less than by the artist's pencil. At some point, a look that gels together as a coherent entity is likely to be reached but how and when exactly this result is achieved is never a foregone conclusion. Along the way, each element — however minute or mundane — is accorded equal respect without any facile skimping on finishing touches for which much commercial animation is sadly infamous.

Allied to unremittingly stylish direction and an original take on logline, the visual strategies outlined above imbue Gainax's productions with an energetic appeal that has seldom gone unnoticed by their viewers — whether or not such viewers have cherished the problematic stories and proverbially inconclusive endings that have come to be regarded as almost synonymous with the name "Gainax" or else fled them in sheer exasperation. What ought to be clear to anybody whose inclination is *not* to run away but rather to engage, both as a fan and as a scholar, with a body of works so unconventional as to verge on the bizarre is that an appreciation of the studio's storytelling and rhetorical ploys requires a parallel grasp of the graphic techniques brought to bear upon the animation — here literally intended as the infusion of life into the inanimate. In this respect, a broad range of reciprocally sustaining materials calls for thorough inspection. These encompass not only the animated products but also the concept art, line art and model designs underlying them. In addition, art books supplying character designs of individual personae and ensembles provide precious insights into both the creators' aesthetic values and the psychologies of the people portrayed, as well as a distinctive sense of the genius loci wherein they act and interact.

No less crucially, careful scrutiny of the motion pictures themselves demands patient viewing, not infrequently in slow motion, of the more complex montages whose import cannot be fully comprehended in real time. The grayscale sequence of stills presented in *Gunbuster*'s climactic battle, *Evangelion*'s legion composites and collages, and the effervescent switches from naturalistic to caricatural styles in *His and Her Circumstances* aptly confirm this proposition. To some potential audiences who are still to sample the studio's oeuvre (or to be persuaded to progress past the sampling stage) the foregoing remarks might suggest that Gainax's productions should come with a health warning. Undoubtedly, a comprehensive grasp of the company's unique approach to anime only seems likely as the outcome of a scrupulous labor of love. The rewards, it is here proposed, are nonetheless well in excess of the toil.

◆ ◆ ◆

Gainax's works evince markedly introspective proclivities on both the thematic and the formal planes, resulting from the animators' steadfast determination to foreground the devices utilized in the construction of the visual narrative. (The technical implications of this proclivity will shortly be returned to.) As a consequence of this inward-looking ethos, the studio has often been regarded as largely responsible for the spawning of a distinctive "otaku" mentality.[1] Originally, as Eng explains, the term "otaku" means "'your house,' and more generally it is also a very polite (distancing and non-imposing as opposed to familiar) way of saying 'you.' ... The basic idea is that the word is used to explicitly indicate detachedness from who you are speaking to." Such an attitude came to be automatically expected of people whose passions would inevitably be conducive to their spending a lot of time on their own, developing introverted attitudes and hence failing to socialize. Concomitantly, "otaku" little by little came to designate a subcultural fandom phenomenon associated with fetishistically addictive consumers of anime, manga and video games. Although the otaku's isolation is not in itself a fearful crime, it was incrementally demonized and even, in extreme instances, equated to perversity insofar as it contravened a major cultural imperative: "Not unlike American adult society ... Japanese adult society has long had anxieties about its youth culture becoming more individualistic and isolated and less interested in fulfilling mainstream social duty" (Eng 2001).

The assumption surrounding otaku is that they are bunkered in and hence socially inept people who have taken refuge in their favorite products to avoid confronting the harsh realities of their cultural milieu. However, much as zealous fans could be seen to lead atomized lives, they are by no means the only members of postindustrial regimes enduring such a fate. Atomization, in fact, is a ubiquitous condition that dominant ideologies endeavor to conceal in order to foster the illusion of harmonious sociality. What makes otaku suspect in the eyes of many non-otaku is the fact that they, by contrast, do not seek to efface that condition but actually wear it on their sleeve. Historically, this conduct largely resulted from a pervasive sense of psychological unease ensuing from unresolved tensions between regional traditionalism, on the one hand, and multinationally oriented modernization, on the other.

However, otaku's tainted reputation was not to endure indefinitely. In fact, as Gilles Poitras maintains, "in the early 1990s" the term "began to lose its negative meaning. In fact, it even picked up some positive connotations as the power of the otaku audience (and the vast sums of money it spent on its hobby) made itself known in the entertainment business." It is also noteworthy that "there's another term in Japan for a dedicated connoisseur of some obscure subject: *maniakku*, or maniac.... Why two terms for the same thing? The difference essentially lies in degrees of obsession. 'Maniacs' can enjoy fairly normal lives while devoting a portion of their energies to their hobby.... otaku ... devote their entire lives to their interest" (Poitras, p. 71).

Closely connected with the otaku sensibility is the aforementioned notion of "*moe*." As Jonathan Clements and Helen McCarthy explain in the entry devoted to "Argot and Jargon" by their *Anime Encyclopaedia*,

> *Moe* is a fetishistic obsession with a particular topic or hobby, entering modern parlance as a replacement for otaku.... Toshio Okada has written that a *moe* fan need only be obsessed, while a true otaku actually develops background knowledge. Its etymology here is related to *moeru*, to burn with enthusiastic fervour. Also often associated in anime fandom with one particular kind of *moe*, an intense attraction to cartoon characters, particularly young and innocent girls that need to be nurtured and may be looking for a brotherly protector. Its etymology here is more related to *moederu*, to sprout or bud [Clements and McCarthy, p. 31].

Hence, it could safely be surmised that "*moe*," initially a way of designating any fixation, gradually came to be equated to the otaku disposition, and eventually acquired specifically erotic nuances. (The concept of "*moe*" will be examined in some depth in the chapters devoted to

Mahoromatic — Automatic Maiden and *This Ugly Yet Beautiful World*, the two Gainax shows wherein the formula is most overtly and imaginatively deployed.)

Interestingly, Western anime fans were, by and large, more inclined than their Japanese counterparts to embrace the word "otaku" enthusiastically even when in Japan it was being used as the equivalent of "nerd" or "geek" at best and "pervert" at worst. What this indicates is that perceptions of fandom are inevitably culture-bound: in using "otaku," a Western consumer is not merely appropriating an element of Japanese culture but also reinscribing it with reference to his or her own socioeconomic context. This phenomenon is especially important when assessed in relation to a studio, like Gainax, whose output carries transcultural relevance and whose fans, accordingly, will be approaching its works from multifarious and feasibly even discordant cultural perspectives.

The danger, while this process unfolds, is that Western fans might indulge in a spurious "Othering" of Japan grounded in slapdash misreadings of its traditions and mores. However, Gainax's productions bravely challenge this unsavory prospect by simultaneously perpetuating indigenous tropes and presenting us with materials that are intimately related to Western pop culture. Therefore, even as a Western audience might arbitrarily appropriate anime's images and codes, thereby somewhat distorting their import, that audience will concurrently see its own cultural parameters displaced and defamiliarized. As a result, the intrinsic plasticity of all forms of cultural embodiment will become obvious and all attempts to colonize foreign imports with reference to parochial values will openly declare their preposterousness.

(An understanding of Gainax's works — and arguably of Japanese animation at large — is certain to gain from some examination of the origins of the word "otaku," its evolution and mutating cultural connotations over time in both Japan and the West, as well as its connection with the broader experience of generational crisis. The chapter devoted to *Otaku no Video* will revisit this intriguing topic extensively.)

The emotional and psychological ordeals, contorted psyches and troubled sexualities presented by numerous Gainax productions with varying degrees of explicitness undoubtedly echo the otaku mentality by virtue of their inward-looking and self-reflexive proclivities. These stylistic tendencies, moreover, are perspicuously evident across the studio's entire corpus even where it seemingly indulges in unfettered blitheness. It is vital to appreciate, however, that Gainax's distinctively introspective approach does not deliver a vapidly self-gratifying vision and cannot therefore be unproblematically dismissed as an effete concession to otaku escapism. In fact, the self-reflexive approach is ultimately conducive to a radical explosion of all sorts of established codes whereby the art of anime itself is irreverently deconstructed. Myriad intertextual allusions to both seminal and marginal works in both the animated and the live-action domains, interwoven with in-jokes that are at times blatant and at other times only recognizable by inveterate fans, abet the mission.

In the process, full animation frequently gives way to snippets of an artist's sketchbook, crayon scrawls, scribbles, squiggles and doodles, collages, cutouts, newspaper clippings, live-action footage and stills, as well as starkly black-and-white manga panels, minimalist line drawings and myriad expressions of typographical prowess. Ultimately, therefore, Gainax's productions could be described as inherently ironical enterprises wherein the characters' subjective enclosures are both mirrored by the stories' metacommentaries on their own interior workings, and yet audaciously ruptured through a drastic displacement of the conventions of mainstream anime. The outcome is a galaxy of alternate worlds that are invariably enchanting and baleful in equal measures.

Gainax's self-referential tendency to lay bare the material foundations of its works by foregrounding the various stages of the creative process from the storyboard to the screen entails that in some of the studio's most experimental productions, one gets to witness the very evolution of the animated image over time. The eye is thus regaled with rough pencil sketches corresponding to the image's inceptive form; examples of the translation of the sketches into either grayscale pictures or line drawings with neatly defined black contours; images revealing the sequential steps taken in the incorporation of colors, shades and highlights into both the backgrounds and the characters moving against them; and samples of the visuals as they are incrementally enhanced by either the diligent application of pigments with a brush or the flooding of selected portions with washes of variable density. (Assiduous as the employment of such self-referential techniques undeniably is, it must be stressed that the effects thereby achieved are subtly varied across Gainax's opus. Therefore, specific examples pertaining to particular productions will be considered in the course of the individual case studies.)

Some of the roughest sketches presented in the formally self-reflexive sequences are especially effective in conveying the dynamic properties of the characters they represent. Hence, even though they may at first be thought of as the least realistic components of the overall process at the purely mimetic level, they actually constitute the lynchpin of that magical illusion of movement that the art of animation as a whole seeks to evoke. It is the intrinsic energy of those drawings, moreover, that imparts a potent impression of dynamism even to scenes in which Gainax refrains altogether from the rendition of motion in the orthodox sense in favor of montages and collages based on the sequential filming of emphatically *still* images. What the sorts of visuals described above enable us to sense with palpable intensity is the sheer joy that Gainax's artists derive from their unwavering approach to animation as an art with an unparalleled potential to reinvent its representational scope virtually ad infinitum.

Gainax's incorporation of *kanji* (Chinese characters) and both *hiragana* and *katakana* (syllabaries comprising sets of phonetic symbols), rendered in a wide variety of fonts and styles matching the mood of a scene, deserves special attention. Far from simply constituting a flourish of virtuosity, this strategy attests to the studio's allegiance to a semiotic sensibility steeped in Eastern tradition, and particularly in pictographic and ideographic forms of writing. Pictograms are fairly unambiguous representations of objects in the real world executed in a stylized fashion. Ideograms are also inspired by empirical referents but these are less instantly recognizable in ideograms than they are in pictograms. *Kanji* (and, by extension, the syllabaries deriving from them) partake of both signifying modalities, at times exhibiting close connections with actual objects and at others relying on extreme stylization. Either way, the characters underscore the material substratum of language by retaining the physical underpinnings of words in their visible shapes. Words do not, of course, simply designate objects. No less frequently, they refer to intangible categories of thought and feeling. However, even in those cases, *kanji* and their derivatives come across as concrete images that symbolically evoke such categories without becoming, *in themselves*, immaterial.

Like all systems of written signification, pictograms and ideograms rely on the mechanism of metaphor: the creation of relations between material and immaterial entities. In the West, credit for this exercise has generally been accorded to the human mind's capacity for logical abstraction and related ability to divorce thought from physical reality. Nevertheless, as Ezra Pound has persuasively argued in "The Chinese Character as a Medium for Poetry," the model at the basis of metaphoric linkage is actually provided by Nature:

> primitive metaphors do not spring from arbitrary *subjective* processes. They are possible only because they follow objective lines of relations in Nature herself. Relations are more real and more important than the things which they relate.... Nature furnishes her own clues. Had the world

not been full of homologies, sympathies, and identities, thought would have been starved and language chained to the obvious [Pound].

This proposition is memorably conveyed in Charles Baudelaire's "Correspondances":

> La Nature est un temple où de vivants piliers
> Laissent parfois sortir de confuses paroles;
> L'homme y passe à travers des forêts de symboles
> Qui l'observent avec des regards familiers.
> Comme de longs échos qui de loin se confondent
> Dans une ténébreuse et profonde unité,
> Vaste comme la nuit et comme la clarté,
> Les parfums, les couleurs et les sons se répondent.
> [Baudelaire]
>
> [*Nature is a temple where living pillars*
> *Let sometimes come forth garbled words.*
> *Man walks through these forests of symbols*
> *That observe him with knowing eyes.*
> *Like prolonged echoes blending in the distance*
> *In a dark and deep harmony,*
> *As vast as night and light,*
> *Perfumes, colors and sounds converse with one another.*]
> [My translation]

Just as the interrelations fashioned by Nature have concrete foundations, so do the metaphorical associations forged by language. Regrettably, in keeping with its programmatic enthroning of disembodied concepts over anything corporeal, Western logic goes to considerable lengths to efface that concreteness:

> Languages today are thin and cold because we think less and less into them. We are forced, for the sake of quickness and sharpness, to file down each word to its narrowest edge of meaning.... We are content to accept the vulgar misuse of the moment. A late stage of decay is arrested and embalmed in the dictionary [Pound].

Emphasizing the autonomous aesthetic value of pictographic and ideogrammatic forms of textuality through the integration of *kanji, hiragana* and *katakana* into their animations, Gainax's artists palpably assert the enduring materiality of language. The use of shots in which the regular anime register gives way to explicitly drawn images rendered in pencil, charcoal, chalk or pastel bolsters the studio's commitment to the cultivation of a tersely pictographic mode of expression. The more allusively oblique flashes of printed, painted or scrawled text, for their part, are more akin to ideograms. Whilst perpetuating a distinctively Eastern legacy, these strategies also hold the potential for alerting Western audiences to the intrinsic, albeit latent, concreteness of all forms of language and especially writing the world over.

CHAPTER 2

Royal Space Force: The Wings of Honneamise (Ouritsu Uchuugun— Oneamisu no Tsubasa)

Director: Hiroyuki Yamaga (1987)

The first film from the Gainax studio features a nobody as the hero—a nobody who makes you look through the sky, past the weather, and into what is possible.
— Patrick Drazen

Wings of Honneamise's protagonist, Shirotsugh (Shiro) Lhadatt, does not even vaguely resemble the standard sci-fi anime hero—if the phrase is taken to designate, as it frequently is, a valiant soul abetted by either material or mental superpowers. In fact, Shiro is a quintessentially average young man who, having aspired to fulfill his childhood fantasy of flying by joining the Honneamano Navy but having failed to obtain the required grades, has ended up joining the Royal Space Force instead. Regrettably, this organization turns out to amount to little more than a dolefully underfunded group of elderly rocket scientists, dropouts and lazy young recruits, fabricated as a publicity stunt and diplomatic pawn by the royal family and by the government. As it happens, nobody has ever even made it into space and the technology necessary to achieve this feat is far from realization. Shiro's life in the Royal Space Force is riddled with humiliations, repetitively useless chores and debilitating forays into a vapid pleasure industry, which unsurprisingly plunge him into apathetic inertia.

His attitude changes drastically upon meeting the idealistic young missionary Riquinni Nondelaiko, the first person he has ever come across to react enthusiastically to the notion of space travel. He thereby transcends his existential malaise, is able to rekindle the dormant embers of ambition in his spirit, and commits himself passionately to the attainment of the Force's putative objective by becoming indeed the first man in space. It is also noteworthy, even though autobiographical concerns do not come explicitly into play in *Wings of Honneamise*, that director Hiroyuki Yamaga was only twenty-four years old at the time he embarked upon the execution of this epoch-making cinematic extravaganza, and that his task therefore amounted to a bold excursion into the virtually unknown comparable to Shiro's own venture.

Shiro's fascination with Riquinni is not wholly Platonic, however, and much as he endeavors to sublimate his libido to loftier values, there comes a point when his instincts gain the upper hand and he attempts to force the young woman into sexual intercourse. Far from providing a slice of dubiously voyeuristic fan service, the scene plays an important role in *Wings of Honneamise*'s overall diegesis insofar as it serves to throw sharply into relief the clash between two incompatible worldviews: the earthbound hedonism of a frustrated and painfully human bloke, and the asceticism of a blindly devout foundationalist whose striving for otherworldliness is ultimately no less of a testament to her human limitations. Thus, the film is not merely a story about humankind's ascent into space — it is also, no less importantly, a story about descent into the murky depths of characters that are both unsure about their future goals and haunted by a legacy of thwarted fantasies. These characters' psychological and emotional turmoil is consistently conveyed, from a dramaturgical point of view, not only by conversations about daunting issues such as war, poverty, material and spiritual corruption and, ultimately, life itself but also, often more effectively, by frames in which dialogue is overtly marginalized. In such shots, the film opts for a deliberately low-key tone intensified by pregnant pauses and a focus on facial expressions that lend themselves to multiple interpretations.

The action follows the struggles of the Royal Space Force to launch Shiro into orbit amidst countless budget cuts and attempts on the prospective pilot's life meant to sabotage the operation. What does not transpire until it is almost too late is that the military forces do not wish the project to succeed but rather intend to use the rocket as a means of provoking a neighboring kingdom into attacking them in order to capture the weapon, hence giving the Honneamano army itself a pretext to invade. Shiro's ship, propelled just as the invading army approaches the launch site, rises majestically above the conflict below into cosmic infinity. The launch scene is realistic, and indeed almost indistinguishable from live-action footage of actual sequences of its kind. Fieldwork conducted by the troupe at Cape Kennedy and the Air and Space Museum no doubt abetted the accomplishment of this visual feat. Vividly redolent of Stanley Kubrick's *2001: A Space Odyssey* (1968), the sequence powerfully intimates that space flight as conceived of in *Wings of Honneamise* does not merely constitute a physical journey but, more crucially, also a psychological odyssey of self-understanding and maturation.

Hand-drawn frame by frame, *Wings of Honneamise* is nonetheless technically innovative on numerous counts, enthroning Studio Gainax's acclaimed preference for dizzying perspectives, bizarre camera angles, sensational backgrounds and, most memorably, meticulously executed montages of unparalleled complexity, particularly in the emphatically impressionistic sequence following Shiro's launch into orbit. An elaborate sequence of images, beautifully painted by the fine artist Nobuyuki Ohnishi, is here used to evoke a recapitulation of the protagonist's life as it flashes before his mind's eye. This microcosmic dimension is then echoed by a macrocosmic series of pictures proposing in telescoped guise the growth of human civilization from prehistory through the industrial era to the age of flight. Ryuichi Sakamoto's stylish soundtrack, combining electronic music and string melodies, evocatively enhances the action's epic momentum without ever swamping its pathos. *Wings of Honneamise*'s employment of impressionistic drawings invested with painterly tactility foreshadows Gainax's use of the same technique in *Nadia: The Secret of Blue Water*, most dramatically in the acherontic montages that fill the show's pre-credit sequence.

Integrating numerous motifs typical of Japan's traditional visual and performance arts (from the ink scroll and the *ukiyo-e* to Kabuki and Noh), the overtly hand-drawn images presented in Yamaga's movie tenaciously abide in memory by virtue of their intensely artisanal feel. In this respect, they act as a prelude to a style to be subsequently developed by Gainax as one of the studio's most distinctive trademarks. An unflinching passion for manually crafted visuals indeed permeates the company's output across productions as diverse as *Neon Genesis Evangelion* and *His and Her Circumstances*, *FLCL* and *Mahoromatic—Automatic Maiden*, in spite of its progressive integration of state-of-the-art digital tools and techniques into the production process.

Yoshiyuki Sadamoto's character designs, whilst unequivocally detailed in the rendition of both naturalistic and cartoony personae, are not undilutedly attractive — especially in comparison with the designs later executed by the same artist for *Nadia* and *Evangelion*. Snub noses and overelongated chins, for example, are not somatic traits to which seasoned anime lovers will automatically warm. The final character designs resulted from the director's request for a markedly realistic style, while Sadamoto's original drawings had been much more graceful (and much more to his own liking). This is confirmed by the concept art included in the "Art and Music" bonus on the Manga DVD, as well as the color plate portraying the film's main characters presented in the artbook *Der Mond*. More importantly, however, deliberately uncomely character designs serve as iconographic clues to the moral baseness of Honneamano's society. As "Scoot" maintains,

> the entire cast is *ugly*. Racked with the cowardly, greedy vulgarities which make us human, they are a million miles away from the clean-cut, huge-eyed peacocks which preen and strut through the majority of modern productions. Here we see character development in a corporeal way: never do we resent the cast for thinking of themselves first — instead we relate to them, which in turn makes us care for them all the more, flaws and all ["Scoot"].

Often the costumes, more than the characters' physiognomies themselves, succeed most eloquently in conveying both individual and group identities. In capitalizing on an inspired synthesis of traditional Eastern and Western fashions (including Chinese, Indian and Native American motifs), martial garb and civilian dress, muted and lurid palettes, fluid and stark lines, the costumes consistently communicate the impression that Honneamano is an alien culture and yet eerily similar to our own world. They do so not so much by recourse to explicitly outlandish stylistic markers as through the inclusion of subtly marginal oddities (asymmetrical suspenders and epaulets, for instance) or else of garments that appear to combine the attributes of disparate forms of attire from the actual world (e.g., collars and mantles, balaclavas and helmets, breeches and skirts).

Where the film unquestionably triumphs, at the level of art direction (a task undertaken by Hiromasa Ogura), is in the backgrounds representing both Nature and architecture. In an astoundingly elaborate world-building enterprise, every aspect of the film's fictional culture is punctiliously crafted down to the most prosaic details: its language and alphabet, currency and units of measurement, popular games, funeral rites, drinking customs, cuisine, ticket-vending machines — the list could potentially stretch over several paragraphs. It is ultimately up to the individual spectator to take the time to explore the movie's semiotic density and accordingly appreciate its simultaneous similarity to and departure from the actual world. As the *AAW* review of the film maintains, "at its heart this is a quiet movie for those with imagination, for people who see more than the simple hustle and bustle of the world around them, and who look for something bigger in life" (Marc 2003).

The gorgeously detailed artwork underpinning both the natural and the architectural backgrounds is studiously interwoven with the characters' emotional struggles, whilst concurrently playing an instrumental role in the film's seamless orchestration of the familiar and the unfamiliar. Moreover, *Wings of Honneamise* uses the popular elements of Art Deco — trapezoidal, zigzagged and tumbled shapes, as well as fractionated, crystalline and prismatic patterns — allied with sweeping curves that at times supplement and at other times supplant the more gently sinuous and whiplash lines, largely based on stylized organic forms, characteristic of Art Nouveau. The pervasive utilization of elements derived from Art Deco and Art Nouveau in the creation of vibrant urbanscapes replete with myriad ornamental fixtures evokes a relatively recognizable stylistic realm. However, the application of analogous motifs to the rendition of vehicles and assorted machinery causes Shiro's world to often come across as tantalizingly uncanny. An ostensibly marginal but unforgettable touch consists of the design of the wiper arms for the local transport system (trolley convoys of sorts) in the shape of Art Deco "leaves" so delicately molded as to appear almost ethereal.[1]

Characterized throughout by curvilinear and undulating architectural structures, the city rises to the role of protagonist in several scenes. Its prominence is exuberantly proclaimed by a fanfare of roaring and rolling vehicles, a labyrinthine network of winding cobblestone alleys and meandering canals, and a veritable flurry of stairways, catwalks, gangways, archways, bridges, overpasses, funicular railways, battlements, domes, lobbies, pillars, wrought-iron railings, kiosks and food stalls, as well as a deluge of street signs, billboards and graffiti depicted in elegantly modulated hues. Specifically, technological aspects of each available scenario are conveyed with a cornucopian profusion of eagerly crafted details. At times, the machines exude an ominous sense of crushing gravity. At others, their exquisitely delineated contours recall the grace of filigree with its lace-like intertwined wires.

The oscillation of the two contrasting modalities of familiarity and estrangement at the level of style is mirrored by the film's pace. Indeed, the action deftly alternates between sequences of effervescent dynamism (i.e., in its breakneck chases and in the more challenging aspects of Shiro's training), and quieter moments devoted to the characters' domestic contexts and daily routines, as well as to technical evaluations of the scientific project in hand. It would be preposterous to deny, however, that the film's tempo occasionally flags to the point that the action would come across as excruciatingly ponderous were it not relieved by unflinchingly rich visuals. Aesthetically satisfying in the more intimate scenes, these rise to authentically sublime proportions in the representation of large-scale soaring vistas.

Most notably, *Wings of Honneamise* never tilts conclusively toward either the energetic or the meditative poles, maintaining throughout a delicate balance. The same could be said of its guiding message. At the same time as it contrasts generous idealism, on the one hand, and cynical rapaciousness, on the other, the movie intimates assiduously that the noblest of intentions are always in danger of degenerating into bigotry — and hence into no less blinkered a mentality than the one fostered by power-hungry politicians. This is patently borne out by the ill-defined — though seemingly staunch — spiritual goals pursued by Riquinni, whose philosophy often exudes adolescent fervor rather than mature conviction. Shiro is himself trapped in a thorny ethical dilemma. Whereas flying is his driving personal ambition, he is well aware of the iniquity poisoning the venture to which he has devoted himself and ill-disposed toward the government-led propaganda he is enjoined to fuel. When, at the end, he addresses humanity from orbit and messianically invites all people to pray and thank god for every step they take, it is also clear that he has not uncritically bought into the myth of space travel as a universal panacea. In fact, having alleged that warfare may be the result of humans feeling "confined," and that by entering cosmic infinity, they might be able to transcend the dread of enclosure and the attendant drive to fight, he remains resolutely pragmatic. Hence, he is wise enough to point out that were more and more people to follow his first steps into space, they would soon begin to wreck it through selfishness and belligerence.

Additionally, as Shiro passionately asks whether anybody is listening to his exhortation, we are given precious little indication that this might indeed be the case. In fact, as his words recede into the background, the screen is filled by images of ordinary life on Earth portraying mindless and brawling humans utterly oblivious to any peace-promoting message. In this decidedly unpreachy and inconclusive finale, it is made patently clear that the world of Honneamano (like the real world itself) may be on the verge of realizing one of mankind's grandest ambitions but is no less poised to face the possibility of utter annihilation by war.

An undisputed landmark in the evolution of space opera, *Wings of Honneamise* has inspired more or less directly numerous anime productions in later years. In its articulation of a whole mythology of cosmic exploration underpinned by meticulous world-building, Yamaga's feature has indeed imprinted its vestigial signature even on explicitly futuristic worlds, which take the human colonization of distant galaxies for granted, in terms of tone if not in those of narrative development. A case in point is the television series *Crest of the Stars* (dir. Yasuchika Nagaoka, 1999), in which "United Mankind" wage war against the "Abh," a race of aliens reminiscent of Tolkien's Elves. *Crest of the Stars* does not bear any obvious plot connections with *Wings of Honneamise*, yet it echoes Yamaga's movie in its ethical stance. The film, as shown, does not unproblematically enthrone the penetration — and possible domination — of space as a heroic quest guided by undilutedly noble principles. The finale makes this perfectly patent. In *Crest of the Stars*, similarly, the human race's objectives are presented as dubious and as hampered by tunnel vision. Above all, the human characters appear incapable of conceiving the so-called enemy in any terms other than narrowly human ones. Driven by an eminently teleological notion of cosmic expansion as the guarantee of steady progression toward higher and higher ends, humans simply cannot grasp the Abh's own worldview: as it happens, the alien race has no interest in dominance per se but actually regards the conquest of space purely as a means of gaining the freedom to roam it and to fathom its inexhaustible beauty. (The inappropriateness of judging non-humans by entirely human criteria is a theme that Gainax will revisit in greater depth, most notably in the *Evangelion* saga and in *This Ugly Yet Beautiful World*.)

Traces of *Wings of Honneamise*'s take on the development of astronautical technology and its military utilization can also be detected in Shouji Kawamori's *Macross Plus—The Movie* (1995) — a film that concurrently reverberates with Yamaga's fascination with intensely painterly natural imagery whose pastoral charm stands in ironic contrast with the technological equipment's sinister connotations. In the specific domain of natural backgrounds, one of *Wings of Honneamise*'s most worthy successors in recent years is undoubtedly the feature *The Place Promised In Our Early Days* (dir. Makoto Shinkai, 2004). In this work, virtually each of the frames depicting the environment is so stylishly lit as to appear endowed with an inner glow. Undoubtedly, many art lovers — and not merely anime enthusiasts — would like to see a still of one such frame on their wall. A mysterious column soaring tens of miles into the sky (which eventually turns out to be a parallel-universe generator powered through the hypersophisticated application of quantum physics) supplies the concomitantly magnificent and forbidding catalyst around which the visuals cluster, spiral and scatter by turns — in much the same way as Shiro's rocket provides an economically graphic pivot in Yamaga's movie. It is also worth pointing out that *The Place Promised In Our Early Days* shares several typically Gainaxian preoccupations. Set in an alternate-history postwar Japan and chronicling the principal characters' struggle to keep their teenage dreams alive, while both personal and collective crises insistently thrust them into a bleak adult reality, the film indeed provides an elegant interweaving of a solid sci-fi theme with an unsentimental exploration of convoluted psyches, tortuous relationships, unfulfilled promises and longings, and large-scale political intrigues.

Influential, yet still unique, *Wings of Honneamise* endures in anime history as a fascinating reinscription of classic science fiction into a story that some may regard as an adventure and others as a sermon but that ultimately stands out, first and foremost, as a grittily human and resolutely open-ended speculation on the engagement between man and machine. The spectacle it thereby offers, stark and serene by turns, resonates throughout with rhapsodic wonder at the mystery of the unfathomable beyond.

CHAPTER 3

Gunbuster (Top o Nerae!)
Director: Hideaki Anno (1988)

> Royal Space Force: The Wings of Honneamise
> *was a critical success but failed to attract the theatre audience needed
> to recoup [Gainax's] investment.
> How did they get back in the black?
> With* Gunbuster, *the first massively popular straight-to-video anime
> and one of the most influential titles of the '80s.*
> ...
> Gunbuster *created a mould that was followed by dozens upon dozens
> of OVA releases in the ensuing years*
> —"Gunbuster—*The OVA That Defined OVAs*"

The six-episode show *Gunbuster*—or *Top o Nerae!* (literally, "Aim for the Top!")—is a seminal work in the history of OVA production and a landmark in the evolution of *mecha* anime. It is also, however, the series to which fans ought to be grateful as the work responsible for Gainax's survival past their first work—and hence the panoply of stunning animations we have today. Hideaki Anno has commented thus on his directorial debut:

> If I hadn't made *Top o Nerae!*, this company might not be here today. You've got to make products [implying Gainax could not just dwell indefinitely on the *Wings of Honneamise* experience], or the staff won't stick around. The company isn't the one that makes these works—it's the staff that makes them. If you don't have a staff, you can't make the product [quoted in "(inside) Gainax"].

Gunbuster was released on DVD in a special three-disc collection by Bandai Visual USA in 2007 as part of their long-term commitment to the launch and promotion of "high-quality versions of historically significant anime titles" ("*Gunbuster*—The OVA That Defined OVAs"). This fully attests to the stature achieved by the 1988 OVA on an international scale.

Gunbuster is almost unanimously regarded as Gainax's first classic—not only due to its impressive balance of storytelling, psychologically convincing character development and sci-fi world-building but also because it ushers in a topos destined to become one of the studio's most enduring preoccupations, namely, the cardinal importance of maximizing one's potential so as to develop a mature sense of interpersonal responsibility. Set in a not-too-distant future, the story follows the exploits of a group of talented men and women picked from special training academies in charge of a fleet of *mecha*. Their mission is to confront and, ideally, destroy a breed of invading "Space Monsters"— gigantic insect-like aliens that roam the galaxy planting their eggs on practically every planet they encounter. Their key goal appears to be the total eradication of humanity and it is therefore vital to prevent them from pinpointing Earth's precise location.

The story opens in the year 2023, not long after humans' first fight against the extraterrestrial foe, and chronicles closely the growth of the tentative and seemingly inept teenager Noriko Takaya. This initially unlikely heroine strives to live up to the legendary reputation achieved by her heroic father — an admiral whose ship, the *Luxion*, was destroyed by the aliens at the cost of his own life — and hence comes to excel at the art of piloting despite having set out as the least promising trainee at Okinawa Academy.

The plot gains depth and intensity as this cute and sweet-tempered but also awkward and deeply insecure adolescent gradually learns to look inside herself and to accept what she sees, bravely accommodating both her capabilities and her shortcomings and eventually becoming a genuinely top-notch fighter willing to make enormous sacrifices. Thus, the OVA could be said to tackle a quintessentially Gainaxian preoccupation in proposing that no credentials, however distinguished, ever "make" a person unless they are bolstered by self-understanding and that self-understanding, in turn, is inevitably a laboriously accomplished outcome requiring both courage and humility. Other key characters beside Noriko include Kazumi Amano, unquestionably the most sympathetic and amiable crew member but also an indomitable fighter whose abilities emanate from diligent training no less than from natural aptness; Coach Ohta, a survivor from Admiral Takaya's ship determined to help Noriko fulfill her full potential; the valiant but doomed pilot Toren Smith (to whom Noriko becomes emotionally attached); and Jung Freud, the star of the Soviet Space Force, who antagonizes Kazumi and Noriko bitterly and insolently by turns until she recognizes their undeniable worth and resolves to befriend them.

Noriko's clumsy performance in the story's early parts would appear to indicate that *Gunbuster* constitutes a burlesque distortion of the *mecha* genre. The shots centered on giant robots, dubbed RX-7 units, doing calisthenics (including push-ups), pulling huge tires and running laps are especially amusing, in this respect. As manga artist and illustrator Haruhiko Mikimoto — the OVA's character designer has stressed — it is indeed instantly clear, upon encountering the series, that Hideaki Anno's intention was to approach the *mecha* genre from a radically "different direction," wherein the "parody aspect" was intended from the start to take center stage (Mikimoto, p. 43). However, in spite of its comedic entrée (replete with nods to the *shoujo* and cuties-in-space genres), *Gunbuster* soon offers an unexpected turn in the direction of serious drama, focusing on the protagonist's psychological turmoil amidst dysfunctional romances, torturous rivalries and other angst-ridden relationships.[1]

Moreover, the school-comedy formula, a set of conventions with a potentially facetious thrust, acquires sinister undertones when several of the other girls' perception of Noriko as an untalented pupil speciously receiving preferential treatment results in undilutedly cruel bullying. (This theme will be revisited in the course of the episode analysis offered later in this chapter.) Also prominent throughout *Gunbuster* is the absent-parent topos, one of Gainax's recurring concerns throughout its history. In this instance the absentee father does not elicit revulsion in the way the callous parents portrayed in *Neon Genesis Evangelion* and *This Ugly Yet Beautiful World* do, insofar as he has no choice but to dedicate himself wholeheartedly to his profession for the sake of humanity (in this respect, he comes closer to the parental figure presented in *Mahoromatic — Automatic Maiden*). Nevertheless, the fact remains that Noriko sees him only once a year as long as he is alive and that his ghostly presence looms like a giant shadow over her whole life well after his demise.

As the *AAW* review of the series indicates, *Gunbuster*'s dramatic poignancy owes much to Anno's deliberate prioritization of the action's raw affective qualities over and above its dynamic import: "The fight feels desperate more than heroic, difficult choices are made, and when tragedy strikes, it often does so without fanfare. Among the best moments is a subtly powerful scene that exchanges the theatrics that usually accompany the death of a character for nothing more than sudden radio silence" (Marc 2005). The scene here alluded to is the one in Episode 3 where Toren Smith suddenly vanishes without Noriko being able to get so much of a single shot to assist him.

Thus, the series transcends the formulaic boundaries of the *mecha* show and the school comedy alike, capitalizing on its creators' artistic sense to translate the potentially banal into a viewing experience that is engaging and refreshing in equal measures. At the same time, *Gunbuster* deserves special attention due to its radical redefinition of anime's technical purview through the establishment of the OVA format. Inaugurated by Mamoru Oshii's *Dallos* in 1985, this constitutes one of the most effective means of maximizing the medium's marketing opportunities and thus abetting its dissemination the world over.

The mood conveyed by *Gunbuster*'s early episodes is relatively blithe compared with the subsequent installments and some viewers may deem the affective switch jarring. Yet, it could be argued that it actually serves the purpose, within the show's overall diegesis, of accentuating by ironic contrast the pathos of the more serious segments of the action. As Kevin Gifford maintains, it is Anno's unique directorial signature, ultimately, that imparts *Gunbuster* with its unmistakable visual identity. Anno's style becomes especially palpable in the late installments, as "*Gunbuster* morphs into a sort of proto–*Evangelion*, complete with sudden flashes of text and a variety of weird, experimental storytelling methods" (Gifford 2007a, p. 152).

It could hardly be denied that in reenvisioning the familiar theme of the kid piloting a giant robot through the infusion into the action of highly innovative techniques, introspective and melancholy musings on emotional dislocation, and a genuinely frightening take on the horrors of its mammoth-scale battles, *Gunbuster* constitutes the closest antecedent to Gainax's most illustrious anime. As in *Evangelion*, the magnitude of the threat looming over the human species is overtly conveyed by means of the attackers' sheer size. It should suffice to note, in this regard, that the smallest insectile specimens presented in *Gunbuster* measure at least ten meters in length while the largest reach one hundred meters. Thus, even though the aliens' weapons are wholly organic rather than mechanical, their dimensions (allied to their stratospheric number) more than compensates for their lack of "technology" as humans understand it.

It is also noteworthy, in assessing *Gunbuster*'s connection with *Evangelion*, that several characters from the OVA anticipate characters subsequently developed for the TV series: Noriko, specifically, foreshadows the timid Shinji; Coach Ohta, like Gendou Ikari after him, is a distant man driven by a stormy past; Jung Freud presages Asuka by virtue of her fiery temper; Kazumi is an obvious forerunner for Misato both stylistically and narratively. (Please note that whereas *Gunbuster*'s characters were designed, as mentioned earlier, by Mikimoto, the artist behind the distinctive psychophysiognomies of *Evangelion*'s personae is Yoshiyuki Sadamoto. The role played by Sadamoto on the *Gunbuster* production team was that of animation director. On the purely stylistic level, Sadamoto favors lissome proportions, while Mikimoto appears to harbor a preference for slightly more robust shapes.)

As the chapters to follow demonstrate, this book works on the premise that providing episode-by-episode analyses is hardly likely to benefit the reader in the case of protracted series including numerous installments. In the case of a capsulated six-episode show like

Gunbuster, however, evaluating the adventure's flight path through sequential analysis seems appropriate insofar as each installment constitutes a distinctive stage in its advancement. Accordingly, the ensuing paragraphs supply a chronological assessment of the OVA's episodes seeking to bring out the show's axial concerns while also commenting on some of the visual effects utilized in order to invest those thematic preoccupations with a peculiar graphic density.

The opening credits sequence offers a paradigmatic illustration of Gainax's penchant for encapsulating visually a whole adventure's dramatic import by the most economical means through a montage alternating three distinct types of images: frames focusing on individual characters in order to highlight particular physiognomic and dynamic traits; vistas of the galaxy's overwhelming immensity; moments extrapolated from the series' pivotal action sequences.

Episode 1—"Unbelievable! Amano and I are Pilots?"—opens with a voiceover from Noriko played against the background of a series of stills. The screen fills with a bright photograph portraying the heroine and her father in an idyllic setting as Noriko reads out her elementary school essay celebrating Admiral Takaya's achievements, followed by newspaper clippings confirming his stature and culminating with a full-color portrait of the smiling officer. The image is seamlessly replaced by a somber version of the same photograph, now in monochrome and within a black frame, as Noriko describes her father's death. A further set of newspaper clippings documenting the incident lend documentary weight to the girl's personal report. By means of its carefully orchestrated chromatic shift, the sequence provides an eloquent affective contrast. The link between its conflicting sets of visuals is Noriko's determination to follow her dad into space. Her closing lines indeed are: "I want to be a space pilot, too."

Many of the show's key themes are introduced in the opening installment despite its seeming levity. Most crucially, Episode 1 emphasizes the importance of discipline and intensive training over and above natural talent. When Noriko, who regards Kazumi as the ultimate role model, tells the older girl "You're a natural," Kazumi tersely replies: "No, Takaya. It's hard work.... If you work at it, you'll succeed.... Hang in there." Noriko's admiration for Kazumi verges on fetishistic infatuation: This proposition is jocularly underscored through a parody of the typical *shoujo* mode in the scene where we are offered glimpses of Kazumi as Noriko perceives her, namely, a quasi-angelic being surrounded by an unearthly pastel-tinted glow against a background of sensuous red roses. The protagonist continues to communicate her respect for Kazumi by addressing her throughout the story as "*Oné-sama*."[2]

The paramount value of discipline, promulgated by Kazumi in the dialogue mentioned above, is reinforced by Coach Ohta later in the episode. When Noriko opines that her selection as a pilot was a "cruel" action, he ripostes: "You think you're not cut out to be a pilot...? But Amano is? come with me." Ohta then shows Noriko her role model as she climbs a steep flight of stairs with massive weights attached to her shoes and states: "It's true that Kazumi is good. But what's more important is the work she puts into it. You're not good yet. Not disciplined enough. But you have the raw talent it takes. That's why I picked you. Work hard. Let your natural abilities surface. Make decisions from your heart. In space ... depend only on yourself."

Bullying also plays an important role in Episode 1, its unsentimental depiction often reaching realistically sadistic extremes. This results from the pupils' belief that Noriko is the undeserving beneficiary of favoritism. The girl's assets are indeed far from obvious at the beginning of the story: in the course of the first training session under Coach Ohta's supervision, in particular, Noriko is utterly incapable of coordinating her movements with her *mecha*'s control systems and is made to run the fifty laps which the other pupils are performing in conjunction with their respective training robots all by herself. It is on the very next day, however, that her choice as a future pilot is announced: Ohta has obviously recognized her potential worth. The young trainees' responses to Noriko's selection exude equal measures of dismissive haughtiness and vituperative jealousy. "Her father was a captain of the ship where the crew was killed," one of the pupils announces. "She's got connections, that's why they picked her.... She's the coach's pet." The girls' animus is so intense that they even nickname their victim *"zenmetsu musume"* (the "daughter of defeat"), and place nasty graffiti all over Noriko's RX and drawing pins on the seat of its cockpit to further torment her.

The heroine's brutal persecution reaches its climax as the skilled pupil Kashiwara challenges Noriko to a duel in their training robots. Initially overwhelmed, the protagonist suddenly remembers Ohta's advice to follow her personal instinct in emergencies: She turns off the *mecha*'s monitor so as to depend exclusively on her own senses and vanquishes Kashiwara by performing the "Thunder Kick" (*"Inazuma Kick"*) — a feat deemed well beyond the capabilities of a rookie. It is worth dwelling for a moment on Anno's characterization of Noriko's antagonist: for all her hostility, Kashiwara is not portrayed as undilutedly evil but as actually capable of forgiveness and respect for others' abilities. This is attested to by the closing airport scene, in which Kashiwara can be seen waving enthusiastically as Noriko, Kazumi and Ohta leave Okinawa, bound for the Silver Star Station in Earth's orbit. The same ethical suppleness is later applied to the portrayal of the aliens as creatures that are not so much adversarial as simply oblivious to the human race's plight. (The alien culture "Saint" against which humanity is pitched in *Mahoromatic — Automatic Maiden* is similarly characterized.)

Episode 2, "The Challenge of the Fearless Girl Genius," opens with a sequence dramatizing the *Luxion*'s final moments. Noriko's father is apologizing to his beloved child for not being able to join her for her birthday, addressing an animated snapshot of the little girl, which he replays over and over again. There is only enough time left for one survivor to evacuate the ship, and Admiral Takaya forces Ohta to leave while he stays behind as the *Luxion* blows up. On the *Exelion* at last, Noriko and Kazumi meet Jung Freud, a character initially so competitive as to challenge Kazumi to a fight during their first training session. The duel is about to finish in a draw when Noriko, who has been following the fighters, accidentally opens a secret area of the base where an alien's remnants are kept. As Noriko realizes that the creature was the cause of her dad's death, we are treated to a flashback in which she recalls Admiral Takaya's visits for her birthday. To emphasize the imaginary feel of these frames, the animation introduces an element of intentional jitteriness, a subtle blurring of the figures' contours and explicitly hand-drawn graphics.

An unidentified object moving at a rate close to the speed of light is detected soon after, and Noriko and Kazumi are sent to investigate it by Ohta who wishes to get them used to light-speed flights in consideration of their future employment as Gunbuster pilots. The object in question turns out to be the wreck of Admiral Takaya's vessel. Noriko enters the *Luxion* when only two days have effectively elapsed since its destruction (due to the temporal vagaries inherent to *Gunbuster*'s entire adventure) and sees the horror of the attack in all its starkness. Ohta, who would have very much liked to spare Noriko this experience, personally engineers her rescue.

The episode's closing portion provides one of the entire show's most moving moments as Noriko and Kazumi, for whom the mission only occurred one hour earlier, find that six months have actually elapsed for their associates. Noriko, acknowledging that her own birthday would have occurred six months earlier, addresses her departed father with the wish to celebrate it "today" nonetheless, just with him. (*Gunbuster*'s idiosyncratic approach to the temporal dimension will be discussed in detail later in this chapter.)

In Episode 3, "First Love, First Sortie," we are introduced to one of *Gunbuster*'s most intriguing scientific tropes: "warp." During "warp," we are told, ships go into "subspace" and the "ether becomes plasma." No activity is allowed onboard and the crew are therefore confined to their cabins where they wait patiently for the warp to come to an end: The atmosphere is similar to the mood of those scenes from classic war movies in which soldiers simply wait for the next attack whiling the hours away with games and tales. Jung Freud maintains that a connection exists "between subspace and the spirit world" and accordingly regales her captive audience with legion scary stories.

As an additional pastime, crew members engage in tests of courage ("*kimo dameshi*") — a motif revisited some years later to memorable effect by Shouji Saeki's *This Ugly Yet Beautiful World*. Noriko, specifically, is charged with the task of venturing down the *Exelion*'s darkened corridors to leave a marker of her presence in a remote corner of the ship. As she wanders through the forbidding gloom feeling utterly puny and defenseless, Noriko is surprised by an apparition, which she at first mistakes for a ghost. In fact, the vision amounts to a flesh-and-blood youth, Toren Smith, who is undertaking a test akin to Noriko's. Discovered by Ohta, the pair are punished by being made to polish the *Exelion*'s seemingly countless laser lenses.

The action undergoes an abrupt change of pace as an enemy fleet moves in relatively close proximity to the ship, thus engendering a mighty magnetic storm. In the buildup to the operation meant to keep the aliens at bay, *Gunbuster* bears full witness to Anno's passion for meticulously executed technological equipment: the *Exelion*'s headquarters, with their myriad monitors, dials, graphs and diagrams, directly anticipate the depiction of the NERV HQ in *Evangelion* while also obliquely foreshadowing the command center of the *New Nautilus* in *Nadia*. Occasionally, the equipment presented in *Gunbuster* incorporates deliberately anachronistic touches. The monitors, for example, appear to be lit by neon lamps. The use of relatively old-fashioned cableways in Episode 6 conveys comparable retrofuturistic effects.

Wondering what her personal role in the imminent battle might be, Noriko feels totally devastated when she accidentally finds out that Kazumi wishes her partnership with the younger girl to be "disbanded," in the belief that Noriko is not fit to go into space and would certainly die were she to do so. Smith endeavors to console her and urges Noriko to pair up with him instead. Not long after the new team has entered the fray amidst ever-proliferating hordes of aliens, Smith vanishes without his partner being able to come to his assistance. This tragic incident affects profoundly the heroine's perception of herself and of her duties, and accompanies her to the very end as both a cautionary reminder of her human limitations and a potent motivating force no less influential than Noriko's determination to live up to her father's reputation. In sharp contrast with the bleak inescapability of the protagonist's predicament, the image of the alien presented at the end of the installment provides one of the OVA's most striking pictorial gems. The creature is especially notable by virtue of its eerily beautiful amalgamation of disparate organic forms and concurrent evocation of an exquisite sense of dignity and grace.

A dispassionate assessment of the aliens' ethical stance is provided in Episode 4, "Launch! The Uncompleted Final Weapon," by means of a speech delivered by a scientist to the *Exelion*'s Council. For aliens, the expert explains, humans are akin to "bacteria" and "to the galaxy, human actions serve no known or useful purpose"— people are merely "flotsam in the sea of space." The installment also offers *Gunbuster*'s first spectacular climax as the enemy armies manage to attack in subspace while the *Exelion* is attempting to return to Earth. As the ship emerges from warp, the human fighters inevitably disclose the location of their home planet, which is exactly what they most wanted to avoid. Noriko, left behind aboard the *Exelion* while her comrades engage in an all-out fight against the aliens, is at first rendered powerless by feelings of utter inanity and bitter humiliation, and she sits on her humble cot weeping profusely. Visually, the girl's grief is succinctly amplified through a studious use of reflections: images of her face reflected in the little mirror placed on the bedpost quietly, yet effectively, duplicate the magnitude of her sorrow.

However defeated Noriko may feel at this stage in the action, her proverbial resolve soon gains the upper hand. She single-handedly activates the as yet unfinished Gunbuster, which she has learned how to pilot through secret and exacting training supervised directly by Coach Ohta, and joins the fray to everybody's absolute astonishment. It is at this point that the ultimate fighting machine's most formidable attributes come resplendently to the fore: a cape-like shield exuding chivalric connotations; fingertip missiles; laser beams and holographic radars. Made of an element exclusively indigenous to the *Gunbuster* universe ("Buster Metal") combined with titanium, the *mecha* measures over 600 feet in height and weighs over 10,000 tons. In specifically dynamic terms, the machine's key properties are the ability to travel at a velocity equating to 99.9 percent the speed of light in normal space and a knack for producing faster-than-light warps. Kazutaka Miyake's design emphasizes the Gunbuster's supple plastic mass by integrating conical and cylindrical shapes that convey awesome strength without pandering to the *mecha*-genre taste for overtly metallic, sharp and rigid surfaces. This almost organic feel is perpetuated — though with striking graphic variations — by later Gainax machines, most notably the Eva Units in *Evangelion* and the Dix-Neuf in *Gunbuster 2*.

Therefore, even though the Gunbuster does not incorporate any explicitly declared biological components, it nonetheless communicates a powerful sense of aliveness. This impression is assiduously reinforced by the direction's emphasis on the coalescence of the pilot's and the robot's bodies: Thus, the *mecha* is not posited simply as a prosthetic adjunct but rather as an indispensable complement to the human operator's own functions. This effect reaches its apotheosis in the scene from Episode 6 where Noriko rips the Gunbuster's chest open to release one of its generators and the structure that appears beneath the robot's metallic skin turns out to look very much like an animal ribcage. The visual metaphor is sustained as the "stripping" of the *mecha* results in half of Noriko's own suit being analogously torn in the pectoral area (with a concession to fan service, incidentally).

In the climax of Episode 4, Noriko spectacularly decimates all the alien units except for the mothership, which is too fast for the Gunbuster to compete with — hence, she decides to let it strike her. No sooner has the unit cut straight through the Gunbuster than its pilot activates the massive electrodes located on the *mecha*'s arms and annihilates it. (The frame in which the Gunbuster is pierced by the alien mothership, incidentally, foreshadows the penetration of the Eva-01 by the "Lance of Longinus" in *End of Evangelion*.) The real Noriko has finally asserted herself beyond doubt.

Set in Okinawa in the year A.D. 2032, Episode 5 — "Please Save Some Time for Love" — throws painfully into relief Noriko's temporal displacement. Ten years have passed on Earth but the girl has only four months' worth of memories from when she was last at the Academy. This state of affairs helps Noriko grasp how her dad must have truly felt upon his annual visits, when he would find her substantially grown from one year to the next while no more than a few days had concurrently elapsed in his own temporal scheme.

Reality hits Noriko brutally when she bumps into her former classmate Kimiko. Whereas Noriko, despite the horrors she has witnessed in space, is fundamentally still a kid, Kimiko is no longer the cheerful and carefree schoolgirl the protagonist remembers. Now a mother concerned with her little daughter Takami's future, she begs Noriko to use her connections in the military in order to secure a place for the girl on the Eltrium, the evacuation ship built in preparation for the aliens' ultimate onslaught within which only a paltry number of humans can be feasibly accommodated.

The age gulf that has formed between Noriko and Kimiko is painful to behold and serves to remind us that no unproblematic glee is to be derived from eternal — or near-eternal — youth. Thus, although Gainax's animations frequently present adults as unpleasant (if not downright obnoxious) creatures, they concomitantly emphasize that indulging in the fantasy of ageless adolescence encapsulated by the "Peter Pan Complex" — a concept formulated by the popular psychologist Dan Kiley — is hardly desirable. In fact, that fantasy is unremittingly punctured by the opposite pull of what could be experimentally dubbed the "Vampire Syndrome," namely, the perception of immortality and never-ending youthfulness as curses. This topos will be revisited in the chapter on *Mahoromatic — Automatic Maiden* with reference to the show of that title, to Gainax's own ancillary production *Petite Princess Yucie* and to the series *Vampire Princess Miyu* directed by Toshihiro Hirano.

While Noriko struggles to come to terms with her private ghosts, the war against the aliens rages on. As their last resort, humans decide to use the decommissioned *Exelion* to create a black hole capable of swallowing the approaching enemy units, which now number in their millions. It is up to the "Buster Machine # 1," piloted by Noriko, and the "Buster Machine # 2," piloted by Kazumi, to defend the *Exelion* in the course of the mission. Kazumi, whose romantic liaison with Ohta has been finally revealed after a scattering of discreet hints earlier in the series, is utterly disheartened by the thought that once the operation is over, six months will have gone by on Earth: by then Ohta, who is afflicted by space-radiation syndrome, might already have passed away.

At one point, she very nearly gives up altogether but Noriko valiantly urges her on: by now, she has not only thoroughly internalized the "*top o nerae!*" lesson as her personal guiding force but also learnt how to communicate its importance to others at times of uncertainty and strife. As Kazumi snaps back to her customary plucky self, the two machines combine to form the titular *mecha*. The sequence matches in both dramatic pathos and sheer graphic vigor the Gunbuster's inaugural launch in Episode 4.

When the Gunbuster lands in the vicinity of the hospital where Ohta is being treated, the animation unobtrusively offers a touch of graphic genius that eloquently attests to Gainax's magisterial attention to details. As the massive robot's feet make contact with the ground, the intensity of the impact is conveyed by a frame depicting the lower leg as though it were seamlessly attached to the foot without the mediation of articulating junctions. When the *mecha*'s body adjusts, the leg correspondingly elongates, revealing an ankle-like area between the foot and the calf. These images exemplify Gainax's proficient use of the technique described by Richard Williams as the "successive breaking of joints." By "bending the joint whether or not it would actually bend in reality" and "doing it continuously ... to make things limber," this strategy enables animators to convey "the effect of curved action by using straight lines," and hence produce "fluid, flowing movement" by recourse to geometrically accurate forms rather than unrealistically "rubbery figures" (Williams, pp. 231–32). No less striking, at this point in the action, is the shot following the landing in which a little door opens in the Gunbuster's left hand whence Noriko and Kazumi hurriedly emerge in their eagerness to reach their ailing mentor without further delay.

Episode 6, "At the End of the Endless Stream," opens at Okinawa Academy like the previous one but is presented in black and white. The year is now A.D. 2048, Coach Ohta is dead and his widow Kazumi stands looking at his grave in the swirling snow. The Earth has been severely damaged by the shockwave caused by the black hole generated in the course of the earlier operation. As all viable resources are being channeled into the production of a

"Black Hole Bomb" intended to eradicate the alien enemy once and for all, large parts of the planet affected by the catastrophe are still unreconstructed.

As for Noriko, her experience of temporal dislocation has by now reached preposterous extremes: although 16 years have elapsed since her last mission with Kazumi, only six months have gone by for the heroine as she remains stationed in outer space. The passage of time is also underscored with reference to technological development, not only at the level of large-scale military equipment but also at the level of civilian consumption. This idea is neatly encapsulated by the contrast between the animated snapshot of Noriko, which her father watches insistently in Episode 2, and the photograph of Takami sent to Noriko, where the figure is actually able to come out of the frame.

The OVA's final episode addresses overtly a thorny ethical question alluded to at several junctures in the story, namely, does humanity have an automatic right to wipe out an entire galaxy and an entire breed of sentient beings? Since peaceful coexistence with the invaders is clearly not an option, humans decide to deploy the aforementioned weapon, a.k.a. "Buster Machine # 3," a bomb in the shape of a monstrously gigantic rugby ball. As the countdown to the deflagration of the Black Hole Bomb starts, the aliens multiply faster and in larger quantities than expected. Their objective is to destroy the Buster Machine # 3, neglecting the remainder of the fleet. The main weapon is marginally damaged but the rest of the human forces incur dire losses, which are vividly depicted by Anno's team in utterly uncompromising tones.

Although the fierce climactic battle is so gorgeously rendered — in both its animated segments and in its series of stills, rough sketches and stylized artwork — as to verge on the aesthetic concept of the Sublime, its visceral violence is never effaced or edulcorated. The overall mood is unsentimental to the point of forlornness. Unexpectedly, at the end of the countdown the bomb fails to activate fully as only 98 percent of its reactors is functional. Noriko decides to enter the Black Bomb with Kazumi in the Gunbuster and infuse the lacking energy into the apparatus by recourse to one of the *mecha*'s two reactors, hoping to use the other one to return to Earth. Having successfully engendered a black hole and thus annihilated both the aliens and the galaxy, Noriko and Kazumi eventually return to their native planet to find it altered almost beyond recognition, at least from a distance: 12,000 years have elapsed since the completion of their last mission.

Ultimately, in veering away from established conventions, *Gunbuster* delivers an anime so rich, sensitive and endearing as to demonstrate that for the Gainax animators, no less than for Noriko, the guiding precept is to "aim for the top." The most audaciously experimentative gesture is provided by the closing episode, presented entirely in black and white (except for the very final frames) by actually executing the images in various shades of gray, instead of simply shooting color animation with black-and-white film as would be both more customary and less demanding for the artists involved. Furthermore, the episode uses an unusual 16x9 aspect ratio, which results in a wider image display and lends the action a distinctively cinematic feel.

Even when *Gunbuster* is not so overtly bold on the technical front, it is stylistically informed throughout by an overt emphasis on the manually crafted qualities and general constructedness of its images, at times foregrounded by the replacement of polychromatic palettes with a grayscale scheme that evokes the properties of pencil and chalk. These characteristics are most notable in the rendition of emotionally intense incidents and flashbacks. Classic examples are provided in Episode 2 by the aforementioned scene in which Noriko remembers her father's annual visits for her birthday and, later, by the shot of the girl's horrified face as she enters the battleship in which the officer met his dismal end. Grayscale filters are effectively used in Episode 1 to heighten the scene's affective impact for the frame displaying Noriko in profile as she learns that Ohta is a survivor of the *Luxion* disaster. Also memorable, in this respect, is the scene in Episode 5 in which the protagonist discovers that Coach Ohta has space-radiation sickness and is therefore unlikely to live much longer. Inspired use of explicitly hand-drawn and hand-painted graphics is likewise made in the closing credits: In this specific instance, elegant pencil sketches and watercolor washes representing simple moments in Noriko's life exude a markedly more light-hearted mood.

Gainax's proficient handling of backgrounds as pictorial feats endowed with autonomous artistic value rather than mere stage sets is consistently borne out by *Gunbuster*. This skill is instantly communicated by the OVA from its opening installment: the background paintings deployed for the sequences that dramatize both Noriko's and Kazumi's training routines, with their glorious skies alternating between dawn and dusk, glittering water expanses, lush vegetation and billowing clouds, are particularly remarkable in their evocation of a genuine sense of the "heroic."

Anno's passion for reflections is palpable throughout. Beside the aforementioned example provided by Episode 4, a further typical instance of that ploy can be found in Episode 2, in the scene where Noriko and Kazumi face Ohta after neglecting to undertake their training duties and entering the top-secret location where classified material is stored, and are spared imprisonment for the simple reason that they cannot be trained if they are locked up. The two women's shapes are here literally "framed" within Ohta's mirror shades. Reflections similarly play a key role in Episode 1, in the scene in which Ohta lectures Noriko about the crucial importance of hard work and self-discipline, as well as in the scene in which the disaffected trainee Kashiwara goes to see the coach to complain about Noriko's selection as a Top Squadron pilot. Kashiwara's body is starkly framed within the rectangle of light created by the opening of a door to Ohta's dusky office, and both are further framed within his glasses.

The fact that one always sees *two* reflections when glasses are involved concisely evokes split identities, equivocal situations and shifting perspectives. This theme is brought to the fore in Episode 2 by the scene in which Noriko sees Earth's newest battleship, the *Exelion*, from afar and states that the vessel looks "small" and then gradually appreciates its overwhelming magnitude. Ohta tersely communicates his relativistic message by stressing that in space objects never quite look their real dimensions—"in space you lose perspective of distance and size"—and implying that in the absence of conclusively dependable referents all certainties must be suspended.

Gunbuster's technological infrastructure is invariably rendered with a characteristically Gainaxian devotion to minute details. The digital equipment, with its profusion of dials, diagrams, graphs and ubiquitous beams is impressive, especially in the sequences that focus on a pilot's computer-mediated perception of the outside world from the cockpit of a giant robot. The *mecha* themselves are lovingly depicted, coming across by turns as awesome and amusing depending on their context. For example, even though Noriko's robot maintains the same basic shape throughout her training, it stands out as the very epitome of clunky clumsiness as long as she is incapable of proper coordination but comes to exhibit an incontrovertibly balletic elegance as her skills become increasingly refined. The scene in which the *mecha*-clad Noriko jogs along the seashore at sunset accompanied by Coach Ohta on his motorbike is a genuine gem among all *mecha* animation ever committed to the screen.

Gunbuster also bears witness to Anno's distinctive utilization of silence as a potent dramatic tool. Indeed, one of the whole show's most effectively moving moments is the totally wordless scene in which Noriko briefly looks into the room where Toren Smith's comrades quietly mourn their lost mate. One senses at once the protagonist's desire to share her grief with the others, respect for their privacy, and a latent feeling of guilt at not being able to protect Smith in combat. Of course, Gainax would not be Gainax without an element of self-reflexivity. The studio's allegiance to this ruse is overtly exposed at the end of the first episode, where the banner displayed by the Okinawa Academy students to wish Ohta, Kazumi and Noriko farewell bears the inscription "*Top o Nerae!*" Moreover, the buildings within the airport compound carry signs that include "Anno" and "Gainax." Self-referential proclivities also make themselves felt at the intradiegetic level. The mugs used on the *Exelion*, for instance, bear a logo that overtly mirrors the star-shaped component of the Gunbuster's head.

Gunbuster is undeniably made memorable by its stunningly detailed settings, originally handled combat sequences, and subtle integration of the sublime grandness of the firmament with the gritty palpability of fear. In assessing the OVA's comedic dimension, however, it should be noted that Anno's provocative utilization of intertextual humor in the guise of legion parodic allusions to other animated and live-action films, as well as disparate facets of popular culture, is also central to its aesthetics. The title itself is a double parody of the classic tennis anime *Aim for the Ace!* (dir. Osamu Dezaki, 1973–1974) and the American film *Top Gun* (dir. Tony Scott, 1986). Additionally, as the *AAW* review points out, the "'Tannhauser Gate' mentioned in one science lesson is a reference to the movie *Blade Runner*—Rutger Hauer's character Roy mentions such a thing in recollecting his time in space," while the "overall plot has also been said to be inspired by *Starship Troopers*, the novel by Robert J. Heinlein" (Marc 2005).

Noriko, for her part, turns out to be an otaku: "Two of her favorite shows were *Space Battleship Yamato* and *Nausicaä of the Valley of Wind*. [In Episode 5, the room she occupies when she returns to Earth for her graduation ceremony flaunts posters of both Hayao Miyazaki's *Nausicaä* and his later film *My Neighbour Totoro*.] She also loved heavy metal music as was evident by the Van Halen poster hanging in her living quarters. There was even a shot of the miniature submarine from the 20th Century–Fox movie *Fantastic Voyage* floating over the hull of the *Exelion*" ("*Gunbuster*: Series History"). The character of Toren Smith, moreover, is named after a real-life person largely responsible for promoting the spread of manga in the United States.

On a more facetious note, *Gunbuster* is also reputed to have ushered in the stylistic flourish known as "Gainax bounce" or "animated jiggle," namely, a buoyantly fluid and detailed representation of breasts in motion. Episode 5 supplies a classic example of this ruse in the scene where Noriko collapses onto her bed and lands heavily on her back. In the rebound, her loose sleeveless vest detaches itself from the body, offering a glimpse of her shapely breasts. Some viewers detest such moments as pure indulgence in fan service. Many others, however, find these frames sensuously appealing, very possibly subscribing to Roland Barthes's proposition that "the most erotic portion of a body" is "*where the garment gapes*," since "it is intermittence ... which is erotic: the intermittence of skin flashing between two articles of clothing..., between two edges" (Barthes 1990, pp. 9–10). Nobody could deny, either way, that the scene succeeds in conveying a relaxed image of the heroine that stands in refreshing contrast with the tension-exuding Noriko seen in the martial and training sequences.

One of *Gunbuster*'s most intriguing aspects — hinted at earlier — lies with its handling of temporal dilation in relation to the protagonist's ability to travel at the speed of light. Based on the "Rip-Van-Winkle effect" implied by Albert Einstein's theory of relativity, this rests on the notion that when one moves at such a rate (approximately 300,000 km per sec), time passes more slowly. As Alessio Soldano explains, "some experimental proofs of this theory" truly exists: "in the high atmosphere, the cosmic rays produce various particles, among which there are the muons." Although these particles' lifespan would not logically allow them to reach the Earth's surface," we are able to receive them ... because time goes by more slowly for the muons, which travel at the velocity of light" (Soldano).

The gap between the actual passage of time on Earth and the passage of time as it is perceived by Noriko, accordingly, grows incrementally with each of her missions, so that although the events recorded in the OVA ultimately span a considerable duration, they are felt by Noriko to have filled no more than a year. When she graduates, for example, in terms of her own sense of time she is merely seventeen but the certificate shows that she is actually twenty-seven. On such occasions, the overall effect is gently amusing if not exactly funny. At other times, however, the dissonance between the heroine's personal perception of life and the actual flow of events strikes painful chords.

A classic moment, as intimated in the course of the detailed episode analysis offered earlier, is provided by the scene in which Noriko finds out that her best friend Kimiko has become a mother: The discovery unsettles her deeply by drawing her attention to all the experiences that have passed her by, leaving her inexorably at the mercy of a "sad and lonely feeling." Temporal dilation is also put to great dramatic effect in the OVA's open-ended finale: Noriko and Kazumi, as mentioned, return to Earth after spending no less than 12,000 years in space. When they finally arrive, they find a "welcome home" message left for them by Jung Freud, which could be seen to allude to a comforting sense of continuity. However, the fact that the last ideogram in the word "*okaerinasai*" is intentionally reversed succinctly hints at possibly momentous transformations in Earth's whole civilization.

Barmy as the concept of time dilation may sound, its foundations are soundly scientific. The phenomenon described by Soldano upholds this proposition and the *AAW* review even more emphatically promulgates it: "in traveling to distant parts of space it would be entirely likely to find yourself moving away from Earth at speeds near the speed of light, which causes time to pass more slowly relative to those back on Earth and would produce a cumulative effect of years of missed time upon your return" (Marc 2005).

The concepts of relativity and time dilation are also used to memorable dramatic effect in *Voices of a Distant Star*, an experimental 24-minute OVA written, directed and executed entirely on his Macintosh computer by Makoto Shinkai in 2002. Universally acclaimed as a groundbreaking intervention in the field of advanced CGI — and, accordingly, the receiver of a panoply of prestigious awards — the film chronicles the long-distance relationship between Mikako Nagamine, a middle school girl who joins the UN Space Army's carrier *Lysithea* as a Special Agent in a war against aliens, and her boyfriend Noboru Terao, who remains on Earth. After Mikako's departure, the couple faithfully goes on communicating across interstellar infinity by email. However, as the *Lysithea* ventures deeper and deeper into space, the messages take increasingly long to reach Noboru, to the point that the time-lag in the correspondence eventually encompasses several years. About half way through the action, Mikako sends an email to Noboru bearing the date 2047 addressed to "the twenty-four-year old Noboru" by "the fifteen-year old Mikako." The message, we are told, would reach the young man only over eight years later.

The scientific metaphor developed by *Gunbuster* is pursued further in the farcical "Lessons" delivered by SD ("Super-Deformed" or "Squashed-Down") versions of Noriko and Kazumi between Episodes 1 and 2, between Episodes 3 and 4, and between Episodes 4 and 5. Although the characters' grotesque appearance, in heightening the humor of these scenes, may suggest that their content is totally fictitious, this is not actually the case. In fact, wholly sci-fi theories surrounding "warps" coexist alongside serious scientific notions such as "black holes," "Lorentz transforms," "cosmic rays" and the "Doppler effect." The series in its entirety, anticipating *Evangelion*'s approach to science, is peppered with references to genetics, astrophysics and geology.

An exemplary instance of Anno's tongue-in-cheek use of both scientific jargon and pseudoscientific patter is offered at the beginning of Episode 3, as the following chunk of hyperbolically dense text scrolls down the screen:

> Extract from Kazumi Amano's speech during the 2021 Japan High School Physics Debate Convention — "Comparing the similarities between quantum, mechanical partition function and statistical mechanical partition function in ordinary form, the net quantum mechanical effect can be expressed as:
>
> $$Z = \{ \exp[i/hl]n[\emptyset]$$
>
> If we interpret this as the fundamental relation, this is actually what Wall proposed and Yang and Mills expounded on in regard to the gauge theory and its result; i.e. the Weinberg-Salam theory unifying electromagnetic and weak interactions. The formation of a unified quantum mechanical theory can be concluded as the most correct interpretation of the ordinary form of the fundamental relation. A good example in the classical interchange is the integral of the isospin resonance in the 10XX GeV region which affects the physical parameter $\emptyset$ and the subatomic structures."

The piece continues in this vein for several paragraphs with a sprinkling of historic names for good measure — Einstein, Hilbert, Fermi, Dirac and Planck, for example. Once again, even though this spiel oozes with mumbo-jumbo, its underpinnings are not entirely fantastical.

The OVA's references to astronomy, specifically, are by and large accurate despite the occasional nod to farcical technobabble. An especially good example of the show's careful use of scientific allusions is supplied by Episode 2 in the sequence in which the wreck of the *Luxion* is detected and an *Exelion* technician states that it is impossible to obtain a precise picture of the object as a result of "its marked Doppler-Lorentz shift." As Soldano points out,

> The reference to Lorentz regards the Lorentz transforms ... and therefore the fact that the object appears much smaller than it is really; ... the Doppler reference regards the so called *red shift—blue shift*: when you observe a body which is moving away or getting near at high speed from a long distance, the measurement of the radiation emitted by such a body shifts towards red or blue. This expedient is used in astronomy to establish whether a certain celestial body is getting near or going away from us.

Black holes are likewise intelligently invoked. Even though *Gunbuster*'s use of these celestial phenomena "more or less as vacuum cleaners for aliens" may seem hilarious, this function is quite consonant with their proven "ability to draw towards themselves everything falling within their field. Everything means really everything, luminous waves included ... the choice made by the *Gunbuster* direction in the moment when the first black hole comes into being in the 5th episode (i.e. perfect silence) is rather well-chosen" (Soldano).

Writing about the novel as both a form and a medium, Susan Sontag has offered a memorably succinct account of fiction writing that elliptically provides an apposite commentary on the art of animation as well — and especially on the aesthetic and ethical experience delivered by a work of *Gunbuster*'s caliber. "A great writer of fiction," Sontag writes,

> both creates — through acts of imagination, through language that feels inevitable, through vivid forms — a new world, a world that is unique, individual; and responds to a world, the world the writer shares with other people but is unknown or mis-known by still more people, confined in their worlds: call that history, society, what you will.

Even more directly relevant to Anno's 1988 OVA is Sontag's emphasis on the artist's ability to take us "on a journey. Through space. Through time," leading us "over a gap" and hence making "something go where it was not." *Gunbuster*'s provocatively original take on the temporal dimension, finally, echoes Sontag's proposition that the process through which authentically inspired fiction guides us "is much more than mere casual sequence, just as lived time — which distends with feeling and contracts with the deadening of feeling — is not uniform, clock time. The work of the novelist [indeed any artist] is to enliven time, as it is to animate space" (Sontag).

CHAPTER 4

Nadia: The Secret of Blue Water (Fushigi no Umi no Nadia)
Director: Hideaki Anno (1990–1991)

> Nadia ... *is a lively adventure, swinging easily from gut-busting hilarity to thought-provoking importance, often within the same episode.... Probably the most notable feature of the series is its characters. Director Anno Hideaki ... paces the series well, and gives every character we meet time to develop. There are no cardboard cut-outs in this series; every person, from Jean and Nadia to the mysterious villain Gargoyle, is three-dimensional, with a personality of their own.*
> —T.H.E.M. Anime Reviews

Loosely based on the novel *20,000 Leagues Under the Sea* by Jules Verne (1828–1905), *Nadia* is set in 1889, and depicts a steampunk-inspired alternate realm wherein the Industrial Revolution appears to have taken over unchallenged and to be avidly consuming the world with its newfangled technologies and contraptions. The action chronicles the adventures of a fourteen-year-old circus acrobat and orphan, the titular character, whose past is shrouded in mystery. Her only companion when we first encounter Nadia is the pet lion cub named King, whose language she is able to understand. The sole clue to the heroine's provenance seems to be "Blue Water," a gem in her possession that two sets of unscrupulous enemies appear determined to obtain at all cost.

The first is a trio of jewel thieves comprising Grandis Granva, once the fabulously wealthy daughter of an aristocratic Italian family rendered destitute by a perfidious suitor who has turned to crime out of a perverse passion for jewels; Sanson, her former chauffeur and now a formidably muscly (if incorrigibly vain) fighter; and Hanson, the family's erstwhile mechanic. Sanson contributes sheer physical strength to the "Grandis Gang," whereas Hanson is a resourceful inventor whose major achievement is a multiskilled machine-vehicle known as the *Gratan* (although Grandis insists on calling her the *Catherina* in the belief this is a far more stylish designation). The apparatus is capable of morphing from a tank into a hot air-propelled flying contraption, a seaworthy vessel and even a submarine, depending on the circumstances at hand. Sanson and Hanson are the sole members of the Granva household's original retinue not to have deserted Grandis upon her fall from grace. Nadia's second — and significantly more dangerous — foe is a man named Gargoyle who wants the precious stone as a means of controlling the fate of the entire planet. Blue Water is indeed deemed instrumental to the full activation of the "Neo-Atlantis" forces over which the villain presides.

At the World Exposition in Paris, Nadia is hounded down by the jewel hunters and rescued just in the nick of time by Jean, a fourteen-year-old would-be scientist and inventive genius who is deeply captivated by her mysterious beauty. The fugitives lead the villainous posse at their heels on a chase that eventually takes them to the Atlantic Ocean, where they are rescued by an American battleship hunting a vengeful Sea Monster, get washed overboard and finally get picked up by Captain Nemo's submarine, the *Nautilus*. Nemo is utterly consumed by his resolve to annihilate Gargoyle and Neo-Atlantis, and this is practically the only thing we know about the character up to Episode 22 of the series (analyzed in depth later in this chapter), in which his past and secrets are eventually revealed. Nemo avails himself of a remarkably competent crew whose most capable and prominent member in addition to the captain himself is undoubtedly Electra, the *Nautilus*'s First Officer. While appropriating both the name of the character and that of his vessel from Verne's classic novel, *Nadia* provides a substantially different version of the legendary captain. The show's emphasis, concurrently, is to a greater extent placed upon the nefarious activities of the power-thirsty organization Neo-Atlantis and its efforts to achieve global dominance than on the *Nautilus* and its commander as singular agents. Anno's dissection of the villain Gargoyle's machinations, in turn, enables the director to engage in a sustained allegorical critique of despotism of great historical resonance.

In order to adequately contextualize *Nadia*'s generic import, it is vital to appreciate the show's allegiance to the rhetoric of steampunk, namely, a subgenre of alternate-history speculative science fiction, normally set in a pseudo–Victorian culture replete with varyingly preposterous gizmos, appliances and utensils alongside mechanical monsters of mammoth proportions. The aesthetic promulgated by steampunk is fundamentally retrofuturistic insofar as the temporal zone it tends to depict is not the future as one might imagine it today but rather the future as imagined by the techno-visionaries of past eras. The steampunk sensibility usually associated not only with Verne himself but also with the historian and illustrator Albert Robida (1848–1926) spectacularly resurfaced in 1992 with William Gibson's and Bruce Sterling's collaborative novel *The Difference Engine*, an application of the characteristic trademarks of cyberpunk fiction to an alternate Victorian society. Steampunk elements have consistently featured in mainstream manga since the 1940s, as clearly indicated by the science-fiction trilogy by Osamu Tezuka encompassing *Lost World* (1948), *Metropolis* (1949) and *Next World* (1951). Anime, in turn, has eagerly absorbed the narrative lessons divulged by manga, on this as on many other counts, yielding a prismatic range of steampunk-based series and features.

Some of the most notable instances in the domain of feature-length anime are unquestionably offered by Hayao Miyazaki's *Laputa: Castle in the Sky* (1986)—a major influence behind *Nadia*—and *Howl's Moving Castle* (2004), Rintaro's *Metropolis* (2001), and Katsuhiro Otomo's *Steamboy* (2004). The TV series *Future Boy Conan* (dir. Miyazaki, 1978), *Space Battleship Yamato* (dir. Leiji Matsumoto, 1974), *Rose of Versailles* (dirs. Tadao Nagahama and Osamu Dezaki, 1979–1980), *Sakura Wars* (dirs. Ryutaro Nakamura and Takashi Asami, 2000), *Fullmetal Alchemist* (dir. Seiji Mizushima, 2003–2004) and *Elemental Gelade* (dir. Shigeru Ueda, 2005) are also deserving of inspection as apposite ancillary sources.[1] The fascination with an imaginary version of old Europe demonstrated by these and many other anime productions is intimately linked to what the Japanese describe as *"akogare no Paris"* ("the Paris of our dreams"), that is to say, a fictional constellation of that world elaborated through Eastern eyes that is akin to the West's fantastical configurations of the East grounded in the myth of the "exotic." At the level of design, *Nadia*'s own steampunk signature announces itself most flamboyantly in the representation of the spaceship-like submarines punctuating the story's visuals.

Focusing specifically on affinities between Anno's series and Miyazaki's *Laputa: Castle in the Sky*, it should be noted that both Nadia and *Laputa*'s female protagonist, Sheeta, are orphans ignorant of their origins and status in possession of precious stones invested with supernatural powers. In both cases, moreover, the heroines' attempts to retrace their roots are abetted by young males (also orphans) with a passion for flying machines and indeed anything even vaguely connected with flight. (Although Jean echoes *Laputa*'s Pazu, in this respect, at the level of design he is actually closer to Tombo from Miyazaki's *Kiki's Delivery Service* [1989] — another nascent inventor fascinated with airborne vessels of all sorts.) Further similarities can be detected in the representation of supporting characters and aspects of the setting. While visually combining elements of both Jung Freud from *Gunbuster* and Asuka from *Evangelion*, Grandis recalls *Laputa*'s Ma Dola, the head of the sky pirates after Sheeta's gem, just as her henchmen are redolent of Ma Dola's motley crew. Gargoyle and his associates, for their part, are akin to Miyazaki's villain Muska and his retinue — with the distinctive addition of KKK-style hoods and Noh-like masks. The baleful machinery deployed by Gargoyle in order to enhance Neo-Atlantis's strength, additionally, resembles both Muska's fortress and the diabolical infrastructure of the flying island of Laputa itself.[2]

Like *Wings of Honneamise* and *Gunbuster*, *Nadia* employs emphatically hand-crafted frames in sequences of particular symbolic significance or heightened affective substance. This stylistic proclivity proclaims itself right from the start by means of an inaugural, pre-credit sequence orchestrated entirely through montages documenting the horrific shipwrecks, which some blame on Sea Monsters and others on technocratic hubris. Their somber chromatic qualities and boldly sweeping lines emanate an awesome sense of the Romantic Sublime redolent of Gustave Doré's illustrations for Samuel Taylor Coleridge's *The Rime of the Ancient Mariner* (1870).

The director has commented on *Nadia* as an only partial accomplishment, thus demonstrating that Gainax's artists rarely — if indeed ever — gloat about their achievements and are inclined instead to reflect upon their shortcomings as springboards to further development.

> NHK [the broadcasting company]'s vision for *Nadia* was very, very strong. I was able to do what I wanted within that vision, but I couldn't change the basic parts. I was able to do a lot of the things I wanted to, but I couldn't do everything that I'd really wanted to do. Which, I think, gave it the nuance of being a more child-oriented work. And that's why, even though I did everything I possibly could, *Nadia* is a work I still have regrets about [quoted in "(inside) Gainax," p. 16].

The more adventure-based portions of the story up to Episode 22 may indeed fit in with fairly standard fare aimed at kids, although this scarcely applies to the more meditative moments, while the so-called Island Episodes (to be returned to later in this chapter) are sometimes downright silly. It is undeniable, however, that Episodes 35 through 39 strike ominous metaphysical chords that are on a par with *Gunbuster* and anticipate *Evangelion*.

Moreover, even seemingly mundane incidents can unexpectedly lead to something darker and deeper. A case in point is the hyperkinetic sequence in Episode 11, "New Recruits for the Nautilus," in which Jean frantically chases King through the *Nautilus*'s labyrinthian passages after the cub has stolen a piece of lethally spicy fish, and the madcap action accidentally culminates in the submarine's secret and ominous core. We thus learn that at the "heart of the Nautilus" there lies a form of nuclear power that renders the vessel a potential "killing machine." Relatedly, initially cardboard personae incrementally exhibit unsuspected complexity and nuances, especially in the case of the "Grandis Gang" members. Sanson, in particular, develops a genuinely touching affection toward Marie, the orphan "adopted" by Jean and Nadia in the course of their adventures, whom he will eventually marry (as revealed in the show's Epilogue set in the year 1902).

On the other hand, *Nadia* often lightens up the tenor of its narrative by juxtaposing disturbing scenes with moments of delicious humor. A perfect example is supplied by Episode 20, "Jean Makes a Mistake," where a genuinely terrifying display of Gargoyle's soaring power is displaced by the presentation of Marie playing home with King in the role of "Papa"—and suitably garbed in a formal hat and tie—and Sanson in the role of "Baby" equipped with a dummy and lacy cap-cum-bib kit that is hilariously at odds with the jewel thief's brawny frame.

At other times, sorrowful and uplifting visuals seamlessly coalesce. This tendency, so typical of Gainax's style in general and of Anno's signature in particular, is effectively deployed from the very beginning of the series. A paradigmatic example provided by Episode 1, "Girl at the Eiffel Tower," is the sequence in which images of a dejected Nadia, betrayed by the circus master that has callously sold her off to her pursuers, haunted by a crushing feeling of rootlessness, and uncertain as to both her origins and her destination, are seamlessly integrated with pictures of the landscape surrounding Jean's boat as this rolls down the Seine that foreground Nature's beauty at its most glorious by means of a lavishly depicted sunset.

As far as the heroine's moods and feelings are concerned, it must also be noted that although Nadia is capable of communicating highly positive emotions and standing up for herself with both determination and aplomb, an ineradicable undercurrent of pained insecurity courses through her actions. Anno's distinctive inclination to weave serious psychodrama into even the seemingly most lighthearted, good-humored and adventure-driven plots thus comes assiduously to the fore. The slapstick comedy issuing from the jewel hunters' fanciful and increasingly vicious attempts to get hold of Blue Water further throws into relief, by ironic contrast, the gravity of the young woman's predicament.

Although, as indicated, the show's opening anticipates aspects of its visual style and narrative preoccupations to be developed throughout its often tortuous unfolding, it is actually quite innocent and jovial. It is only when *Nadia* begins to warp what at first appeared to be a comfortable world into something alarmingly unfamiliar that the story's true scope fully manifests itself. The adventure then evolves into a much more somber exploration of anxiety, alienation and loss, interwoven with harrowing allusions to racial discrimination and cold-blooded acts of violence perpetrated by frighteningly earnest criminals. Racism, in particular, is thrown into relief in Episode 2, "The Little Fugitives," by the scene in which Jean's aunt refuses to give Nadia shelter, reproaching the boy with the words "Have you seen the color of her skin?" It is worth noting, in this respect, that in the original character designs, Nadia had been endowed with a more explicitly African look. Alterations, as Marc Hairston explains, were necessitated by the proverbial difficulty of animating "kinky hair" (Hairston 1995a).

By venturing into the human psyche's murkiest recesses, *Nadia* concurrently disrupts the *shoujo* element associated with the heroine. As Jonathan Clements and Helen McCarthy emphasize, "despite the sunny color palette of the show and its upbeat pacing and music, the audience quickly realizes that a dark and terrible fate is always waiting just out of shot, threatening to engulf the young couple—the same team's later hit *Evangelion* brought the lurking darkness into the foreground." Moreover, much as Nadia and Jean manage to "learn that their origins are less important than what they make of themselves," as also conveyed by both *Wings of Honneamise* and *Gunbuster*, and that "love can conquer all," they also come to realize that this "doesn't guarantee a happy ending" (Clements and McCarthy, p. 572). At the same time, the characters elliptically come to terms with the zen paradox according to which accepting fate is the sole means of transcending it.

Among the more serious issues explored by the series, the relationship between humanity and technology is especially prominent and appropriately fueled by its steampunk-inspired stylistic underpinnings. Characteristically eschewing conclusive lessons, the show does not incontrovertibly militate in favor of either the pro-tech or the Luddite polarities, choosing instead to choreograph the relationship between Jean and Nadia as a dialectical tension between a techno-optimist who unproblematically trusts machines and gadgets to solve all problems, and a champion of Nature at its most organically spontaneous harboring an intense distrust of anything mechanical. However, the clash between Jean's and Nadia's world pictures offers a subtly modulated friction, not a stark binary opposition.

Nadia's ambivalence regarding technology is foregrounded in Episode 2, in which she repeatedly oscillates between declaring Jean a genius at the sight of his inventions and harshly dismissing them as flimsy and unreliable toys. Episode 3, "The Riddle of the Giant Sea Monsters," offers further insights into this key aspect of the heroine's mentality by revealing that she is a staunch vegetarian and loves unconditionally all living creatures, the Sea Monsters included. In this respect, Nadia echoes the eponymous heroine of Miyazaki's *Nausicaä of the Valley of the Wind* (1984). When Nadia and Jean are picked up by the battleship in the same episode, the two characters' divergent perspectives are tersely conveyed by Nadia's unmitigated hatred of the vessel as an instrument of death, on the one hand, and Jean's fascination with its sophisticated machinery, on the other. This thematic lead is developed in Episode 4, "Nautilus, the Fantastic Submarine," in which Jean is utterly enthralled by the vessel's technological equipment, whereas Nadia suspects that the *Nautilus* might constitute yet another nefarious invention — or indeed the product of malevolent magic.

Episode 6, "Infiltration of the Secret Base," additionally emphasizes Jean's obsession with technology, intimating that the young genius simply cannot help indulging in the inspection and admiration of advanced machinery even at times of extreme peril — a proclivity that Nadia bluntly brands as the symptom of a "one-track mind." Jean's faith in technology receives a severe blow in Episode 15, "The Nautilus Faces Its Biggest Crisis," when his friend Fate, a Nautilus technician, has to face an excruciatingly painful death in the aftermath of a radiation accident. Not even the idealistic and proverbially optimistic inventor can remain untouched by technology's latent malignancy when his personal feelings are brought to trial.

The protagonists' discordant perceptions of technology are paralleled by no less radical differences in their instinctive attitudes to other humans. Thus, whereas Jean is fundamentally trusting and willing to give people the "benefit of the doubt," Nadia is constitutionally suspicious and inclined to think that people — and particularly adults — are intrinsically deceitful and self-seeking. The darkness at the heart of the heroine's ethical vision is corroborated by Episode 5, "Marie's Island," in which the program's tone incontrovertibly shifts toward intense drama as the young couple chances upon Marie just after her parents and pet dog have been brutally murdered by Gargoyle's emissaries. Neither blood nor pathos are spared in the depiction of the installment's most poignant moments. The appalling grandiosity of the villain's domain is also unsentimentally foregrounded, especially in the representation of the elaborate Power Plant that feeds the jewel in Gargoyle's architectural and technological crown: the Tower of Babel.[3]

While Jean's naive passion for all sorts of hi-tech scenarios may seem preposterous, it fades virtually into insignificance compared to the sheer lunacy of Gargoyle's own techno-enthusiasm. Believing that Neo-Atlantis's science is actually capable of surpassing Nature's own achievements (e.g., in the production of immaculately beautiful and unperishable flowers and trees), the tyrant at one point insanely declares: "We are the new gods." Further proclaiming that his "might is beyond measure," Gargoyle aims to "recreate the final night of

Sodom and Gomorrah," and thus "supplant the old gods" and their "paltry" creation in order to regain "Paradise" (Episode 7, "The Tower of Babel").

Accordingly, the villain does not hesitate to destroy an entire island just to demonstrate experimentally the Tower of Babel's technological might, which is hardly surprising given how cold-bloodedly and capriciously he is capable of murdering his own associates whenever this seems apposite. Yet, as Episode 8, "Mission to Rescue Nadia," dramatically shows, Gargoyle still has one obstacle to overcome in his advance toward full-spectrum dominance: Nemo's *Nautilus*. (In Episode 20, the despot explicitly describes the captain and his submarine as the only "thorn" in his "side.") In Episode 8, Nemo actually annihilates Gargoyle's whole compound but the tyrant does not consider himself defeated and in fact remains steadfast in his conviction that Neo-Atlantis has authentically inherited the scientific prowess of the semi-mythical Atlantean civilization of old. (Gargoyle's engrossment with the ancient empire's achievements is confirmed by the maniacal zeal with which he collects and worships ancient Atlantean artworks.)

Nadia is a veritable treasure house of varyingly esoteric symbols and cryptic allusions to both scientific and mythological discourses. (The website "Tamarro Forever," inaugurated in 2000 and assiduously updated thereafter, is a highly recommended source of data covering numerous aspects of the series' symbolic fabric.) Blue Water is the iconographic and narrative crux around which *Nadia*'s intertextual tapestry is woven. The stone's supernatural powers are fully exposed in Episode 16, "The Mystery of the Lost Continent," in which Nadia discovers that she just cannot get rid of it however hard she may try and, having asked Jean to subject it to close inspection, finds that its inner structure resembles intricate circuitry of a complexity never detected before in any natural substance. That this disclosure should occur in Episode 16 is not fortuitous, insofar as the installment as a whole stands out as the show's mythical crux. It is indeed at this point in the action that we are first presented with a vision of Atlantis in the form of a sunken city used as a cemetery for Gargoyle's victims. Among them, Jean realizes, is his own father, whose survival despite a protracted absence the boy has desperately continued hoping for against empirical evidence to the contrary.

No less densely symbolic, Episode 19, "Nemo's Best Friend," takes us into an alternate world situated beneath the Antarctic and harboring the "World Tree." As Jean and Nadia behold the spectacle with awed reverence, Nemo memorably states: "Only man's arrogance assumes that the ground beneath our feet is fixed in place." The alternate-world trope is sustained by a series of shots displaying the "museum in ice" wherein ancient saureans of all sorts are encased, bearing witness to the prehistoric existence of evolved civilizations gradually extinguished by cosmic mutations. The 20,000-year-old whale "Irion" has, however, managed to survive and is able to communicate directly with Nadia's heart by means of Blue Water, advising her to "honor" Nemo's "trust" in her, which he describes as his "last wish" before finally expiring with the parting words "Thank you, children ... inheritors of Blue Water." Returning to the surface, Nemo, Nadia and Jean witness the aurora borealis in its full glory. The captain supplies a strictly scientific explanation for the phenomenon but then emphatically adds: "Of course such theories can never truly describe the beauty of Nature." A refreshing touch of humor follows this intense set of sequences as Jean makes ice cream using what is effectively 12,000-year-old ice, causing Nadia to remark: "It's like we're eating the history of the world."

Nadia's turning point, where both the show's diegesis and its symbolic significance are concerned, resides with the aforementioned Episode 22, "Electra the Traitor," in which Nemo's turbid past is disclosed. In the wake of a furious battle against Gargoyle's subaqueous fleet of "GarFish," the *Nautilus* is reduced to a hunk of sinking metal seemingly beyond all hope of recovery. Nemo decides to split the submarine's main module, where he and Electra are located, from the submodule accommodating Nadia, Jean, Marie and King. Before he pulls the lever enabling the programmed severance to take place, Electra takes center stage, shooting Nemo through his left arm and causing blood to spatter against the instruments in the control room. She then proceeds to recount the chain of events conducive to the present state of affairs.

We thus learn that thirteen years prior to the adventures depicted in the series, Nemo's wife — the queen of Thartessos — was assassinated and that Nemo's friend Gargoyle rose to power, renaming the realm Neo-Atlantis and enthroning Nemo's son Neo as emperor. The new ruler's principal goal was to restore the damaged Tower of Babel. Nemo, unwilling to abet Gargoyle's plan, impeded the restoration, thus causing the Blue Water situated within the tower to explode, spread its energy throughout the surrounding city, and devastate it utterly. Electra miraculously survived the catastrophe and was rescued by Nemo, to whom she remained deeply grateful until she accidentally discovered his partial responsibility for the disaster, as well as the real reason behind her adoption, namely, to provide a substitute for his lost daughter, Nadia. (By an ironical twist of fate, Electra will be seen to be carrying Nemo's baby at the end of the saga.)

Although the thematic and symbolic content of Electra's narrative is itself intriguing, more tantalizing still is its stylistic configuration. The account indeed relies on the time-honored conventions of sequential art — a practice based on storytelling by means of consecutive images that dates back to Egyptian tomb painting. It accordingly minimizes motion in favor of still frames pregnant with emblematic meanings. On the technical plane, the sequence's cumulative impact owes much to the subtle integration of stylized visuals — at times so stark as to appear to have been carved into wood — and a softly somber chromatic register consisting of varying shades of black and white. The mood is, therefore, at once haunting and ethereal. Shadows and silhouettes soaked in harsh light and engulfing darkness by turns draw the viewer's eyes to the focus of each frame with skilful unobtrusiveness.

The pacing is exquisite, allowing the narrative to effloresce delicately even as it depicts horrific occurrences, in much the same way as an intricate origami figure could be expected to unfold. (The sequence's closest antecedent, in stylistic terms, is the climactic battle presented in the sixth episode of *Gunbuster*.)

The following visual motifs are especially worthy of close inspection:

- Stationary drawings of Thartessos with cutouts of banks of fleecy clouds moving across the screen in the foreground set the scene for the conflagration to come.
- Camera pans across views of the city and the surrounding landscape rely mainly on static drawings but the animated details they do incorporate, for example, a billowing wisp of smoke, a tremulous flame, Electra's blinking eyes, are intensely dynamic.
- Images of bloodshed are characteristically still and rendered in black and white but the sense of mounting horror is succinctly conveyed by a spreading pool of vermilion.
- Sound effects, especially gunfire and crowds cheering Gargoyle, are effectively deployed to punctuate the sequence.
- The climax harrowingly juxtaposes caliginous grayscale backgrounds and splashes of green, pink and amber, as well as diagonal lines expressive of the cataclysm's furious energy.
- The climactic shot of Electra, alone on a deserted shore, deploys the severity of grayscale to maximum effect, enhancing its impact through the incorporation of

stretches of sickly yellow scorched land and lurid pink skies, with gnarled tree trunks and crowing ravens set against them.

Episode 22 uncompromisingly shows that Nemo is by no means a hero of immaculate repute. Consequently, his past actions are no less blood-soaked than Gargoyle's in many respects. The captain's ruthless streak survives well into the present, as shown by his relative lack of concern with the welfare of individuals when the *Nautilus*'s survival is at stake. Nevertheless, he does not feel entitled to set himself up as a role model for the young and innocent to emulate. Thus, when Jean insists on becoming an official member of Nemo's crew, the captain denies his wish because he simply does not want the boy to become, by implication, a killer (Episode 17, "Jean's New Invention"). It is at such narrative junctures that we realize, as Hairston observes, that

> Nemo's mission is driven, not by evil, but by guilt.... Haunted by the guilt that so many died while he lived, he can only atone for his sin by continuing the fight to stop Gargoyle. His own deep reverence for life appears when he stops Electra from killing herself after the Nautilus has been destroyed. "NEVER take your life lightly!" he shouts at her. And at the end of the series, his final order to Nadia is one of life, not death. "Nadia, no matter what happens, LIVE!" [Hairston 1995b].

Nadia does not directly develop the narrative strand articulated in Episode 22. In fact, following the intense pathos of Electra's narrative, the audience's attention is redirected to ancillary and eminently humorous events that cover Episodes 23 through 34 (known as the "Island Episodes" because they dramatize Nadia's and Jean's adventures after the shipwreck). Episode 30 and 31, as argued later, are a partial exception insofar as they contain thematic developments destined to contribute to the adventure's denouement in significant ways.

As the *Gainax Pages* review of the series explains, the episodes "sandwiched in the middle of the show ... were not entirely created by Gainax.... [They] were farmed out to anime companies in Korea and are characterized by many as 'filler' material. The episodes have inferior animation compared to earlier episodes and, more importantly, strike a radically different tone from the rest of the show" ("*Gainax Pages* reviews: *Nadia*"). The reason behind *Nadia*'s unorthodox composition is that its tremendous popularity led NHK, the distribution network, to request a greater number of episodes than had been initially intended, and overseas companies had to be brought into play because Gainax was running into financial difficulties (something the studio is notoriously adept at doing, as subsequently indicated by both *Neon Genesis Evangelion* and *His and Her Circumstances*).

The humor-driven "castaway"-style portion of the series is ushered in by one of the most exuberantly comedic moments in the entire narrative (Episode 23, "Young Drifters"). The *Anime Meta-Review*'s assessment of the program colorfully describes the scene as follows:

> Nadia and Jean are in an enclosed room that is filling with water. There seems to be no way to escape and that both will drown. The situation seems serious, and comes at the tail of a rather heavy sequence of events. Jean's answer is to do a weird physical comedy stunt as he attempts to "drink" the water that is drowning them. Swelling up like a weird human balloon until he bursts. It's either a really clever balancing act or the creators just couldn't think of anything better to do ["*Anime Meta-Review—Nadia: The Secret of Blue Water*"].

Some inveterate Gainax fans may contemplate the possibility of watching solely Episodes 1 through 22 followed directly by Episodes 35 through 39 the first time around (possibly with an incursion into Episode 30 and Episode 31 for background purposes), and then sample the "Island Episodes" at a later stage as relatively free-standing material. The setting of the ancillary installments, incidentally, was inspired by Verne's other novel featuring Captain Nemo, *Mysterious Island* (1874).[4]

What is arguably most disturbing about the "Island Episodes" is their dramatization of incidents in which the main personae behave in a stridently out-of-character fashion. Nadia, in particular, evinces an unpleasant streak: despite her tender adoration of Nature, she often acts selfishly and reveals herself prone to sudden anger and underhandedness. Her attitude toward Jean falters capriciously, moreover, as evinced by Episode 25, "The First Kiss," and Episode 26, "King, the Lonely Lion." In the former, when the boy helps Nadia recover from a fever, she treats him to their first romantic kiss but rapidly forgets her gratitude and gives in to unmitigated fury when Jean — having inadvertently consumed some hallucinogenic mushrooms in the following installment — shows no recollection of the event.

Thus far elegantly poised at the intersection of serious drama and gentle comedy, the action gravitates toward overt slapstick in Episode 27, "The Island of the Witch," in which a typhoon brings a new island in close proximity to the one inhabited by the protagonists and the character of Eaton (first seen in the show as an officer aboard the American battleship) reappears in the guise of a semi-deranged drunk possessed by apocalyptic presages. The farcical tone is sustained in Episode 28, "The Floating Island," in which a creature first believed to be a monster turns out to be a crafty disguise through which Grandis, Sanson and Hanson reintroduce themselves into the story. The most incongruous chords, at the plot's tonal level, are struck by the incidents incorporated in Episode 32, "Nadia's Love," Episode 33, "King's Rescue" and Episode 34, "My Darling Nadia." In this segment of the program, the heroine, having crash-landed with her companions in the middle of an African village, falls hopelessly in love with the native Hamahama, King is kidnapped and flamboyantly rescued, and the party eventually leaves to travel to Nadia's homeland. The series resumes its central diegetic thrust, with an unprecedented darkening in mood to boot, with Episode 35 and consistently maintains it to the end. Before examining Episodes 35 through 39, a detour via Episodes 30 and 31 is, however, necessary.

Episode 30, "Labyrinth in the Earth," and Episode 31, "Farewell, Red Noah," are reputedly the only instalments in the "Island" section that Anno would have kept — not surprisingly, given their contribution to the unraveling of the mysteries surrounding Nadia's past. In Episode 30, Jean and Nadia accidentally find themselves in a subterranean chamber. As Jean utters the girl's name, Blue Water suddenly begins to glow and Nadia is drawn through a wall made of the same substance as the jewel. In Episode 31, we discover that the heroine has entered "Red Noah," a space ark supposed to have come to Earth with other vessels of its kind from 277.5 light years away 2,400,000 years earlier. The arks unloaded their passengers onto the planet, where they established the civilization of Atlantis. This, however, incurred brutal annihilation and it is now up to Nadia to gain control over humanity and resurrect the lost realm. Nadia adamantly rejects Red Noah's instructions, knowing that abiding by them would only bring about further strife and, in the face of her tenacity, the ark lets her go — but not without a cautionary parting in which it balefully states that the heroine's fate is unalterable and that they will most certainly meet again.

This strand of the narrative is picked up again, suitably recapped and significantly elaborated in Episode 35, "The Secret of Blue Water." This installment offers crucial revelations, ushered in by a mesmerizingly atmospheric sequence of drawings showing Noah's Ark from the Bible and the animals boarding it. When Nadia and her friends reach their destination, the heroine obtains shocking insights into the nature of the place, its connection with Atlantis and, relatedly, its significance vis-à-vis her own submerged history. We thus learn that there were originally three arks altogether: the Red Noah, the Blue Noah and the *Nautilus*'s ancestor. These came to Earth carrying members of the alien civilization of Atlantis and gradually became caught up in a fateful succession of events, which Nadia summarizes as follows:

> A long time ago, the people of Atlantis began to fight. They hated each other, and killed each other until the very end.... One ark was burned and sank into the sea.... The other ark lost its master, and disappeared somewhere. It was that island. It was Red Noah. Then the last ark lost its power to fly and fell here. The only people to survive were those here, on the Blue Noah.

(The *Nautilus*'s parent ark turns out to be the sunken vessel alluded to above.) The Kingdom of Atlantis — to which Nadia is the rightful heir — was founded in this location.

The girl is fully aware of her powers within Blue Noah, where the entire environment palpably seeks to obey her "every wish," and finds her authority utterly hideous: "I'm afraid to go on," she states, "because I'm afraid to find out who I really am.... The one who holds the Blue Water can become God or Satan, and destroy the world with its power." Not only is the heroine terrified of causing evil but she also claims to be vicious and incapable of taking responsibility for her actions. Although Grandis warmly urges her to "believe" in herself (a quintessentially Gainaxian message), Nadia remains convinced of her intrinsic worthlessness.

Nadia's assessment of her personality in this segment of Episode 35 echoes director Anno's own self-perception as described in a Q & A session conducted among pupils of the Unishimma Elementary, where Anno went to school. "I'm not crazy about myself," Anno reflects. "I'm often told that those who don't like themselves have high ideals, but I think someone who says that doesn't really understand the pain that's involved" (quoted in Sevakis). This comment could be read as symptomatic of a crippling lack of self-esteem, yet could also indicate a modest recognition of one's limitations without which there would be no leeway for improvement, and hence no space for creativity to flourish.

Returning to Episode 35, the action overcomes the affective impasse described above as Nadia learns that the Kingdom of Thartessos never died but actually transformed itself in order to survive and became Neo-Atlantis (as seen in Episode 22). Therefore, she must accept that the Neo-Atlanteans are, after all, her own people, too. At the same time, the girl becomes conclusively conscious of her alien makeup and bravely accepts that she is simply "not a human being."

In Episode 36, "The New Nautilus," Nadia gives herself up to Gargoyle in exchange for his promise that he will spare her companions. It is hardly likely that the girl truly believes, given her constitutional mistrust of people, that the villain will honor his vow. Indeed, Jean and the others are only afforded a diminutive chance to escape. In a memorable coup de théâtre, however, the company is rescued by the "*New Nautilus*" with Nemo and Electra as eager for action as they were in the pre–"Island" instalments. Episode 37, "Emperor Neo," shows a fully refurbished version of the *Nautilus*, with an interior that vividly anticipates the NERV Headquarters in *Evangelion*—while Electra, for her part, foreshadows in design both Rei and Ritsuko from that same show. (The *New Nautilus*'s original name, incidentally, is reported by Electra to have been "*Exelion*," which can be read as an explicit homage to *Gunbuster* on Anno's part.)

Episode 37 offers further vital disclosures regarding the Atlanteans' evolutionary intervention. In this installment, Gargoyle shows Nadia "Adam" (arguably a precursor of *Evangelion*'s "First Angel"): namely, an experimental creature constructed by the Atlanteans two and a half million years earlier in their progressive elaboration of advanced life forms. The Atlanteans, we are told, needed servants and made first the whales, then primates and eventually humans (whom they shaped in their own image) to fulfill that purpose. Having obtained Nemo's own Blue Water as well as Nadia's, the despot considers himself close to total triumph. Confronting the girl in the presence of Emperor Neo — now explicitly presented as Nadia's brother at last — Gargoyle announces his intention of subjugating humanity and asserting Neo-Atlantis's uncontested dominance the world over — a plan he instantly proceeds to carry out with delirious fervor.

Episode 38, "To the Sky," dramatizes Nemo's and his troupe's elaboration of a counteractive strategy: the Gratan is to infiltrate Gargoyle's bastion and take out the power plant that activates the Tower of Babel. In one of the series' most exuberantly adrenaline-pumping sequences, Grandis and her associates indeed manage to accomplish this feat — magnanimously sacrificing the vehicle in the process. In the wake of this success, Nemo resolves to confront Gargoyle face to face. Electra and Jean insist on joining him and the three of them are soon captured and placed upon cylindrical pedestals of vertiginous heights. The tyrant declares that Nemo is to be tried for betraying Atlantis and offers him one last chance to partake of the leadership of Neo-Atlantis. When the captain refuses, Gargoyle orders Nadia — who has been meanwhile brainwashed into total subservience — to shoot her father, which she does cold-bloodedly, though not to mortal effect. Nemo responds by instructing Jean to shoot Nadia in turn, which brings Episode 38 to a cliffhanging close.

Episode 39, "Successor to the Stars," follows straight from this climactic moment. Jean does not, as is only to be expected, manage to bring himself to pull the trigger, aware though he is that Nadia is no longer the girl he knew and loved. Nemo's next ploy is to try to persuade Gargoyle that humans are not an unredeemably inferior species but are actually capable of self-improvement through altruism and compassion. The villain remains utterly unmoved, however, and orders both Nadia and Neo to shoot at their father. It is now Electra's turn to deploy her strategic shrewdness to save the day: by means of a concealed aural device, she instructs the Nautilus crew to fire a beam exactly 60° to her left. When the order is carried out, both Jean and Electra are knocked off their platforms by the momentous explosion, while Nadia loses consciousness and Neo's body is revealed to be almost entirely mechanical.

In what surely qualifies as one of the series' most gloriously irrational and — possibly thanks to this very attribute — most riveting occurrences, Neo breaks free of Gargoyle's mental shackles, unexpectedly remembering everything that the villain hoped to have erased. To Gargoyle's astonishment, the proto-cyborg leaves his chair, trailing a thick cable plugged into his back behind him, and approaches Nadia. Neo's power, regrettably, runs out just as he is about to reach his sister, which renews the tyrant's hopes of success. However, as Nemo cries out his son's true name, Venusis, Neo miraculously self-reactivates and awakens Nadia, who suddenly realizes the magnitude and horror of what she is witnessing.

In a multilayered denouement, Blue Water's powers are deployed one final time. In the process, Nadia is able to bring Jean — who has been gravely injured in the climax — back to life (although this means she will not be able to cure her father's own fateful wounds), while Gargoyle — who has wrongly considered himself an Atlantean when he is, in fact, merely a human raised by Atlanteans — disintegrates into a paltry mound of sand. The company eventually boards the *New Nautilus* once more. The entire crew is forced to leave the vessel when it incurs serious damage at the hands of the explosions destroying Gargoyle's base in order to return safely home — except for Nemo who, like all honorable captains, chooses to stay with his ship to the bitter end and indeed deploy it as the ultimate weapon to annihilate the remaining vestiges of Gargoyle's nefarious legacy.

What is ultimately incontestable about *Nadia*'s retrofuturistic setting is the gravity with which it deploys steampunk rhetoric as a tool for sustained social critique rather than as a pretext for nostalgic spectacle. An apposite point of comparative reference is supplied, on that front, by the pseudo-historical TV series *Le Chevalier D'Eon* (dir. Kazuhiro Furuhashi, 2006–2007). Kevin Gifford has commented on this show's ideological cogency in his review of the first DVD volume, released in the West by ADV Films in 2007. Key to the program's dramatic flavor, the critic argues, is its depiction of a distinctive sociopolitical atmosphere: "a time when life was cheap, the nobility was clueless to the revolution surging in the streets and everyone really *did* wear all that frilly stuff you see in Revolutionary War documentaries."

The show's protagonist is based on an actual historical figure, the diplomat and spy D'Eon de Beaumont in the service of Louis XV in the mid–1700s. Nevertheless, here as in *Nadia*, history gives way to fiction in the elaboration of the series' narrative, in which the hero's allegiance to king and country takes second place to his personal agenda when his beloved sister Lia is found dead in the Seine. This is just one of the story's numerous murders whose victims, it is revealed, are turned by occult means into mercury-bloodied zombies known as "Gargoyles" (a further parallel with Anno's series) at the behest of a cabal of aristocrats devoted to the Dark Arts and a Russian character passing himself off as a fur trader. Though packed with tantalizing action sequences (especially in the swordfighting camp), *Le Chevalier D'Eon*, like *Nadia*, is fundamentally "a sober story laden with history (you really feel the power that both religion and royalty held over Europe three-hundred years ago" (Gifford 2007b, p. 146).

The show's creator and editor Tow Ubukata confirms *Le Chevalier D'Eon*'s historical import as follows:

> I think a lot of biographical works favor the fiction side of the equation. No matter how much they pretend to be presenting you with real-life people, the emphasis is invariably placed on the elements of speculative fantasy they add to it. But I'm the opposite — always trying to bring the story back home to reality.... One thing I had to keep remembering ... is that the main character is not just some random guy from the past, but someone who grew up within the cultural context of premodern Europe [Ubukata, p. 56].

In the execution of *Nadia*, Anno, like Ubukata, was eager to anchor the narrative to a recognizable social reality and hence conceive of his characters as inextricable from a particular social milieu and its shaping agency. This is especially patent in the characterization of Jean: the historical product of a utopian notion of technological advancement driven by the ingenuous ardor of youth, yet increasingly having to confront the grim reality of scientific abuse. As an inveterate Luddite, Nadia, too, is pithily defined as the product of a specific age. Gargoyle and his lackeys, for their part, exemplify what happens when grand political visions fuelled by the ideology of the Enlightenment get ahead of themselves and, in claiming to deploy science and technology as means of eradicating old superstitions, actually erect and idolize dark dreams of their own.

Thus, although neither *Nadia* nor *Le Chevalier D'Eon* allow strictly factual data and dates to constrain the fantasy worlds they seek to evoke, both series consistently endeavor to tease out the cultural vicissitudes of the historical periods in which they are set. As a result, both works steer clear of the stuffy rhetoric of standard period pieces and their ornamental trappings by engaging with the past as a dimension amenable to imaginative reinterpretation through the lenses of overtly fictional visions.

At the same time, the fact-fiction syntheses accomplished by Anno and Ubukata alike also enable them to articulate multifaceted investigations of complex individual psyches. Nadia is a divided character, torn between a present that mercilessly threatens her in a very palpable guise and a past that no less cruelly haunts her with its slippery elusiveness. When she finally discovers her place of origin, Nadia is quite literally split into discordant voices and drives. D'Eon de Beaumont is likewise marked by a schizoid personality. As Amos Wong explains, he is indeed "possessed by his sister's vengeful soul.... Manifesting itself during moments of danger, she brings forth superlative swordsmanship accompanied by shockingly unbridled fury" (Wong 2007, p. 26). D'Eon's heightened physical powers at times of extreme peril echo Nadia's preternatural ability to summon unsuspected skills (such as the opening of passages through solid rock) when she wrestles most grievously with inner turmoil. The use of supporting characters with often obscure motives and hidden agendas, capable of alternately exuding political cunning and chivalric integrity, ruthlessness and elegance, roguishness and glamour, also unites *Nadia* and *Le Chevalier D'Eon*. This ethical ambiguity, moreover, is matched by the masterful integration of esoteric symbolology and cryptic codes alluding to the deceptive nature of language and, by extension, to the unreliability of human communication at large.

Finally, some remarks made by director Furuhashi regarding his show's depiction of a society's tortuous transition to modernity — and of this phenomenon's impact on individual sensibilities — could no less fittingly apply to Anno's show than to *Le Chevalier D'Eon* itself: "The problems stemmed from the fact that no one knew exactly *which* new ideas would lead to greater happiness." Mixed attitudes toward technology amidst *Nadia*'s cast, as seen, reflect an analogous conundrum. "In a word," Furuhashi continues, "they were forced to live under the burden of contradiction." In Furuhashi's series, as in *Nadia*, the only way out of this seemingly intractable impasse is seen to lie with a brave effort to negotiate conflict by transcending manichean dualism and embracing the dialectical tension between opposites instead. As Furuhashi himself puts it, this attitude consists of the "spirit of determination to live through tragedy by transforming contradiction into a new set of values — instead of letting it ruin you" (Furuhashi, p. 31).

Like virtually all of Gainax's previous and subsequent productions, *Nadia* is a stylishly immersive coming-of-age story. Yet, in framing its trajectory within the broader context of a momentous conflict between two sets of individuals with equally powerful convictions, the series surpasses the classic Bildungsroman formula. In addition, while the action invites us to sympathize with Nemo more than with Gargoyle, it boldly explodes the moral reductionism of a story of good versus evil by unsentimentally exposing the captain's own darkness. Ethical relativism, therefore, displaces the simplistic lessons frequently delivered by action-packed anime fare. The show's tempo contributes significantly to its effectiveness as a reflection on thorny ethical issues. Indeed, *Nadia* introduces its more austere themes gradually, at first drawing its spectators into an illusion of jocular levity and then unsettling their perceptions with often vehement briskness. If such a shift of gears will come as no surprise for viewers accustomed to Gainax's genre-bending sleights of hand, what remains surprisingly unique about *Nadia* is its ability to deliver a cinematographical experience that bounteously satisfies the expectations of mass audiences and yet does not sacrifice, in the process, either its ethical validity or its pictorial charm.

CHAPTER 5

Otaku no Video
Director: Takeshi Mori (1991)

A true treat for true fans of any genre, Otaku no Video ("Fan's Video") *is an outrageous mockumentary that combines the superb animation that made Gainax one of Japan's best-loved animation studios with truly strange interviews with "real animation fans." The result is a thinly fictionalized history of Gainax that segues into a truly strange SF adventure.*
— AnimeNfo.Com

As seen in chapter 1, Gainax's history is intimately connected with Otakuism — and hence with the very genesis of the otaku category, its evolution from the early 1980s to the present day, its shifting ideological and ethical connotations, its links with specific social circles and sectors of the entertainment industry, and its incremental appropriation by Western fans. *Otaku no Video* is a powerful testimony to those key components of Gainax's development vis-à-vis a distinctive political and economic milieu. The OVA's full plot unfolds over two installments, set in 1982 and 1985. Its protagonist is Kubo, an average Japanese college student, who initially belongs to a tennis club, is very popular with his classmates and has a gorgeous girlfriend by the name of Yoshiko. This seemingly perfect life acquires an utterly unprecedented turn when Kubo bumps into an old high school classmate named Tanaka and is drawn into the weird subculture to which his friend appears to belong: a parallel universe peopled by anime and manga fans, cosplayers, model makers, information geeks, weapon collectors, martial artists and army enthusiasts — in other words, the otaku subculture. Toying with otakudom for fun, as one might with an innocent after-school hobby, Kubo soon discovers that the lifestyle involved in being a dedicated fan is coming to dominate his whole existence. The protagonist's personal trajectory thus fully corroborates the ominous warning voiced by one of Tanaka's associates early in the story: once you enter otakuland, "you can NEVER get out." Kubo thereafter channels all his time, energy and money into anime, allowing it to shape his entire routine, becomes estranged from his girlfriend (who never quite forgives him), loses his social reputation, and finds that even his health is beginning to deteriorate. Kubo may well choose to reject this exacting regime — but he may equally plausibly resolve to embrace it wholeheartedly and thus become the ultimate otaku: the *Otaking*.

The protagonist does succeed in creating his own anime, opening shops and even establishing a kind of Disneyland specifically designed for the benefit of otaku. However, his prosperity is abruptly brought to an end when a plucky competitor (who, ironically, also happens to be married to the disaffected Yoshiko) takes over the entire venture. Eventually, Kubo falls in love with the manga author Misuzu and, through the sheer energy unleashed by his enthusiastic otaku spirit, manages to overpower the grubby hard-nosedness of lucre-driven entrepreneurs and to assert his presence in the anime universe with the Magical-Girl show "Misty May."

In the exploration of *Otaku no Video*'s cultural backdrop—a task on which any genuine Gainax fan will be eager to embark—Volker Grassmuck's influential article "'I'm alone, but not lonely': Japanese Otaku-Kids colonize the Realm of Information and Media—A Tale of Sex and Crime from a Faraway Place" offers an especially useful source of contextual information. "The etymology of the word," the critic explains, "is not without black holes." At base, the term derives from

> everyday language, and in the original sense means "your home," then in a neo-confucian pars pro toto "your husband," and more generally it is used as the personal pronoun "you" (since a Japanese individual cannot be thought of without his connection to his household).... [T]here are 48 ways to say "I" in Japanese, and just about as many to say "you." ... Otaku is a polite way to address someone whose social position towards you you do not yet know, and it appears with a higher frequency in the women's language. It keeps distance [Grassmuck].

The word gains more problematic connotations when it is employed among peers. On such occasions, it tends to convey a desire to keep one's friends and colleagues at arm's length, which can be interpreted as an assertion of superiority on the user's part proclaimed ironically and even self-derisively rather than in earnest, or else as an inability to communicate openly due to a lack of adequately fostered interactive skills.

In a sense, otaku are a fairly logical outcome of a technology-driven and information-saturated society. Avidly consuming the products seen to embody their burning passions at the expense of intimate social interaction, with often irreverent disregard for fashionable dress (despite its being a veritable fetish among Japanese kids at large), and virtually no concern with either physical exercise or diet, otaku take refuge in the technological equipment that typically clutters their haunts. This grants them constant access to virtual images with which they can identify and which they can, by and by, assimilate as their own personal self-images.

Whether one embraces the idealistic quest for otakuism promulgated by Kubo, or else views the phenomenon as symptomatic of deeply dysfunctional facets of Japan's youth culture, it would be hard to deny the existence of a connection between otaku's social withdrawal and reclusiveness and a broader atmosphere of cultural malaise bred of atomization and disconnectedness, as well as the monumental pressures posed by the overarching imperatives to always do one's best—and succeed. These pressures, ingrained in Japan's philosophy and socioeconomic fabric since time immemorial, have not infrequently led to tragedy, as notoriously attested to by the country's high suicide rates among teenagers failing to meet their academic targets in a veritably exam-obsessed culture. Self-destructive despair appears to be an endemic response to the apprehension of failure, anomie, insecurity, loneliness and the lack of a clear sense of purpose. This proposition has been recently confirmed by some troubling statistics. As David Samuels points out, "From 2003 through 2005, 180 people died in 61 reported cases of Internet-assisted suicide in Japan" (Samuels, p. 1). Intriguingly, although ritualized suicide has featured in Japanese history since at least samurai culture and the related ethos of *bushido* ("the way of the warrior")—with kamikaze pilots later offering a baleful anticipation of contemporary suicide bombers—the "most spectacular manifestation of Japan's exploding suicide culture, Internet group suicide, is unique in that it is rooted in the technologies of the computer age and has no meaningful precedent in traditional Japanese social behaviour" (p. 2).

Takeshi Mori — and Gainax generally — adopt a deliberately ambiguous stance to otakuism. On the one hand, they celebrate the joys of passionate fandom with unbridled glee. It is worth noting, in this regard, that Gainax cofounder Toshio Okada has actually founded an International Otaku University (as well as lectured in "Otakuology" at Tokyo University) as a conceptual space within which fans can interact and learn through their consumption of anime and manga, participation in conventions, festivals and clubs, and involvement in fan art, fan fiction and cosplay. On the other hand, Mori and his colleagues elliptically draw attention to the numbing solipsism to which rabid addiction is only too often conducive. Hence, the studio never unequivocally militates in favor of otaku pride.

The dreamland aspired to by Mori's characters constitutes, at one level, a totally fantastic realm fuelled by sheer escapism — a space, as the character of Tanaka puts it, "where every day is like a school festival." (Gainax's proverbial aversion to the obligation to grow up resonates through Tanaka's Pinocchio-like words.) At another level, the harsh realities of the actual world insistently infiltrate the otaku's imaginary fairground. This is patently borne out by the OVA's tendency to sprinkle references to serious news items across its footage, including the British invasion of the Falklands and countless local and international crimes, political scandals and natural calamities. A vivid mood of reportorial veracity is concisely evoked by the presentation of such items in the form of text typed over a black screen in a white, old-fashioned font.

Otaku no Video instantly announces itself as a formally adventurous project. A two-part OVA alluding to the early history of Studio Gainax itself, the production intersperses its animated portions with mockumentary extracts titled "A Portrait of an Otaku." These offer a sample gallery showcasing otaku of all sorts (e.g., a garage-kit addict, a porno-video fan, an obsessed videogamer, cel thieves, and a cosplayer refusing to own up to his passion) in the form of live-action interviews. The baffling variety of fans included may surprise the casual viewer inclined to believe that otaku's cravings are exclusively anime, manga and computer games. In fact, as the Liner Notes included in the AnimEigo release of the OVA explain, "In Japan, one can be an Otaku of any genre, as the 'Portrait of an Otaku' segments, and some of the specialties of the characters themselves, demonstrate. There is in fact a TV quiz show called 'Cult Q' which is basically a show for Otakus [sic] of all kinds — whether they are experts of tropical fish or ingredient labels of over-the-counter drugs!" ("*Otaku no Video*: Liner Notes").

The animated segments and the "Portrait" interludes differ in tone to the extent that whereas the former tend to celebrate otaku's positive enthusiasm, the latter are more inclined to throw into relief the negative implications of their rabidly all-consuming passions. The denigrating dimension is explicitly foregrounded by the reluctance of certain interviewees to express their opinions and admit to their addictions in public. The partially illicit nature of their pursuits (a corollary of the media's demonization of otaku as perverts) is further highlighted by the incorporation of two strategies typical of the serious documentary style: the retention of the characters' anonymity and the masking of their faces by means of filmic mosaic.

In both the anime and the mockumentary sequences, however, the OVA consistently evinces an ironically self-deprecating stance: even when the fans' joyful fervor is brought to the fore, the latent absurdity of their activities and objectives is tersely underscored by the ludicrously bombastic, mock-epic tenor of the discourse in which they couch their ideals. Kanda Yoshimi's lyrics for the show's theme song, "Tatakae! Otaking" ("Fight! Otaking"), eloquently attest to this trait, as indicated by just the first couple of verses:

> Over the endless wasteland
> I run alone for all I am worth
> embracing the hope
> of an unseen world far away.
>
> ♦ ♦ ♦
>
> The only thing I believe in is glowing passion
> I will be a raging inferno!
> No one will be able to stop
> my heart's beat!

Moreover, as the *Right Stuf* review of the OVA points out, one senses throughout the 100 minutes of its duration that "This is Gainax having a good deal of fun at their own expense" ("*Otaku no Video* DVD"). Nevertheless, even though the studio was unquestionably keen on parodying otakuism, and, by implication, its own practices, it also sought to pay respect to the fan base that had made the company's own establishment and meteoric rise to fame possible in the first place. It is thanks to this commodious disposition that *Otaku no Video* manages to remain good-humored and touching throughout despite its indictment of otaku's least savory proclivities.

Not only does *Otaku no Video* mirror Gainax's own inception and early stages, it is also commonly believed that all the characters included in the mockumentary sections were based on staff employed by the studio at the time of shooting. As explained in the Wikipedia entry for the OVA,

> The first otaku interviewed bore a remarkable resemblance to Toshio Okada, a principal founder in Gainax, in both background and physical appearance. The *gaijin* otaku, Shon Hernandez, has been confirmed to have been Craig York, who with Shon Howell and Lea Hernandez ... were the main staff of General Products USA, an early Western branch of Gainax's merchandising in the early 1990s.... At FanimeCon 2003, Hiroshi Sato, an animator and another Gainax member, mentioned that he had been one of the interviewees in *Otaku no Video*. It is speculated that Sato was the garage-kit otaku, who used a simple reversal of his name for the pseudonym "Sato Hiroshi" for the interview [Wikipedia, the Free Encyclopaedia—*Otaku no Video*].

Additionally, the OVA is rife with anime references of all sorts, mirroring a stylistic propensity already nascent in Gainax's earlier works. As argued in the preceding chapters, *Wings of Honneamise*, *Gunbuster* and *Nadia: The Secret of Blue Water* all stand out as bold redefinitions of established genres: space opera, the *mecha* show, steampunk-inspired historical allegory. In this respect, those productions are inconceivable independently of an aesthetic foundation that brings together successively accreting strata of anime's coral-reef structure. *Neon Genesis Evangelion* will further reconfigure the *mecha* formula while simultaneously taking anime's penchant for serious psychodrama and ideological critique into the stratosphere. *His and Her Circumstances*, for its part, will radically reinvent the parameters of romantic anime by means of daring stylistic gestures and a resolutely unorthodox diegetic orchestration. With *FLCL*, the studio will embark on one of the most flamboyant experiments in brain-twisting anime underpinned by Bildungsroman motifs, whereas *Mahoromatic—Automatic Maiden* will give Gainax the opportunity to deconstruct both maid-based romantic comedy and intergalactic epic. Self-reflexive parody will reach its apotheosis with *Magical Shopping Arcade Abenobashi*—a veritable hymn to multigeneric and multimedia pastiche.

Providing a fully comprehensive list of the myriad productions alluded to in the course of *Otaku no Video* by means of action figures and manga volumes on display on the shelves, posters and costumes donned at festivals and conventions would barely be apposite in the present context. It must nonetheless be emphasized that several highly esteemed classics make an appearance. These include the following titles (here listed in alphabetical order for ease of filmographical reference):

- *Future Boy Conan* (animated TV series; dir. Hayao Miyazaki, 1978)
- *Gauche the Cellist* (animated feature film; dir. Isao Takahata, 1982)
- *Lupin III: The Castle of Cagliostro* (animated feature film; dir. Hayao Miyazaki, 1979) [also alluded to in *FLCL*]
- *Maison Ikkoku* (animated TV series; dir. Kazuo Yamazaki, 1986–1988)
- *Mobile Suit Gundam* (animated TV series; dir. Yoshiyuki Tomino, 1979–1980)
- *Nausicaä of the Valley of Wind* (animated feature film; dir. Hayao Miyazaki, 1984) [also alluded to in *Gunbuster*]
- *Rose of Versailles* (animated TV series; dirs. Tadao Nagahama and Osamu Dezaki, 1979–1980)
- *Space Battleship Yamato* (animated TV series; dir. Leiji Matsumoto, 1974)
- *Super Dimensional Fortress Macross* (animated TV series; dir. Noboru Ishiguro, 1982)
- *Urusei Yatsura* (animated TV series and feature films; dirs. Mamoru Oshii, Kazuo Yamazaki, Satoshi Dezaki and Katsuhisa Yamada, 1981–1991) [also alluded to in *This Ugly Yet Beautiful World*]

In-jokes centered on self-referential allusions to Gainax's previous productions, including the groundbreaking *Daicon 4* opening animation, *Wings of Honneamise*, *Gunbuster* and *Nadia: The Secret of Blue Water*, serve to further reinforce the program's zestfully intertextual nature. The finale renders direct homage to *Gunbuster*.

The DVD cover is itself a paean to self-reflexivity, featuring the character of Misty May as the central figure — modeled on the Bunny Girl from *Daicon 4*— surrounded by her non-magical incarnation, by Tanaka (who is based on Toshio Okada) and Kubo (Hiroyuki Yamaga's avatar), and by a lion cub directly inspired by *Nadia*'s King. Furthermore, the company "Giant X" is Gainax itself in thin disguise, just as the ancillary merchandise manufacturing venture "Grand Prix" clearly echoes General Products. In addition, *Otaku no Video* regales the senses with legion allusions to anime conventions, festivals, fanzines (*doujinshi*), clubs, merchandising ventures and studios, as well as to celebrities in both the music and the cinema industries.

A worthy successor to Mori's classic OVA is the 12-episode TV series *Genshiken*, directed by Takashi Ikehata and first aired in 2004. *Genshiken* constitutes a dispassionate, occasionally farcical but on the whole quietly amusing, dissection of an otaku club's endless quest for geekery. Most of the humor emanates from the club members' totally unself-critical magnification of its trivial goals as valiant missions. The gloriously overinflated episode titles used throughout the show, in particular, blatantly perpetuate the mock-heroic mood conjured up by *Otaku no Video*. The following examples seem especially deserving of citation in the present context:

- Episode 1— Study of the Modern Visually-Oriented Culture;
- Episode 2 — Comparative Classification of the Modern Youth through Consumption and Entertainment;
- Episode 4 — The Sublimating Effects of the Dissimulation Brought on through Makeup and Costume;

- Episode 6 — Theory of the Individual Outside the Boundaries of the Subculture;
- Episode 7 — Aspects of Behavioral Selection in Interpersonal Relationships.

As Chris Johnston observes, "The series provides a fantastic peek into anime/game/manga culture in Japan through Suioh University's Genshiken — a club of dorkus maximus who live, sleep, eat and breathe all things geek. In addition to being informative ... it also holds the mirror up to our own fan culture and reveals some of the quirks of the more hardcore among us" (Johnston, p. 152). Glimpses into the subcultures of cosplay and model-making are also supplied, as are the rules and codes of conduct surrounding attendance at fan-driven conventions.[1]

Analogous themes to those addressed by *Otaku no Video* and *Genshiken* have been recently developed in the TV show *Welcome to the N.H.K.* (dir. Yusuke Yamamoto, 2006). The series pivots on Tatsuhiro Satou, a classic case of the societally dysfunctional type known as "*hikikomori*." The term designates reclusive individuals inclined to lock themselves away for prolonged periods, to fill their days with long spells of sleep and to spend their nights surfing the Internet, playing video games or watching TV. This total withdrawal from social life generally induces *hikikomori* to take refuge in fantasy worlds akin to those favored by otaku, such as manga and anime. Satou is convinced that his condition is the result of a widespread conspiracy initiated by an organization eager to turn everybody into a social recluse. Much as he wishes to break free from his state, Satou is hindered by his sheer inability to face the outside world — until Misaki Nakahari enters his life and commits herself to curing the youth of his obsession.

Otaku no Video, *Genshiken* and *Welcome to the N.H.K.* exuberantly demonstrate, in their distinctive ways, that fandom is not by automatic definition tantamount to insular obsessiveness. At the same time, even as they adopt a predominantly jocular tone, they never quite lose sight of the darker cultural substratum underlying the phenomenon with which they so dispassionately engage. Accordingly, the viewer is regaled with plentiful opportunities to just have a good laugh; yet, he or she is also consistently reminded that otakuism is a cultural phenomenon inextricably intertwined with a profound sense of generational crisis, and is concurrently imbricated with the cognate phenomenon of information fetishism and with Japan's proverbially torrid relationship with technology.

CHAPTER 6

Neon Genesis Evangelion (Shinseiki Evangelion) I — The TV Series

Chief Director: Hideaki Anno (1995–1996)

> Eva. Whether you love it or hate it, you have to admit that it single-handedly redefined the genre, proved to the skeptical American market that animation is not necessarily for kids, and solidly placed ADV films on the map as a force to be reckoned with and feared. Eva is so well known that if a so-called anime fan admits to not having seen it yet, he or she can face social ostracism within the community.
>
> — Neon Genesis Evangelion Review

Evangelion's release history is almost as convoluted and multibranching as its dramatic dimension. The 26-episode TV series, aired in Japan in 1995–1996, climaxed with an unexpected ending as Hideaki Anno, left with inadequate funds to shoot the originally intended script for the two closing installments, resorted instead to a boldly experimental and open-ended finale. Enthusiastically received by fans who had already cherished the director's forays into avant-garde territory in the course of the run, the show's conclusion left others deeply dissatisfied. Feelings not merely of disappointment but also of downright rancor manifested themselves in the guise of death threats anonymously posted on the Internet. *Evangelion* had not, however, thereby come to an end. In fact, Anno resolved to produce an OVA utilizing — albeit with financially imposed alterations — the original script for Episodes 25 and 26 of the show.

Exceptionally generous sponsorship from a consortium of Japanese corporations eventually enabled the director to extend his ambitions to the creation of two feature-length films: *Death & Rebirth* and *End of Evangelion*, both of which were released in 1997. *Death & Rebirth* comprises two segments: the first, *Death* consists of a stylish reimagining of key moments from the series in montage format with approximately twenty minutes of new footage; the second, *Rebirth*, contains wholly novel materials. The scenes presented in *Rebirth* went on to constitute the opening thirty minutes of *End*, namely, an alternate version of the saga's finale to the one offered by the TV program. *End* itself consists of two sections, namely, Episode 25: "Air" and Episode 26: "Sincerely Yours."

In 1998, the *Directors' Cuts* of Episodes 21 through 24, annotated as Episodes 21–24 and featuring extended and improved animation, were released on video. The same year saw the airing on the WoWoW satellite channel of a second version of *Death*, known as *Death True*. This included much of the footage from the aforementioned *Directors' Cuts*. In 1998, a further theatrical release also took place in Japan: titled *Revival of Evangelion*, the movie included a third edit of *Death* dubbed *Death True^2* and the *End* film.

In 2003, Gainax embarked upon a thorough remastering of the original show headed the *Renewal Project*. Undertaken almost ten years after initial planning for the series had started, this developed under Anno's chief direction. New life was thus imbued into a chapter of anime history that had already yielded a global fandom phenomenon of unprecedented magnitude and vigor — to a considerable extent due to its shocking conclusion in both the televisual and theatrical formats. The world of the saga was reprocessed by recourse to the latest digital technology, eliminating jittery transitions and rendering the backgrounds more clearly detailed and defined. Acoustic effects were also boosted by completely remixing the dialogue and soundtrack in 5.1 stereo. The *Renewal Project* included the footage from the original episodes, the *Directors' Cuts* of Episodes 21 through 24, *Death True^2* and *End of Evangelion*. Multifarious ancillary merchandise was also released in the course of the *Renewal Project*. This included CDs, video games, cel-art illustrations and collectible models of all sorts (e.g., musical dolls, soapdish and bottlecap figurines, wedding-cake statuettes and incredibly detailed Eva Units with legion articulated joints).

In the United States and Europe, the series has been distributed by ADV Films, whereas the license for the features has been held by Manga Entertainment. The first DVD release by ADV Films was the 8-disc *Perfect Collection* in 2002. This contained the original 26 installments. In 2004, ADV released two DVD compilations titled *Neon Genesis Evangelion: Resurrection* and *Neon Genesis Evangelion: Reborn*, encompassing the directors' cuts of Episodes 21 through 23 and Episodes 24 through 26, respectively. The second DVD release of the series by ADV, incorporating both the remastered original 26 installments and the *Directors' Cuts* of Episodes 21 through 24, took place in 2005. Named the *Platinum Collection*, this was adapted from the *Renewal Project*, though it left out the theatrical releases.

In November 2006, ADV UK released the *Neon Genesis Evangelion Platinum Limited Edition R2 Collection*, arguably the most impressive European release of the saga to date. The collection contains all the materials produced by ADV for the purposes of the *Platinum* edition encased in a stylish tin box uncannily redolent of platinum and elegantly decorated with engravings of the three protagonists' eyes. A year later, the same package was released in the United States by ADV alongside Limited Edition metal-cased sets of *Nadia: The Secret of Blue Water* and *Magical Shopping Arcade Abenobashi* with the accompanying slogan "Full Metal Jacket Collections from the Bad Boys of Anime."

This chapter examines the TV show's diegetic premises, stylistic attributes and thematic preoccupations, providing illustrative examples drawn from individual installments. It deliberately avoids a sequential episode-by-episode analysis. This is because a substantial amount of information about the series is supplied in chapter 7 in the context of a detailed assessment of its reconfiguration in the first part of the feature *Death & Rebirth*. The reason for adopting this format is that it seems appropriate to address the original program and its theatrical reimagining in tandem as alternate, yet complementary, versions of the saga rather than as totally discrete enterprises. A comparative approach is thereby pursued.

The main portion of the plot unfolds in the course of the year 2015, fifteen years after the Second Impact, an apocalyptic cataclysm ostensibly caused by a meteor strike but actually unleashed by human arrogance, has melted the Antarctic ice cap, tilted the Earth's axis and wiped out half of the planet's population. The surviving humans and their offspring are tentatively beginning to recover from those horrors just as a new formidable menace descends onto the scene in the guise of polymorphous and seemingly invincible biomechanoids dubbed the "Angels." Conventional armaments are completely powerless in the face of these portentous creatures, the only available weapon consisting of another breed of biomechanicanoids known as the Evangelions or Evas.

The Japanese word used in the saga to designate the Angels is "*shito*," namely, "messenger," which corresponds to the original (pagan) meaning of the Greek word "*angelos*." The Japanese term for heavenly creatures closer in character to the angels in the Judaeo-Christian tradition is "*tenshi*." The Angels invoked by Anno have nothing in common with either Western painting's solemnly ethereal Gabriel visiting Mary with its baffling announcement or the plump cherubs in the Baroque style. Nor do they come equipped with wings, harps and haloes. In fact, they are invariably enormous, multiweaponed and downright scary.

The Evas are produced by the paramilitary organization NERV and piloted exclusively by chosen "Children" born after the Second Impact who are given very little choice in the matter.[1] As the saga develops, it emerges that the actual cause of the disaster resides with the hubristic evolutionary schemes promoted by the shady organization SEELE ("soul" in German): the Second Impact was not instigated by a meteor but by mankind's contact with the First Angel, Adam, and by the being's resulting explosion. Yet more unsavory truths come to the surface as it is unveiled that although NERV is supposed to exist in order to prevent a probable "Third Impact" from occurring, both NERV and SEELE are in fact *planning* a Third Impact in their separate ways. Furthermore, SEELE seeks to engineer a macrocosmic metamorphosis through the implementation of the "Human Instrumentality Project," which entails the merging of all people into a single undifferentiated mass akin to the primordial life soup.

Wings of Honneamise charts at once humanity's rise into the promises of cosmic infinity and its plunge into tormenting emotional and ideological dilemmas. *Gunbuster* transforms the formulae of both *mecha* anime and high school comedy into an intense quest laden with ethical implications. *Nadia* analogously transcends the conventions of action-adventure to deliver a dark and thought-provoking epic. *Evangelion* extends exponentially the genre-twisting proclivities of these earlier productions. Translating its *mecha* element into an allegorical correlative for the characters' inner struggles, the saga yields a hard-core psychodrama capable of matching David Lynch's convoluted imagination at its most baleful.

Like many *mecha* shows, *Evangelion* features action sequences interspersed with massive-scale urban destruction and occasional dabs of comedy. Unlike other series, however, it delves dispassionately into the characters' twisted personalities, as the fear of abandonment and betrayal, the omnipresent phantom of loneliness and a no less ubiquitous sense of disconnectedness from their world persistently threaten to paralyze them beyond remedy. The result is a deeply estranging yet engrossingly familiar mosaic of emotional turmoil.

Anchored to their legacy of childhood loss and rejection, Anno's personae are relentlessly haunted by an acute sense of dispossession that cannot be adequately relieved by any promises of restoration or compensation. Relatedly, although they feel a desperate need for love and acceptance, they are terrified of being hurt and hence erect impervious affective barriers. This condition eventually involves a total devaluation of social bonds and of language whereby everything becomes meaningless or, conversely, everything becomes equally and overwhelmingly meaningful. As a result, the characters are incapable of grasping any clear notion of relationality and, though repeatedly forced to occupy communal contexts, are unable to open up to others and hence interact positively. They feel warped and stigmatized by their atomized insularity, which would seem to point to a state of undiluted solipsism, and yet, ironically, continually acknowledge the existence of others insofar as they tend to feel exploited and hated by them or, at best, dependent on their bond to others for their very existence.

The Angels themselves could be regarded as concretizations of the principal characters' anxieties and fears. Their insistent intrusions, moreover, provide a metaphorical correlative for the compulsive repetitiveness with which the afflicted personae circularly return to their feelings of crisis throughout the narrative. Just as the defeat of all seventeen Angels does not lead to a neat resolution but rather to a chain of elusive riddles, so the characters' quest for emotional stability remains inexorably inconclusive.

The various emotional maladies experienced by *Evangelion*'s dramatis personae are economically condensed in Anno's bold characterization of the protagonist, the "Third Child" Shinji Ikari. According to Mike Crandol, the saga's protagonist embodies the typology of the "Tragic Hero." Prone to spiral into depressive acedia and to relate to others in a purely mechanistic and apathetic fashion, "Shinji is a departure from the more idealistic heroes commonplace in *mecha* anime (or adventure fiction in general, for that matter). Adventure heroes customarily represent the audience's aspirations: they are people we'd like to be. Shinji, conversely, is representative of the audience's realizations: his flaws we recognize in ourselves" (Crandol).

Susan Napier corroborates this point by proposing that despite its concessions to the conventional trappings of the *mecha* recipe, *Evangelion* actually subverts their import right from the start through its utterly uncompromising characterization of the saga's protagonist. Whereas the typical *mecha* hero customarily embodies an adolescent male fantasy of technologically enhanced omnipotence, Anno's tragic hero is intensely repelled by the task laid before him by his callous father Gendou Ikari — NERV's chief — and his associates: "It is as if Shinji were looking into a distorting mirror and is horrified by the self that he finds there" (Napier, p. 97).

Confirming the saga's unorthodox adventurousness, Anno's storyline incrementally reveals levels of complexity far greater than any skeletal plot delineation may superficially indicate. Repeat viewings of the TV series (including the directors' cuts) indeed disclose a rather convoluted story arc. Outlined below is a chronological reconstruction of the saga's *fabula*.

[*Approximately 4 billion years ago*:]
- The First Impact takes place — this refers to the splitting of a godlike being into the Angels Adam and Lilith and concomitant emergence of the White Moon, which contains Adam and is embedded under Antarctica, and the Black Moon, which contains Lilith and is embedded under Tokyo-3, the saga's key setting. The latter will later become the giant hollowed-out cavity hosting the "Geofront." This is a deep underground conglomeration spreading below Tokyo-3. The NERV Headquarters are situated in the middle of the Geofront, and are surrounded by woods and a subterranean lake. The numerous high-rise buildings that hang downwards from its ceiling are the same buildings that stand in Tokyo-3 and are retracted below the city's surface during Angel onslaughts. Some of these, dubbed "Armament Buildings," are Eva support structures containing launch and recovery gates, sockets and weaponry storage facilities.

[*1999*:]
- Professor Kohzou Fuyutsuki, expert in metaphysical biology at Kyoto University, meets the highly talented research student Yui Ikari and the roguish troublemaker Gendou Rokubungi. In the autumn of the same year, Yui and Gendou start dating (upon their marriage, Gendou will adopt his wife's family name).

[*2000*:]

- On 13 September, the Second Impact takes place. Officially presented as the result of a meteor strike, this cataclysm causes sea levels to rise and inundate the Earth, concurrently shifting the planet's axis and wreaking havoc on the ecosystem. Famines, plagues and wars instantly escalate. The Katsuragi research team is in Antarctica at the time of the Second Impact and its sole survivor is Dr. Katsuragi's daughter, Misato. Gendou, who has also been part of the team, fortuitously leaves Antarctica the day before the disaster.
- Far from constituting a natural disaster, the Second Impact turns out to have been instigated on purpose by Lorenz Keel and by the international cabal SEELE over which he presides. Keel and SEELE are guided by a prophecy included in the "Dead Sea Scrolls," an ancient document containing descriptions of the seventeen invading Angels. Keel's ultimate aim is specifically to trigger the Third Impact, and he knows that this cannot come to pass unless mankind has confronted seventeen trials in the form of seventeen Angels. The Second Impact, in this perspective, is instrumental to the unleashing of the Angels. Adam is exploited as the energy source necessary to cause the Second Impact in the first place. The First Angel is subsequently captured, shrunk to embryo size and eventually appropriated by Gendou, who proceeds to merge with the creature by having its chrysalis grafted upon his very body.
- It should be noted that the saga posits two kinds of Third Impact: the "Destructive Impact," meant to occur if an Angel returns to Adam and expected to annihilate mankind altogether; and the "Constructive Impact," in which all people are supposed to merge into a single being and Lilith plays the pivotal part. It is initially assumed that in order to allow the Constructive Third Impact to take place, mankind needs to defeat all seventeen Angels, to contain Adam and Lilith and to possess the "Lance of Longinus"— a giant spiral-shaped dart, also known as the "Spear of Destiny," that is capable of piercing an A.T. (Absolute Terror) Field, namely, the portentous defensive barrier deployed by both the Angles and the Evas. However, matters become rather more complicated as it transpires that the key characters foster quite different plans. This aspect of the saga's storyline is fully developed in *End*.
- What must be emphasized at this stage is that both SEELE and Gendou pretend to be endeavoring to prevent the Third Impact by destroying the Angels — and hence eliminating the threat of their return to Adam — when, in fact, they are eager to initiate it. The depth of their mendacity is tersely exposed by the revelation that the Angel imprisoned and crucified in NERV's hidden bowels is not Adam but Lilith, the Second Angel. Hence, the danger of an invading Angel rejoining its "father" has never obtained but only served as a convenient fabrication meant to keep hosts of loyal employees in thrall.

[*2001*:]

- Yui and Gendou Ikari have their first and only child, Shinji.

[*2002*:]

- Fuyutsuki visits the South Pole on a formal investigation of the Second Impact at the UN's request. In the course of the expedition, the professor meets Gendou again and learns that he and Yui have married and become parents. Fuyutsuki, already suspicious as to the real causes of the Second Impact and to Gendou's personal motives, discovers that the official documents recording the cataclysm have been severely manipulated. The true nature of the Second Impact, therefore, has been unscrupulously concealed from the public.

[*2003*:]

- Fuyutsuki obtains further confirmation for the formidable lies surrounding the Second Impact and for the role played therein by Gendou, who works for SEELE as chief of research of the Artificial Evolution Laboratories (AEL). When Fuyutsuki visits the AEL and threatens Gendou with a public revelation of the truth, Gendou leads Fuyutsuki to "Central Dogma," a massive cavity situated beneath the laboratories. There Fuyutsuki meets Dr. Naoko Akagi, an employee of the SEELE-sponsored organization "Gehirn" (the German word for "brain") and the ultimate authority in the field of biocomputers. Gendou invites Fuyutsuki to join his team and the professor, after careful consideration, accepts the offer. About half of the Eva-00 has by now been built — this Unit will eventually accommodate elements of Naoko's mind.

[*2004*:]

- Yui Ikari is absorbed into the body of the Eva-01 during an experiment before the very eyes of her son Shinji. Gendou vanishes for a week and upon his return informs Fuyutsuki that he has recommended the "Human Instrumentality Project" (a.k.a. "Human Complementation Project" or HCP). This consists of SEELE's plans to instigate the Third Impact so as to reconfigure drastically the boundaries of human existence. After Yui's disappearance, Shinji is placed by his uncaring father in the custody of a teacher until 2015.

[*2005*:]

- The victim of agnosia for five years, Misato is beginning to recover from her trauma. At Tokyo-2 University, she meets Ritsuko Akagi, daughter of the renowned Dr. Naoko Akagi, and Ryohji Kaji, a man who reminds her of her father and will soon become her lover. (Tokyo-2, incidentally, is the city built after the destruction of the original Tokyo in the Second Impact as a temporary capital while the architecturally more advanced Tokyo-3 is being developed.)

[*2007*:]

- Misato and Kaji separate: Kaji, it transpires, resembles Misato's father too much for the relationship to work healthily.

[*2008*:]

- Asuka Langley Sohryu is selected as the "Second Child." On the same day, her deranged mother hangs herself.
- Dr. Akagi completes the basic theory for the biocomputer "Magi." The Magi system consists of three interrelated computers — Melchior-1, Balthasar-2 and Casper-3 — and decisions are reached as a result of their conferring together. The Magi houses the thought patterns of its developer, with Melchior-1 corresponding to Naoko as a scientist, Balthasar-2 to Naoko as a mother and Casper-3 to Naoko as a woman. Ritsuko joins Gehirn, is assigned to the "E [Evangelion] Project" and learns that her mother and Gendou are having an affair. (A few years later, Ritsuko will take her mother's place in Gendou's private life.)

[*2009*:]

- Misato joins Gehirn and is stationed at the German Third Branch.

[*2010:*]
- The Magi system is completed. (There will eventually be five more Magi supercomputers under the command of SEELE in China, America and elsewhere. However, only the original trio will ever contain Naoko's personal notes detailing additional program stratagems and shortcuts.)
- The First Rei Ayanami visits Gehirn with Gendou, who claims that she is the child of an acquaintance. Rei (the "First Child") contains DNA from Yui Ikari and from Lilith. (SEELE's counterpart to NERV's Rei is the Seventeenth Angel Tabris—the Angel of Choice and Freedom—that contains Adam's DNA.) Naoko recognizes Yui in the child and finds that she has no records. Having learnt from Rei that Gendou is merely using her skills and has no regard for her feelings, Naoko strangles Rei and then kills herself. The next day, SEELE disbands Gehirn and moves the entire team to a new organization, "Special Agency NERV." SEELE's agenda thus enters a new phase.

[*2012:*]
- On the eighth anniversary of Yui's death, Shinji visits his mother's grave with his father.

[*2014:*]
- The Second Rei Ayanami transfers to the Tokyo-3 First Municipal Junior High School.

[*2015:*]
- Summoned by his father, Shinji comes to Tokyo-3. On that same day, the first Angel attack occurs: its perpetrator is the Third Angel encountered by mankind (Sachiel, the Angel of Water). Shinji is hastily placed inside the Eva-01 to defend the city and narrowly defeats the enemy.
- The Angel invasions continue and are countered by NERV by means of the Eva Units 00, 01 and 02 and of the First, Third and Second Children employed to maneuver them respectively (i.e., Rei, Shinji and Asuka). The "Fourth Child," Touji Suzuhara, is selected as the pilot of the Eva-03. During the initial activation test, the Unit turns out to be the Thirteenth Angel (Bardiel, the Angel of Lightning and Hail) and is dealt with as such by Shinji's Eva-01. After this incident, Shinji rebels against his father and quits piloting but the advent of the Fourteenth Angel (Zeruel, the Angel of Power) compels him to return to the front lines. The Eva-01 goes berserk during this fight and devours the enemy, thus acquiring its "S^2 [Super Solenoid] Engines"—the mechanisms that allow biomechanoids to operate independently of external energy supplies.
- Kaji, who is supposed to be working for NERV's "Special Inspection" department but also appears to be secretly investigating NERV's activities at SEELE's behest, as well as acting as a spy on behalf of the Japanese government, is assassinated. Misato's enduring attachment to her college lover despite her protestations to the contrary becomes blatantly and painfully obvious.
- The Eva-00 uses the Lance of Longinus in the battle against the Fifteenth Angel (Arael, the Angel of Birds), effectively vanquishing the enemy but also losing the weapon for good. (The Lance is recalled from the moon by the Eva-01 in *End*.) Rei's

Unit subsequently self-destructs in an effort to eliminate the Sixteenth Angel (Armisael, the Angel of the Womb) and protect Shinji. The Second Rei is also destroyed in the explosion, and soon replaced by the Third Rei.
- Embittered by the breakdown of her relationship with Commander Ikari, Ritsuko betrays NERV and destroys all the Rei clones ("dummy plugs"), except the one currently functional.
- Asuka vanishes and although she is found before long, it is obvious that she is no longer able to pilot an Eva. The "Fifth Child," Kaworu Nagisa, arrives at NERV as a replacement for Asuka. Despite his humanoid appearance, he turns out to be the Seventeenth Angel and to be aiming to enter "Terminal Dogma," presumably with the intention of coming into contact with Adam and thus initiating the Third Impact. However, what Kaworu finds is not Adam but Lilith, and hence chooses to be crushed to death by the pursuing Eva-01. Following this climactic occurrence, the TV show and the feature films proceed to offer alternate, though arguably complementary, endings.

In overturning many of the expectations traditionally surrounding its parent genre, *Evangelion* also questions, at times quite acerbically, dominant power structures and power relations. This is borne out by Episode 7, "A Human Work," in which Ritsuko (in her capacity as NERV's head scientist) first reveals to Shinji the actual occurrences underlying the Second Impact. In the same installment, a corporation critical of NERV's methods performs the activation test of a pilotless and supposedly "superior" biomechanoid powered solely by nuclear energy, the creature goes on the rampage, and it is up to Misato, Shinji and Unit 01 to save the day. The installment brings forth a trenchant critique of corporational elites, exposing their greed, mendacity and myopic vision. In this instance, the *mecha* formula is turned into a vehicle for active engagement in political and economic satire.

The ending, moreover, discloses that Gendou himself has surreptitiously triggered the machine's malfunctioning, which adds a further level of complexity to the episode's unpalatable ideological message. The dramatization of wheels-within-wheels conspiracies is undoubtedly *Evangelion*'s forte. A germane topos is articulated in Episode 10, "Magma Diver," in which Gendou is determined to retrieve the embryonic Eighth Angel (Sandalphon, the Angel of Unborn Children) from the bottom of a volcano. The mission is dramatized as a metaphor for pecuniary and territorial expansionism. Typically, Gendou pursues his goal with scarce concern for the mission's potential outcomes, which could amount to another planetary upheaval of no smaller a scale than the Second Impact.

Evangelion's generic distinctiveness is also borne out by its refusal to comply with the typical *mecha* show's passion for hard metallic surfaces. In fact, it is rooted in the intractable reality of the flesh. This is attested to by the designs for the Evas, executed by Ikuto Yamashita, as biomechanoids whose organic components are ultimately capable of breaking through the mechanical restraints meant to curb and encase them with shocking repercussions, thereby emphasizing the bestial drives coursing beneath their sleek façades.

The series provides a number of clues to the animal nature underlying the Evas' restraining plates from an early stage. In the flashback to Shinji's first battle supplied in Episode 2, "The Beast," for example, the Third Child catches a glimpse of Unit-01's vibrant aliveness in the guise of a reflection of its bright green eye in a mirror-fronted edifice. The same image occurs in Episode 14, "Weaving a Story," in the context of Rei's stream-of-consciousness reflections, in which the gigantic eye stares out of a grotesquely zoetic skull. As Dennis Redmond emphasizes, the Evas depart radically in their design from conventional *mecha* made of "stacks of mechanical boxes and tubes which approximate a human figure" and actually "look and move like quasi-living creatures, thanks to extensible necks, tapered waists (very similar to anime characters themselves), gracefully elongated arms and legs, and unusually thin shoulder guards" (Redmond, p. 247).

The Evas' animateness is not only communicated by the full-fledged Units in action. It is no less powerfully (though less sensationally) exuded by the unfinished prototypes seen in Episode 23 "Rei III." In the installment's initial version, the remains of each failed model are neatly laid out on the floor of a remote section of the NERV HQ, and their organic nature is alluded to by most of the flesh having rotted away, leaving little more than spinal chords and odd bones in its wake. In the directors' cut of Episode 23, the rejected Evas' body parts are amassed in circular waste pits symmetrically arranged on the sides of a huge cross-shaped cavity, which echoes the show's governing iconography. Shinji poetically describes the space as a "graveyard" for Evas but Ritsuko characteristically sees it as merely a "dumping ground." The scientist's terminology mirrors NERV's hubristic attitude to their weapons: although both Gendou and Ritsuko know full well that the Evas are organic entities capable of achieving self-awareness to horrifying extremes, they do not hesitate to handle them as lifeless automata. Rejects consisting of heads from which sinuous backbones ensue are presented in *End of Evangelion*, in which the creatures' latent aliveness is hinted at by the remarkable degree of variety in facial layout that they exhibit. Three incomplete and unarmored Units (stored in the "Pribnow Box") are also shown in Episode 13, "Lilliputian Hitcher," where they are hacked into by the saga's most formidable menace: the Eleventh Angel Iruel, the Angel of Terror.

Evangelion's indigenous vocabulary likewise foregrounds the material dimension of its universe. The "entry plug," a capsule-shaped cockpit accommodating the Eva pilot within the biomechanoid, is vividly redolent of a womb-like receptacle. Posited as a protective chamber throughout the majority of the Eva pilots' exploits, this location nonetheless holds less than benevolent proclivities. Following Unit 01's ingestion of Zeruel's S^2 Engines (Episode 19, "Introjection"), Shinji is indeed swallowed by his Eva as though its entry plug were an all-engulfing ancestral womb.

At the same time, the very process of activating an Eva is an intensely physical operation insofar as it requires the insertion of the entry plug into one of its most sensitive body parts, namely, its cervical vertebrae. The principal neural connector between a pilot and an Eva is the A10 nerve, a nerve that "travels from the brain stem through the hypothalamus ... related to high level brain functions such as memory, recognition, and carrying out motion, as well as emotions such as anxiety, fear, happiness, and pleasure. It is also said that it plays a vital role related to the feeling of love between family and lovers" ("Glossary"). The privileging of this vehicle within the series is amply justified by *Evangelion*'s psychological dimension.

(Please note that a pseudo-entry plug developed so as to activate and operate an Eva without the intervention of a human pilot is dubbed a "dummy plug." The personal thought patterns inscribed in Rei's mind in the case of NERV, and those hosted by Kaworu Nagisa's brain in that of SEELE, are transferred onto the plug to make it functional.)

The uterine analogy is reinforced by the term describing the cord used to energize the Eva from an external source, the "Umbilical Cable." Just as a fetus receives nutrients through the blood vessels extending from its navel to the placenta, so the Eva receives electric power through the Umbilical Cable. Furthermore, each of the main Evas appears to behave under the influence of the soul of the maternal figure whose vestiges it carries: Naoko's in the case of the Eva-00, Yui's in that of the Eva-01 and Asuka's mother's in that of the Eva-02. The most potently physical element repeatedly invoked by the saga is the "LCL"—"Link Connected Liquid"—a viscous substance endowed with an unmistakably blood-like odor. LCL fills "Terminal Dogma," namely, NERV's nethermost area, situated at the bottom of the 7-kilometer deep "Central Dogma."[2] It also floods the Eva's entry plug and plays a key role in enabling activation. When the LCL is traversed by an electric current, its molecular arrangement alters and allows it to connect mentally and affectively the pilot and the Eva. Suggestively, the composition of the LCL is also posited as analogous to that of the ancestral life soup.

In portraying the Evas as entities pivotal to humanity's survival, on the one hand, and bloodthirsty monsters, on the other, *Evangelion* throws into relief Gainax's take on the relationship between humanity and technology. Influenced by animistic beliefs of Shintoist orientation, the saga suggests that technology can never be unproblematically regarded as an ensemble of inert tools amenable to total control by humans. Everything, in fact, is endowed with at least potential aliveness, and humanity and technology are accordingly situated on a continuum from which ethical and moral values ensue. As Frédéric Kaplan observes, this worldview entails that "Japanese people do not oppose the natural and the artificial but on the contrary very often use the artificial to recreate nature." This idea is exemplified by the contrast between "Western fountains" and "small Japanese cascades." Whereas the former seek to prove humanity's "mastery over nature" by capitalizing on an entirely "unnatural movement," the latter "mimic as closely as possible the way water naturally flows." Ironically, despite their "modest" appearance compared to Western waterworks, "the hydraulic mechanisms underlying them turn out to be technically superior" (Kaplan, p. 5).

Stylistically, *Evangelion* marks Anno's introduction into the realm of anime of forms of camera work virtually absent from earlier TV shows. These include the *plan séquence* (a shot in which the camera shifts focus from one plane of depth to another as the actors move about, allowing for a realistic rendition of both middle ground and background activity); off-frame action (the intimation of the presence of people or objects that are actually outside the frame, which extends an audience's grasp of the story beyond the boundaries of the visible); a close focus on static details intended to encapsulate metonymically the tenor of an entire scene. These tropes are seamlessly amalgamated with more conventional anime techniques, which Anno boldly resituates within a decidedly contemporary—and arguably postmodern—vista.

Alongside intrepid choreography, a further aspect of Gainax's experimentative mission deserving of attention is *Evangelion*'s handling of typography. Gainax had already shown a proclivity to incorporate textual elements prior to *Evangelion*. This is demonstrated, for instance, by the pivotal scene in *Gunbuster* in which Ohta lectures Noriko about the part to be played in humanity's future by her and Kazumi's courageous efforts and by the composite prowess of their *mecha*. The message is silently bolstered by the abrupt appearance of the kanji for "heart" and "double fire," starkly rendered in black ink over a white background. In *Nadia*, Gainax's fascination with textuality manifests itself in the guise of cryptic characters and engravings alluding to the heroine's submerged past and to the vicissitudes of her race, while in *Otaku no Video*, text is brought into play in the course of parodic interviews with all manner of rabid fans.

Evangelion develops the studio's attraction to textual elements into a full-fledged passion, utilizing superbold kanji in the Mincho font in the actual footage and design work in the Ryumin and Matisse fonts for the video and laserdisc covers created by Norihiko Nezu. The saga's unique handling of typography, which caused quite a stir when the series was first broadcast, bears witness to Anno's commitment to an aesthetic vision wherein every single graphic element is accorded a vital part. Following *Evangelion*, both *His and Her Circumstances* and *FLCL* will again emplace textuality as a major performative agent by means of scrolling and flashing letters and compounds presented in a variety of styles, whereas *Mahoromatic—Automatic Maiden* will harness typography to the evocation of a broad range of moods and generic situations.

Evangelion also brings textuality into play in the form of stills of newspaper clippings and pages from official reports regarding the Second Impact and related occurrences. Such pseudo-documentary evidence adds dramatic weight to SEELE's and NERV's allegations (and lies) in a dispassionate fashion. This would have been hard to achieve if events had been considered solely through the eyes of individual personae without any external mediation. At the same time, the obviously distorted nature of the information divulged by the authorities reminds us that putatively objective sources are no less subjective — and biased — than personal perceptions.[3]

Increasingly, as the series advances toward its shocking finale, temporal suspension and stasis dominate large portions of the action surrounding the hyperkinetic fight sequences. To some extent, the attenuation of *Evangelion*'s dynamic dimension is a direct result of budgetary restraints (felt by the troupe most severely from Episode 19 onwards). Yet, it would be ungenerous not to acknowledge that the unhurried rhythm exhibited by the show in its closing third contributes vitally to the communication of Anno's unique style. The director was indeed able to translate what some would consider a flaw into a virtue, making deliberate pacing and even inaction into key expressive vehicles, and thus exploding the Disney-based assumption that animation must necessarily be rapid, bouncing and tumultuous.

This animational style is ideally suited to *Evangelion*'s diegetic mold: an intricate thriller that discloses its secrets in a highly methodical, and, at times, excruciatingly oblique, fashion. Although sensational coups de théâtre are not rare, the show's essence more often emanates from suspenseful drama wherein the action element is minimalistically refined. The incredibly varied soundtrack, created by the composer, conductor, arranger and producer Shiro Sagisu, contributes crucially to the overall mix.

The main characters' psychological struggles are most effectively conveyed, on the cinematographical plane, by means of animated trips across their psychic terrains. Perplexingly surreal analyses that gradually increase in frequency as the saga progresses, these sequences fathom dispassionately the characters' minds to the point that these dissolve into digitized fragments of sheer color, language and light. The closing episodes, in particular, offer an uncompromising anatomy of the characters' minds by deconstructing the art of animation itself. First, we witness a breakdown of the action's flow into vignettes of the main personae intercut with flashbacks and flashforwards. Increasingly, the emphasis falls on various symbolic correlatives for their anxieties and fears in the guise of abstract sketches, collages, montages, still photographs, impressionistic blotches and flickering lights, as well as starkly minimalistic line-drawings and monochrome typographical elements.

The key message here conveyed is that people inhabit not *one* reality but rather multiple coexisting realities — or, more accurately, "reality effects." Any one narrative shape that one's life acquires is only a minute drop in an ocean of interplaying narratives — all of which are ultimately lacunary and arbitrary. What happens to fall into shape could have been something quite different: the apprehension of potential difference renders the contingently realized circumstances inexorably precarious, stressing their inextricability from legion might-bes and might-have-beens. What must be emphasized, in order to do the director's accomplishment the justice it deserves, is that these experimental sections would appear pointless or even unbearable were they not underpinned by rigorously crafted, and hence utterly credible, human personalities, the disparate facets of which are brought into focus by Anno's diligent attention to the various characters' alternately somber, challenging or downright disturbing interrelations.

Psychedelic concatenations of visuals occur consistently at fraught junctures in the series. A case in point is Episode 16, "Splitting of the Breast," where Shinji and his Eva are mysteriously suctioned into the dark shadow cast by the Twelfth Angel Leliel (the Angel of Night), namely, a gigantic zebra-striped ball. As Shinji resignedly waits for the life-support system to run out of energy, curled up inside his Unit, he falls into a slumber and is instantly assaulted by troubling visions.

In one of these, he finds himself in a subway car with his own double seated opposite him. One image corresponds to Shinji's own perception of himself, the other image reflects the perceptions of Shinji held by those around him. These impressions are varied and even conflicting but none of them is ultimately more correct than any of the others. This same subway-car scenario is used elsewhere in *Evangelion* as the setting for moments of intense introspection, its yellow-orange glow, consistent use of a soft focus and fish-eye lenses, and suspension of the passage of time deliberately lending an eerie atmosphere of unearthliness to the character's emotional ordeals. Fleeting scraps of disjointed reminiscences fill the screen, interspersed with newspaper headlines reporting Yui's death and allusions to Gendou's possible responsibility for the tragedy. When Shinji eventually wakes up, he realizes that he is still trapped inside the Eva-01 and that he has no chances of survival. Suddenly, however, the image of an ethereally beautiful woman reminiscent of his mother fills him with unwonted hope. Red streaks rapidly spread over the captor's surface and Unit 01 bursts out of its prison, covered in blood.

Besides offering an unsentimental portrayal of Shinji's disturbed psyche, this climax is also important to the saga's overall logic, insofar as it throws into relief the Evangelions' ultimately impenetrable nature. NERV's own understanding of its biomechanoid weapons is scanty and its mastery of the Units' mentalities lamentably limited. The ghastly image of Unit 01 emerging from its captor indeed induces Asuka to wonder *what* exactly she is piloting, while Misato expresses apprehension about NERV's true purpose. Ritsuko, who knows full well that the Evas are intrinsically ferocious beasts, anxiously wonders whether the Units are "really on our side" or rather "hate" us. Another paradigmatic example of Anno's penchant for dissecting his characters' psyches by recourse to allegorical animational journeys is supplied by Episode 20, "Weaving a Story 2: Oral Stage," in which Shinji is ostensibly "taken into" the Eva-01's being, having lost his "ego border" altogether and merged with the LCL in a replica of the "primordial soup" from which all life is held to have proceeded. As the NERV staff tries desperately to release Shinji, only to have the "eject code" declined time after time, the pilot himself is assaulted by a barrage of mental images.

The Unit has already exhibited an uncanny ability to operate of its own volition in the sequence dramatizing the climax of Shinji's first mission (Episode 2,), and flaunted the Beast-Within in all its brutal magnificence in Episode 18, "Ambivalence," and Episode 19. It now appears determined to have things its own way once again. The images to which Shinji is incrementally exposed include recurring flashes of seawater (a further reference to an ancestral life-giving force), snapshots of people he knows, menacing pictures of his "enemy" (first in the guise of Angels he has battled and eventually in that of his father), flashing polychromatic text, quavering lines, splotches of pure hues, and hand-drawn sketches (including a highly allusive one of Shinji as a baby at his mother's breast). This almost overwhelming array of images powerfully conveys the protagonist's continuing confrontation of his inner demons with unsurpassed graphic vigor.

Analogous techniques are employed in Episode 22, "Don't Be," in which Asuka's mind is "raped" by the invading Angel, and the horrors of her childhood cascade upon it in the form of visually disorienting whorls, squiggles, zigzagging lines, overexposed and solarized shots, and lurid chromatic juxtapositions. Flickering snatches of text are again employed as a means of succinctly encapsulating the character's torment by means of semiotically laden captions. The images are invested with additional pathos by their recurring juxtaposition with images of Asuka as a bereft and helpless child, most notably in the directors' cut of the episode. In the latter, the magnitude of Asuka's agony is surrealistically underscored by the scene in which she walks backwards across desolate rail tracks and is gradually swamped by a crowd of hooded figures whose garments hide not actual bodies but masses of blood-red swirls.

Quite a different kind of psychological excursion is offered by Episode 14 with a focus on the most elusive of the saga's personalities: Rei. The installment constitutes an adventurous piece of cinematography right from the start, as each of the Angels' attacks to date is recapitulated by means of a palimpsest of data supplied by various characters' reports, notes, testimonies and diary entries. The collage-like form adopted in the first part of the episode is exponentially intensified by the transition to an oneiric sequence in which Rei reflects, in an associative fashion, on the ultimate meaning of Nature in its multifarious manifestations. The vision is sparked by a compatibility test in which Rei is synchronizing with Unit 01, and the Eva's feedback system seeps into her consciousness. Rei's musings fluidly travel from the contemplation of mountains, the sky, the sun, water, flowers and blood, to a meditation about creation — the creation of cities, of Evas, and of humans. As her voiceover unfolds, to the accompaniment of a haunting musical score combining choral and instrumental melodies, the following images consecutively fill the screen: a misty ravine, a summer sky framed by puffy clouds, sun-kissed rice fields, and Van Gogh–style sunflowers (these images are intertextual "borrowings" from Episode 4, "Hedgehog's Dilemma").

With a subtle shift of visual mood, the picture then moves to a glass beaker (a detail associated with Rei throughout the saga), a blood-smeared hand, a nocturnal panorama of Tokyo-3, a gigantic moon, a close-up of Rei's eye, a row of Rei clones, close-ups of Shinji, Misato, Ritsuko, Rei's classmates Kensuke, Touji and Hikari, Asuka and, finally, Commander Ikari's spectacles. The sequence reaches its climax with shots of the First Child herself, of the Eva-01 without its constraining faceplate, of one of the Eva's green eyes and of a human eye, as Rei repeatedly asks: "Who are you?" The sequence thus indicates that Rei's personal "I" is inextricably intertwined with the simultaneously singular and plural "you" she incantationally invokes.

The sorts of mental images implanted into Rei, fully documented by the sequence in Episode 14 here described, and alluded to by Ritsuko in Episode 23, are hauntingly captured by several of the works included in *Die Sterne* and *Der Mond*. The First Child is repeatedly associated with images of a full moon dappled with roaming flecks of vaporous clouds, cool palettes dominated by all conceivable shades of blue, green and lilac, both still and flowing water and, at least in one case, fireflies whose transience fittingly echoes the ephemeral status of Rei's own being.

Episode 25 and Episode 26 are undoubtedly the portions of the series in which hallucinatory excursions through the characters' psyches come most prominently to the fore. In Episode 25, "Do you love me?" Shinji is persecuted by guilt as he struggles to justify his destruction of Kaworu — the only being ever to have told him "I love you" — but can find no satisfactory solution. He is aware that Kaworu wished for death and that he had to kill him because he was an Angel, an enemy, but he can derive no conclusive solace from this knowledge. Seeking absolution from others and receiving no such thing, Shinji discovers that what he fears most, ultimately, is his own self and the hatred that his being may provoke. He then wonders why he pilots the Eva, and realizes that he does it exclusively to get appreciation from others. There appears to be no natural inclination, in the character's makeup, to do anything of his own accord and this, it is intimated, may well be the ultimate cause of his unhappiness.

The focus then shifts to Asuka: curled up in her Eva underwater (an anticipation of a scene in *Rebirth* and of its reprisal in *End*), she dolefully reflects on her worthlessness as an Eva pilot and, by extension, as a human being. Asuka, too, appears unable to gauge her personal value independently of other people's recognition of her abilities, terrified that she will lose her identity altogether if others abandon her.

The next "case study" addressed in the episode is that of Rei. Her various incarnations — products of her repeated cloning at Commander Ikari's behest — discuss the nature of their respective identities, the First and Second versions maintaining that they are all "Rei Ayanami" because that is what other people call them. They also claim that the Third Rei is endowed with an entirely fake body and soul but she adamantly asserts that she is simply "herself." The First and Second Reis, however, go on insisting that Rei III is merely Gendou's fabrication, that she exists only because of his need for her, and will return to nothingness when she is no longer of any use. This portion of Episode 25 comes to a close as Gendou enters the room and tells Rei to follow him, for this is the day for which she was created (*End* is again foreshadowed by this shot.)

The scene returns to Shinji, as he struggles to make sense of the engulfing feeling of nothingness into which he believes to have sunk. Episode 25 now provides its first overt reference to the Instrumentality Project, with Gendou telling his son that what he senses as nothingness actually signals a return to a primal state. Ritsuko elliptically praises Instrumentality as a corrective to the feeling of incompleteness that unrelentingly haunts the whole of mankind, whereas Misato berates it as an entirely artificial means of controlling human life to which no scientist should feel automatically entitled. Misato becomes the center of the episode's attention in the ensuing scene: Unresolved internal conflicts rooted in infancy instantly begin to surface, as it becomes patent that the character's professional brilliance, sense of humor and playfulness belie a tormented personality. Seeking relief in erotic gratification has only served to magnify Misato's deep-seated dissatisfaction with herself. Like Shinji, Asuka and Rei before her, Misato, too, ends up admitting that the presence of other people is pivotal to her self-validation.

At the end of the episode, Instrumentality is brought into focus once again as Misato apprises Shinji that the situation he is now experiencing — this vacuous world he can barely grasp and clearly gives him no comfort — is of his own making, regardless of his father's master plan: wishing for a closed universe in which he could keep wholly to himself to avoid pain, the boy has spawned a forbiddingly lifeless prison.

Episode 26, "Take care of yourself," develops its predecessor's dramatic premises. Set in the year 2016, the installment first focuses on Shinji's deeply ingrained conviction that he is unwanted and therefore worthless. Misato opines that wallowing in this belief is ultimately akin to running away, and concedes that she is also persecuted by the spectre of failure. She further maintains that all humans, deep down, feel lacking and struggle to fill in the gaps at the core of their being by merging with others. Instrumentality, ideally, provides a means of materially erasing the barriers separating one individual from another. However, the question of why one exists in the first place is still to be answered. Asuka suggests that one exists only in order to find out that one exists. In response, Shinji concludes that if such a discovery is to be made, the quest for self-understanding must never be abandoned and this entails ceasing to run away. The problem here is that for Shinji, not running away has meant just agreeing to pilot an Eva, which he sees as the guarantee of being accepted and even praised by others. This does not really amount to self-understanding since it depends on an external validating agency, which, as Ritsuko stresses, cannot be unequivocally relied upon.

As the animation shifts to an increasingly stylized modality, Shinji's being is translated into spartan drawings expressive of other people's perceptions of his identity and actions. Shinji, in this respect, is fundamentally an aggregate of fragmentary interpretations instrumental to his own sense of self. Were he to dissever himself from this web of partial readings, he could be free to do anything he wished but would also, in the process, divorce himself from others and hence preclude any chances of interaction, which is pivotal to the achievement of self-understanding, and hence to the psyche's acceptance of its one unavoidable quest.

Thus far, the images presented in the final episodes have conveyed the notion that *all* the characters, though most pointedly Shinji, have taken refuge in insulated dark rooms of their own making so as to protect themselves from further anguish. However, they have thereby merely succeeded in rendering their lives even bleaker. As Shinji puts it in the climactic moment, a world in which he can do anything he fancies but only with himself on the cast is untenable because it lacks other people's acknowledging agency: "It's as if I'm here but not here at all." Insofar as it accommodates "no difference between me and nothing," a reality with only "me" in it ultimately amounts to an entropic field of unrelieved negativity in which one might as well not exist at all.

Suddenly, Anno offers an alternate scenario in which, conversely, a number of parallel realities dialectically coexist. In one of these possible worlds, Shinji inhabits a context utterly incongruous with the rest of the show, governed by the lighthearted conventions of domestic and school comedy. In this dimension, the Second Impact has clearly not occurred and no trace of either Evas or Angels can be detected. Gendou and Yui are just the sort of parents one would expect to encounter in stereotypical anime fare. Misato's pet penguin Pen-Pen (a.k.a. Pen^2) is reimagined as a plastic doll. Asuka is Shinji's childhood friend and her main concern seems to be to get him out of bed in time for school (following some scolding occasioned by the "objectionable" state he wakes up in). Even Rei is a ditzy bundle worried mainly about avoiding unwanted exposure of her lingerie. This last point of departure from the saga's principal tenor sums up the magnitude of the last installment's uniqueness. As for Misato, she is a gorgeous teacher whose attitudes bring out in a comedically magnified fashion aspects of her character seen in Episode 7 when she visits Shinji's school in her capacity as his legal guardian.

If Shinji can accept *this* world, it is suggested, then he can feel entitled to occupy *any* available world without unrelentingly feeling he has to either hide or run away. The realization gains him unanimous approval from the rest of the cast, as each character treats him to a gleeful "Congratulations!" to which he responds with heart-warming gratitude. Previously trapped in a reality he could only perceive as hostile, the protagonist now seems willing to concede that no reality is utterly fixed or inexorable — not even the apparently all-encompassing visions construed by powerful bodies such as SEELE and NERV. Anno has commented on the proposition advanced in *Evangelion*'s finale in a letter originally published in *Anime FX*, Issue 10: "It is said that 'To live is to change.' I started this production with the desire that they [i.e., the characters] and the world change by the time the story reaches its conclusion" ("Ikari Gendo's Ultimate EVA FAQs about the TV Series").

The ADR director and English language producer of *Evangelion*, Matt Greenfield, has put forward an imaginative interpretation of Episodes 25 and 26 according to which the series as a whole is "a flashback from the last two episodes ... as opposed to what's happening" (Greenfield). The axial importance of the numbers 25 and 26 within *Evangelion*'s diegesis is confirmed by their recurrent flashing on Shinji's portable audio player. It is almost as though, with the show's finale, Anno were telling us that the story we thought we were following was not really the story he was telling.

As Redmond notes, one of Episode 25's most salient formal features is its extensive use of "theatrical tropes — spotlights, character monologues, and simple stage props.... During Misato's own moment of self-reflection, for example, her childhood photograph is shown repeatedly, each time looking slightly more torn and frayed than before" (Redmond, p. 284). No less remarkable is the choreographing of flashbacks in such a fashion that they do not merely capture fragments from the past of the scene's focal persona but also illuminate their perception by other characters as actual participants in the retrospective experience. Thus, in the presentation of Misato's flashback to some intimate moments with Kaji, "Shinji silently watches them from *within* the flashback, accompanied by the steady rocking of a subway or train," and punctuated by "shots of a whirring fan" (pp. 284–285). This kind of device serves to highlight, in a quasi–Brechtian manner, the staged nature of the action. In the final installment, the constructed status of the mise-en-scène is further underscored. Especially memorable is the shot in which Shinji's monochrome silhouette is flooded in rapid succession with polychromatic snippets of frames from other episodes.

Evangelion abounds with biblical allusions, including "Eve," "Adam," "Lilith," the "Lance of Longinus" and, of course, the "Angels." The image of the Crucifixion, moreover, is iconically pivotal to the show in the rendition of both spectacular lighting effects and peripheral decorative details. Reference is also sporadically made to the Kabbalah, and particularly to its "Sephiroth": the "Tree of Life" depicting the ten emanations of the divine principle. Babylonian mythology is also invoked in the use of the name of the deity "Marduk" to designate the institute held responsible for selecting Eva pilots but actually consisting of 108 dummy corporations. (108, incidentally, is the number of sins believed to afflict humanity in Tibetan Buddhism.) Although *Evangelion*'s religious frame of reference may at first appear dominated by a fundamentally Judaeo-Christian repertoire, oblique allusions to Shinto[4] are also notable and may, in fact, play more instrumental a role in the overall diegesis than their biblical and Kabbalistic counterparts. As Patrick Drazen observes, in this respect, even though in the saga "much is made (though little is explained) about the Lance of Longinus," this may have "less to do with the weapon of a Roman centurion than with the jeweled Spear of Heaven, given by the gods to Izanagi and Izanami, the male and female Shinto deities responsible for creating the Earth" (Drazen, p. 306).

It should also be noted that the saga's use of religious imagery of Western derivation is neither entirely nor preeminently serious. Asked to comment on *Evangelion*'s biblical symbolism, Kazuya Tsurumaki has explicitly underscored the playfully utilitarian character of its employment: "There are a lot of giant robot shows in Japan, and we did want our story to have a religious theme to help distinguish us. Because Christianity is an uncommon religion in Japan we thought it would be mysterious. None of the staff who worked on *Eva* are Christians. There is no actual Christian meaning to the show, we just thought the visual symbols of Christianity look cool" (Tsurumaki 2001).[5]

◆ ◆ ◆

The latest product of Gainax's ongoing reinvention of the *mecha* genre is the TV series *Tengen Toppa Gurren Lagann* (translatable as *Making Breakthrough Gurren Lagann* or *Breakthrough to Heaven Gurren Lagann*), which aired in Japan from April to September 2007. The show's dominant attribute is high-octane action that allows relatively little leeway for introspective and romantic elements. Director Hiroyuki Imaishi, who is renowned for the kind of colorful and hyperkinetic style found in *FLCL* (to which he contributed as animation director), has underscored this point, describing *Gurren Lagann* as "full-on, balls-to-the-wall, guy-oriented drama" (Imaishi, p. 59). Nevertheless, the series does elaborate some serious motifs pivotal to Gainax's cachet that occasionally invite quiet reflection. The orphaned hero left to his own devices in an obdurately exploitative world and brutal adults hell-bent on crushing youthful idealism are cases in point.

Moreover, even though *Gurren Lagann* thrives on sensational explosions and stupendous transformations as its primary visual effect, it is often from the gentler scenes that the story derives dramatic density. Most remarkable, in this regard, is the use of chromatic and textural contrasts, which, in defining diverse ambiences, also evoke conflicting emotions — for example, the suffocating gloom of the subterranean settings, the airiness of the aboveground locations, the hostility of scorched plains and rocky terrain, the rapture of starry skies beckoning the eye to the unknown, the vanilla-hued softness of urbanscapes canopied by billowy clouds, the smoke-saturated noxiousness of blasted battlefields.

At the level of *mecha* design, *Gurren Lagann* is especially original in its use of a face-based motif in the ideation and individuation of its numerous robots. Simultaneously, the show revamps to good effect iconographic elements associated with classic space opera: for instance, Leiji Matsumoto's *Space Battleship Yamato* (1974). Structurally, the program's most intriguing feature is its division into two story arcs separated by a seven-year time gap. This strategy enabled Imaishi and his team to chronicle various characters' physical and psychological development as they endeavor to complete their quests, and thus present shifts in emphasis and perspective that a more conventional chronology could not have afforded.

Set in the distant future, the show depicts a depleted planet where people struggle for survival in claustrophobically murky subterranean villages under the constant threat of earthquakes and attendant landslides.[6] The timid and introverted fourteen-year-old Simon unrelentingly digs away at the edges of his beleaguered underground town, Jiiha, until the day when a massive seismic upheaval sends a giant robot crushing through the ceiling. Simon's life takes a drastically new direction as he and his mate Kamina — the charismatic leader of the punkish Gurren gang aiming to break through to the Earth's surface — are enjoined to protect the community against the invading *mecha*. Help comes, no less unexpectedly, in the guise of the gorgeous Yoko, who drops through the crack opened by the robot's fall equipped with a mighty rifle. Her mission is to hunt berserk "Gunmen," robots such as the one terrorizing Simon's home town.

As chaos escalates, Simon reveals to Kamina and to Yoko another robot that he had previously unearthed: the titular Lagann. Simon's plan is to deploy the robot, piloted by Kamina, to vanquish the rampaging *mecha* from above. However, events take an unforeseen turn as Simon approaches the face-shaped entity and the crystalline "core drill" he wears as a pendant begins to interact with the Lagann, thereby bringing it to life. As a powering device, the luminescent drill proves instrumental to the impending quest and to its protagonists as they embark upon a perilous journey above the ground in the Lagann. The other *mecha* referred to in the show's title, the Gurren, is acquired by Kamina in the course of the adventure. The Lagann and the Gurren are capable of combining into a single formidable creature by means of a favorite trope of *mecha* anime: the "*gattai*," which literally translates as "combination." (This term will be discussed in detail in Chapter 13.) In their subterranean existence, reaching the surface was Simon's and Kamina's ultimate ambition but the situation they encounter when they emerge into the open does not deliver the utopia of their fantasies. In fact, the place is caught up in the clutches of war and despair.

Central to *Gurren Lagann*'s diegesis is the multipronged conflict between three factions:

ordinary humans, Spirals and Anti-Spirals. Spirals are beings that embody the power of limitless evolution and have been relentlessly persecuted by Anti-Spirals fearing the expansion of that power. The Spirals' champion, Lord Genome, is reputed to have deployed the aforementioned Gunmen —*mecha* powered by Spiral energy whose designation simply means "face"— against the enemy. The Lagann was one of Lord Genome's principal weapons. The Gunmen's pilots, dubbed "Beastmen," are non–Spiral creatures cloned by Lord Genome that rely on solar powered batteries (which renders them unemployable at night).

Defeated by the Anti-Spirals, the Spiral troops were forced to retreat to their original homes, continually threatened by the prospect of the "Spiral Existence Extermination System": a program installed on every planet harboring Spiral beings. (It is worth noting that the extermination plan dramatized in *Gurren Lagann* is elliptically reminiscent of SEELE's Human Instrumentality Project in *Evangelion*.) The danger posed by ordinary people, in this pugnacious climate, was that they might grow in number and strength and set off the Anti-Spirals' System, which would result in the annihilation of their race. To avert this risk, Lord Genome decided to relegate humanity to the underground areas where, due to scarcity of resources, the species' population level could remain low and hence be unlikely to trigger disaster.

In terms of sheer drama, a poignant moment is provided by Kamina's death — an event that leaves Simon in a state of bitter depression. It is upon meeting the ethereally mysterious Nia and drawing inspiration from her disarming kindness and innocence that Simon begins to recover. Gradually, the youth ascends to leadership status, puts an end to the war, and is chosen commander in chief of the freshly founded Kamina City: humanity's first proper aboveground settlement in a long time. Unfortunately, as the city flourishes and its human population accordingly grows, so does the threat of the Extermination System. When the one millionth human child is born, the Anti-Spirals indeed sanction that the time has come at last to wipe out the race.

One of the most memorable scenes in the entire series comes about two-thirds of the way through the narrative when Nia herself, to whom Simon has become deeply attached and to whom he eventually proposes, appears to be humanity's most lethal enemy. It is indeed Nia who, deployed as the Anti-Spirals' vehicle, cold-bloodedly announces that humanity's extermination has been conclusively decreed. As Kamina City and the rest of the planet in its wake are thrown into civil unrest, it is up to Simon and to his new ally (and former antagonist), the Beastman Viral, to launch into deep space to put an end to the conflict with the Anti-Spirals once and for all.

◆ ◆ ◆

To commemorate *Evangelion*'s tenth anniversary, a special collaborative project named "Eva At Work" enlisting the talents of numerous Japanese artists from disparate fields was set up in early 2006 under the general supervision of curator Shinya Furui. The gallery thus assembled includes a textile design based on graphical symbols associated with the saga's Angels, executed by Mizuki Totori; a food platter by Studio Big Art focusing on the explicitly tactile aspects of *Evangelion*'s imagery via the metaphor of food (appositely served on a Lilith-shaped platter); a folding screen by the traditional painter Yoshitoshi Shinomiya displaying a minimalist version of an Eva fight; *bento* (i.e., lunch-box) arrangements by Junko Terashima containing realistic references to several *Evangelion* characters — Pen-Pen included; a meticulously detailed stained-glass lamp featuring symbolic allusions to the show by glass artist Takaaki "Pucci" Tsuchiya; as well as various multimedia installations, a wedding-dress adorned with motifs from the saga and a full-back tattoo. The project culminated in December 2006 with a Noh performance inspired by the theme of Shinji's emotional ordeal and by the related topos of maternal love, and featuring a gorgeously stylized Eva-01 mask, crafted by Shouhei Yamashita.

If *Evangelion* remains a pinnacle in anime artistry after over ten years since its original airing, which few would dispute, this has much to do with its flair for integrating conventional tropes derived from science fiction, romance and postmodern dystopia with mature themes associated with psychoanalysis, sociology, politics and anthropology. This synthesis would not, in and by itself, deliver engrossing spectacle, however. What enables *Evangelion* to yield a philosophical vision that does not at any point degenerate into dry sermonizing but succeeds, in fact, in drawing the audience into a vortex of eminently sensuous experiences is Anno's determination never to let the conceptual deaden the concrete or, conversely, to let palpable dramatic effects trivialize the adventure's abstract import.

CHAPTER 7

Neon Genesis Evangelion (Shinseiki Evangelion) II — The Movies

To find happiness, a man need only live in the moment; he need only live for the moment. But if he wants meaning — the meaning of his dreams, his secrets, his life — a man must reinhabit the past, however dark, and live for the future, however uncertain.

— Jed Rubenfeld

Neon Genesis Evangelion: Death & Rebirth (Shinseiki Evangelion Gekijouban: Shito shinsei)
Directors: Hideaki Anno, Masayuki, Kazuya Tsurumaki (1997)

This chapter presents a close analysis of the films *Death & Rebirth* and *End of Evangelion*, followed by a review of the currently developing four-part project *Rebuild of Evangelion*. The first part of the chapter focuses on the relationship between *Death* and the TV series. A schematic delineation of links is offered and a detailed comparative evaluation subsequently provided. The rationale underpinning the decision to incorporate this analysis deserves elucidation. This is because it might be tempting for some readers to regard it as just a game of "I-spy" worthy only of obsessive otaku who have watched *Evangelion* more often than is salutary. In fact, what this chapter proposes is that a study of formal and conceptual correlations between *Death* and the original show can contribute significantly to a grasp of the saga itself and of Gainax's artistic preferences.

Thanks to its capsulated format, *Death* pithily throws into relief the show's themes and techniques, drawing the viewer closer to the heart of *Evangelion*'s psychological and philosophical preoccupations. At the same time, in offering a discrete take on the story, *Death* illuminates all of the most salient aspects of Gainax's vision as a sustained experimental purview of the realm of animation and of what this medium alone is capable. *Death* and the series are like the Lance of Longinus's two prongs: distinct, yet capable of converging to magnificent effect.

Death provides a radically alternate version of the TV program's diegesis by extracting key moments from its episodes and reassembling them in a novel order. Far from constituting a mere re-edit of the original show, the film actually yields a bold cinematographical feat to be appreciated by its own merits. The detailed study of *Death* in relation to the TV episodes offered below will hopefully appeal to both relatively new viewers, who are likely to benefit from an exposition of internal correspondences among different segments of the saga's universe, and established fans, for whom the analysis ought to bring together disparate strands of *Evangelion*'s complex arc.

The new footage produced for *Death* encompasses three categories. First, there are the sequences set in the school gymnasium and auditorium in which Shinji, Asuka, Rei and Touji play their musical instruments. These scenes do not explicitly contribute to the advancement of the action but rather constitute pauses for reflection abetted by an inspired use of string pieces that elliptically comment on the characters' interrelations and on their diverse perceptions of their functions within a group. Key aspects of their personalities are thereby exposed: Shinji comes across as more relaxed and generally more in control of his emotions in these scenes than anywhere else in *Evangelion*. Learning to play the cello, after all, is the only activity he has persevered in by choice rather than exclusively in compliance with another person's expectations or demands.

Asuka, constitutionally hell-bent on asserting her superior worth so as to exorcize a deeply ingrained sense of inadequacy, sees music as just another means of flaunting her skills: Accordingly, she glorifies her role as a violinist and reviles Shinji as a mere player of "arpeggios." Rei, in keeping with her habitually compliant disposition, simply gets on with it and executes her viola piece: It is not for Rei ever to question the value of a task laid before her. Touji's role in *Death*'s musical interludes is merely ancillary, as indeed it is in the domain of Eva piloting. However, just as Touji's one hapless fight carries crucial repercussions for the narrative's overall development, so the scene in which he features vitally completes the set of musical sequences by offering a complete String Quartet instead of individual performances.

Second, *Death* proposes a number of retakes of shots from the TV series intended to improve the initial image quality. Recognizing these scenes is an arduous task even for the seasoned *Evangelion* fan, which attests to the immense care devoted to their execution and integration. Although they mesh seamlessly with the remainder of the footage, the retakes were exceptionally labor-intensive, requiring the team not only to redo the drawings but also to repaint whole backgrounds and then film the various elements all over again. Third, there are a few images that were not originally created for the TV series in the form in which it was actually aired but rather for the directors' cuts. These are especially useful in fathoming the characters' intersubjective roles in a markedly meditative, rather than kinetic, mode. Through its combination of unedited shots from the show and new scenes of the three types outlined above, *Death* evinces a Godardian impatience with linearity. The TV series already pointed to this proclivity in the allocation of the Angels across its first twenty-four installments in a fashion that, though broadly chronological, allowed for digressions. *Death* boldly takes this trend to brain-twisting extremes.

The extent to which *Death* disrupts linearity in favor of systematic and swiftly moving cut-ups is eloquently attested to by its deft shuffling of myriad images and lines of dialogue from the series. The titles used by the Manga Entertainment DVD (2004) as headings for *Death*'s eleven chapters are, in this respect, deliciously misleading. With the exception of the first three segments, which employ a thematic point of reference ("01. Second Impact") or terms derived from the musical register ("02. Overture" and "03. First Movement"), the various chapters are headed by the given name of one of the principal characters: "04. Misato," "05. Asuka," "06. Rei," "07. Yui," "08. Ritsuko," "09. Touji," "10. Kaji" and "11. Kaworu." These designations may induce the viewer to assume that each part includes snippets from the series that highlight the specific personality and experiences of the named character. In fact, although each segment may partly take the titular persona as its point of departure, the ways in which the textual cut-ups are therein orchestrated actually underscore a vast and intricate architecture of interconnections within which no character conclusively emerges as a singular or privileged presence. This is quite congruous with the saga's thematic emphasis on the tenacity of interpersonal bonds despite their ostensible tenuousness.

At the technical level, *Death*'s most prominent trait consists of its assiduous use of montages. Two main versions of this technique can be observed: (1) the concatenation of a seemingly unrelated series of frames, causing one scene to dissolve into the next and conveying a compressed sense of the passage of time; (2) the collision of existing frames, orchestrated so that they join up, blend or overlap. (Segment 02. of *Death* exemplifies the former modality, Segments 04., 05., 06., 08. and 10., the latter.) The unique cinematographical advantage yielded by the montage lies with its ability to communicate a greater deal of narrative and symbolic information than any individual portion of the cluster may ever aspire to capture by capitalizing on metaphorical condensation at the expense of metonymic contiguity.

As a result, the various images — juxtaposed, superimposed or shown in rapid succession with little regard for sequential logic — are capable of presenting an idea or theme that far surpasses the sum of their individual messages. Operating in tandem, the cut-up and the montage enable the animating troupe to interrogate the universe by recourse to the cinematographical equivalents of scissors and a pot of glue. *Social Fiction*'s evocative assessment of Anno's favorite ruse indirectly supplies an apposite description of *Death* in its entirety: "The cut-up renders the subliminal flows of information, information hidden from our conscious modes of perception, visible ... the cut-up disturbs space-time causality and the future leaks into the present. The cut-up becomes the Delphic exercise of the interpretation of signals adrift in time" ("On the Cut-Up").

The following web of correspondences between *Death* and the series can be detected by means of numerous viewings:

Death Segment	TV Episode(s)
1	12/21(DC)
2	1/20/21/22/22(DC)/24
3	1/2
4	1/2/3/4/21/22(DC)/23/24/25
5	8/9/10/15/19/22/22(DC)/24
6	2/5/6/16/19/22/23
7	15/21(DC)
8	13/15/16/19/20/21/23/24
9	3/4/17/18
10	5/8/9/15/18/19/21/24(DC)
11	21/23/24

DC = Directors' Cut

What follows is a detailed examination of *Death*'s eleven chapters, assessing the movie's connections with, and departures from, the parent source and thereby documenting Anno's distinctive approach to anime — an approach, arguably, that consistently proclaims its caliber as a cutting-edge enterprise regardless of whether it deploys traditional or innovational techniques.[1]

Segment 01. "Second Impact"

Death goes straight to the core of *Evangelion*'s narrative weave by focusing on the Second Impact itself. The date is "15 August 2000" and the setting is the "UN Underground

Base 02" in Antarctica. The center's seemingly rickety structure shudders helplessly in the grip of the intense atmospheric turbulence destined to culminate in the Second Impact just under a month later. Fragments of conversation fill the background, as faceless voices comment on the Katsuragi expedition and accuse scientists of being trapped in "petty speculations," as they struggle to impose order on the "chaos of the cosmos." The verdict reached is unequivocally unflattering: Scientists are said to be "losing touch with reality." The looming form of Adam, whose explosion is held to have triggered the catastrophe, is at one point visible in the background. This portion of *Death*'s first chapter is drawn from the directors' cut of Episode 21, "He was aware that he was still a child," where it is situated prior to the opening credits. Episode 21 (in both its original version and its marginally expanded and technically polished configurations) plays a key role in the saga as a whole in that it provides, by means of flashbacks and intercutting, a semichronological reconstruction of the events that unfold between 1999 and 2015 (as itemized in Chapter 6 in the delineation of *Evangelion*'s underlying *fabula*). The episode will be returned to a number of times in the course of the present analysis.

The escalating disturbance portrayed in the opening moments of *Death*'s inaugural segment reaches its climax in the form of a titanic explosion that leaves in its wake a blazing crater. In the ensuing sequence, we see a young Misato, obviously injured, inside an escape pod into which she has been placed by her father. Upon emerging from the capsule after an unspecified length of time, Misato appears to be already wearing the cross-shaped pendant that she dons throughout the series. Images of the girl are juxtaposed with those of gigantic glowing wings that stretch upwards toward the sky: a potent allusion to the First Angel. This part of *Death*'s opening chapter is derived from Episode 12, "She said 'Don't make others suffer for your personal hatred.'"

Episode 12 is axial to *Evangelion*'s world insofar as it supplies unique insights into Misato's personality at both the personal and the professional levels. It is indeed in this episode that we learn of her ambiguous reasons for joining NERV and combating the Angels. Prior to the Second Impact, her relationship with her father had been fraught with difficulties due to his neglect of familial bonds and attendant weakness in the handling of emotions at large: a trait Misato had come to detest so acutely that she could only laugh at the man when her mother had eventually resolved to divorce him. Mr. Katsuragi's sacrifice and heroic struggle to save his daughter's life at the time of the cataclysm gave rise to mixed feelings in Misato's heart, as a result of which she cannot now be conclusively certain whether she is committed to the annihilation of the Angels because she wishes to avenge her father's death, or whether she actually aims to eliminate the enemy in order to be rid of the past and its legacy.

It is also in Episode 12 of the series that Misato's skills as an exceptionally shrewd strategist shine forth in their full colors. As both Commander Ikari and Professor Fuyutsuki are absent from NERV on business at the South Pole, it is solely in Misato's hands to annihilate the Tenth Angel, Sahaquiel (the Angel of the Skies). The major accomplishes the task with both poise and humor by deploying all three Eva Units in a consorted effort to intercept the enemy that exudes scintillating athleticism.

Segment 02. "Overture"

Death's second chapter introduces the viewer to the saga's principal personae in an intriguingly disorienting fashion, by selecting disparate moments from the series with a ludic disregard for chronological consistency and by reorganizing the pieces according to the idiosyncratic logic of the cut-up. The segment encompasses seven sequences, as follows.

2015 Misato and Kaji are seen in bed together, as Misato comments somewhat ruefully on her lover's lack of concern for others — an aspect of Kaji's personality that, fond of him though Misato undoubtedly is, disturbingly reminds her of her father. The scene is drawn from Episode 20, in which it provides emotional relief in the aftermath of Shinji's thirty-one-day entrapment inside the Eva-01 and of Misato's anxiety about the boy's fate.

9 months earlier A scene from the directors' cut of Episode 22, this portion of *Death*'s second chapter pivots on Kaji and Asuka gazing at a nocturnal sky side by side on the eve of the Second Child's move to Japan, where she is about to take up her piloting job. Asuka's attachment to the older man is openly revealed by her emphatic declaration that her "heart belongs" to Kaji. On the whole, however, the scene is emotionally subdued, whereas its source explicitly exposes Asuka's vulnerability as she endeavors to sexually allure her guardian, is appropriately held at bay, and is thence assaulted by crippling memories of childhood rejection.

7 years earlier A younger Asuka runs home to announce her selection as an Eva pilot to her mother. As she approaches the dwelling, she proudly proclaims: "They chose me! ... I don't feel lonely any more!" What awaits her upon her return, alas, is the bloodcurdling silhouette of her mother hanging from a rafter. This sequence comes from Episode 24, "The Beginning and the End, or 'Knockin' on Heaven's Door.'"

2015 Asuka's synchronization ratio with her Eva is rapidly deteriorating, which entails that her viability as a pilot can no longer be taken for granted. Hard as she tries, demons from her past keep flooding her psyche with indomitable cruelty. Episode 22 is the source of this snippet.

2010 Gendou takes a child version of Rei (the First Rei clone, that is) to the Gehirn Headquarters and introduces her to Naoko and Ritsuko as the daughter of an acquaintance. In Episode 21, from which this fragment is taken, the older Dr. Akagi instantly recognizes Rei's physical resemblance to Yui, inspects the child's records and discovers that they have been entirely erased.

2015 As in Episode 1, "Angel Attack," Shinji is vainly trying to make a call from a public phone (Misato turns out to be the person he is attempting to contact), as the Third Angel makes his sensational appearance. Just as he is flung into total mayhem by this hulking monstrosity, which is indifferent to the fire of hordes of armored vehicles, Shinji catches a glimpse of Rei standing on the road ahead. The next portion of this sub-segment is also drawn from Episode 1 of the series, and takes place in the NERV area where the Eva-01 is housed (to which Misato has taken Shinji once they have finally managed to meet). A massive blast produced by the invading Angel causes the entire center to rock dismally. Rei, who is heavily bandaged and barely conscious, is dislodged from her hospital bed and Shinji succors her, deeply moved by her agony. Upon beholding Rei's blood on his hand, Shinji utters for the first time in the film a line destined to reverberate throughout the entire story: "I mustn't run away."

The transition from the street scene to the NERV scene would be hardly comprehensible for spectators unacquainted with the TV show. For one thing, they would have no inkling as to how Shinji has shifted from one location to the other. Moreover, they would not be aware of the reason for Rei's presence at the HQ, namely, Shinji's refusal to pilot Unit 01 and Gendou's compassionless decision to use the injured First Child instead (arguably as a form of emotional blackmail targeted at his son).

2015 (Twenty-three episodes and fourteen Angels later.) This portion, imported from Episode 24, focuses on the climactic moments in Shinji's doomed relationship with Kaworu Nagisa, who has joined NERV in the presumed capacity of Fifth Child but is actually the Seventeenth Angel, Tabris. As an Eva pilot, Shinji has no choice but to vanquish the creature, much as his personal emotions militate against his professional duty. Kaworu urges him on, however, declaring that he welcomes death as "the only absolute freedom."

Death's second segment provides a paradigmatic illustration of the *Evangelion* team's penchant for elaborate montages. At the same time, the piece tantalizingly juxtaposes a series of scenes characterized by technically and stylistically disparate tendencies. For example, the minimalist mise-en-scène used for the scene revolving around Misato and Kaji contrasts sharply with the sophisticated camera work used for the shots focusing on Asuka as a child. Relatedly, the highly pronounced chromatic and linear refinement of the urbanscape in which we first encounter Shinji overtly pays homage to the time-honored pictorial conventions of traditional Japanese engravings and scroll paintings. With the Third Angel's advent onto the scene, however, CGI come to play an unexpectedly prominent part.

Segment 03. "First Movement"

This segment opens with the first of the musical interludes executed specifically for *Death*. The scene takes place eighteen months prior to the events presented in the closing portion of the foregoing segment and is set in the school gymnasium-cum-auditorium. Shinji plays the cello, performing Johann Sebastian Bach's "Suiten für Violoncello solo Nr. 1, G-dur, BWV. 1007, 1. Vorspier." The film's opening credits follow. The action then shifts to the present, displaying the climax of Episode 1, where the Eva-01 is deployed against the Third Angel. The actual fight, which in the series is presented in Episode 2 as a flashback, ensues: The Eva has "trouble maintaining activation," is severely damaged and soon breaks down altogether. Quite unexpectedly, however, the giant biomechanoid reactivates itself spontaneously (showing that mankind's authority over its weapons is very precarious indeed), penetrates the enemy's A.T. Field and destroys it with glee.

The sequence, quite apart from being technically remarkable as a piece of masterfully orchestrated dynamism, makes imaginative use of typographically varied text (in both Japanese and English) as an animational tool in its own right. Indeed, the action is consistently interspersed with captions — so fleeting as to be hard to register at first sight — that boldly augment the battle's breakneck pace. The words complement the action, moreover, by drawing attention to key aspects of the saga's indigenous vocabulary — for instance, "Test Type," "Eva-01 Lift Off," "Absolute Terror Field," "The Beast" — as well as consecutive stages in the duel, such as "First Sortie," "First Activation," "Emergency," "Head Injury," "Bloodshed," "Silence," "Reactivation," "Running Berserk," "Counterattack," "Hand-to-Hand Combat," "Panic," "Explosion." Vector graphics play a key role in this sequence, reminding the audience of the origins of this tool in media directly connected with writing and printing technologies. The film could therefore be said to be commenting metacinematically on the nature and provenance of its chosen techniques.

Segment 04. "Misato"

Death's fourth chapter is a veritable paean to the cut-up technique abetted at once by conventional and state-of-the-art techniques. The opening scene, drawn from Episode 2, shows Shinji's arrival at Misato's flat, where the NERV officer has decided to accommodate the boy after his father has categorically announced that he has no intention of living with his son. Shinji is at first hesitant but Misato's disarming kindness rapidly ingratiates him, as borne out by the following exchange:

Shinji: "I ... don't want to intrude."
Misato: "Shinji, this is your home now."
Shinji: "I'm home."
Misato: "Welcome home."

Two flashbacks follow in rapid succession. The first, set in the year 2002, is taken from Episode 21 of the show, and portrays Misato as a young girl in a state of shock. Professor Fuyutsuki explains that she has not spoken since the Second Impact: her physical wounds could be healed but the psychological trauma has proved far less tractable because "she saw hell first hand." The second flashback, also drawn from Episode 21, is set in 2005 and shows Misato's and Ritsuko's first encounter as students. As the two young women sit together over lunch, a voiceover reciting the text of one of Ritsuko's letters to her mother Naoko comments on Misato's background, explaining how she used to be mute but now talks relentlessly as though to make up for lost time.

As the action returns to the present, offering a scene from Episode 2 in which Shinji sits with Misato in the kitchen of her junk-infested apartment while the hostess guzzles down beer after beer, we find that Misato's emotional problems predate the Second Impact. A voiceover, adapted from a sequence in Episode 25, gives us an auditory glimpse of Misato as a child struggling to convince herself that she must be a good girl and refrain from crying, seamlessly superseded by the character's adult voice and the words: "But I hated my father, and I hated being a good girl." The scene culminates with a shot of the nocturnal setting also used in the second sequence of Segment 02., taken from the directors' cut of Episode 22, in which Asuka proffers a censorious assessment of Misato's lifestyle. (Asuka's original lines have been amended for the purpose of the movie.)

Asuka's judgment is instantly countered by a shot of Shinji in the bath (from Episode 2), in which he reflects that Misato is not really a "bad person." We then move to the sequence from Episode 3, "A Transfer," in which Shinji decides to return to pilot the Eva-01 after its controversial defeat of the Third Angel. As Shinji engages in a simulation intended to refine his skills, the film supplies a characteristic example of *Evangelion*'s self-referential use of computer technology, insofar as the video game-style images of the Eva-01 and of Sachiel employed by the NERV personnel in the exercise are indeed computer-generated to a substantial extent. A voiceover yields part of the conversation presented in Episode 24 in which Shinji tells Kaworu that prior to being summoned by his father to Tokyo-3, he used to live with his teacher, which was utterly uneventful but "fine" by him. He felt comfortable with a routine that did not require him to endure much interpersonal contact, yet he was all the time haunted by one dominant emotion: "I really hated my father." (Please note the parallel between Shinji's and Misato's backgrounds, in this respect.)

The visuals stay with Episode 3 and the script itself now shifts to the same episode, as NERV employee Maya observes Shinji's totally robotic approach to training and wonders why the boy has come back after all. Ritsuko states that he just does what he is told to do, and that this is his way of "getting through life." The Eva-01's defeat of the Fourth Angel — Shamshel, the Angel of Daytime — ensues. Likewise taken from Episode 3, this sequence shows an initially losing Unit 01 bereft of its Umbilical Cable. The Angel unceremoniously grabs the Eva with one of its whip-like limbs and flings it across the landscape. Although he is about to run out of energy, Shinji releases the Unit's "Progressive Knife" and stabs the enemy, yelling like a lunatic.

The following portion of *Death*'s fourth chapter comes from Episode 4 and depicts Shinji's abortive attempt to run away. Central to the sequence is an exquisitely slow train journey in the course of which Shinji, oblivious to those around him, sits alone listening to music — here, as indeed throughout the saga, tracks "25" and "26" are endlessly replayed, possibly as a correlative for the open-ended Episodes 25 and 26 of the series. One by one, the passengers get off until the boy is the only one left. We next see Shinji wandering around the outskirts of the city in a series of wordless shots that economically capture both the melancholy and the splendor of the abused but reviving habitat. The sequence following Shinji's purposeless peregrinations offers a stunning example of *Evangelion*'s passionate dedication to the depiction of the natural environment in ways that refuse to pander to the tenets of classic realism — by foregrounding stylized shapes and unmistakably hand-painted sets — yet succeed in conveying a more genuine sense of Nature than any strictly photorealistic sequence could presume to achieve. The camera moves used to film the sequence, preeminently the pan, tilt and follow, contribute vitally to its overall mood.

In Episode 4, Shinji's wandering also takes him to a movie theater where grade-B sci-fi films based on the Second Impact are showing. This self-referential gesture parallels the sequence in Episode 3 in which Shinji's teacher describes the cataclysm to his pupils, who are oblivious to their mentor and intrigued instead by the discovery that Shinji is an Eva pilot. (The Second Impact is again the subject of the lesson in Episode 17, "Fourth Child.")

Shinji is then seen camping at night in an isolated spot with his school friend Kensuke Aida, who clearly envies him for having the gorgeous Misato as a flat mate. We are next treated to an emotionally intense flash-forward following Shinji's return to the NERV Headquarters after his vain escape, presenting an exchange between Misato and Shinji. The boy has severe misgivings about his job but concedes that it would be unfair to place the entire burden of Eva piloting upon Rei's shoulders. (Please note that at this stage in the series, Asuka has not yet been introduced, and Shinji and Rei are therefore the sole available pilots.) The NERV head of operations reacts angrily, insisting that Shinji should ask himself what *he* wants to do instead of merely acting according to other people's orders or expectations.

The action shifts to an image of Shinji playing the cello (exclusive to the movie) against the background of the words spoken by his classmate Touji Suzuhara in Episode 4 at the railway station, where Shinji has been forcibly taken after being officially retired from NERV. As a farewell, Touji tells him that if he leaves Tokyo-3, others will also have to leave in his wake (implying that without his Eva's intervention the city would be defenseless). Touji also remarks that neither he nor Kensuke blame Shinji for leaving, however, having seen how he suffered in the Eva. These words would undoubtedly baffle viewers unfamiliar with the TV show, as they would not be aware that Touji and Kensuke had actually been inside the Eva-01 in the climax of Shinji's fight against the Fourth Angel — having been taken into the cockpit by the pilot after sneaking out of their shelter in the hope of witnessing an Eva-versus-Angel battle.

Shinji's ensuing words would likewise be puzzling: Just before being dragged off to his special train by NERV agents, he says that he is a coward and that he is the one who deserves to be hit. The boy is here referring to a scene in Episode 4 preceding Touji's farewell words, in which Touji apologizes to Shinji for hitting him sometime earlier (Episode 3), and asks him to punch him in the face so that they may be even. As the image of a road's dusty tarmac and its bright yellow markings (a recurrent image also seen, for instance, in Episode 23) flashes past, Misato's voice fills the background, advising Shinji not to run away, to confront his father and, most crucially, to confront himself. These words come from the key scene in Episode 1 in which Shinji is first instructed to pilot Unit 01 and is understandably reluctant to do so, having ascertained that the only reason for which Gendou has sent for him is that he now has a "use" for his son.

The action moves from Misato's words to the scene in Episode 2 in which Commander

Ikari unconditionally rejects Shinji and decrees that the boy shall live on his own, which is in turn followed by another memorable scene from Episode 2. Misato here shows Shinji the awe-inspiring sight of Tokyo-3's mushrooming edifices at sunset, as these majestically resurface after being retracted to be spared from the invading Third Angel. CGI unobtrusively enhance the scene's magnificence without even remotely impairing the cels' tactile painterliness. Touji's farewell words can again be heard in the background, followed by Misato's own statement to her charge: "This is our city, and it is the city you saved." Misato praises the Unit 01 pilot once more in the following shot (also from Episode 2), in which Shinji is in his bed and she lingers by the door on the way to her own room to tell him that in defeating the Angel he has performed a "noble" action of which he should be "proud." (As to whether Shinji is capable of such a feeling, this remains a moot point all the way through to Episode 26 — and beyond.)

In the fourth segment's coda (from Episode 4), we discover that Shinji ultimately resolves not to leave the city and his duties. As Misato meets him at the station, obviously relieved by his decision, the lines of dialogue already exchanged by the two characters in the opening scene are reproposed, lending the chapter a markedly symmetrical shape:

Shinji: "I'm home."
Misato: "Welcome home."

Segment 05. "Asuka"

The second of *Death*'s music-centered scenes opens this segment, with Asuka executing Bach's "Partita III für Violino solo, E-dur, BWV. 1006, 3. Gavotte in Rondo." The setting rapidly changes from the gymnasium to Misato's flat, where we are treated to a delightful shot of Misato's pet penguin Pen-Pen raptly listening to a tune he appears to be greatly enjoying. The shot comes from Episode 15, "Those Women Longed for the Touch of Others' Lips, and Thus Invited Their Kisses," in which Pen-Pen is actually listening to Shinji as the latter practices the cello. A scene from Episode 9 — "Both of You, Dance Like You Want to Win!" — seamlessly ensues: Asuka collapses next to Shinji as he pretends to be asleep, and the boy is overtaken by a sudden desire to kiss her. As he is just about to make contact, he is put off by Asuka's mouthing of the word "momma," which leads him to conclude dismissively that Asuka herself is "just a kid."

We then see Asuka upon her first appearance in the series (Episode 8, "Asuka Strikes!") aboard a UN Pacific Fleet warship, as a substantial proportion of the Navy appears to have been mobilized for the purpose of delivering the Eva-02 to Tokyo-3. While Rei's personality parallels Shinji's propensity for introspection, the new girl — brimming as she is with energy, personal initiative and unsentimental pragmatism — embodies the active side of the boy's character: an aspect that has been dormant since infancy but will increasingly prove central to his maturation as an individual and as a member of a tangled skein of relationships. A black-and-white montage of images portraying Asuka in various poses and contexts follows, with a rather damning assessment of her personality resonating in the background.

The shot of Asuka presented in the immediate aftermath of the black-and-white sequence contrasts sharply with the picture of the assertive, conceited and hyperconfident persona evoked by the earlier shots: An utterly suicidal Second Child lies in the tub of a derelict bathroom, with Kaworu's haunting message about the inevitability of pain and loneliness tolling in the background. Both the visuals and the Seventeenth Angel's words are imported from different stages in Episode 24.

Asuka is restored to her ebullient self in the next scene of *Death*'s fifth chapter, taken from Episode 8, in which she is engaged in conversation with Kaji on the warship's colossal deck. Although she claims not to find the Third Child in the least remarkable, even the arrogant Asuka cannot help being impressed when her companion informs her that Shinji's sync ratio was over 40 percent with no prior training. A shot from the same Episode-24 scene presented earlier follows the exchange in which Asuka, devastated by the utter loss of her own ability to synchronize with Unit 02, disconsolately comments: "I can't be the Second Child anymore." The shot functions as a daunting reminder of Asuka's intrinsic vulnerability despite her insistent claims to uncontested superiority in the earlier parts of the series.

The action returns to Episode 8 once again, with the Second Child showing off the Eva-02 to Shinji in all its pristine glory — a sight to which the boy sarcastically responds with the bathetic comment: "I didn't know it was red." Asuka triumphantly points out that her Unit is the first to have been "created for actual combat conditions" (00 having constituted the prototype and 01 the test type). Asuka's claims to excellence are soon tested as the Sixth Angel Gaghiel, the Angel of Fish, appears on the scene heralded by phenomenal undersea shockwaves. With Asuka and Shinji huddled together in its cockpit, the Eva-02 engages the Angel, hopping from ship to ship and then diving into the ocean. Although Gaghiel nearly manages to swallow the Eva, Misato's expeditious plan saves the day: She forces the Navy to sink two unmanned warships, gets Asuka and Shinji to open the enemy's mouth just wide enough to enable the vessels to enter it, and instructs the ships to self-destruct once they have accessed their destination.

In *Death*, the original incident is considerably telescoped and followed in rapid succession by shots from further missions involving the Eva-02. The first (from Episode 9) focuses on Asuka's assault upon the Seventh Angel — the Angel of Music Israfel — in which she smartly slices the monster in half. (In the episode, Israfel evinces a lamentable knack of self-regenerating into two exact replicas of its original form.) The second, from Episode 10, shows Unit 02 descending through broiling lava. The third comes from Episode 19, and displays Asuka's vain attempt to destroy the Fourteenth Angel as a result of which she very nearly loses her life. The fourth shot, from Episode 22, focuses on Asuka's breakdown as the Fifteenth Angel invades her mind, and the Eva-02 reacts by convulsing spasmodically and hopelessly losing coordination. The Second Child survives but has to be placed in quarantine as a result of her contamination: at this point, she conclusively precipitates into inconsolable abjection.

The shift to a scene from Episode 9 counterbalances the sadness of the preceding frames, as Asuka flamboyantly taunts Shinji in the school grounds and then approaches Rei with the proposition that the two of them should be friends, on the grounds that it would be "convenient" — a suggestion to which the First Child responds with dismissive indifference. The action moves to another moment from Episode 9, set in Misato's apartment, in which Shinji and Asuka are made to engage in harmonization drills intended to enhance their ability to work as a team (which, earlier in the episode, they have embarrassingly failed to do in their confrontation with Israfel). The training appears to be yielding very poor results, which does not please Asuka in the least. Unsurprisingly, her mood does not improve when Misato asks Rei to try out the same exercise as Shinji's partner and the outcome is impeccable coordination. (In the actual episode, it is worth noting, Asuka and Shinji do finally succeed in operating in unison, and their next go at the Seventh Angel delivers a performance that amounts to nothing short of a balletic exploit.)

One more shot of the prostrate Asuka from Episode 24 ensues, juxtaposed with the image of the rag doll which her mother hanged upon killing herself in a pathetic simulation of a double-suicide pact (*shinjuu*). This comes from the directors' cut of Episode 22. Rei's voice accompanies the shot with a line from Episode 22: "I am not a doll." (In the episode, the First Child speaks this line in response to Asuka's accusation that she is merely a wind-up doll prepared to do anything she is instructed to do, including killing herself if necessary.)

The closing portion of *Death*'s fifth segment derives wholly from Episode 22 of the show, with additional editing and agile intercutting. Asuka's sync ratio appears to be plummeting exponentially. Misato tries to justify the girl's unsatisfactory performance by pointing out that "it's her period" but Ritsuko clinically maintains that this is no excuse, for physiological factors are not supposed to interfere with an Eva pilot's synchronization capacities. The problem, the scientist rightly believes, lies in Asuka's "'subconscious." Additionally, as Misato observes, Asuka feels "beaten" specifically by Shinji. It should be noted, in this respect, that Asuka's relationship with her male colleague is further problematized by her ambivalent feelings toward him. Although she customarily dismisses Shinji's probing questions about the meaning of Evas, Angels and the pilots' role in the entire game by means of a strident "What are you, stupid?" Asuka herself is persecuted by uncertainty — not least about her self-worth. Moreover, there are indications that she does care about Shinji's safety despite her nonchalant profession of indifference. (Asuka's emotional ambivalence characteristically peaks in the climax of Episode 10, in which she is grateful to, and resentful of, the Third Child in equal measures for intervening in a mission that would almost certainly have resulted in her death.)

As the exchange between Ritsuko and Misato draws to a close, the scene shifts to a sequence in which Asuka and Rei stand together in an elevator for a seemingly interminable length of time. (Rei, in the foreground, faces the viewer, while Asuka stands in the rear right-hand corner in profile, arms folded resolutely across her chest.) A veritable jewel of anime at its most audaciously wordless, this emotionally charged scene supplies a paradigmatic instance of the fix, namely, the type of cut in which the camera does not move. The sequence lasts 46 seconds (54 in the parent installment) and the only motion punctuating the overwhelming stillness is Asuka's blinking eye and determined shrug (the latter is introduced in the film). When Rei eventually speaks, advising her colleague to open her mind to the Eva, the Second Child literally explodes, accusing Rei of being no better than a "wind-up doll" (as seen above). One can palpably sense the atmosphere of mounting frustration and barely suppressed ire that progressively fills the lift, growing floor by floor, and Asuka's outburst, disturbing as it undeniably is, comes as something of a welcome relief.

Segment 06. "Rei"

The third of the scenes set in the school gymnasium, the opening part of *Death*'s sixth segment focuses on Rei as she executes a piece entitled "Viola — Third String." A close-up of Shinji's face gazing intently at the First Child is then offered. This frame has been imported from the scene in Episode 2 in which Shinji stares at the injured Rei as the trolley carrying her is wheeled past him in the NERV hospital corridor, shortly after his recovery from the fight against the Third Angel. Rendered in a blue-grey monotone in the series, the image presented in *Death* has been edited to full color, as well as flipped horizontally.

From this shot, we are led to another frame in which Shinji is likewise absorbed in silent contemplation of Rei. The latter (from Episode 5, "Rei I") is part of a sequence set in the school sports grounds, where Touji and Kensuke mercilessly tease Shinji about his obvious fascination with the azure-haired girl. The Third Child defends himself by maintaining that what actually intrigues him is Rei's unremitting solitariness, and his classmates indeed concede that she has had no friends in all the time she has been a pupil at their school. As these lines of dialogue are spoken, the action moves to another scene from Episode 5 set in the NERV Headquarters: From the cockpit of his Eva, Shinji inadvertently witnesses a warm exchange between Rei and Gendou that instantly kindles his resentment and jealousy.

As Shinji's eyes get wider and wider at the unwelcome sight to which they are accidentally exposed, a snippet of a conversation between Ritsuko and Shinji concerning Rei's personality is heard in the background:

> Ritsuko: "She's a nice girl but she's like your father. She's not very adept at..."
> Shinji: "She's not very adept at what?"
> Ritsuko: "Living, I guess."

In Episode 5, this exchange takes place in Misato's flat over dinner. It is in this same scene that Ritsuko asks Shinji to deliver Rei's new security card to his colleague. The next portion of *Death*'s sixth segment accordingly consists of the sequence in which Shinji visits Rei's derelict building and enters her apartment. Scattered around its single room are several bloody bandages bearing witness to the horrible injuries suffered by the First Child just prior to Shinji's arrival at NERV. (In the series, the cause of those injuries is revealed in the opening moments of Episode 5, set twenty-two days earlier, in which the Eva-00 goes berserk and Gendou himself releases Rei from the capsule, severely burning his hands and damaging his spectacles in the process.)

In *Death*, as in Episode 5 of the show, Shinji sees his father's cracked glasses on a table in Rei's room and tries them on just as the girl emerges from the shower garbed merely in a towel. An embarrassing situation ensues in which Rei walks over to Shinji and removes Gendou's glasses, whereupon the boy trips and tumbles on top of Rei, his left hand unwittingly coming to rest upon her right breast. With a character other than Rei into the equation, the scene might well have delivered rambunctious slapstick. As things stand, the action just shifts to a later portion of Episode 5 in which Rei and Shinji travel together on one of NERV's mammoth escalators. Shinji asks Rei whether she is scared of piloting after the aforementioned accident, to which she responds by asking Shinji: "You are Commander Ikari's son, aren't you? ... Shouldn't you trust him?" When the Third Child heatedly exclaims "No, of course not! How could I ever trust him again?" Rei resolutely slaps him.

In Episode 5, this shot is followed by the sequence in which Rei is supposed to undergo a test in her freshly repaired Unit 00 and the arrangement is disrupted by the advent of the Fifth Angel Ramiel (the Angel of Thunder)—a floating blue polygon. The Eva-01 is launched and the Angel almost immediately manages to fry a hole into its chest by means of a formidable energy beam. The episode ends as Shinji screams in horror and pain. In *Death*, the escalator scene is followed by a scene from Episode 6—"Rei II"—in which Shinji lies in a hospital bed with Rei hovering over him. This image would inevitably surprise viewers not familiar with Episode 5 and its ending, as they would have no inkling of the reasons behind Shinji's hospitalization.

In the scene offered in the movie, Rei mechanically informs Shinji that they are both expected to board their Evas imminently in order to confront the Fifth Angel once more. In the TV show, this sequence is colorful, highly detailed and shot from a variety of angles. It even contains a touch of humor in the guise of a gentle sexual innuendo. In *Death*, the mood is altogether more somber, and the composition is accordingly starker, more static and chromatically more uniform. The emphasis falls primarily on the formal contrast between Shinji's recumbent shape and Rei's sternly standing body.

Shinji expresses his unhappiness at the prospect of piloting again and Rei, utterly unimpressed, states that she will take charge of Unit 01 instead, adding that Dr. Akagi is ready to reprogram it for this purpose. As Shinji, stunned by the unexpected news, utters "Ritsuko?"

the screen changes to a close-up of the NERV head scientist taken from the opening part of Episode 5 as she screams: "It's gone berserk!" Ritsuko is here reacting to the incident in which the Eva-00 cuts away from its pilot and starts thrashing madly around the laboratory allocated to its testing. In Episode 5, Ritsuko suspects that the rampaging Eva was specifically aiming to hurt *her*. The explanation for this seemingly illogical suspicion lies with the Unit's biological composition: The presence in its makeup of elements of Naoko's being entails that the Eva is partly controlled by Naoko's psyche, and it is feasible for the Eva's behavior to emanate from the dead scientist's vengeful feelings toward her daughter, namely, her own ex-lover's current companion. It is worth observing, in this regard, that Naoko incontrovertibly betrays Ritsuko in *End* with nefarious repercussions.

(The Eva-00, it should be noted, goes on the rampage again in Episode 14 during a compatibility test in which it is piloted by Shinji, responds to his presence by flooding his mind with memories of Rei and then attacks the observation room. Ritsuko appears again to consider herself the intended victim but, in this instance, Rei is no less likely a target, as the Unit's violence could have been triggered by Naoko's resentment toward the First Child as Yui's replica and hence a competitor for Gendou's affection.)

In *Death*, the Eva-00's rampage is followed by a shot from Episode 6 providing a close-up of Rei saying "goodbye" from the same installment. Images drawn from the Eva-00 and the Eva-01's joined confrontation of the Fifth Angel show the enemy's brutal mangling of Rei's Unit as she deliberately places herself between Ramiel and the Eva-01 to protect Shinji. Accompanying the sequence is a voiceover (replicating an exchange that in Episode 6 occurs just before the Evas are launched) in which Shinji asks Rei why she pilots the Eva and she replies: "I'm bonded to it." Shinji wonders whether Rei means that she is bonded to his father, to which she ripostes: "To all people." She then adds, in a touching afterthought, that she has "nothing else." Having eventually vanquished Ramiel, Shinji rips out the Eva-00's entry plug and steps into the capsule to check whether Rei is still alive. Hugely relieved to find out that she is, he starts crying and tells her never to say she has nothing other than her job to live for, and never to say "goodbye" upon leaving on a mission: "It's just too sad."

The First Child is unsure how to react and frankly tells her colleague that she does not know what to do at a time like this. He tells her just to try "smiling," which evokes a fleeting image of a kindly looking Gendou in her mind and indeed triggers an ambiguous Mona-Lisa smile. (In Episode 6, Gendou's brief apparition is followed by a more overt smile replete with emphatically hand-drawn expression lines.) In both the TV installment and the movie, the sequence just examined demonstrates Anno's tendency to foreground delicate character interactions, even as titanic battles fill the screen. The action element, therefore, unquestionably enriches yet never threatens to asphyxiate the affective import of events.

Venturing further into its distinctive cut-up mode, *Death* then shifts to the scene from Episode 19 in which Shinji, having decided to quit piloting in the aftermath of a mission that has required him to inflict irreparable damage upon his friend Touji, sees the Eva-00 approaching the Fourteenth Angel in the distance. Rei's background words unsentimentally state that it does not matter if she dies because she can be "replaced." In the voiceover that ensues, we hear Rei asking: "A dream?" and Asuka acidly replying: "Yeah, don't tell me you don't dream either." This brief exchange, succinctly encapsulating the elemental conflict between the First Child's and the Second Child's personalities, comes from the scene in Episode 19 in which Shinji and Touji are recovering in hospital in the wake of Touji's one doomed sortie as an Eva pilot, in which his Unit actually turns out to be the Thirteenth Angel. In the TV installment, Asuka opines that to Shinji the entire experience may feel no more solid than a dream. Touji's own delirious visions are also highlighted.

The action moves to the climax of Episode 22, in which NERV has to face its most intractable opponent yet, namely, the Fifteenth Angel. Gendou instructs Rei to fetch the Lance of Longinus from Terminal Dogma and to deploy it against the enemy, which her Unit does with aplomb, throwing it like a javelin straight through Arael's A.T. Field. As the Eva deals with the invader, we hear this snippet of conversation from Episode 16:

> Rei: "You can rest now. We'll take care of everything."
> Shinji: "But I'm feeling just fine now."

The final part of *Death*'s sixth segment is derived from Episode 23 and focuses on the Eva-00's battle with the Sixteenth Angel, Armisael. As Rei enters this fatal fight, Ritsuko's voice fills the background, reproposing the lines from Episode 5 in which she states that the First Child's "past has been eradicated, all her personal records have been erased." Unit 02 is launched to assist Rei's struggling Eva but proves utterly useless due to Asuka's lamentable sync ratio. At this point, Commander Ikari resolves to take Unit 01 out of cryostasis (where the Eva was placed after its defeat of the Fourteenth Angel and attendant consumption of the enemy's flesh and controlling mechanisms). Armisael begins to invade Rei's body and psyche: As the contamination spreads and each blood vessel in the girl's body pops up and threatens to burst, the Angel lures Rei into believing that she wishes to merge with Shinji (which may well be the case anyway) in order to facilitate its own nefarious plan. So vivid is the illusion that at one point she can even "smell" her colleague.

Insofar as Unit 01 contains elements of both Lilith (as part of its original constitution) and Adam (as a result of its ingestion of Zeruel), were the Sixteenth Angel to succeed in merging with the Eva via Rei, the outcome would consist of an alliance powerful enough to instigate the Third Impact. This idea is even more dramatically conveyed in the directors' cut of Episode 23, in which a fluid, diaphanous and gigantic female shape redolent of both Rei and Yui tries to infiltrate Shinji's Unit. The Eva-01's contamination is rendered pointedly horrific by the shot in which the engorged vessels on its/Shinji's left hand take the semblance of miniature Rei/Yui heads and upper bodies. An anticipation of the cosmic phenomenon presented in *End*, the form alludes to an engulfing primordial force that symbolically combines maternal and erotic drives, as borne out by the shot in which it literally enfolds the Eva.[2]

In Episode 23, Rei visibly splits into two entities: the actual Rei, determined to be herself regardless of the suffering this may entail, and the Angel's simulation of Rei, striving to tempt the First Child with the promise of a future without loneliness. Set in a pool of saffron-hued liquid, with the two Reis facing each other in the rhetorical equivalent of mortal combat, the sequence offers one of *Evangelion*'s most compellingly surreal mental excursions through a deft blend of conventional camera work and state-of-the-art chromatic and lighting effects. Considerably shortened and telescoped, the movie version is less graphic than its televisual antecedent but makes up for what it may lack at the level of visual details by means of its cryptic allusiveness, challenging viewers to formulate their own interpretations of Rei's predicament. Ultimately, the Eva-00's pilot bravely withstands Armisael's polluting onslaught and self-destructs in order to save Shinji and his Unit. (In the directors' cut of Episode 23, the Eva-00 and the enemy it has managed to contain by choosing to self-destruct assume the aforementioned colossal shape again just before exploding. At this point, it appears to be reaching out toward an image of Gendou that Rei has perceived as her terminal recollection.)

Segment 07. "Yui"

Set in the year 2003 and imported from the directors' cut of Episode 21, *Death*'s seventh segment opens with one of the entire saga's most overtly Japanese images: a garden dominated by a magnificent cherry tree (though not in bloom) overlooking a glittering lake with a Shinto gate on its shore. Professor Fuyutsuki and Yui are engaged in conversation about SEELE's plans, as Yui lovingly tends to a toddler version of Shinji in his buggy. Although the setting is idyllic, we are informed that not all is well with the planet: The seasonal cycle has been severely impaired by the Second Impact, steeping the country into something of an eternal summer. Fuyutsuki comments somberly on this state of affairs, noting that the disappearance of autumn has rendered Japan's habitat more melancholy. (In the series, interestingly, one of the scenes set in 1999, when the professor and his promising student first meet, exhibits gloriously autumnal palettes.)

In the course of the exchange, we also learn that the Third Impact is expected to occur in less than ten years hence. Fuyutsuki believes that Yui's intentions are noble but is suspicious of those of her employers, SEELE, and firmly objects to the young woman's involvement in the next major experiment as test subject (the very experiment that will result in her disappearance). Yui, however, is convinced that she has a role to play in the grander scheme of things, and states that she is ultimately happy to work for SEELE for her son's sake. Yui's assertion, in the light of subsequent developments, is concurrently apposite and ironical.

The scene then switches to the present, proposing a fragment of Episode 15 in which Gendou and Shinji stand in a huge, windswept graveyard. Shinji observes that he has not visited his mother's grave since running away three years earlier. Gendou, for his part, is proud to stress that he does not even own a photograph of his deceased wife for he treasures all the valuable memories in his very "heart."

Segment 08. "Ritsuko"

This segment opens with a scene from Episode 21 set in 2010 in which Naoko shows her daughter the recently completed Magi supercomputer. In a voiceover reproducing part of Episode 13, Ritsuko explains to Misato that Naoko implanted three complementary aspects of her personality (scientist, mother, woman) into the Magi in order to make the system acquainted with the "dilemmas of human experience." The footage from Episode 21 continues, now accompanied by dialogue featuring in the same televisual installment. Naoko and Ritsuko exchange a few words about the younger woman's excessively analytical outlook, until Ritsuko leaves the room. Shortly after her departure, the child version of Rei appears at the door of Naoko's office and explains that she has lost her way. When the scientist offers to escort her back to her dwelling, Rei proceeds to dismiss Naoko as an "old hag"—a designation, the child avers, coined for Naoko by Commander Ikari himself. Overcome by jealous rage, the scientist strangles the First Child in a montage of psychedelic exuberance. The last shot of Rei's upside-down face as she is being throttled is fleetingly intercut with a drawing of Kaworu's mien from the Episode-24 scene in which Rei wonders: "The Fifth Child ... In what way are he and I alike?"

We next catch a glimpse of Shinji, drawn from Episode 16, in which the boy sits helplessly in the Eva-01 cockpit after being swallowed by the Twelfth Angel, gazing at a twinkling azure glare akin to the reflection of candlelight in a puddle. *Death*'s eighth portion then focuses on the climax of Episode 19, in which the Eva-01, having been badly damaged by Zeruel and used up its entire energy supply, spontaneously reactivates, replaces the arm cut off by the Angel earlier in the sequence and breaks sensationally through the adversary's A.T. Field. Shinji's sync ratio is found to be inexplicably over 400 percent and, as the NERV staff look on in horrified awe, Ritsuko declares that the Eva is "'aware." We now discover crucial aspects of the Evangelions' genuine identity, which Gendou and Ritsuko have thus far managed to keep carefully under wraps: The plates encasing an Eva's body are not solely an armor but also "restraints" used by NERV to control the creature in the first place. As things stand, the Unit is actually "breaking free" by "removing the web that binds it to our will," as Ritsuko puts it. In the process, we are shown explicitly human features of the Eva — most notably, an arm and hand that appear to consist of actual flesh. (A hint at the Eva-01's human hand is also offered, early in the series, in Episode 3 during its fight against the Fourth Angel.)

Having subdued the enemy, Shinji's Unit proceeds to devour it with grotesque gusto — at one point in the course of the feast turning to look defiantly at the appalled onlookers — and thus takes into itself the Angel's S2 Engines. The incident constitutes the gory culmination of Unit 01's consistent displays of independence: In Episode 1, it moved of its own accord to protect Shinji; in Episode 2, it reactivated autonomously to attack the Third Angel; and in Episode 20, it will keep its pilot imprisoned in the LCL for an entire month. At this stage in the narrative, "the Beast inside the Eva is out at last."

These events confirm that NERV possesses only a very limited understanding of the weapons of which it is supposed to be in unequivocal control, and that it is only through hubris that Commander Ikari pursues his schemes without compunction. As Kaji watches the scene from his garden, he wisely points out that SEELE is not going to accept the incident without asking lots of unsavory questions. (In Episode 21, the SEELE Committee will explicitly declare that through the Eva-01, mankind has created a deity, and that such an act can be regarded only as an intolerable and blasphemous aberration.) It is feasible, however, that Gendou himself perceives the recent developments as beneficial to his personal cause: His cryptic comment, delivered with more than just a hint of self-satisfaction, is indeed: "This is the beginning."

In sharp contrast with the flagrantly polychromatic clamor of the preceding sequence, the next frame delivers a subdued blue-grey multitone shot of a bandaged Rei. This image comes from Episode 20 and portrays the First Child as she is recovering from the severe damage inflicted upon her Unit by the Fourteenth Angel. The scene travels to another image of a bandaged Rei from Episode 23: The temporal transition is, at first, only noticeable if one observes that in the first shot the gauze draped over the girl's face covers only the left eye, whereas in the second she wears far more elaborate surgical dressing alluding to more serious injuries. In this fragment from Episode 23, Rei appears to have no recollection of her self-sacrificial defeat of Armisael and, even though Shinji is eager to thank her for saving him and the Eva-01, she remains oblivious. Her tentative explanation for her current state is that she must be "the Third." (Indeed, this is the third clone of the First Child presented in the saga.)

Following on this reference to Rei's synthetic identity, *Death* moves to a later scene from Episode 23 in which Ritsuko, Misato and Shinji are standing by a tank of dummy plugs containing a host of floating, unconscious and vacantly smiling Rei simulacra. The NERV head scientist goes on to explain the true nature of these eerie entities, maintaining that the Rei lookalikes are the "cores of the dummy plugs ... empty vessels, nothing but spare parts, spare Reis." She then supplies a history of NERV *in nuce*, as follows:

> Mankind found a god and man, in his folly, tried to make the god his toy. For that arrogance mankind was punished. That happened fifteen years ago. And the god that man found was lost

but man continues to attempt to resurrect the god and from that god, Adam, man attempted to make a man who was like a god himself, and that is Eva.

Shinji, astonished by the intimation that the Evangelions are human, asks Ritsuko for confirmation and the head scientist indeed provides an affirmative answer: "Inside the empty shell of each Eva is a human soul."

As Ritsuko's explanations unfold, the scene switches from the images of the First Child's artificial replicas, bathed in yellow-orange light, to black-and-white shots of the third Rei in her dreary apartment, helpless to grapple with her existential conundrum. The original scene, also from Episode 23, tells us that Rei feels as though she were perceiving her surroundings for the first time, and yet senses that this is not truly the first time. At one point, she finds herself crying without grasping the cause or nature of her tears. In *Death*, we can clearly see that the character is speaking but her words are drowned by Ritsuko's.

The screen fills once more with pictures of the glowing aquarium and then seamlessly changes to a frame from Episode 15 in which Shinji stares transfixedly at Rei as she wrings a cleaning cloth: the episode explains that the image vividly reminds the boy of his mother — an impression that causes Rei to blush, most uncharacteristically, when Shinji discloses it to her. (The only other instance of blushing on Rei's part occurs in Episode 17, in which Shinji tidies up her room out of sheer kindness and she finds herself using words that, on her own admission, she has never used before: "Thank you.")

In the closing moments of *Death*'s eighth chapter, Ritsuko destroys the dummy plugs — an act triggered by jealousy and frustration in much the same fashion as her mother's murder of the First Rei was. The segment as a whole thus pivots on the symmetrical mirroring of two analogously destructive actions inspired by resentment against Gendou's ongoing attachment to Yui despite his amorous liaisons with first Naoko and then her daughter.

Segment 09. "Touji"

Death's ninth segment opens with the fourth and last of the musical interludes executed specifically for the movie, as Shinji, Asuka, Rei and Touji perform Johann Pachelbel's "String Quartet, Kanon — D-dur." The piece is played as the background to a montage of images of the school's classrooms, corridors and grounds, of a kind also proposed in Episodes 3, 17 and 18, that drift smoothly across the field of vision. A typical anime technique, sliding holds the advantage of conveying dynamism without having to rely on a large number of cels.

The scene then travels to a frame from Episode 18 intended to foreground Touji's dejection: The boy has just been selected as the Fourth Child and is decidedly unenthusiastic about the prospect of piloting an Eva. We then see the boy brutally hitting Shinji — a scene first shown in Episode 3 and then reproposed as a flashback in Episode 18 — for putatively causing his younger sister's injuries, received by the child during the Eva-01's fight against the Third Angel.

The segment rapidly shifts to the Episode-18 action sequence in which the Eva-03, piloted by the reluctant Touji, is undergoing an activation test and, in the process, is found to be a lethal enemy: the Thirteenth Angel, Bardiel. The creature first attacks Unit 00, infiltrating its left arm, and Gendou orders that the limb be amputated before the contamination can spread. Since Rei's neural connection with the Eva is active, the mutilation causes excruciating pain to the proverbially long-suffering First Child. Shinji is curtly instructed to attack Bardiel but refuses to do so: He does not know that the Eva-03's pilot is Touji but is in any case restrained by the unequivocal knowledge that "there's still a person inside that thing."

Totally unmoved by his son's ethics, Gendou instructs the NERV personnel to put the dummy plug inside Unit 01 into operation — even though the mechanism has not yet been officially approved by Dr. Akagi — and let the Eva do its job regardless of Shinji. We soon discover that an Eva run by a dummy plug is bestiality incarnate — even though, paradoxically, Unit 01 will reveal itself capable of comparable ferociousness in its handling of Zeruel (as seen in *Death*'s eighth chapter). The Eva-01 breaks the Thirteenth Angel's neck and blood literally begins to inundate the landscape. As the battle rages on, Kensuke's voice is at one point heard in the background: Touji's little sister, he claims, was furious at her brother's treatment of Shinji, asserting that the giant robot actually "saved her" (the line comes from the camping sequence in Episode 4.)

The sequence effectively communicates with harrowing realism both the fluidity and the tangibility of the blood that saturates it. At the same time, however, the lure of the hand-drawn component makes itself felt, as the camera dwells on a vermilion stream of Turneresque sublimity. As the horror escalates, Touji's classmate Hikari, who is inexplicably besotted with the churlish boy, wonders what to cook for his lunch — a darkly ironical touch of the kind Anno seems to relish. At the end of the chapter, as Shinji finally beholds his friend, Misato's words fill the background: "The pilot of Unit 03 is ... The Fourth Child is...." In the version of the scene presented in Episode 18, Shinji screams in dismay as he sees Touji's body, whereas in the film the pathos is deliberately more restrained and possibly even more disturbing: The Third Child completes Misato's statement by simply uttering the word "Touji."

Turning an Eva into an Angel does not simply constitute a clever plot twist allowing for screenfuls of breathtaking dynamism — although it is undeniably one of the show's most dramatic ploys. In fact, it is also a means of exposing the inherent iniquity of the system in which both NERV and SEELE participate. Episode 17, in which Touji's selection as an Eva pilot is first announced, reveals that the Eva-03 has been expeditiously conveyed to Japan from the United States without, it is hinted, adequate preparations as a result of the mounting paranoia caused by the inexplicable disappearance of NERV's second branch (located in Nevada) just as a prototype S2 Engine was being installed in an experimental Eva-04. These events unequivocally demonstrate that in mankind's war against the Angels, the safeguarding of territorial stability and the attendant concealment of diplomatically thorny situations are priorities that far exceed any ethical considerations. Touji, Rei and Shinji are casualties of this ruthless ideology.

Segment 10. "Kaji"

Central to this segment of *Death* is one of *Evangelion*'s most enigmatic personae: an unaffectedly handsome, ponytailed and permanently stubbly young man whose apparently carefree personality belies a grave disposition and a deeply inquisitive spirit — so searching, indeed, as to lead him to fathom both SEELE's and NERV's darkest secrets, and eventually be murdered as a result. Kaji's role as a dispassionate questor is mirrored by the cinematographical style used in the chapter's opening portion, in which the adoption of black-and-white images capturing key moments in the saga lends the footage a distinctively documentary flavor.

In a heady dalliance with the cut-up at its most intrepid, the sequence moves from a shot of Gendou rescuing Rei from her entry plug, originally included in Episode 5; through two shots imported from Episode 21 depicting first a young Gendou with Professor Fuyutsuki and then Naoko kissing Gendou; through a shot from Episode 19 portraying Shinji in the NERV cell where he has been imprisoned after disobeying his father's orders; to a shot of Kaji and Misato kissing passionately in a NERV lift from Episode 9. From here, the sequence switches to the scene from Episode 5 in which Kaji, visiting Kyoto on business, discovers some unpalatable truths about NERV. (The episode itself reveals that the Marduk Institute, namely, the organization supposedly responsible for selecting the Eva pilots, is in fact an ensemble of ghost companies run exclusively by Gendou.) As the sequence unfolds, the voiceover offers a conversation between Kaji and Shinji, drawn from Episode 18, triggered by the boy's urge to understand what Gendou is really like. Kaji, in response, patiently explains to Shinji that "people can't even really understand themselves, much less each other."

The transition to the next part of the segment is signaled by Ritsuko asking Kaji what he has been doing in Kyoto, at which point the screen shifts to full color and displays a scene from Episode 15 in which Ritsuko and Kaji are attending a friend's wedding reception together. Misato's voice fills the background, as she communicates her frustration about the past and deep-seated dissatisfaction with her management of personal relationships. The words come from a subsequent Episode-15 sequence in which Kaji walks a severely drunk Misato back to her apartment. The sequence clearly exemplifies Anno's ability to transcend stereotypical characterization. While Misato may at times unproblematically come across as a boisterously sexy leader, there can be little doubt that insecurity and unresolved conflicts haunt her soul.

The screen returns to the black-and-white mode, reproposing the Kyoto scene mentioned earlier with a voiceover containing the message left by Kaji on Misato's answering machine just prior to his assassination. Endeavoring to sound casual to the bitter end, Kaji is essentially proffering a final farewell. In the same communication, he also advises Misato to trust her own judgment: "Katsuragi, the truth is with you. Don't hesitate. Move ahead." The voiceover continues as we move to a scene from Episode 8 in which Kaji delivers Adam's frozen embryo to Gendou, so as to aid the commander in the advancement of his dubious goals. With a sudden transition to full color, the camera then delivers a close-up of the embryo in Kaji's briefcase. A shot from the directors' cut of Episode 24 is then supplied in which a close-up of Gendou's right hand shows that the creature has been grafted onto his very person. (In the episode, this shot occurs at the point where Commander Ikari addresses the Eva-01 as though he were talking to Yui, promising that the day of their reunion is nigh.)

A frame exhibiting an overtly hand-drawn sketch of Kaji, Misato and Ritsuko as students — also presented in Episode 21—flickers by in the ensuing shot. The closing part of Kaji's message to Misato is then played, followed by her own words — "you fool" — and by blatant indications that she is weeping. As Misato's words are heard, the screen switches to the setting of Kaji's assassination. This whole fragment comes from Episode 21. In the next shot, following a black screen, we see Shinji trying to get Asuka to accept once and for all that Kaji is dead. The distraught Second Child, however, reacts to Shinji's statement by vitriolically accusing him of being a "liar." This shot has been imported from the directors' cut of Episode 24, in which a seemingly less irate and more careworn Asuka merely whispers "no."

Segment 11. "Kaworu"

Death's closing chapter opens with a scene from Episode 24 displaying a view of the ruins of Tokyo-3 at sunset. As a disconsolate Shinji gazes at the blasted landscape in all its lurid glory, haunting memories of the grieving Misato (Episode 21), of Asuka's breakdown, and of Ritsuko's dejection after her destruction of the Rei dummy plugs (Episode 23) surge through his mind. His right arm hangs limply by his side, the hand exuding a sense of pent-up tension: This aspect of the Third Child's body language is used recurrently throughout the series to convey nervousness and anxiety.

Death's eleventh segment is closely based on Episode 24. Shinji suddenly becomes aware of a boy around his own age sitting on a rock nearby and humming Beethoven's "Ode to Joy." Having declared that this aria constitutes the "highest achievement of the Lilim culture," the youth goes on to introduce himself as Kaworu Nagisa, the "Fifth Child." (The term "Lilim" designates mankind as Lilith's progeny.) The exchange comes to an end as Kaworu's words from a later part of the episode are played — "It is time. Let us go, Adam's dark shadow, servant of the Lilim" — and the action travels to the NERV Headquarters, where Kaworu shows himself able to activate Unit 02 (which he is indeed addressing with those words) even though the Eva is "unmanned." (Please note that Asuka is in intensive care by now.) The Fifth Child's true identity as the last of the "angelic" enemies to be confronted by mankind is hence revealed. Professor Fuyutsuki comments: "SEELE has delivered an Angel to us," to which Gendou impassively riposts: "The old man [i.e., SEELE'S head, Lorenz Keel] wants to advance his schedule using us as his tools."

A snatch of a meeting held by the SEELE Committee, specially adapted for the movie through additional dialogue, instantly corroborates Gendou's suspicions: "We must take the fate of the future into our own hands. Unit 01 will be our instrument." (How exactly SEELE intends to exploit the Eva-01 will not become evident until *End*.) The NERV personnel struggle to keep Kaworu from accessing Terminal Dogma but the intruder quite effortlessly reaches his intended destination. Shinji is left with no alternative but to confront the boy, who has meanwhile become his friend, and annihilate him. Kaworu himself is adamant as to the ineluctability of this climax. As Units 01 and 02 fight fiercely in NERV's secluded underbelly, the Seventeenth Angel reflects:

> The Eva series was born from man's antithesis. And yet the Lilim will utilize that which they hate most of all in order to survive? I do not understand... Your Evas and I are composed of the very same matter. Born from Adam, I can synchronize with it easily, as long as there is no dominant soul.

While they prepare to destroy the entire Headquarters should Unit 01 fail, the NERV staff detect another A.T. Field besides those of the struggling adversaries: At this point, Rei is shown, looking upon the scene from the chamber's upper area. The reason and meaning of her presence are left open to interpretation. Finally, Kaworu realizes that the Angel concealed underneath NERV is Lilith, not Adam, and entreats Shinji to kill him so that he will no longer be doomed to "live forever." Only one species, he maintains, is ultimately allowed to survive, for the Angels and the Lilim are not capable of coexisting. It is for Shinji's species to survive, according to Kaworu, for the "future" is "what you Lilim live for." The tantalizingly protracted, wordless and motionless sequence in which the Eva-01 clutches Kaworu before eventually destroying him, first presented in Segment 02. of *Death*, is here reproposed, to the accompaniment of Beethoven's "Ninth Symphony."

◆ ◆ ◆

The *Rebirth* segment placed after *Death* consists of wholly new footage and is reproposed as the first half hour of *End*. The animation opens with a wordless preamble of stunning compositional elegance and lyrical grace in which Shinji gazes at the sunken ruins of Tokyo-3. The atmosphere of utter desolation conveyed by the urbanscape contrasts ironically with the sublime tranquility of the turquoise skies above, investing the scene with a deeply haunting beauty. The sequence's climax offers a bird's-eye view in which the reflection of a white-hot sun in the water is framed by the concentric circles formed by ripples spreading upon its surface, by the reflections of the fleecy clouds and by the emerging tips of the derelict edifices. *Rebirth* enters the action proper with Shinji visiting the comatose Asuka in hospital, desperately begging her to help him and then masturbating by her bed: an action that leads him to observe that he is now truly "fucked up." This sequence employs a minimalistic palette, yielding muted multitones based on the softest of blues and blue-greens, with gentle touches of toned-down warm hues for Asuka's hair (its pale rusty brown a remote echo of the erstwhile blazing mane) and for the fluid by means of which the patient is intravenously fed. Chromatic minimalism is matched by the linear simplicity of the explicitly two-dimensional character designs.

The scene then switches to the NERV HQ, as the personnel puzzle over the reasons for the current state of "first level alert" to which they have been consigned in spite of the fact that all the Angels are supposed to have been destroyed. A brief scene centered on Misato, sitting alone in her car at night, addresses the concept of Instrumentality as the phenomenon that "will manufacture the evolution of man's separate entities into a single composite being." The Major's mien clearly indicates that she objects to this scientifically engineered metamorphosis of the human race, echoing the reservations expressed by the same character in Episode 25 of the TV series when the "Human Instrumentality Project" is first mentioned in an explicit fashion. Misato also points out that the tool meant to instigate Instrumentality will not be Adam, as had originally been suspected, but the Evas themselves, which makes the need to hide them and their pilots from SEELE and its emissaries absolutely vital if mankind as we know it is to survive.

SEELE's intention to use the Evas is confirmed in the next scene, as the Committee states that in the absence of the Lance of Longinus (lost in Episode 22 of the series; Segment 06. of *Death*), the Eva-01 (which contains elements of Lilith as well as the empowering S2 Engines acquired by feasting upon the Fourteenth Angel) will be utilized instead. Gendou retorts that this was not part of SEELE's original plan but the Committee is adamant about the appropriateness of exploiting any available means in order to "free us all for rebirth." Gendou, however, insists on peddling his personal philosophy, asserting that "mankind exists because it has the will to live," and then cryptically adding: "After all, that's why she chose to remain in the Eva." The "she" in question is Rei, and the choice referred to by Commander Ikari is her decision to self-destruct in Episode 23 of the show (*Death*'s sixth segment) so as to save Shinji and Unit 01.

Fittingly, the scene now moves to a close-up of Rei in the dingy NERV room where her various clones are said to have been "born" (Episode 23 of the TV show; Segment 08. of *Death*). An intensely atmospheric view of the nocturnal sky, dominated by a majestic full moon and powdered with lacy clouds, symbolically alludes to the mental images with which Rei's mind is synthetically infused. As the First Child leaves the room, we are given a close-up of Gendou's ubiquitous glasses, now more substantially damaged, on the floor: Rei appears to have finally ceased regarding the object as her most precious possession, which succinctly anticipates her later refusal to comply with Gendou's self-aggrandizing schemes. (In the TV series, a relatively early clue to Rei's latent dissatisfaction with Gendou's agenda is offered by Episode 11, "The Day Tokyo-3 Stood Still." In this installment, as the pilots approach the NERV HQ in preparation for the battle against the Ninth Angel — Matariel, the Angel of Rain — Asuka accuses the First Child of being the commander's pet and Rei tersely states that the treatment she gets is far from enviable.) A shot of a dejected Shinji, compounded with the image of a misty landscape replicating the nebulousness of the boy's psyche, is rapidly followed by a scene in which Misato conclusively ascertains the nature of the lies surrounding the Second Impact.

In the ensuing scene, SEELE learns that Gendou has duped the Committee, pretending to advance its agenda but actually pursuing his own private version of the Human Instrumentality Project. In order to hinder him, SEELE hacks into the Magi supercomputer based at the HQ by deploying other Magi systems located around the world, at which point Ritsuko is summoned to set up "additional defense programs." In spite of Ritsuko having been heartlessly rejected by Gendou and kept locked up in one of NERV's obscurest nooks as a result of her destruction of the Rei dummy plugs (Episode 23 of the TV show; Segment 08. of *Death*), she does not hesitate to help — though she remains baffled by the illogicality of the "interaction between men and women" — and is indeed able to stop the hackers for sixty-two hours. As Ritsuko leaves the supercomputer's inner chamber, she enigmatically remarks: "Well, mother, I'll see you soon." The meaning of these words becomes clear in *End*, in which it transpires that Ritsuko has not only installed the powerful "type 666 firewall" but also meddled with the Magi for her own nefarious purposes. (The allusion to the "Number of the Beast" is intriguing.)

As time is running out, SEELE realizes that in order to get to the Evas, it will have to resort to force. It therefore resolves to send in the JSSDF (Japanese Strategic Self-Defense Forces), who effortlessly infiltrate the NERV HQ and proceed to butcher mercilessly all the staff they encounter. The NERV personnel make a last stand in the Command Center, where the Magi system is situated. Asuka is launched in Unit 02 and stored at the bottom of the lake surrounding NERV. Rei, meanwhile, is seen floating in a vast tank filled with a radiant fluid. As for Shinji, he is stuck in a remote section of the complex, seemingly beyond reach.

The bulk of this portion of the film is devoted to rapid-fire action sequences that cumulatively amount to a tumultuous ride: The violence is pervasive and the camera even lingers on execution-style assassinations as blood pours, oozes and gushes by turns. Intercut with the scenes documenting the attack is a sequence in which Rei looks intently at the gruesome dummy-plug fragments floating aimlessly about in the wake of Ritsuko's murderous act. Gendou approaches her and confidently states: "The time has come. Let's go."

Meanwhile, Misato saves Shinji from certain death at the hands of the JSSDF, and although the Third Child appears to have precipitated into a condition of terminal apathy, she insists on dragging him to Unit 01 to persuade him to pilot it just one more — decisive — time. It is at this point that the JSSDF relinquish any lingering sense of moderation and drop an "N2 bomb" onto Tokyo-3's ruins. Non-nuclear to the extent that it is designed not to cause fallout or radiation, the explosive is nonetheless as powerful as a regular nuclear weapon and hence tears a huge hole in the Geofront that leaves the NERV HQ fully exposed.

Misato painstakingly explains to Shinji that SEELE wants the Third Impact to occur, that mankind is in fact the "Eighteenth Angel," born of Lilith, and that the Eva-01's pilot must "destroy the rest of the Eva series" as this is "the only way to stay alive." As the Major's narrative unfolds, an exquisitely composited montage fills the screen. This moves from a medium shot of the Eva-00's inceptive skeleton to a shot of an array of spinal cords issuing from countless Eva craniums and reaching into a vat of sanguine goop. This image is next intercut with a chain of flashing shots, so fast as to be almost unnoticeable unless the footage is viewed in slow motion. These include images of the glowing crater generated by the Second Impact, Adam as a radiant giant, Adam as an embryo, the graveyard where Yui is commemorated, the graph displaying the Angels' biophysical similarity to mankind, a pencil sketch of Kaworu's face and a still of Rei in her piloting suit. In a sense, this montage could be said to deliver a potted history of *Evangelion* as a whole.

Curled up in the Eva-02's cockpit, Asuka gradually awakens to find herself under attack by the JSSDF troops. At first merely able to mutter mechanically the incantation "I don't want to die," she finally discovers the truth about Unit 02 (and, by implication, about each of the other Evas), namely, that it possesses a soul and, specifically, the soul of Asuka's own mother, whose voice can be heard gently infiltrating the girl's robotic mantra. The Second Child's epiphany is dramatized by an unforgettable montage, unleashing vertiginous juxtapositions and superimpositions. The sequence recalls Asuka's mental rape in Episode 22 (especially in the directors' cut version).

The shots include images of Asuka as a child, her mother's rag doll, her own stuffed toy and, most startlingly, a decaying and maggot-infested female face. The various shots are by turns broken up into fragments analogous to the contents of a kaleidoscope, solarized, overexposed or desaturated. The montage culminates with the shot of a seashore (an image that also plays a vital symbolic role in Episode 16 and Episode 20). This is followed by a patently hand-crafted sketch of Asuka's mother, approaching the girl with a tender smile on her face and open arms, and by a shot of the young Asuka in a dark wood — where her and her mother's hands eventually touch. The transition from one image, or cluster of images, to the next is so fast that it is only by means of multiple viewings that its import may be fully gleaned. It also transpires, when the sequence is played in *very* slow motion, that it capitalizes on subliminal impulses, as images are often quite literally hidden inside other images.

Strengthened by the realization that her mother's spirit has always been with her in the Eva, Asuka boldly arises from her stupor and plunges into the fray, determined to defend the NERV HQ. She is eventually deprived of her Umbilical Cable but manages nonetheless to vanquish the attackers in a display of determination, martial prowess and sheer passion not seen in the saga since at least Episode 9 of the TV show.

Deploying their final and most lethal weapon, SEELE now launches the new Eva Mass Production Models 05–13 against Unit 02: *Rebirth* terminates with a close-up of the Second Child looking up at them in surprise. The new Evas possess S2 Engines, which entails that they do not need an Umbilical Cable to operate, and wings. Each Unit is piloted by a dummy plug based on Kaworu's mental patterns and equipped with a weapon based on the Lance of Longinus. The sequence in which the nine colossal freight planes transporting the mass-produced Evas first appear would have been practically unachievable by recourse to conventional anime camera work. However, through the incorporation of CG cuts into the animation, it was possible to portray the planes from a bird-eye's perspective, and to have them overlap with one another or slide gracefully in subtly differentiated directions.

Neon Genesis Evangelion: End of Evangelion (Episode 25: "Air" Episode 26: "Sincerely Yours") (Shinseiki Evangelion Gekijouban: "Air"/ "Magokoro wo, kimi ni")
Directors: Hideaki Anno, Kazuya Tsurumaki (1997)

End is an entirely novel development of the saga's finale, offering an alternate conclusion to the one provided by the last two episodes of the TV show. Pointedly action-oriented, Episode 25: "Air" interweaves two complementary narrative strands: Asuka's heroic confrontation of the horde of bloodthirsty Eva Mass Production Models 05–13 with no scruples about ravaging their own kind, and Misato's courageous death in her effort to protect Shinji and thus secure his participation in the final chapter of humanity's struggle. Having reproposed the contents presented in *Rebirth*, about one quarter of which were shot again to improve technical quality, *End* offers wholly new footage from the point at which the Evas 05–13 descend upon the Geofront and attack Asuka's Unit 02. The Second Child's slaughter of the Mass Production Models administers one of *Evangelion*'s most sensational sequences. As the Eva-02 pilot's fervor builds up to a veritable paroxysm of ferocity, disturbingly heightened by her savage body language and frenzied facial expressions, the action brings about an uncanny synthesis of gruesome brutality and graphic elegance.

Episode 25 eloquently attests to Anno's characteristic passion for dexterously edited cut-ins. As Asuka butchers the Evas 05–13, the fight is repeatedly intermingled with shots that dramatize the events concurrently unfolding within the NERV HQ. We see Misato and Shinji being shot at by the JSSDF troops, and Misato's final effort to rouse a terminally aboulic Shinji just before dying—a deeply moving moment mysteriously witnessed by an apparition of Rei in her school uniform. Asuka's fight is subsequently intercut with scenes pivoting on Shinji in the Eva-01's "cage," on Gendou and Rei by Lilith's crucified body in Terminal Dogma, and on Ritsuko's abortive attempt to blow up NERV.

This last scene is especially worthy of consideration insofar as it brings to a dramatic end the narrative strand based on the NERV head scientist's ambiguous relationship with her mother Naoko. In equipping the Magi with the type 666 firewall, as seen earlier in the discussion of *Rebirth*, Ritsuko has also tampered with the supercomputer so that it will cause the obliteration of the NERV Headquarters at her pressing of a button. Intended as Ritsuko's ultimate revenge upon her ruthless ex-lover, the plan boomerangs when, at the appointed moment, Casper—and thus Naoko via Casper—betray the disillusioned scientist. Gendou shoots Ritsuko, who back-flips spectacularly into NERV's blood-red subterranean waters. *Evangelion*'s inspired use of classical music is fully attested to by the use of Johann Sebastian Bach's "Air on G" for the part of the sequence in which the fight between Unit 02 and the Mass Production models is displayed, intermingled with the confrontation between Gendou and Ritsuko.

Asuka's battle is brought to a nasty close by the appearance of a duplicate Lance of Longinus produced by SEELE and its lethal piercing of the Eva-02 through the head. The new Evas, alas, are capable of regenerating in virtually no time at all regardless of the degree of mutilation incurred. Thus, though severely damaged by Asuka, they heal themselves almost instantaneously and proceed to rip Unit 02 apart while its pilot sits powerless in the entry plug in absolute agony.

News of Asuka's death (an occurrence that subsequent events will call into question) and Shinji's attendant invocation of his mother cause the Eva-01 to self-activate and rise with its pilot to the surface amidst a terrifying storm. The Unit's stylized facial features, redolent of a traditional Japanese mask, are jarringly superimposed over a photorealistic sky traversed by magnetic waves and ominous crows. A brief exchange between two astounded onlookers economically sums up the scene's drama:

"Evangelion Unit 01...."
"The devil himself."

Upon seeing the Eva-02's disemboweled remains, its vividly rendered dangling eyes and festering entrails, Shinji emits an ear-piercing scream, which brings "Air" to an arresting end.

Though replete with spectacular sequences of alternately ebullient and methodically paced dynamism, the second segment of *End*—Episode 26: "Sincerely Yours"—comes across less as an action piece than as a metaphysical exploration. Indeed, the struggle it dramatizes amounts to a choice of apocalyptic proportions, the responsibility for which falls squarely on Shinji's shoulders — a rather infelicitous outcome, when one considers that this character appears constitutionally incapable of making choices as a result of his ingrained conviction that since all he ever does "is hurt other people," he would "rather do nothing at all."

At this point, *End* engages with a fundamentally existentialist issue in proposing that although a choice inevitably represents an act of violence, namely, the elimination of possibility, probability and suspension, a person only really exists insofar as he or she is able to act, and to act inexorably means to exercise the faculty of choice. The choice faced by Shinji — not, it must be emphasized, as an individual character so much as an allegorical, Noh-like emblem for humanity at its most fleeting and vulnerable — is whether it is preferable for individuals to eclipse their bodily and mental boundaries and merge into one entity or else learn how to live with themselves and with others as distinct monads.

The dominant powers, that is, SEELE and NERV, are ardently committed to the former option. SEELE's goal is to engineer a Third Impact that will result in the fusion of all people into a primordial mass, and regards this move as instrumental to mankind's achievement of its final evolutionary form; Gendou, for his part, is not willing to see his own separate identity erased and aims instead at a Third Impact that will invest him with godlike powers and reunite him with his beloved Yui. Although SEELE's and Commander Ikari's respective agendas differ, both parties are driven by the same all-consuming desire for absolute power and by a pseudo-ethical stance earlier defined by Professor Fuyutsuki in uncompromising terms as "self-righteous arrogance" (Episode 12). NERV and SEELE alike seek to transcend individuality as a means of suppressing any intimations of alterity — and hence any threats of resistance or opposition to their grandly deterministic teleological visions.

In the opening scene of Episode 26, Gendou urges Rei to release her A.T. Field and merge with him — having already incorporated Adam's embryo, he now hopes to stage the forbidden fusion of the First and Second Angels by bringing Adam into intimate contact with Lilith, whose genes are encoded in Rei's DNA. However, just as the fusion — graphically ushered in by Gendou's literal penetration of Rei's left breast with his right arm, where Adam's embryo resides — is under way, the First Child begins to sense Shinji's need of her. Shinji himself, meanwhile, faces the ultimate crisis: The real Lance of Longinus returns from the Moon and reaches Unit 01, its tip menacingly poised at the Eva's throat.

The SEELE Committee now feels officially entitled to initiate the Third Impact, solemnly declaring: "Let the sacrament begin." Represented, as is customary throughout the saga, in the form of a dark room wherein each Committee member is epitomized by a basalt-black monolith bearing a glowing red number, the SEELE HQ provides a startling visual contrast with the foregoing frame, in which the Eva-01's chromatic opulence and the baroque palette of its background literally flood the senses with a feeling of the sublime. The action then shifts to the Mass Production models as they capture Shinji's Unit by means of replica Lances, bear it aloft and place themselves around it so as to form a colossal Sephiroth. Concurrently, a momentous explosion causes the Geofront to resume its primordial shape, namely, that of the Black Moon or Egg of Lilith. The rendition of massive shockwaves, first resembling a gigantic eye and then condensing into a purple-black globe is especially memorable.

It is at this juncture that Rei conclusively withstands Gendou, stating that she is not his "puppet," and resolves to assist the Commander's son instead. Rei's decision to disassociate herself from Gendou and thereby defect to his son's side represents the culmination of a gradual process that reveals a developing mistrust of the elder Ikari and growing attachment to Shinji. "Ikari is calling me" are her last words before she proceeds to merge with Lilith. The Second Angel's release from the table upon which it has been forced to lie, crucified, for so long offers an outstanding instance of morphing as Lilith's hands extricate themselves from the huge nails used to keep them in place, and each layer of skin and flesh smoothly detaches itself from the restraints. A giant and diaphanous Rei — the result of her merging with Lilith — rises grandiosely from the depths of Terminal Dogma to pervade the NERV Controls Room and then emerges into the sky to join the Eva-01.

No sooner has the giant Rei reached Shinji's Unit that the Evas 05–13 start merging with the creature, yielding a sensational scenario of large-scale morphing that matches Lilith's release from Terminal Dogma. Most enthralling, in this regard, are the emergence of faces bearing stylized traits of Rei's own countenance from each of the creatures' skulls, and the attendant sprouting of multifarious analogous faces from their rapidly transmuting bodies. A montage swiftly juxtaposing Shinji's memories of Rei by recourse to frames taken from various TV installments seamlessly ensues. Morphing also plays a central part in the following sequence, in which the mammoth Rei develops two distinct torsos and heads, one of which goes on bearing Rei's semblance, while the other acquires Kaworu's features. Faced with the image of the only person (except, plausibly, his long-departed mother) who has ever professed love for him, the despairing Shinji gratefully smiles, as tears simultaneously well up in his eyes. It is at this point, the action obliquely suggests, that the Eva-01 pilot relinquishes his individuality and chooses to merge with what he seemingly perceives as an unbroken stream of warmth and tenderness. The Lance of Longinus, thus far positioned just inches away from the Unit's body, at last penetrates its core as though to ratify Shinji's shedding of personal boundaries. Kaworu next metamorphoses into a second Rei that may also, however, stand for a simulacrum of Yui — as intimated by Shinji's ensuing evocation of mental images of his mother, interleaved with shots of his childhood self.

Following Shinji's childhood recollections, the screen switches to a series of scenes set in a playground. These are rendered deeply uncanny by their amalgamation of lighting effects intended to convey a mood of oneiric suspension, of symmetrically placed lines and stark geometrical primitives whose perfection is so excessive as to feel uncomfortably eerie, and of a self-reflexive exposure of cinematic artifice. As a child version of Shinji tearfully builds a pyramid-shaped sandcastle (probably an allusion to the NERV HQ's architecture) and then proceeds to demolish it, his movements measured by the steady oscillation of an unoccupied swing, film lights surround the playground as though to underscore its status as a film set.

Multiple montages centered on snapshots of Asuka, Misato and Rei follow, interspersed with the harrowing sequence in which Shinji strangles Asuka as if to put an unrescindable seal on his tale of affliction. (This incident will be returned to later in this chapter.) The Unit 01 pilot's private musings culminate with a shot in which Shinji's distorted features are crisscrossed by a proliferation of inky lines, as though the animation were endeavoring to erase his identity in much the same way as a kid would seek to obliterate a disappointing drawing. This introspective sequence is drastically displaced by the screen's return to a frame of macrocosmic magnitude in which the giant Rei holds the Egg of Lilith between her cupped hands and sprouts multitudinous wings. The apparition seen at the scene of Misato's death, that of a normal-size Rei garbed in her school uniform, reproposes itself next in plural incarnations amidst the corpses left behind by the JSSDF in a NERV corridor, as a voiceover from Rei ponders the pervasiveness of sorrow, loneliness and emptiness in human life.

The borders separating individuals (mankind's own A.T. Fields) finally dissolve as the NERV employees — and, by implication, *all* people — come into contact with a vision of the person they have loved most passionately and unrequitedly (e.g., Yui in Professor Fuyutsuki's case and Ritsuko in Maya's) and then vanish with a gentle popping noise, leaving merely a splurge of viscous matter in their wake. By and by, each and every person's discrete shape is sucked into the heady mix.

Gendou's own experience of the Third Impact does not even remotely approximate anything he could ever have wished for. Visions of Yui, Rei and Kaworu in turn indicate that the commander's fear and loathing of intersubjective bonds — most brutally evinced by his treatment of his own son — now precludes him from merging with other creatures. This, Gendou recognizes, is his "retribution." He finally utters the words "Forgive me, Shinji," and is snatched up and devoured whole by a simulacrum of the Eva-01—an appropriate executioner when one reflects that the Unit allegorically personifies both Yui and Shinji.

End's most awesome metaphysical sequences ensue, regaling the eye — and indeed the entire sensorium — with a dense visual poetry so multilayered as to invite endless speculation. The nine Mass Production Evangelions pierce their hearts by means of as many facsimiles of the Lance of Longinus, thereby yielding yet more memorable instances of morphing. The world's collapse into a state of utter undifferentiation is symbolically encapsulated by the scene in which Rei places her hands around the Egg of Lilith once again and the latter assumes the guise of a globular mass of twirling red corpuscles (each dot signifying the soul of a human being) that gradually metamorphoses into a seemingly infinite flow of energy. Concomitantly, legion cruciform lights inundate the Earth, their fluorescent green in jarring contrast with the red of the ocean of particles emanating from Rei's hands.

While the world undergoes its momentous metamorphosis, Shinji's psyche appears to be caught in a liminal domain between individuality and undifferentiation, which suggests that his acceptance of Instrumentality cannot yet be taken for granted. The character's internal ordeal is communicated by means of two complex montages. The first of these consists of a barrage of extremely fast-paced juxtapositions and superimpositions of shots from the TV series, pencil sketches, character studies, collages and abstract shards of color. Following a brief intermission offering close-ups of Shinji's, Misato's and Rei's profiles, the second montage focuses quite blatantly on Shinji's specifically sexual anxieties, displaying protean representations of the human body (which include elements of live-action footage) distorted by recourse to filters that emulate the look of watercolor washes. This is played out against the background of disjointed lines uttered in turns by the three key women in Shinji's adolescence, the erotic import of which is unquestionable.

The screen is then abruptly taken over by live-action footage. This includes prosaic images of the urban environment, with its amorphous crowds and impersonal buildings, pylons, signs, graffiti and a tortoiseshell cat — as well as a real-world counterpart of the animated swing presented earlier — that are rendered intensely lyrical in spite of their drabness by the camera's melodic suppleness and stupendous musical accompaniment. Images of the *seiyuu* (voice actresses) for Rei (Megumi Hayashibara), Asuka (Yuko Miyamura) and Misato (Kotono Mitsuishi) also feature, as does the fleeting apparition of a blue-haired pedestrian vividly akin to Rei (possibly a deftly edited cut-in from the anime, possibly a shot of an actual person engaged in "cosplay"). Toward the end of the sequence, we are additionally supplied with flickering scans of death threats targeted at Anno via the Internet by frantic fans dissatisfied with the TV show's ending. The soundtrack for this part of the film is "Jesus bliebt Meine Freunde" by Johann Sebastian Bach. Anno's consistent recourse to the work of this composer can be attributed to its eminently visual appeal: a trait of Bach's opus that the physician and musician Albert Schweitzer described as distinctively "painterly," or "pictorial" (Schweitzer).

The pivotal image used in the live-action footage is that of a capacious movie theater. This recurs throughout the sequence, alternately empty, filling and packed with spectators. While the image self-reflexively reminds us of *Evangelion*'s artificial nature as a cinematic product, it also tangentially alludes to a metaphorical analogy between film-viewing and dreaming by means of visual effects that impart the auditorium with an elusively oneiric feel. The analogy is sustained by the background dialogue, the main topic of which is indeed the nebulousness of the dividing-line between reality and dreams:

> Shinji: "What are dreams? ... I don't understand what reality is."
> Rei: "You can't bridge the gap between your own truth and the reality of others."
> Shinji: "I don't know where to find happiness."
> Rei: "So you only find happiness in your dreams."
> Shinji: "Then this is no reality, this world where no-one exists?"
> Rei: "No, it is only a dream."
> Shinji: "Then I don't exist here either."
> Rei: "This convenient fabrication is your attempt to change reality.... You are using fantasy to escape reality."

Rei is here suggesting that the world of undifferentiation into which Shinji appears to have chosen to immerse himself is purely a construct intended to exorcize the dread of separation and hence loneliness. Shinji is anxious to discover why he cannot simply dream that he is "not alone" and Rei explains that this would not be a dream but rather "a substitute for reality." Loneliness, as noted by her multiple apparitions earlier in the film, is an inevitable aspect of being human: Nowhere is a person *not* alone, at least potentially, for the spectre of loneliness is ineradicable even when the actuality of that state is temporarily alleviated.

The exchange reaches its climax with the following lines:

> Shinji: "So, where is my dream?"
> Rei: "It is a continuation of reality."
> Shinji: "But where is my reality?"
> Rei: "It is at the end of your dream."

A constructive dream, it is here intimated, is a vision that seeks not to flee reality but rather to generate an imaginative extension of reality. The art of animation itself, in this respect, could be said to epitomize such a dream. This hypothesis is formally corroborated, albeit evasively, by the action's return to the anime mode precisely on the tail of Rei's proposition.

Shinji's "dream" has consisted of a plunge into a primeval ocean wherein each creature is "everywhere" and "nowhere" at once. Even though he has willed such a fantasy, he now feels that it is "wrong." In a tantalizing scene in which Shinji's and Rei's bodies are literally fused together as a seamless entity, the boy frankly acknowledges that there is "nothing good in the place I escaped to," and that he longs to see again the people he has so far endeavored to flee as individuals in their own right, regardless of the sorrow they may occasion him.

In the closing parts of the sequence, Kaworu features steadily beside Rei, the two characters symbolizing, in conjunction, the element of "hope" buried in Shinji's own heart. The sequence's focal message is embodied by Kaworu's assertion that "reality exists in a place unknown and dreams exist within reality," and by Rei's ensuing statement: "And truth lies in your heart.... The power of the imagination is the ability to create your own future and the power to create your own flow of time." Rei's closing words hint at a further affinity between productive, as opposed to escapist, visions and the art of animation, insofar as the ability to manipulate the temporal flow with no obligation to emulate the normal passage of time constitutes animation's greatest asset, and exuberantly celebrates its disengagement from the laws of gravity and logic.

Shinji's initial acceptance and eventual rejection of the state of entropic inertness ushered in by Instrumentality are encapsulated by two key scenes dramatizing his interaction with

Asuka. In the acceptance phase, Shinji's urge to suppress all vestiges of otherness — and hence separation from his fellow humans — is brutally communicated by the strangling episode referred to earlier: if he cannot rely on Asuka's unconditional support (something she is patently unwilling to provide), Shinji would rather destroy her altogether. The fear of being abandoned here gains the upper hand.

In *End*'s final scene, Shinji is seen lying on a desolate seashore next to an ostensibly catatonic Asuka. His first impulse is to strangle her, as though to reassert the message conveyed by the previous sequence. However, the moment he feels Asuka's caress — a gesture reminiscent of the shot presented a few frames earlier in which Yui lovingly strokes her son's cheek — Shinji releases his hold on the girl's neck and starts weeping profusely over her face. The act seems to repulse Asuka but at least she voices her feelings by simply terming Shinji's behavior "disgusting" and not by slapping the boy or calling him an "idiot," in keeping with her customary conduct throughout the saga. This change would seem to allude to increased maturity on the Second Child's part. Concurrently, Shinji's ability to refrain from his initially destructive impulse arguably indicates that he is now prepared to accept the existence of a separate other, even if this inevitably entails the possibility of reproach and disapproval — as Asuka's verbal reaction indeed shows. In this respect, the scene intimates that both characters may have finally attained to a more variegated and less monolithic world picture.

It is important to recognize that the earlier strangulation scene, set in Misato's flat, does not constitute an actual event so much as a hypothetical projection of Shinji's feelings akin to a dream (in much the same way as the events presented in Episodes 1 through 24 of the series could be regarded as imaginary flashbacks processed through Shinji's psyche). For one thing, the scene does not logically fit in the *Evangelion* timeline, which makes it a surreal appendix rather than an integral addition to the saga's narrative trajectory. The proposition that the scene offers an externalization of the contents of Shinji's own psyche and not an empirical occurrence is corroborated by Asuka's mocking interjection: "Idiot! I know about your jerk-off fantasies of me. Do it again ... I'll even stand here and watch." These words give voice to Shinji's own feelings of guilt and shame, not Asuka's actual resentment: in "Air," as mentioned, Shinji does masturbate over Asuka's unconscious body and feels quite disgusted with himself, yet the girl could not plausibly have been cognizant of his actions. Nor could she be commenting on the incident in the context of Misato's apartment (with Pen-Pen lurking in the background), as this setting predates Asuka's hospitalization and subsequent developments in the story.

The reality of the closing scene cannot be taken for granted either, as the chance of Asuka having survived the Evas 05–13's onslaught is extremely slim. The scene's ambiguity is reinforced by the fact that although the bandages worn by the Second Child are consonant with the injuries she appeared to suffer in the course of the attack, they are also akin to those worn by Rei both at the beginning and toward the end of the TV series, which obliquely suggests that the character may actually constitute a composite fabrication emanating from Shinji's own mind. Furthermore, a puzzling shot of Rei (analogous to the image of the First Child incorporated in the depiction of Misato's death), at one point makes a flickering appearance over the water, which further interrogates the scene's empirical substance.

It is in any case undeniable that by encompassing a broad range of both positive and negative human affects and interactions, *End*'s closing scene does not bestow conclusive answers, and chooses instead to celebrate *Evangelion*'s stature as an enduring monument to the collusion of action, mystery and pathos. Moreover, the scene makes sense in relation to the lesson conveyed both by Rei earlier in the film and by the TV show's final installment, as it may dramatize an alternate reality wherein Asuka has not been savaged by the enemy, any more than separate humans have been aggregated into an undifferentiated lump.

Asked whether Shinji could be said "to have reached a sort of settlement regarding troubles of the heart" by the end of the second movie, Kazuya Tsurumaki has pithily stated: "Well, my personal view is, 'Do we really need to complement these troubles of the heart?' Regardless of whether or not we are complemented, have troubles, or find our answers, interpersonal relations exist, and the world goes on. I thought the last scene meant to say that life goes on" (Tsurumaki 1997).

Throughout the TV series, its reprisal in *Death* and the first portion of *End*, Shinji is continually plagued by his failure to relate adequately to other people — hence, his pathological tendency to withdraw from all intercourse, deep sense of discomfort in the mere presence of boisterous conviviality, and even occasional proclivity to hurt others in order to punish himself. In the second segment of *End*, as shown, Shinji's frustration escalates (at least figuratively) into naked brutality when he fantasizes about strangling Asuka to give full vent to his emotions. Shinji's difficulties in interacting with others, and specifically women, have been complicated from the saga's inception by the fact that he harbors latently erotic feelings for all of the three female characters (Misato, Rei and Asuka) with whom he is in regular contact, yet can only translate those affects into varyingly explicit expressions of embarrassment or vexation. This is largely a corollary of his ongoing dependence on the maternal figure he so brutally and prematurely lost. In *End*, Shinji is given one final opportunity to negotiate and understand his separateness, and willingly embrace it as a fate of his own choice rather than a punishment.

Through its prismatic metaphysical tropes, *End* proposes that interaction is integral to the achievement of a sense of self-identity and inexorably entails a grasp of the demarcations that separate one individual from another. Hence, the plan to exterminate alterity cannot ultimately prevail, since life itself is engendered by dynamic oppositions requiring the existence of multiple subjectivities, of frictions and of tensions — as well the tenacious endurance of the spectres of disappointment and failure. The world, the film intimates, is what one makes of it: a matter of ineluctably tentative and rescindable interpretations. Thus, although *End* constitutes a profoundly innovative contribution to the saga and is undoubtedly sustained by a distinctive visual rhetoric, it should be noted that its pivotal message is essentially consonant with the lessons elliptically proposed by the TV show.

As noted, the image of a movie theater, interwoven with speculations about the nature of dreams, is pivotal to *End*'s multimedia climax. It could, in fact, be argued that the *Evangelion* saga in its entirety functions as a commentary on the affinity between film-viewing and dreaming as cognate expressions of the flimsiness of the real. In constructing an elaborate universe that is at once autonomous and imbricated with the actual world, *Evangelion* offers an alternate dimension in much the same fashion as a dream does. At the same time, in inviting the audience to become absorbed in that parallel world by supplying a uniquely engrossing (and occasionally exacting) viewing experience, the saga draws us into a space akin to that of a dream. Hence, both the narrative form evinced by *Evangelion* and the communicational modality it fosters could be said to partake of oneiric discourse.

The destabilizing power of dreams, and particularly nightmares whose troubling essence eludes description or quantification, is fully captured by *End*'s emphasis on psychological estrangement, lack of balance and cognitive insecurity. These oneiric traces are at times so acute in *Eva*land that the plausibility of ever feeling "at home" anywhere is seriously called into question. Looked at within a specifically Eastern perspective, Anno's vision echoes the message promulgated by Hindu myths in which dreams are deployed as a means of defamiliarizing reality by positing the incongruous and the absurd as no less vivid and palpable than commonsense-driven empirical realms. If Anno resembles Lynch in the treatment of psychodrama, no less potent a link between the two directors is their commitment to the discourse of dreaming.

In watching *Evangelion*, as in dreaming, we are given opportunity to access an alternate realm and lose ourselves for a while in the dramas unfurling before and through our senses. It can only be hoped that upon emerging from the experience, we shall feel in some way elevated — and that upon endeavoring to write about it coherently, we shall at least grasp why it moved us as it did. In proposing that the realities presented at various stages in its trajectory amount to Shinji's dreams, moreover, *Evangelion* prompts us to ponder the question posed by Bruce Kawin: "If a film, which is already both the dream of its maker and the dream of its audience, can present itself as the dream of one of its characters, can it finally appear to dream itself?" (Kawin, p. 5).

Rebuild of Evangelion (Evangelion Shin Gekijouban)
Directors: Hideaki Anno, Kazuya Tsurumaki (2007–2008)

Cumulatively titled *Evangelion Shin Gekijouban*, namely "*Evangelion New Theatrical Version*," the *Rebuild* project encompasses four movies:

1. *Evangelion Shin Gekijouban: Jo* ("Preface": *Evangelion*: *1.0 — You Are [Not] Alone*);
2. *Evangelion Shin Gekijouban: Ha* ("Breaking-Up");
3. *Evangelion Shin Gekijouban: Kyuu* ("Rush");
4. *Evangelion Shin Gekijouban* ("Final Movie"; title yet to be announced).

Jo, *Ha* and *Kyuu*, as *Newtype USA* explains, are analogous to "the Western storytelling concepts of setup, climax and conclusion, but with slightly different emphasis. *Jo* ... means 'prologue,' what happens before the real story begins.... *Ha* ... is when the story really begins. The literal meaning of *ha* is 'destruction' — swift, violent action that rips apart everything that came before.... Normally, *kyuu* marks the end of the story" ("What's in a name," p. 65).

According to the Wikipedia entry for *Rebuild*, *Jo*, *Ha* and *Kyuu* are also musical terms corresponding to the Western concepts of first, second and third movement. These are derived from *Gagaku*: the "elegant music" performed at the Imperial Court for centuries and held to have exerted a major influence on the development of Noh (Wikipedia, the Free Encyclopaedia — *Rebuild of Evangelion*). The new films thus perpetuate the musical pattern adopted in *Death*.

This large-scale project involves Hideaki Anno in the capacity of general director, Kazuya Tsurumaki in that of director for the first film, Yoshiyuki Sadamoto as character designer and Ikuto Yamashita as mechanical designer. To create *Rebuild*, Anno established an independent production company named Khara. The first three films provide an alternate retelling of the TV show incorporating several new scenes, settings and characters, while the fourth installment offers a wholly new conclusion to the saga. Producer Toshimichi Otsuki has commented thus on the project: "Twelve years is enough time for you to be able to look back on earlier works objectively.... [Anno] and his team have gained a lot of experience.... They've matured as animators and as people.... They've gotten older, but they're still full of energy. It's almost like watching kids prepare for a holiday celebration" (Otsuki 2006, p. 30).

The first film was released on home turf in September 2007 and the ensuing features are slated for domestic exhibition over 2008. *1.0* dramatizes the war against the Angels from the first attack seen in the series through to the fifth, culminating with an enhanced version of "Operation Yashima," the mission central to Episode 6. In the series, "Operation Yashima" originates in the advent of Ramiel and realization that the Evas' standard weapons are insufficient to vanquish the invader, to which Misato responds by requisitioning a pioneering positron rifle from the UN forces and powering it with Japan's entire electricity supply. (The mission, incidentally, is named after a tale regarding a seemingly impossible feat to be achieved by recourse to a bow and arrow.) The execution of "Operation Yashima" in *1.0* offers a paradigmatic example of the team's determination to accomplish goals to which it had already aspired in 1995 but could not have realistically pursued at the time. Otsuki indeed maintains that far from constituting "mere sealed-up versions of the TV series," the new films realize "basic ideas and images" that Anno already had "in mind twelve years ago" (Otsuki 2007, p. 63).

While capsulating the action by expunging some of the slower moments, such as protracted pans, and replacing them with shots of greater pithiness, the film nonetheless pays homage to the parent text's episodic format by means of an interstitial and a preview placed after the closing credits. Where casting is concerned, two significant departures from the original show are hinted at. In the closing moments, we see Kaworu awakening at SEELE's behest and declaring his desire to meet Shinji, which suggests that the character will play a more prominent part in *Rebuild* than he did in the series. In addition, the preview briefly introduces a brand-new female character with a very distinctive look.

It is often by graphic and tonal amendments that the new movie asserts most effectively its stylistic autonomy. A case in point is the depiction of Ramiel. Through the implementation of CG effects unavailable when the TV show was produced, Anno's troupe were able to invest the giant shape with variable levels of transparence and translucence, thus potently enhancing the Angel's vibrant aliveness despite its patently inorganic geometry. This example shows that digital technology does not merely lend itself to the generation of eye candy and pyrotechnics: when conscientiously utilized, it can actually produce subtle nuances of great dramatic vigor. The compositing of reflections and lighting effects used in the portrayal of both the Angels and the Evas confirms this proposition. Innovative tools also came into play in the representation of the conventional weapons deployed (to no avail) against the enemy. These display a markedly more three-dimensional presence and textural density. The machinery supporting the Evas in the course of the fight scenes and the infrastructure of Tokyo-3's metamorphic architecture are likewise developed in the movie to communicate a palpable sense of their unique technological properties.

A further change worthy of notice involves character design: Many facial expressions have been intensified, mellowed down or made ambiguous so as to invest the characters' interactions with a wider range of affective gradations. A notable illustration is Rei's mien in the scene (imported from Episode 6) in which she briefs Shinji regarding "Operation Yashima." In the show, the First Child's expression is sternly impassive, which emphasizes the character's proverbial commitment to professional duty over and above personal emotional considerations. In *1.0*, by contrast, Rei's expression is gentler, even concerned, as though to intimate a capacity for compassion and an understanding of Shinji's troubled psyche. Thus, the film capitalizes at once on a thorough integration of CGI to amplify the suppleness and tactility of its action sequences and related equipment, and on character designs that enrich the quieter moments by drawing attention to the complexity of the actors' emotions, and hence to the untold story lurking behind the scenes.

It would be preposterous to assume that one could do justice to *Rebuild* as a whole solely on the basis of a cursory inspection of *1.0*. Patiently awaiting the future movies, we may at least draw inspiration from Anno's words: "'*Eva*' is a story that repeats. It is a story where the main character witnesses many horrors with his own eyes, but still tries to stand up again. It is a story of will; a story of moving forward, if only just a little. It is a story of fear, where someone who must face indefinite solitude fears reaching out to others, but still wants to try" (quoted in "*Gainax Pages: Rebuild of Evangelion*").[3]

CHAPTER 8

His and Her Circumstances (Kareshi Kanojo no Jijou)[1]
Director: Hideaki Anno (1998–1999)

> *Unlike a Gainax anime, there are no mecha battles nor any overt biblical references. Like a Gainax anime, there exists only a provocative psychological and sociological study in its purest form ... from a male and female perspective. Who better to undertake such a daunting task of forming a coherent product out of seemingly random braincandy than the master of obtuse anime himself Anno Hideaki, the man behind* Neon Genesis Evangelion *and a card-carrying member of the original* Honneamise *bratpack?*
> —His and Her Circumstances—*Anime Academy* Review

Director Hideaki Anno has claimed that what attracted him most potently to the manga by Masami Tsuda on which *His and Her Circumstances* is based was its "comedy" (quoted in "[inside] Gainax," p. 16). Nonetheless, in this series as in Anno's whole opus, comedy unfailingly becomes the conduit for the exploration of convoluted psychologies. In this specific case, the darkest facets of human nature are thrown into relief by the show's emphasis on inherently duplicitous personalities. The show's female lead is Yukino Miyazawa, a model student and excellent athlete blessed with immaculate looks who, unsurprisingly, is an object of both admiration and envy for all her classmates. What is more, Yukino never seems to host any doubts as to what she wants from life and how to achieve it. Her dedication to both academic tasks and physical training subjects her to an exacting routine, which she keeps carefully under wraps in order to make her accomplishments appear to be an artless outcome of natural talent.

In fact, everything about Yukino is studiously constructed. Even her publicized tastes in literature and music are minutely tailored to this effect. For example, she pretends to be perusing Salinger while sitting on a bench in the school grounds where everybody can see her and admire her literary preferences. In fact, the book's only connection with Salinger is the cover: Yukino's favorite texts are actually how-to-become-a-millionaire publications such as *Fortune*. Likewise, she claims to have a passion for classical music, and especially Brahms, when in fact she only enjoys pop hits. Yukino's flawless appearance is therefore no more than a veneer that the girl tenaciously maintains in public in order to gain praise. In private, however, she is actually a solipsistic, self-absorbed and praise-hungry slob tormented by insecurity and fear. As Carlos Ross and Eric Gaede have noted, "whenever Yukino goes home, off comes the '*ojousama*' ["queen" or "princess"] façade — and on go the headbands, reading glasses, and sweats. Miss Congeniality is in fact a conniving, petty con artist with a streak of absolute nerdy bliss" (Ross and Gaede). Having enthroned herself as an unparalleled idol, moreover, Yukino lacks any genuine friends.

The only attenuating circumstances one may invoke in Yukino's favor have to do with her exposure to parental pressure: the injunction to excel at all sorts of scholarly, artistic and athletic pursuits appears to have loomed large over her entire childhood. As already noted, culpable parents are never far from Gainax's thematic range. At times, they are presented as overtly callous and exploitative (*Evangelion, This Ugly Yet Beautiful World*); at others, as remiss by default (*Gunbuster, Nadia*); at others still, as blameworthy due to an excess of zeal in the apparent promotion of their offspring's best interest (*His and Her Circumstances*). Ironically, Yukino's younger sisters, Tsukino and Kano, come across as exceptionally laid back, which would seem to indicate that the parents in question somehow managed to work their longing for a perfect daughter out of their system first time around and are quite prepared to leave Yukino's juniors in peace. (Parental attitudes will be discussed in greater details later in this chapter.)

Yukino's hitherto uncontested dominance within the educational domain is challenged when she applies to get into the Hokuhei Senior High School in the industrial suburb of Kawasaki, and comes second in the entrance exams to Souichirou Arima, a handsome, generous, charismatic and academically brilliant young man — in other words, a person who seems to genuinely *be* everything that Yukino has thus far merely *pretended to be*. However, Souichirou harbors a secret no less embarrassing that Yukino's own hidden existence. Reputed to come from an illustrious medical family, the boy actually lives with his aunt and uncle, who took him into their care following the disappearance of Souichirou's biological parents: a pair of petty criminals embroiled in blackmailing and stealing operations. With the sole exception of the boy's foster parents, his entire family takes sadistic glee in intimating that this despicable conduct is to be blamed upon the boy, whom they brand as the "black sheep" of the family (Episode 18, "Progress").

Although Yukino initially vows to pulverize Souichirou's reputation through hard work and titanic determination, driven by her inveterately vindictive disposition, the two duplicitous adolescents actually end up falling in love with each other. The romantic element, it must be stressed, is originally handled, in keeping with Studio Gainax's penchant for redefining deconstructively the conventions of established genres. The series' form-muddling tendencies are overtly emphasized by the "Producer's Notes" contained in the first disc of the *His and Her Circumstances* DVD Box Set released by The Right Stuf International in 2002. Importantly, said notes concurrently stress another key feature of the show, and indeed of Gainax's oeuvre at large, namely, its deliberate withholding of conclusive explanations for its characters' actions, motivations and ultimate objectives: "How to explain *Kare Kano* to someone who has never seen it before ... that's a bit like trying to describe an elephant to a blind person.... As you progress through the series, don't be too surprised to find out that you have to re-evaluate your opinions of many of [the] characters. Finally, don't be too surprised if you ... catch yourself looking through open windows at rainy nights and thinking of the past" ("*His and Her Circumstances*: Producer's Notes").

As Yukino and Souichirou become acquainted with the occluded — and not too pleasant — aspects of their respective personalities, they gradually learn how to be true to their natures and circumstances beyond the sanitized self-images they project in the public domain. In the process, the program charts the ups-and-downs in their relationship as they are persistently tested by school, family problems, and friends. At the same time, the series works as effectively as it undoubtedly does insofar as it is consistently able to counterbalance its deeply introspective moments with outbursts of undilutedly hilarious comedy. Thus, the storyline asserts itself as a delicately balanced blend of sincere romance and exuberant humor, while Anno's directorial style imparts each and every scene with the individual atmosphere it needs in order to strike the required chords. In the course of a single installment, one may experience glee, annoyance, melancholy and irritation in equal measures, without the shift from one mood to another ever feeling arbitrarily forced.

His and Her Circumstances echoes *Evangelion* on the technical plane in its deployment of Anno's favorite expressive strategies: collages, montages, swiftly flashing text, lengthy static scenes and frames from the parent manga. This is not especially surprising when one considers that *His and Her Circumstances* was the first animated show directed by Anno since *Evangelion*. Whereas *Evangelion* uses relatively gentle distortions of its characters at points of heightened emotional intensity, *His and Her Circumstances* adds explicitly SD (i.e., super-deformed or squashed-down) caricatures of the normal personae to the heady brew of its graphic repertoire. Capitalizing on overtly cartoonish and grotesquely infantilized versions of the characters, these aim at exposing their foibles by recourse to parodic humor. Monstrous caricatures depicted in aggressive hues, specifically, come to the fore in shots where unfettered anger dominates the show's precarious balance of emotions.

It is also worth noting, in this regard, that super-deformity of the kind seen in *His and Her Circumstances* is also deployed to comparable dramatic effect in the TV series *Paradise Kiss* (dir. Osamu Kobayashi, 2005). On the whole, the show adheres to the style characteristic of the manga by Ai Yazawa on which it is based, as well as on that of the semi-prequel *Gokinjo Monogatari* (a.k.a. *Neighbourhood Story*) created by the same author and adapted into an animated series by Atsutoshi Unezawa (1995–1996). Accordingly, it exhibits a marked preference for elegant lines in the rendition of the characters' bodies and costumes and arresting facial expressions. Occasionally, however, the SD mode takes over and blatantly unrealistic caricatures gain center stage. What is unusual — and perhaps most memorable — about Kobayashi's use of this technique is its application to serious or painful moments.

Most importantly, *His and Her Circumstances* does not starkly oscillate between realism and distortion but rather offers subtly modulated gradations of both typologies. For example, characters may be portrayed as exhibiting more childlike features and reduced dimensions at moments of uncertainty or embarrassment without actually morphing into *chibi* (i.e., "child body" or "mini-body") versions of the characters in a full-fledged sense of the term. Refined deformation also encompasses the use of silhouettes that are unquestionably realistic yet also highly stylized due to the elimination of all somatic details, or mere retention of one feature intended to heighten a specific personality trait (more often than not, a hobbyhorse of some kind). Another form of distortion used by Anno is the abrupt translation of a character's body from a harmoniously proportioned and smoothly articulated physical frame to a rubberized doll — this is especially useful in communicating emotional helplessness or sheer fatigue. At the same time, a character's own warped perception of her or his environment is frequently conveyed by means of exaggerated perspective, for instance, in frames in which the character in question is shot from below and the only portion of the body one can see is a pair of seemingly huge thighs looming over tiny feet that appear to be yards way from the hips: a distinctively Alice-in-Wonderland look.

It would, of course, be preposterous to deny that numerous formal experiments undertaken in the execution of the show were partly due (especially from Episode 15 onwards) to Gainax's notorious tendency to run out of funds about halfway through a series (both the 39-episode *Nadia* and the 26-episode *Evangelion* provide illustrious antecedents, in this respect). Nevertheless, the financial constraints faced by Anno and his team indubitably constituted something of a blessing in disguise insofar as they were conducive to some of the most dexterous feats to have graced the screen in the entire history of anime. These include the use of paper cut-outs of characters attached to and moved about by means of sticks (Episode 19). The same technique, incidentally, is also deployed to great dramatic effect in Kenji Kamiyama's *Minipato* (2001). Additionally, whole segments of the narrative — most notably in Episode 26 — are told by recourse to manga panels extracted directly from Tsuda's original. The manga-style sketches, in their unsurpassed simplicity, are a lasting testament to the potential held by a lovingly crafted drawing to express more than thousands of words ever could.

It should also be noted, in this respect, that although the show owes its uniqueness as an anime experience to Anno's directorial touch, "Some have argued that Tsuda Masami's wonderfully lively and energetic manga translates into anime form almost by itself" ("*His and Her Circumstances*"- *Anime Academy* Review). As Fred Patten maintains, moreover, the anime's alternation between contrasting graphic modalities is deeply influenced by Tsuda's own style. In his review of the second volume of the manga, in particular, the critic observes: "The art seems to flip-flop between realistic and super-deformed styles, and this sharply differentiates between when the characters are letting themselves be controlled by their emotions ... and when they are acting thoughtfully—a visual sliding scale between the id and the superego" (Patten, p. 186).

Also notable is the employment of stylishly understated grayscale drawings with overtly two-dimensional qualities as backdrops against which a more solidly rendered presence in full color can be made to stand out for dramatic emphasis. The alternation and juxtaposition of still images and animated frames are concomitantly brought into play to achieve a variety of effects depending on contingent circumstances. They may lend the action a farcical edge in scenes in which they display the repercussions of violent collisions (often laced with jocular hints at various martial arts) and of severe vexation, or else they may be deployed to evoke particular emotions with minimalistic restraint and even convey a sense of epiphanic disclosure.

Anno's visual cocktail is simultaneously spiked by the integration of myriad glowing lights, twirls, whorls and spirals, as well as swathes of both even and graded watercolor washes and impressionistic splotches or splashes of pure pigment. All manner of media bolster the show's graphic density—pencil, pastel, wax crayon, chalk, charcoal, felt-tip—as indeed do numerous tools, including brushes, palette knives and airbrushes. Slow pans across banks of stylized roses are recurrently utilized to connote a romantic mood (for both serious and comical purposes), while hearts are incorporated into various frames to symbolize not only romantic attraction but also affection generally (including toward siblings) or the sheer appreciation of beauty in another person (both of the other sex and of one's own). A succinct summary of the show's graphic adventurousness is offered by the following review: "The animation is an integral part of the story and in many ways functions as a completely independent character with its own personality and point of view.... Quite often a character will say one thing only to have the art or text contradict or twist the meaning, providing a deft and efficient method of adding nuance to the story" ("*His and Her Circumstances Anime Web Turnpike* Review").

Also worthy of notice, from a stylistic point of view, is the employment of live-action footage in the closing credits of several episodes. These primarily feature high school interiors shot from intrepid angles. The closing-credit sequence for Episode 19 is among the most dramatic, as it presents cels from the installment being set on fire. Also memorable are the live-action image of a toy train moving through an auditorium-like space filled with dangling lights (Episode 24) and the shot of the ship sailing through icy seas (Episode 26). An overtly self-reflexive moment is supplied by the next episode preview placed at the end of Episode 23, which focuses on a Gainax employee at work in the studio. The next episode previews generally feature the voice actresses for Yukino and her younger sisters Tsukino and Kano reading the script in the recording studio. From Episode 15 onwards, the scenes are starkly minimalized, offering solely the performers' voices over images.

Although some of the more daring stylistic strategies come into play once the show has advanced past the halfway mark, there is plenty of evidence that experimentation had been a vital part of Anno's aesthetic agenda right from the start. This is clearly borne out both by the opening-credit sequence and by Episode 1, "Her Reasons." The former constitutes an adventurous visual preamble of autonomous artistic value, regardless of its thematic connections with the show itself. All of its key images either counterbalance or supplement one another by moving in either opposite or analogous directions. Ascending and descending patterns of motion are concurrently alternated, as are vertical and horizontal orientations. Elegant chromatic harmonies and contrasts aptly enhance the tag's visual impact in conjunction with compelling variations in the pacing of shots.

The theme of Yukino's and Souichirou's duplicitousness provides the sequence's leading thread. This is assiduously communicated through classic visual tropes typically utilized in the articulation of the divided-self topos: doubling, pairing, shadowing, splitting, mirroring, parallelism, juxtaposition and contrast. Additionally, these motifs are interwoven with a plethora of images alluding, contextually, to the characters' cultural setting and, intertextually, to Gainax's own creative trajectory. For example, a portion of the sequence is filled by intensely solarized stills from the live-action footage proposed in the final part of *End of Evangelion*, with its distinctive snapshots of the urban environment at its most prosaic — lustreless buildings, pylons, billboards — as well as a memorable cat that could be regarded as Anno's own avatar.[2]

Episode 1, in turn, instantly proclaims the director's penchant for intrepid juxtapositions of scenes shot in a relatively realistic fashion (by anime standards, that is to say) and jarringly experimentative shots. At times, the transitions from one modality to the other are smooth, even gentle, and the audience is therefore comfortably eased into the action's shift of pace and tenor. At others, they are so abrupt as to feel almost like assaults upon the optic nerve. (*His and Her Circumstances* is most definitely *not*, incidentally, an anime to be watched in excessive proximity to the screen.) The opening episode offers some paradigmatic examples of such brusque transitions. For instance, we are first introduced to Yukino by means of a fairly standard "corridor scene" of the kind one often comes across in school-comedy anime, as she is being profusely adulated by her peers and condescendingly "accepting" their flattery. Then, suddenly, we are treated to a highly stylized rendition of Yukino's self-idealizing mania in which her image rises, literally larger than life, above a crowd represented in the guise of anonymous cardboard cutouts.

A further abrupt shift occurs as Yukino's normal mien is snappily subject to super-deformation: a concomitant of her ire at Souichirou's popularity. Likewise notable is the later scene in which the protagonist admits to being a "fake" and a "lie": as the Yukino one sees in the school sequences, whom she describes as "the elegant me," swiftly turns, the screen changes to an SD version of the coarse and obnoxious Yukino one sees in the domestic domain. The two types of images are also vividly contrasted at the graphic level: while the shots focusing on the "public" Yukino exude an eminently cinematic aura, the SD shots of the "private" Yukino come across as overtly hand-drawn and almost artlessly pigmented.

Yukino's and Souichirou's relationship develops so tentatively and ponderously, threatened by setbacks no less often than it is blessed by progress, that viewers may occasionally feel that the show's animation machinery is sputtering on the verge of switch-off. Nonetheless, the methodically lingering pace adopted by Anno is part and parcel of an intensely realistic portrayal of the characters' evolving feelings and corresponding attitudes. The realism is never impaired but, if anything, enhanced by the director's flamboyant forays into graphic stylization. Key to this engaging depiction is the emphasis placed by Anno on oscillations in preference to neatly defined trajectories and unequivocal peripeteias. The action, accordingly, has no choice but to follow a desultory and discontinuous rhythm as it charts the ebb and flow of human interaction.

As indicated in the analysis of Episode 1, this formal trait declares itself from the very beginning of the show. Episode 2, "Their Secret," for its part, is especially notable in its presentation of the protagonists' both apparent and hidden motives, on the one hand, and of the inchoate nature of their laboriously evolving emotions, on the other. The installment offers two complementary perspectives on Yukino's personality, highlighting both her resentment toward Souichirou and her budding attraction to the boy. Fearful that Souichirou, having accidentally penetrated her devious fabrication, will expose her, Yukino is at first immensely relieved when she finds that he is, in fact, prepared to guard her secret. Relief turns into aggravation, however, once the girl discovers that her schoolmate's silence comes at a high price: She has no choice but to undertake massive extracurricular tasks on Souichirou's behalf (particularly in the area of tedious paperwork pertaining to the countless committees in which he is involved), which makes her feel as though she had effectively become "Arima's servant."

Simultaneously, Yukino realizes that Souichirou's dubious behavior places him on the same shaky moral grounds on which she herself has been so persistently standing. Yukino further senses that this affinity may indicate that she and Souichirou are somehow made for each other and that she might, ironically, be falling in love with him. Having, up to this point, been in absolute control of all her moves, the girl now dispiritedly concludes: "It feels like I've lost touch with reality." At this stage in the story, the heroine may appear weaker than her male counterpart due to her inner dividedness in the face of his seemingly unequivocal agenda. Nevertheless, nothing is ever black and white in the microcosm of *His and Her Circumstances* (as in the macrocosm of Anno's opus at large), and it soon transpires that the boy, who has liked Yukino for quite some time, is actually using his blackmailing ruse as a pretext for spending more and more time with her as they wade through mountains of forms, documents and data.

In Episode 3, "His Reasons," it is Souichirou's turn to step to the foreground as his own murky past is unsentimentally exposed. In a particularly moving sequence, we are presented with a shot of Souichirou as a small child, huddled and weeping in a dark room as the rain comes pelting down, followed by images of the toddler getting brutally spanked and then sitting alone in a snowfall. The frames derive considerable pathos from the alternation of a gloomy grayscale in the representation of the interiors and of the snowy scenery, and lurid juxtapositions of red and black in the depiction of a gnarled tree and of ominous metallic structures. From this point onwards, rain, concrete and steel rendered by recourse to those chromatic schemes will recur as objective correlatives for Souichirou's depressive episodes. It is also noteworthy that Anno, revamping a ploy previously utilized in *Evangelion*, portrays infantile and teenage versions of the same character within a single scene as an economical means of evoking the sense of a split personality. This is clearly borne out by *Evangelion*'s Episode 22, in which the strategy is applied to the depiction of Asuka as she is about to touch her psychological nadir. The sequence is also intensely redolent of the playground scenes from *End of Evangelion* in which a toddler-sized Shinji dispiritedly erects and then knocks down a sandcastle to the unnerving accompaniment of a steadily oscillating swing.

Souichirou's ghosts also take center stage in Episode 8, "Her Everyday/Beneath the Blooming Forest of Cherry Blossoms," in which the character reflects on the numbing sense of loneliness that haunted him prior to meeting Yukino despite his unparalleled popularity. Echoing Shinji's account of his life before becoming an Eva pilot, Souichirou observes that in the pre–Yukino days, life tended to go peacefully by without any real emotions ever coming into play.

The split-self trope foregrounded in Episode 3 is again invoked in Episode 24, "Different Story 1," in which Souichirou feels increasingly dragged back into the tenebrous past in which nobody wanted him — or even tolerated his presence — and recognizes with trepidation the ever-escalating degree of his dependence on Yukino. In the episode's most poignant moments, Yukino gently but forcibly encourages her companion to enter the dreaded psychic territory — symbolized by a pitch-black sky ruptured by blood-red clouds — in which Souichirou's infantile incarnation is stranded, utterly alone and dejected. Souichirou at first tries to order the child to emerge from the dismal space in a peremptory tone, which only causes his younger self to cry harder. Yukino reminds him that this is not how he would have wished to be treated when he was indeed a small kid, and Souichirou gradually realizes that his sole hope of rescuing the weeping toddler — in other words, of allowing his submerged self to surface and accepting it once and for all — is to break through the barrier he has so carefully erected between his current and former personae and reach out to the bereft child with kindness and tenderness.

The frustratingly gordian nature of Souichirou's and Yukino's romance is incisively communicated by Episode 4, "Her Problem," where the protagonists are shown to have reached an awkward phase in their relationship in which they are obviously more than just friends, yet less than a dating couple. Although they have bravely resolved to drop their masks, they are so used to playing roles in preference to acting spontaneously that an affective barrier persists. Yukino, who has always accomplished anything she ever set her eyes upon rapidly and with panache, can barely believe how arduous it is for her to confess her feelings without disaffecting Souichirou or else getting hurt. Yukino's sister Kano wisely opines that Yukino's emotional deadlock is a corollary of her constitutional tendency to give precedence to her personal feelings over anything else.

The extent to which intersubjective duties weigh upon the main characters' personal lives is vividly demonstrated in Episode 5, "Days of the Labyrinth," in which Yukino and Souichirou are required to supervise the preparations for the school's "Sportsfest," which inevitably draws them apart. To further complicate matters, the character of Hideaki Asaba begins to interfere with the relationship, claiming Souichirou for himself. Yukino initially detests Hideaki, not least due to his brash remarks on her unalluring looks, justifying her feelings on the grounds that the boy intends to "use" Souichirou as his "wingman" in the construction of the ultimate harem. The truth, however, is that Yukino sees Hideaki as a competitor threatening to take Souichirou away from her. Having got off on the wrong foot, Yukino and Hideaki spontaneously befriend each other the moment they realize they are not so dissimilar after all but actually share some vital personality traits — primarily, a shamelessly manipulative streak.

Having expanded its purview with the addition of the peacocky Hideaki to the cast, *His and Her Circumstances* ventures further into the realm of interpersonal relations in Episode 9, "Atonement for the Moratorium," and Episode 10, "Everything from Now," in which Yukino discovers a lethal enemy in the person of her classmate Maho Izawa. Maho suspects that Yukino has been merely playing a studiously scripted part all along, and never truly acted in accordance with natural inclinations. By means of astute argumentation and persuasive rhetoric, the girl manages to convince her classmates of the veracity of her account and, relatedly, of the validity of her character assassination. Yukino, accordingly, is rapidly cast in the role of the class pariah. With refreshing humility, she accepts her fate and tersely states: "I brought this down on myself ... I deceived them ... I guess I have to pay for it now." As pragmatic as ever, however, the heroine establishes that there is simply no point in morbidly regretting her past actions without initiating any positive change and resolves to disclose her genuine identity at last: "This is the beginning of my real self," she proudly announces at a climactic juncture in Episode 9. It is as a result of this courageous decision that Yukino begins, at last, to make some real friends who are not exclusively concerned with obtaining her assistance on academic matters.

Anno's passion for multilayered personalities driven by tangled motives sonorously asserts itself when it later transpires that Maho, too, has been pursuing an unpalatable agenda in her public humiliation of Yukino. Episode 10 indeed reveals that her principal objective has been to manipulate the other girls in order to achieve a position of power over them and that the deceitful Yukino has simply supplied her with a pretext for carrying the scheme through to fruition. When Maho's own shenanigan is uncloaked and it becomes blatant that she and Yukino are not vastly unlike after all, the two girls commodiously open up to each other. The seeds of an enduring friendship have thus been sown — laboriously, no doubt, but then none of the emotional journeys portrayed in *His and Her Circumstances* is ever anything other than toilsome.

The kind of dramatic twist orchestrated in Episode 5, with a focus on the enmity between Yukino and Hideaki, is reproposed with variations in emphasis and tone toward the end of the series, when Yukino becomes gradually acquainted with Takefumi Tonami. (This novel addition to Anno's cast is a transfer student introduced in Episode 19, "Fourteen Days 1.") Initially antagonistic toward each other, Yukino and Takefumi come to discover crucial affinities in their intrinsic natures. Feeling connected, specifically, by the realization that they both had to conceal their authentic identities for a long time, they eventually become close friends. The decisive shift occurs in Episode 22, "Fourteen Days 4," in which we also find that in keeping with the dramatic logic pervading the entire composition of *His and Her Circumstances*, no resolution is without a downside. Thus, although the outcome of Yukino's and Takefumi's initially conflictual relationship is positive, it is nonetheless clouded by Souichirou's suspicion that Takefumi is after Yukino's heart — ironically, Takefumi in fact regards Souichirou himself as the unsurpassable role model.

The emotional impasse dramatized in Episodes 4 and 5 is partially overcome in Episode 6, "Your Voice That Changes Me," in which Yukino and Souichirou are drawn closer and closer together. Nevertheless, the two characters' knotty personalities still prevent them from fully opening up to each other even once they have managed to transcend the original stalemate. Souichirou is baffled by Yukino's "selfish" and "twisted" disposition, yet incongruously wonders whether he is truly "worthy" of her love. Yukino, for her part, appears to doubt that she will ever fathom the boy's secret depths. Stylistically, this installment provides an intriguing formal experiment in that it dramatizes the same events from Yukino's and Souichirou's points of view by turns, thus embracing a multiperspectival approach that both recalls *Evangelion* and anticipates *FLCL*.

Episode 7, "Their Estrangement," provides an outstanding example of the transformation brought upon the two teenagers by their relationship (and attendant desire to redefine the values and ambitions they treasured prior to its inception), showing that Yukino and Souichirou do not care in the slightest about the mediocrity of their exam results — a consequence of their constant dating. Yukino has dropped to thirteenth position and Souichirou to third, which leads the girl to suspect that her boyfriend has been studying in secret. However, Yukino's lingering competitiveness does not prevent her from frankly stating her priorities. Hence, although the school authorities regard the couple's paltry achievements as a very serious problem indeed, maintaining that dating is incompatible with success in life, Yukino responds by persisting in her intention to be her real self at last and accordingly place personal feelings above academic obligations. The situation deteriorates to the point that the parents are summoned. Episode 7 makes it abundantly clear that in the protagonists' cultural milieu, no personal relationship is allowed to unfold without external interferences resulting from overarching social and moral expectations.

As noted throughout this study and hinted at earlier in this chapter, it is a recurrent component of Gainax's cachet to depict selfish adults blind to their offspring's needs and aspirations. *His and Her Circumstances* is no exception: Souichirou is obviously the victim of parental abuse of the direst order, while the subplot revolving around the supercute but quite unsocialized persona of Tsubasa Shibahime serves to consolidate the theme of familial neglect. Souichirou's guardians' and Yukino's parents' magnanimous response to the sudden deterioration in their charges' academic performance provides a refreshing change of tone on Anno's part. Yukino's father, whose behavior is typically more akin to that of an older brother than to that of a full-fledged parent, does not at first exhibit an especially mature attitude, insofar as he essentially regards the school's reprimand as an opportunity to "fight for love." He does, however, persuasively argue in defense of his daughter's rights, indicating that it is precisely because he cares deeply about her intellectual and emotional autonomy that he does not wish to dominate her choices. Thinking and feeling for oneself, Mr. Miyazawa believes, far surpasses in value any kind of material or scholastic success. Voicing Gainax's own philosophy, Yukino's father adamantly maintains that "a single day in high school is far more precious than a month is in adulthood." It is through a quintessentially Annoesque touch of dramatic genius that the character is enabled to morph from a peripheral actor bordering on the figure-of-fun category into a full-rounded sensibility.

The liberal outlook embraced by both of Yukino's parents could at least in part be attributed to personal experience: They married young against the wishes of Mrs. Miyazawa's father — whose relationship with Mr. Miyazawa is still of a cat-and-mouse nature — and know how crucial it is to learn to recognize one's authentic feelings and to treasure them against all odds. A prequel to the portrayal of Yukino's parents presented in Episode 7 is retrospectively provided by Episode 16, "Perpetuating Line," in which it is revealed that Mr. Miyazawa, like Souichirou, was parentless and left bereft at a relatively young age by the death of his grandfather and guardian — a crisis that his wife to be helped him overcome with equal doses of compassion and courage.

When, in Episode 7, Souichirou's foster father endorses Mr. Miyazawa's position, pithily declaring "our son is a gift," the faculty adviser for freshmen Mr. Kawashima (responsible for convoking the adults in the first place) concedes that he, too, has something to learn from younger people and that he is delighted to be finally dealing with students who can "think for themselves." The character of Mr. Kawashima will incrementally display a truly endearing personality as the series develops. This shines forth in its full colors in Episode 23 "Fourteen Days 5," in which he agrees to sponsor the play, written by Yukino's friend Aya Sawada (a budding author of great promise), in which Yukino, Maho and Tsubasa are meant to perform in the course of the imminent school festival.

His and Her Circumstances gains increasing dramatic momentum with the introduction of the aforementioned character of Tsubasa, her putatively well-intentioned but dolefully immature father and her stepbrother Kazuma Ikeda — a charismatic punk rocker. The Tsubasa story arc encompasses Episode 11, "At the End of the First School Term," Episode 12, "The Place of Happiness," and Episode 13, "On the Subjectivity of Happiness." These installments are replete with humor in the representation of the girl's father's utterly irrelevant excursions into film criticism (when he should actually be confronting a major familial crisis), and of Tsubasa's furious reaction when Kazuma addresses her as "little sister" even though — albeit petite — she is actually his senior. Nonetheless, painful chords are struck by the depiction of the girl's gradual negotiation of her demotion from unique object of worship on her dad's part to a rather marginal position within the reconfigured familial structure, and concomitant decision to accept her new role in a brave attempt to be "happy" after all.

An elaborate intersubjective web is incrementally spun as the series progresses through the integration of yet more supporting personae and secondary narrative trajectories. Particularly intriguing is the subplot pivoting on Takefumi and his personal aspirations, articulated progressively over Episodes 19 through 26. This diegetic strand attests to the richness and diversity of the relational tapestry woven by Anno's show. Quiet, composed and handsome, Takefumi is actually animated by an all-consuming desire for revenge. The object of his machinations is Yukino's friend Tsubaki Sakura — a tomboy endowed with remarkable athletic abilities but lamentably scarce academic aptitude — who shielded Tonami throughout his early school years from fierce bullying triggered by his obesity. Tsubaki's protective behavior, misinterpreted by Takefumi as a sign of sincere concern, turned out to be merely the outcome of a teacher's instructions, and this painful discovery provoked the boy's yearning for vengeance. Eventually, Takefumi recognizes that his pathological aversion to Tsubaki is, in fact, craftily disguised affection, while Tsubaki herself (having thus far professed a preference for girls) discovers that she reciprocates the feeling.[3]

A further digression into the broader network of relationships unfolding around the protagonists is offered by Episode 25, "Different Story 2," in which Yukino's youngest sister Kano is convinced that she is being stalked by a girl from her school. Kano turns out to be mistaken, her imagination having been arguably overstimulated by the fiction to which she is practically addicted. The humorously overinflated tone in which the adventure is couched, bordering on the mock epic as it does, provides one of the entire show's most felicitous touches. Most significantly, such "digressions never turn into distractions ... and always manage to add something to Yukino and Soichiro's [sic] relationship" ("*His and Her Circumstances Anime Web Turnpike* Review").

While endeavoring to expand the scope of its psychological investigation through the inclusion of a galvanizing gallery of ancillary characters, *His and Her Circumstances* concurrently offers a bold formal experiment in its periodic recapitulation of the events dramatizing the developing bond between its protagonists in varyingly condensed or telescoped fashions — most notably, in Episode 14, "The Story Until Now (Part 1)," and Episode 15 "The Qualities That Appear Beyond That Voice," in which virtuoso distillations of the most salient components of Episodes 1 through 8 and Episodes 9 through 13, respectively, are proposed.

No less commendable a facet of Anno's style lies with his use of humor as a means of preventing potentially oversentimental scenes from deteriorating into mawkish melodrama. A paradigmatic example is supplied in Episode 17, "His Flitting," by the scene in which Souichirou returns from a Kendo tournament that has kept him away from Yukino for several days and a moment that could only too easily have come across as soap-operatic actually yields a comic flourish. The Miyazawa family dog Pero Pero indeed manages to reach Souichirou and kiss him before Yukino has even fully realized that the boy is on the scene, which renders her characteristically furious. The humor, as is often the case throughout *His and Her Circumstances*, is intensified by a stylistic shift to the caricatural modality.

The series' finale, and especially Episode 26, "Fourteen Days 6," is unresolved. The protagonists have evidently not reached a conclusive stage in their maturation, which, given their ages, could hardly be expected, and are therefore still very much *in medias res*. This is demonstrated by the fluctuating nature of their reciprocal feelings. Souichirou, having embarked upon his relationship with Yukino as the seemingly more rational and self-possessed party, is now increasingly haunted by his abysmal past and tends to cling to Yukino as his only anchor to reality. As a result, he wishes to possess her and cut her off from the rest of the world even though, paradoxically, he realizes that this longing is utterly incongruous with his admiration for the girl's freedom of spirit as one of her most commendable qualities.

These meandering emotions drag him further and further into the "darkness" he has so scrupulously sought to keep at bay since childhood. Yukino, for her part, remains deeply loyal to Souichirou and indeed aspires to spend more time with him but her obsessive need for his constant presence little by little gives way to the realization that the boy is a "separate" being with an autonomous existence of his own and that she, too, must foster new interests beyond both her formerly school-driven self and her recently developed romantic life. She and Souichirou may well be together "forever"— accordingly, it is possible that the main characters' teenage romance will evolve into an adult relationship in the same way as the liaison between Yukino's parents did.

Alternatively, they may end up parting with or without a modicum of angst to be negotiated in the process. As Yukino puts it in Episode 24, it is feasible that she and Souichirou met in the first place so that they could alter each other for the better through a mutual encouragement to understand and come to terms with their true personalities. However, this does not automatically entail that they will be bound together permanently: as they meet new people and open up to fresh influences, they are destined to continue changing. The development foreseen by Yukino is, therefore, ineluctably indefinite. Anno does not presume to know what will happen to his personae past the series' closing installment, which is ultimately what makes *His and Her Circumstances* such an endearing and captivating story.

In its treatment of the murkier facets of human relationality, *His and Her Circumstances* could be said to echo *Evangelion*'s own concern with the inextricability of the individual from a tangled network of interpersonal obligations. At the same time, its somber moments bear affinities to the overall tone exhibited by the TV series *Rumbling Hearts* (dir. Tetsuya Watanabe, 2003–2004). This show's themes are far more overtly harrowing than any of the narrative ingredients brought into play by *His and Her Circumstances*. Its take on the interdependence of singular and collective destinies is, however, comparable to Anno's.

Instantly distinguished by endearing character designs and impeccably executed backgrounds for both its urbanscapes and its natural scenery, *Rumbling Hearts* demonstrates how generic formulae can be bent and reimagined when they fall into the hands of an inspired director and a talented animation team. The series indeed sets out as a fairly standard school romance, peppered with touches of slapstick and allusions to sports-based drama and furnished with a fundamentally predictable cast: the cocky teenage girl Mitsuki, her timid female counterpart Haruka, the laid-back youth Takayuki and his sidekick Shinji. However, *Rumbling Hearts* morphs into something much darker and deeper as the main characters' whole lives are suddenly disrupted, and their aspirations shattered beyond any hope of repair.

Disaster hits when Haruka, who has had a crush on Takayuki for as long as she can remember and just lately started going out with the boy (largely thanks to Mitsuki's efforts on her behalf), becomes the victim of a car accident that precipitates her into a three-year-long coma. Plagued by guilt, having indirectly caused Haruka's involvement in the accident, Takayuki is thrown into a numbing depression. Mitsuki, who also feels deeply guilty due to her own oblique responsibility for the tragedy, endeavors to rescue the young man from his state of inertia, and the two become gradually involved in a tortuous romantic liaison. As they struggle to rebuild their lives, Takayuki and Mitsuki tentatively alternate between a proclivity to hold onto to the past and a longing for fresh beginnings. In the process, viewers are both encouraged to empathize with the characters and to acknowledge the extent to which they are personally accountable for their predicament, acknowledging their altruism, on the one hand, and self-dramatizing egotism, on the other.

On the diegetic plane, the show is most remarkable in virtue of its resolute avoidance of sequential linearity and adoption instead of a multilayered perspective that allows the narrative to travel back and forth in time. This ploy powerfully highlights the emotional tug-of-war at the heart of the story. The interweaving of tropes derived from the time-honored traditions of mythology and fairy tale with a dispassionate dissection of some of the most contorted sensibilities in the entire history of anime imaginatively enhances the series' density.

Rumbling Hearts pursues the dark side of romantic anime so trenchantly, yet not monolithically, delved into by *His and Her Circumstances*. Indeed, with the exception of a sprinkling of slapstick gags revolving around Takayuki's waitressing coworkers, the series is unequivocally pathos-laden. Another popular anime romance of the early 2000s, the TV show *Peach Girl* (dir. Hiroshi Ishiodori, 2005), based on Miwa Ueda's cherished manga series of the same title, recalls several of the more lighthearted moments in Anno's series. The English versions of both *Rumbling Hearts* and *Peach Girl*, it should be noted, were directed by Zach Bolton, which in itself invites a comparative assessment of the two programs as embodiments of the conflicting sides of anime romance.

The narrative of Ishiodori's program pivots on high-school student Momo (the Japanese word for "peach," incidentally), as she tirelessly endeavors to dispel the image conveyed to her schoolmates by her glamorous looks (including a too-die-for suntan and a flaming mane that result not from vanity but from a staunch commitment to swimming). Branded by many as a tarty bimbo, and cast very much against her will into the role of outsider within the school community, Momo is actually a conscientious and motivated student. Her only friend, the apparently innocent and well-meaning Sae, quickly turns out to be a ruthless antagonist, hellbent on accruing everything Momo possesses to her own personal image and discredit Momo herself in the process.

Cheesy as this may sound, *Peach Girl* manages to deliver a dispassionate and realistic anatomy of secretiveness, jealousy, vanity and greed, which is precisely what links it most overtly with Anno's show. Indeed, it could be argued that in its more intense episodes, *Peach Girl*'s content is dramatically on a par with the emotional and psychological turbulence explored in *His and Her Circumstances*. The ethical lesson communicated by *Peach Girl*, moreover, directly echoes the message promulgated by Anno in his own typically idiosyncratic fashion, namely, the exigency to trust honest and impartial communication as an ultimately more dependable — though no doubt demanding — guarantee of genuine relationality than any amount of Machiavellian scheming.

CHAPTER 9

FLCL
(FLCL)

Director: Kazuya Tsurumaki (2000)

"Bizarre" and "random" are understatements of unimaginable magnitude. Nevertheless, regarding the plot, FLCL bats a thousand. Naota's futile struggle to live a normal life is at once hilarious and harrowing, a conflict that lays the foundation for a fantastic animated journey. The bizarre premise functions perfectly within the series' frantic pacing, and the diverse offerings of fascinating characters invite the viewer's empathy.

— Jonathan Mays

This six-part OVA follows Naota Nandaba, a schoolboy inhabiting a motherless home with his baseball-coaching grandfather Shigekuni and his licentious father Kamon in the imaginary and initially peaceful town of Mabase, a nondescript conglomerate if one excepts the monstrous factory "Medical Meccanica," believed to produce medical machinery, that is situated on its edge and shaped like a giant, steam-emitting iron. (Please note that although the spelling "Meccanica" is used in the show itself, for example, in the scene in which the character of Haruko breaks into the factory early in the story, DVD covers tend to use the alternate spelling "Mechanica" as do reviewers. The location is hereafter referred to as M.M.)

Naota is in awe of his older brother Tasuku (who remains unseen in the story), a baseball champion who has moved to the United States to play the game professionally. Naota's quotidian schedule includes going to school, dealing with his brother's sexually unfulfilled girlfriend Mamimi Samejima (perhaps an orphan or a homeless runaway), and returning to the parental dwelling, with utterly tedious, suffocating repetitiveness. One of the most endearing facets of the protagonist's personality lies with his insistent reiteration, episode after episode, that nothing ever happens in Mabase — even as preposterously extraordinary events unfold.[1] On the one hand, this disposition reflects the mind-set of an insecure kid struggling to understand himself and his environment and adopting a blasé attitude as a defense mechanism. Impersonating with little conviction what he regards as a truly mature character is, ironically, the primary cause behind Naota's resistance to growing up. On the other hand, the boy's seemingly incongruous stance encapsulates the pervasive sense of the absurd, and attendant rhetoric, exhibited by *FLCL* as a whole. Naota's predicament, in accordance with the broader worldview presented by the OVA at large, alludes to an existential condition of unremitting mutability and uncertainty. At the same time, it calls attention to the sheer *joy* entailed by the construction of a raucous and scattergun assortment of disconnected incidents as a worthy quest in its own right.

Naota's routine is upset early in Episode 1 when he is hit by a Vespa driven by the exuberantly insubordinate Haruko Haruhara (a.k.a. Raharu Haruha), a pink-haired young woman wielding a 4001 Rickenbacker bass guitar with a pull-start motor, which she uses to hit the boy on the head. Nicknamed by Naota's mates the "Vespa woman," Haruko is reputed to carry a curse destined to blight anybody and anything she comes into contact with. It soon becomes obvious that regardless of any such rumors, she is hiding some troublesome secrets. Matters are not helped by the eruption out of Naota's skull of shapes that hatch into sizeable techno-monsters. Hints are dropped right from the start at the possibility of Haruko being some kind of secret agent harboring more than a casual interest in the iron-shaped factory. It eventually transpires that the mysterious young woman is an alien who has come to Mabase to get hold of an entity named "Atomsk," held captive by M.M., with whom she intends to merge so as to absorb its powers. Atomsk, also known as the "Pirate King," is an alien force so mighty as to be capable of kidnapping entire planets. The character's name is derived from the title of a political thriller created by the science fiction author Cordwainer Smith (a.k.a. Paul Myron Anthony Linebarger, 1913–1966).

Naota would appear to be Haruko's surreptitious means of opening up a special conduit or portal—dubbed "N.O. Channel"—held to abet her mission. As explained in the fan site *Ultimate FLCL*, the "power of N.O. is what lets items be pulled out of characters' foreheads. N.O. comes from the cooperation of the right and left sides of the brain. When it is activated (usually from extreme scenarios, including stress and duty) things can be pulled from anywhere in the universe" (*Ultimate FLCL: FAQ*). Pretending to be an itinerant housekeeper, Haruko moves in with Naota and his guardians—adults whose conduct, in a characteristically Gainaxian vein, evince questionable moral standards. Kamon, in particular, sees Haruko's presence as an opportunity for engaging in some sexy "*FLCL*" (more about this word later) and grows resentful, in the course of the show, as his son and the "maid" show signs of mutual affection. The tension escalates into glaring bellicosity in Episode 5, in which Naota and Kamon engage in a potentially lethal war game.

Haruko's origin and intentions become clearer following the introduction into the story of Amarao, commander of the Interstellar Immigration Bureau—a secret department of the government's Foreign Embassy whose principal task is to keep aliens away from humans. Amarao is hell-bent on boycotting Haruko's mission not only for professional reasons, however. In fact, he appears to have also a personal axe to grind as a result of a past liaison with the alien girl likely to have been very similar to Naota's present relationship with Haruko; hence, Amarao's warnings to the boy regarding older women. Whatever the precise nature of the officer's connection with the alien, there can be little doubt that his self-confidence and masculine pride have not emerged from it unscathed. In fact, his insecurity is exposed by the pathological attention he devotes to his self-image: He exercises obsessively even in the midst of delicate operations, is deeply concerned about getting the precise shade of his hair dye just right and relies on his eyebrows to confer him an aura of authoritative manliness.

The latter constitute Amarao's most distinctive feature and consist of wafers of *nori* (dried seaweed). Practically everybody the officer comes into contact with, and especially his assistant Kitsurubami, finds this attribute not just puzzling but even downright repulsive. Haruko remains unimpressed, however, cheekily dismissing this accessory as a feeble indicator of virility and maturity. (It should be noted that the commander also uses his artificial eyebrows as putative protection against N.O. Channels.) The alien girl is most stridently disdainful in the scene in which Amarao's head (for a change) sprouts an elliptically phallic growth and she comments on its paltry size — indeed, claiming that Naota can do better than that.

Amarao's solipsistic — and Haruko-dominated — take on reality is confirmed by his account of Atomsk's activities, which is accompanied by an image of the alien entity in the shape of a muscly giant covered in an enticing pattern of brightly colored stripes. At the end of the OVA, however, Atomsk's true form is revealed to be that of a huge crimson phoenix-like bird. Amarao has obviously projected his personal fantasies onto the creature, investing him with literally larger-than-life masculine connotations as a result of his conviction that Haruko is in love with the Pirate King and the mighty alien must therefore resemble a human competitor.

One of the creatures springing out of Naota's cranium, a two-meter tall robot with a television set for a head and formidable metamorphic powers, is named "Canti" and becomes another regular occupier of the Nandaba residence. Employed largely in the undertaking of household chores and as an errand boy, the robot (the first specimen in the category to have been designed by Yoshiyuki Sadamoto) also appears endowed with radiological skills. (At one point, this talent enables Haruko to establish that Naota's head does not contain a brain.)

Canti has actually been manufactured by M.M. and contains Atomsk, as borne out by the fact that the Pirate King's symbol appears on the *mecha*'s TV screen when he combines with Naota and thus enters its martial dimension. It is suggested that Atomsk has used Canti to escape from M.M., and that Haruko has inadvertently sabotaged the Pirate King's plans by splitting its core between Naota and Canti. The idea that Naota and Canti are complementary parts of one and the same entity is corroborated by the sequences in which the otherwise meek and clumsy *mecha* (brain-damaged by Haruko's smashing of his TV head) merges with the boy and thus morphs into a formidable fighting machine — the red sphere Canti shoots out in its cannon mode, notably, is Naota himself. It also transpires that M.M. had intended to use Canti — and Atomsk's power hosted therein — to activate its numerous ironing plants and thus flatten out whole planets. The reasons behind this scheme are not overtly explained, though Amarao suggests that ironing out the creases of entire lands is akin to eliminating a human being's cerebral folds and thus suppress the ability to think.

The robot, however, is believed by Mamimi to be a supernatural entity — possibly as a result of the halo and wings it flaunts in the scenes in which it roams the desolate suburbs at night. It is indeed Mamimi that dubs it Canti after "Cantide-sama," the "god of dark things." The girl's fantasies are nourished by the portable video game she plays obsessively — a pursuit, it is intimated in Episode 2, that might be ominously linked with the ever-increasing cases of arson disrupting the town. The link between Mamimi and fire is reinforced by the revelation that the first case of arson occurred six years prior to the events presented in the show, and that its object was the school where she and Tasuku met as small kids. Spine-chilling shots of the fire-centered rituals in which the girl indulges — apparently in order to honor Canti — complicate that speculative connection to surreal extremes. But then, what is *not* surreal about *FLCL*? The title itself is a baffling conundrum. As the *Gainax Pages* review of the OVA explains, "*FLCL*, or *Furi-Kuri* (or *Fooly Cooly*) ... derives from the Japanese habit, especially among modern teenagers, of creating new Japanese words by combining the first syllables of English words.... 'FLCL' doesn't actually stand for anything specific, however. It's used deliberately ambiguously ... to connote sexual, exciting, and random things" ("*Gainax Pages* reviews: *FLCL*").

Like *Gunbuster*, *FLCL* invites episode-by-episode analysis. This is largely because, like the 1988 OVA, Kazuya Tsurumaki's show discloses its thematic and visual complexity incrementally, with each installment contributing a distinctive twist, complication or elucidation to the cumulative story arc. One further reason is that *FLCL*, like *Otaku no Video* before it, is not only an autonomously developing series but also a parodic metacommentary on Gainax's evolution up to the point of its production. The OVA's director has emphasized this proposition in an interview conducted by Owen Thomas on behalf of *Akadot*: "For *FLCL* I wanted to portray the entire history of Gainax, and each episode has symbols of what happened behind the scenes on each of Gainax's shows" (Tsurumaki 2001). Although it is not absolutely indispensable to be acquainted with Gainax's prismatic output in order to enjoy *FLCL*, it is undeniable that total lack of familiarity with external points of reference garnered from other productions is likely to breed frustration. In the course of the analysis offered in the paragraphs that follow, parallels between particular *FLCL* episodes and previous Gainax productions will be drawn.

Episode 1, "Fooly Cooly," opens with a perfect example of *FLCL* at its most mellow, focusing on an exchange between Naota and Mamimi set in the vicinity of the bridge destined to become one of the show's most recurrent locations. The only drama, so to speak, consists of Mamimi's efforts to make out with Naota on the pretext that unless she gives vent to her erotic drives, she will "overflow," as a result of which "something amazing" might happen. Naota remains quite self-possessed, however, adamant in his conviction that nothing remarkable ever occurs in Mabase. Once the boy's life has been taken by storm by the appearance on the scene of the unruly Haruko, he faces a chain of inexplicable events. As if getting run over by a super-powered Vespa and hit on the head with a bass guitar were not unsettling enough, he soon discovers a peculiar growth on his brow (this will turn out to be a *mecha*'s finger). Additionally, when he goes to the hospital to have his condition examined, he is once again set upon by Haruko disguised as a nurse — and eager to whack him again. The seamless blend of freaky horror and cuteness exhibited by the portrayal of the alien girl in these scenes represents one of *FLCL*'s most inspired graphic flourishes.

Having escaped in the nick of time and believing he has left Haruko behind for good, Naota reaches the parental home for a well-deserved rest. His peace is not to last, however: When he descends to the kitchen for dinner, he finds Haruko comfortably stationed at the table wolfing down noodles and deep in nonsensical conversation with Naota's father (whom she also appears to have run over in the meantime) and grandfather. The conversation is rendered in manga format in a sequence that blatantly glories in intertextuality. This is attested to by references to the seminal *mecha* franchise *Gundam* (1979 and beyond) and to its creator Yoshiyuki Tomino, as well as allusions to Jean-Luc Godard, the champion of the "cut-up" technique so consistently favored by Gainax's animators. The OVA's director has explained his decision to break out of conventional animation and use manga panels instead on the grounds that he enjoys "manga, not only to read, but the visuals. The pen drawings, the frame breakdowns and layouts" (Tsurumaki 2001).

Haruko is obviously determined to take Naota's life over for good. Yet, she is not the only woman in the boy's existence to give him cause for concern: in fact, once he discovers that Mamimi has visited the family bakery and left some photographs documenting Naota's accident (Mamimi deploys her camera obsessively), he dashes off into the night to find her, presumably worried about her own well-being. In the nocturnal bridge sequence that follows, we are treated to a remarkable illustration of *FLCL*'s penchant for producing humorous situations out of dialogue in which characters speak at cross purposes:

> Mamimi: He gave me a lot. [*She seems to be alluding to the stale bread which Kamon has given her at the Nandaba family bakery.*]
>
> Naota: Did he send you a letter? Hasn't he contacted you at all? My brother, I mean, how much do you like him?

[*Naota has obviously taken Mamimi's statement as a reference to her relationship with his sibling.*]
Mamimi: It's hard...
[*She might still be talking about the bread or else have switched to the topic introduced by Naota and referring to her feelings about Tasuku's absence.*]
Naota: You saw the sign at our bakery — that bread's old.
[*Now it is Naota's turn to shift gears inconsequentially and reverse the drift of the dialogue whereas Mamimi would appear to have moved on.*]

In the wake of this relatively quiet segment, the action gains momentum, revealing the true nature of Naota's mysterious, horn-shaped bump. Two robots spectacularly emerge from it amidst the clamor of siren noises issuing from M.M.: One is the aforementioned Canti while the other merely amounts to a gigantic hand that Canti severs from its body before the full-fledged *mecha* has a chance to materialize, belonging to a creature meant by M.M. to prevent Canti — and hence Atomsk — from escaping their precinct. The second robot is destroyed by Canti, which thereafter becomes a member of the Nandaba family, as noted. Interestingly, Canti is red in the fight sequence, which reflects his hosting of Atomsk's powers, but fades to blue once the enemy has been vanquished. From now on, Canti will regain the Atomsk-related coloration only upon combining with Naota, who contains the other half of the Pirate King's essence. In this episode, Naota is actually rescued from the inimical *mecha* by Haruko herself, whom he briefly visualizes as the brother he both misses and envies in the action's climactic instants.

Episode 2, "Fire Starter," consolidates the character portrayals ushered in by the first installment, highlighting Mamimi's rootlessness, Haruko's admixture of sagacity and plain weirdness, Naota's vulnerability to forces over which he has no control, and Kamon's self-obsessed conduct. An especially entertaining sequence pivots on Naota's and Kamon's disagreement over Canti's presence in the Nandaba household: The boy is worried about the eccentric image projected onto the public by accommodating a robot within a supposedly normal home, whereas his father simply does not care what people think and even invokes some convoluted pseudo-sociological theories to support the desirability of having Canti around the place — something that Naota explains as consonant with Kamon having once written an "*Eva*" book." Gainax's self-mocking proclivities are here succinctly conveyed. (In the meantime, passers-by are seen to vanish from the screen to indicate their total obliviousness not only to Canti but to their entire environment, which communicates a ubiquitous mood of apathy and unreflectiveness.)

Seemingly casual remarks that occupy no more than a few seconds of screen time often strike *FLCL*'s most hilarious chords. Episode 2 offers a typical example in the snippet of conversation in which Naota accuses Haruko of being weird and she tersely ripostes: "At least I didn't sprout a robot out of my head ... like some people."

It is in this episode that Mamimi develops her quaint hypotheses regarding Canti's divine status with the inspiration of the handheld video game "Fire Starter": a ludic venture whose goal is burning down a whole city. This can be achieved, within the logic of the game, only with the aid of the mighty spirit "Cantide-sama," Canti's prototype. As hinted at earlier, Mamimi honors Canti by means of a spooky ritual in which she sits in the middle of a circle of lit cigarettes pointing to the sky. It is not surprising, given *FLCL*'s iconoclastic thrust, that decidedly unholy fags should take the place of what, in proper ceremonies, would customarily be incense. Moreover, Mamimi's tendency to "sign" the cigarettes she smokes (a brand inexplicably expensive for a stray teenager) with the phrase "Never Knows Best" could be said to encapsulate the show's overall spirit. In omitting a syntactically logical subject, the phrase invites us to contemplate the elusiveness of knowledge in a universal sense, implying that *any* subject could be inserted and that *any* subject would be equally unlikely to "know best." In a complementary interpretation of the phrase, "Never" itself functions as a subject, suggesting that if *anything* can be presumed to "know best," this may only be conceived of as an unfulfilled and unfulfillable state of affairs.

As evidence of Mamimi's responsibility for both the fire that destroyed her elementary school six years earlier and the recent acts of arson escalates, the M.M. sirens start blaring once again and the two horns that have been gracing Naota's head since the beginning of the installment morph into a massive *mecha*. This consists of the M.M. robot whose hand got ripped off in the previous episode. Naota, Mamimi and Canti are now at the mercy of an ostensibly invincible foe but the action abruptly changes direction as Canti swallows Naota, absorbing the Atomsk-based powers contained by the boy and suitably turning red. In the immediate aftermath of the fusion, the Canti-Naota robot, equipped with a built-in cannon to boot, quite effortlessly defeats the attacker. The *mecha*-centered action dramatized by this sequence hints at moments from the *Evangelion* TV series based on three discrete Angels:

- the Fifth Angel (Ramiel, the "Angel of Thunder" — presented in Episodes 5 and 6 — equipped with a drilling weapon);
- the Seventh Angel (Israfel, the "Angel of Music" — presented in Episode 9 — with its giant-mollusc appearance);
- the Twelfth Angel (Leliel, the "Angel of Night" — presented in Episode 16 — whose zebra pattern *FLCL* mimics. The scene in which Naota is unceremoniously expelled, moreover, mirrors an analogous moment from the same *Evangelion* installment).

What Naota seems most concerned with, at the end, is Mamimi's welfare: not only has he been instrumental to keeping her away from the firefighters (and hence the danger of public exposure as a juvenile delinquent), he also resolves to "stay by her side forever." This does not mean, however, that Naota automatically believes it is his duty to look after the girl. In fact, the episode teems with references to Naota's conviction that people should act in accordance with their age and grown-ups, therefore, ought not to indulge in immature pursuits. Just as his father should finally start leading his life in keeping with adult mores and stop fooling (or "fooly-cooly"-ing) around, so Mamimi should behave like a proper high school student, not a half-witted tramp. What further complicates matters is Naota's feeling that he has inherited his absent brother's role as Mamimi's protector, which adds to his uneasiness about his supposedly more capable sibling.

FLCL has a knack of enriching its action not so much by developing threads put in place early on in a sequential fashion, as by unexpectedly foregrounding characters and situations that at first appear to be peripheral. This is attested to by Episode 3, "Marquis de Carabas," in which the pivotal agency is the hitherto marginal persona of Naota's classmate Eri Ninamori. As shown in some detail later in this chapter in relation to the show's treatment of adults, the girl is the casualty of familial discord. Much as she endeavors to preserve the public image of a calm and composed person, Eri is actually deeply troubled by the crisis and not quite successful in repressing her angst by prioritizing her involvement in the school performance of *Puss-In-Boots*.[2] While hinting at the possibility of a nascent romantic relationship between Eri and Naota, the episode uses the school play as a catalyst through which various emotional and psychosexual tensions interact.

On the self-referential front, the installment echoes *His and Her Circumstances* in its handling of the discrepancy between a person's real self and the public image divulged in order to maximize one's charisma and popularity. This topos is underscored by the scene in which

Eri, who is spending the night at Naota's, turns out to be a much more homely girl than one has thus far been led to believe by her adoption of an irreproachably elegant façade. Like Yukino, she secretly wears spectacles and is adamant in her determination to get *exactly* what she wants regardless of the degree of manipulation or mendacity that this might involve. We thus discover, for example, that she has cheated in order to obtain the lead role in the school play. Naota sternly rebukes her: "You've been hiding things."

At this level of the diegesis, the episode elects quiet — and often subtly humorous — psychodrama as its main vehicle. Naota's accretion of cat ears as the latest growth is an exquisite touch, in this context. Mamimi's mirroring of Naota's metamorphosis through her own acquisition of feline headgear is no less elegantly orchestrated. On another level, ebullient action gains the upper hand: The public revelation that Eri has rigged the election, in particular, unleashes one of the most kinetic sequences in the entire OVA. *Evangelion* again supplies the frame of reference for parodic distortion, as borne out by the visual allusions to the Ninth Angel (Matariel, the spidery "Angel of Rain"), introduced in *Evangelion*'s Episode 11.

When Naota exposes the voting illegality, the whole school is plunged into mayhem. The M.M. sirens blast deafeningly in the background as Naota loses his fluffy appendages and Eri sprouts a monstrous *mecha* that uses her body to control the situation without the girl being able to resist its dominance. Eventually, the Naota-Canti hybrid (cannon included) overmasters the enemy. At the end of the installment, the action's focus returns to Eri's duplicitous personality: She is standing on the school stage wearing glasses, which could be read as a concession to her previously concealed identity, yet claims that they are fake — the self-dramatizing urge has clearly *not* left her for good.

Although the feline topos is most explicitly invoked in Episode 3, allusions to cats abound across the show's iconographic fabric. As pointed out in the essay "Feline Delight" posted on the *Easy Target* fan site, "Throughout the series, usually after she had just said something very witty or sly, [Haruko]'ll have one of these cat faces with the puffy upper lip and whiskers on her cheeks.... [In Episode 5,] Haruko communicates via Miyu-Miyu [the house cat of the Nandaba family] to the Galaxy Space Police Brotherhood.... [In Episode 2,] Mamimi befriends a stray kitten that she names Takkun.... on the bakery flag-sign [in Episode 3] there's a cat's face! ... [Also in Episode 3,] the teacher lectures the class about cats at school."

These are just a few instances, prominent even upon first viewing, of a pervasive trend that may or may not carry symbolic connotations. As with practically everything else in *FLCL*, it is up to the individual spectator to decide what meanings — if any — that ploy may communicate. According to the essay quoted above, the cat theme is deployed in a fundamentally tongue-in-cheek vein: "Besides from being sneaky and sly, cats are also very independent creatures.... Ironically, as a whole, all the characters are interconnected with each other and do rely on each other. For example, Haruko ... is a very unique character, but not independent.... she needs Naota's head as an N.O. portal to accomplish her own goals" ("Feline Delight").

Episode 4, "Full Swing," reverberates with sci-fi imagery of the kind deployed in *Gunbuster*. This is most explicit in the shots dramatizing the precipitous approach of a satellite toward Mabase. Sadamoto's fans may also be interested in the subtle ways in which Kitsurubami's design foreshadows Lal'C in *Gunbuster 2*. Self-reflexive parody intended to poke fun at the entire realm of Japanese animation, not merely at Gainax's own output, is evident throughout *FLCL*. Episode 4 offers a characteristic instance:

Naota: Who are you really?
Haruko: I'm an illusory manifestation of the feelings in your adolescent heart.
Naota: Where did you get *that* one from? Anime?

In the installment's opening scenes, we find that the performance of the Mabase baseball team (the "Mabase Martians") has been grievously declining in quality since Tasuku's departure without the younger Nandaba boy being even remotely able to stand in as a competent successor. The situation deteriorates as Haruko joins the competition and helps them beat the home side nothing short of sensationally. Naota's grandfather responds by recruiting Canti onto his side, while Haruko herself (paradoxically) encourages Naota to start swinging the bat with real determination if he wants to discover his true potential. Quite apart from disliking Haruko's patronizing attitude, the boy is also thrown into a vortex of jealousy and repugnance when he finds out that the alien girl and Kamon — or, at any rate, what would *appear* to be his father — have been heartily fooling around.

However, it transpires that Haruko has actually constructed a robotic version of Kamon to play with and, plausibly, to arouse Naota's rivalry and desire for action. This is an unusual way of dispelling pubescent listlessness but this *is FLCL* after all, and we are never allowed to forget it for long. Haruko's and Kamon's saucy dalliance is farcically dramatized in the scene in which Naota returns home after a frustrating baseball session and finds the artificial Kamon gratifying the alien in a fetishistic fashion by massaging every single inch of her body with his spiky beard, followed by some titillating sharing of fried eggs across mouths.

Naota's sense of confusion escalates with the arrival in Mabase of the enigmatic Amarao, who sternly cautions him against Haruko. We next see the officer at the Central Command Center of the Immigration Bureau, dismayed by the discovery that the organization has lost control of one of its satellites, which is carrying a bomb and is heading straight for Mabase. (One of Haruko's insanely powerful balls is reputed to have escaped Earth's gravity and hit the satellite.) The following day, Naota finds the robot-Kamon in the middle of a self-congratulatory spiel about Haruko's favors and gets sufficiently irate to hit the TV set with his bat, disconnecting the robot in the process. He then discovers his real father in a closet, seemingly dead and teeming with roaches but capable of resurging as a malevolent spectre. After a frantic chase involving said ghost and the boy, Naota manages to throw his father into the bath tub and properly revive him, at which point Kamon remembers that the cause of his apparent demise was Haruko's abortive attempt to exploit his N.O. powers.

In the totally disconnected scene that ensues, Amarao questions Naota about his behavior toward his father, opining that his bat-aided attack points to murderous desires of latently Oedipal orientation. The scene is set in a disquietingly austere room and provides a veritable gem of intertextuality, reverberating at once with the visual and dialogical formulae of film noir, hard-boiled crime fiction and Cold War spy movies, as well as hints at the gangster thriller and at the dystopian brainwashing routine.

Following a frantic scene in which Haruko pulls a 1967 Gibson Flying V out of Naota's head, the boy reveals unsuspected valor in the intensely suspenseful sequence in which he single-handedly saves Mabase (and possibly the whole planet) from the satellite-bomb by hitting it with his bat just as it is about to collide with Earth. Atomsk's symbol glows bright on his forehead at this juncture, as it does on Canti's screen, although the two characters do not, on this particular occasion, actually merge.

It is in Episode 5, "Brittle Bullet," that the generational conflict mentioned earlier is explicitly dramatized by means of a blatantly carnivalesque set of sequences in which Naota and Haruko engage in a fight with airsoft guns against Kamon and Canti. Kamon eventually challenges his son to a duel, which is interrupted by the appearance of Naota's classmates — Eri, Gaku and Masashi — as they drive a delivery van along the riverside. The scene provides a quintessentially *FLCL*ish, deliciously preposterous touch in showing a trio of elementary school kids running a business clearly intended for grown-ups: something that Naota superciliously points out but his friends casually dismiss. It is in scenes such as this that the show accedes to the heights of absurdist drama without encumbering the action with redundant details.

Quite a different comedic mood is conveyed, in the course of the same installment, by the scene in which Naota walks in on Haruko as she is talking to her superiors via Miyu-Miyu as a communication device, and tries to deflect the boy's attention from the conversation by suddenly flaunting an Elvis costume and hairdo while spewing out a fusillade of references to pop music. Naota turns to face the audience in a genuinely Brechtian vein, declaring he has no idea what is going on and wondering whether *we* do.

Returning to the riverside scene, it is also worth noting that this supplies a fond parody of moments from *Evangelion* in which Shinji's pals wax lyrical about his heroism, as Gaku and Masashi deliver a paean to Naota's role as the savior of their town professing undying admiration for his "awesome" performance. The scene is overtly redolent of Touji's and Kensuke's glorification of Shinji in Episode 4 of the *Evangelion* TV series in both tone and register — complemented by the infusion of a generous dose of sarcastic humor.

At this point, a newly sensed feeling of power gets to Naota's head, causing him to act in what he sees as a manly fashion. His first move is to literally drag Mamimi along for a dinner date in order to show her that he does not really care about Haruko. Trying to emancipate himself from the alien girl's influence is clearly something that Naota deems axial to his psychosexual maturation. Mamimi, however, does not warm to this novel incarnation of the little boy whom she has only ever regarded as a miniature version of Tasuku to be toyed with at leisure. Amidst this emotional turmoil, a new physical threat emerges as a further monstrosity — this time donning a stylish trench coat — springs from the protagonist's head. Mamimi, to the boy's chagrin, calls out to the absent Tasuku for help, which causes Naota to muster his recently acquired confidence to demonstrate conclusively that *he*— and not his brother — has been playing a genuinely protective role vis-à-vis both Mamimi personally and Mabase at large.

The action sequence that follows is so jam-packed with both interconnected and purely coincidental occurrences as to require patient repeat viewings to be adequately absorbed. One of its highlights is the bewildering materialization of yet another guitar as Canti pulls a 1961 Gibson EB-0 out of his head, which is presumed to be Atomsk's own instrument. (As to the use a gigantic phoenix-shaped alien might feasibly have for such an object, it is left to the viewer to imagine.) The sequence's outcome is Canti's defeat of the latest robot, which gets deprived of its supposedly vital "terminal core," destined to take on a life of its own in the final episode. The behemothic entity's remnants congeal in the shape of a colossal hand looming over M.M.

Episode 5 is peppered with examples of self-referential mockery targeted at Gainax's own productions. Among the most colorful is Haruko's appearance in a Bunny Girl costume screaming "Daicon 5."[3] Additionally, the episode's treatment of the war topos could be regarded as a playful variation on the martial elements invoked by *Honneamise* and *Nadia*. The emulation of stylistic traits typical of video games in some of the military exploits, for its part, anticipates *Abenobashi*. Finally, like Noriko in *Gunbuster* (and her direct successor Nono in *Gunbuster 2*) and like Shinji in *Evangelion*, Naota is an unlikely hero yet is able to pull out a top-notch feat in extremis.

However, the works of other studios are also alluded to: The prodigy featuring in the installment's climax, for instance, is redolent of the Forest God "Didarabocchi" from Hayao Miyazaki's *Princess Mononoke* (1997). Besides the reference to *Mononoke*, a further allusion to Miyazaki's opus can be spotted in the scene in which Naota puzzles over Kamon's weird garb (alluding to the underpants vaunting a garish heart pattern) and the older man, presuming his son is referring to his shirt, asks the boy whether he prefers the "green version," the "*Castle of Cagliostro* version." (The reference is to *Lupin 3: The Castle of Cagliostro* [1979].) At the same time, Episode 5 parodies live-action cinema no less irreverently in the scene in which Amarao spawns a plethora of clones reminiscent of Agent Smith's replicas in the *Matrix* films (1998–2003). In the same sequence (as indeed elsewhere in *FLCL*), a cinematographical technique immortalized by the Wachowskis' trilogy is also deployed, namely, bullet-time photography.

Episode 6, "FLCLimax," opens with an incongruous and ironic homage to Japanese tradition centered on a school lesson in which Naota's teacher praises the benefits of chopsticks in comparison with sporks — in the process revealing herself quite inept at the art of picking up food with the supposedly superior implements. The episode's tone darkens as Naota walks out of the classroom and comments on Mabase's ominous atmosphere since the appearance of the giant hand and the concomitant enshrouding of the entire town by a noxious fog. The boy feels that Mabase is now utterly isolated from the rest of the world, which might just as well not exist.

While Mabase as a whole seems cut off from the outside world, Naota's own personal sense of isolation, allied to a large dose of despondency, is exacerbated by the sudden disappearance of Haruko and Canti, who are on the run from Amarao and his agency. Mamimi, meanwhile, is also experiencing the pangs of loneliness as she realizes that her pet cat Takkun is nowhere to be found. A replacement soon materializes, however, in the guise of a dog-like miniature *mecha* whom the girl adopts and also names Takkun. As shown by the robot's enthusiastic consumption of Mamimi's mobile phone, the creature has a hearty appetite for everything mechanical and a knack of growing exponentially with each repast. Mamimi obliges it by providing gargantuan amounts of not only small gadgets but also sizeable appliances and whole vehicles, which causes Takkun to balloon into a techno-monster in its own right.

As this strand of the plot unravels, Naota's life takes yet another unexpected turn when Haruko returns to the Nandaba home claiming to have been on holiday in Hawaii. The sequence dramatizing the alien girl's reintroduction into Naota's family is rendered in manga format, supplying a neatly symmetrical counterpart for the analogous sequence presented in Episode 1 when Haruko is first emplaced in the household. The manga sequences presented in both Episode 1 and Episode 6 are two of the most flamboyant moments of generic self-reflexivity in the entire OVA. The exchange offered at the end of the Episode 6 sequence is worthy of notice:

> Kamon: Let's stop! Let's go back to normal. C'mon, let's be a normal anime.
> Naota: Anime?
> Kamon: To be in manga form takes time and a lot of work. After the first episode they asked us to stop this craziness. Even so, people accused us of being lazy.

When the action resumes its customary style, an intense exchange between Naota and Haruko takes place, which demonstrates that, in spite of the latently erotic nature of the boy's feeling toward the alien, he has missed her in very much the same way a kid would miss a maternal presence. Scared that Haruko might leave him again, Naota accepts the girl's invitation to run away with her on her Vespa. While the elopement itself is a low-key affair, which merely takes Naota and Haruko back to Mabase (and to improvised sleeping arrangements on a lowly bench), the scenes showing the two characters in motion across a lovingly depicted landscape are memorable on the pictorial and cinematographical planes.

Takkun, meanwhile, has grown so enormous that Mamimi is no longer capable of controlling its movements. The *mecha*'s true identity is now revealed as coinciding with the "terminal core" gone missing in the previous installment. The action escalates to hyperbolic extremes as Canti fuses with the terminal core and lands over the giant hand with Amarao in hot pursuit, Haruko and Naota descend upon the hand on the Vespa, Haruko pushes Naota toward the terminal core, and the boy is incorporated by it. The terminal core then begins to fill a hole in the hand, thereby activating it and enabling it to grab the M.M. iron meant to flatten the planet. However, Naota pulls himself away from Canti, absorbing all of Atomsk's stupendous energy and leaving the *mecha* suitably blue. Haruko is still determined to conquer Atomsk but cannot gain the upper hand on Naota, who valiantly blocks her final blow and overcomes her. The protagonist then releases the Pirate King's powers hosted within his body, allowing the alien to regain its genuine form and to zoom off into outer space.

Haruko, acknowledging her defeat (at least for the time being), drives off, having offered to take Naota along but concluded that this would be inappropriate since he is still, after all, "a kid." Whether Haruko's behavior is to be read as that of a callous adult or that of a pragmatic and responsible person is left to the viewer to decide. What seems more important is that the protagonist, having finally proclaimed an ability to act of his own free will, remains quite unmoved by the alien's parting words and is seemingly prepared to just get on with his life (tedious though this may be). The closing scenes show that Mamimi has left school and managed to pursue a photographic career—a magazine picture of Naota with his guitar, accompanied by the caption "Foolly Coolly," attests to this development. Naota and his mates, for their part, have progressed to the next stage in their education and returned to a normality of sorts.

Even though *FLCL* excels at overt—at times even crude—humor, Episode 6 demonstrates that some of the most felicitous moments result from gentle mockery. Its target, notably, is often Gainax's own opus. A paradigmatic example is supplied by the scene in which Amarao and Kitsurubami gaze at the huge hand looming over M.M. and grandiosely conclude that it *is* indeed a hand, as though they were not stating the nakedly obvious but actually disclosing some esoteric truth:

> Kitsurubami: It's a hand, isn't it?
> Amarao: It's a hand.

It is primarily their overinflated tone that renders these lines so utterly ludicrous. The exchange parodies the scenes in *Evangelion* in which Gendou and Fuyutsuki discuss the nature of an impending threat and pompously declare it is an Angel, which is, after all, only to be expected. (*FLCL* also contains references to the color "blue" as synonymous with danger, echoing *Evangelion*'s association of that hue with the chemical composition of Angels.) Such moments underscore the self-aggrandizing nature of the characters involved, suggesting that they cannot even begin to consider the possibility of their tasks being anything other than momentous. In *Evangelion*, they often are but in *FLCL*, the gravity of a situation can never be automatically taken for granted.

Extrapolating the OVA's key "facts" from both the panoramic synopsis and the episode analyses offered above, it is possible to reconstruct a logline consisting of two intertwined threads.

I. Sci-fi Thread:
1. M.M.—a manufacturer not of medical equipment as its name indicates but rather of machinery designed for essentially nefarious purposes—captures the alien entity Atomsk (a.k.a. the Pirate King). Atomsk is contained within the *mecha* Canti.

2. The alien girl Haruko arrives in Mabase with the intention of freeing Atomsk and merging with it to gain enormous powers. To fulfill her goal, she needs to open a channel through which Atomsk may travel unhindered. She activates such a conduit within the head of the schoolboy Naota, as a result of which Canti erupts from his skull. In the process, Atomsk's essence is split between Naota and Canti. Though both are quite powerless individually, they become immensely effective when they combine, recreating Atomsk's whole core.
3. Commander Amarao intervenes on behalf of the Interstellar Immigration Bureau to hinder Haruko for his own dubious reasons no less than out of political duty.
4. Naota continues to be the victim of *mecha* infiltrations but also discovers, gradually, the existence of unsuspected powers within himself. Thus, he is able to stop a satellite headed straight for Mabase and, with Canti's support, to defeat various attackers.
5. Naota's triumph comes with his resolve to stand up to Haruko and impede the realization of her dream by releasing Atomsk for good rather than just dishing its powers out from one captor to another.

II. Domestic/Urban Thread:
1. While Naota negotiates his personal anxieties, his absent brother's girlfriend, Mamimi, struggles to cope with her own hazy dreams, painful memories and criminal urges.
2. Naota's classmate Eri, in turn, finds herself confronting the harsh reality of parental neglect despite her elevated social standing.
3. The Mabase baseball team run by Naota's grandfather has its own nightmares to face, while Naota's father Kamon floats amidst self-inflating and sexually tantalizing fantasies.
4. As these events unfold, a modicum of maturation is supposed to be achieved. Whether this apparently ordinary task is any less tall an order than saving whole galaxies, it is for *FLCL* to test and for its spectators to judge.

FLCL's unconventional diegesis, with its titanic appetite for intertextual allusions and postmodernist non sequiturs, subtle in-jokes, legion references to often obscure facets of Japanese pop culture and fashion, religious and mythological undercurrents tangentially inspired by Shinto beliefs and morsels of popular psychology (to mention just a handful of its key components) sometimes makes it arduous to ascertain beyond doubt even the most elementary foundations of its construction. The director's own comments on the story's putative "meaning" are worthy of consideration in this respect: "I'd like you to think of *FLCL* as imagination being made physical and tangible, just as it is for me when I take whatever is in my head and draw it" (Tsurumaki 2001). Another reason for which *FLCL* may — at least at first — feel confusing is Tsurumaki's approach to editing in this OVA, namely, an MTV-like style, characterized by very rapid cuts and an occasionally wobbly camera. As a result, some of the smallest details may go past the eye so swiftly as to remain initially unheeded. Even spectators who have watched *FLCL* several times admit to be still detecting snippets of information with each further viewing.

Additionally, as documented by the *FLCL World* website, "Part of the fun with *FLCL* is all of the hidden references and frames, some of which are very easy to miss unless you play back the episode frame-by-frame." Illustrative instances of *FLCL*'s employment of hidden frames include the following:

[Episode 1:]
When zoomed in on Mamimi's cigarette, some say they can see an image of two people in the smoke....

[Episode 3:]
When the monster comes out of Ninamori's head ... Canti tries to keep her under control but removes her shorts in the process.... In [a] scene, Naota's face turns into the "Scream" mask.... When Haruko finds Canti in the closet, he loses his cool and fairies come out of his head....

[Episode 4:]
After Haruko tells Mamimi that Canti is playing baseball, Mamimi leaves — and you briefly see Naota remove her panties....

[Episode 6:]
After the "manga" scene, Shigekuni ... is spotted flying into the night sky ["Hidden Frames"].

It should not be unreflectively assumed, however, that *FLCL*'s formal eccentricities preclude its incorporation of serious concerns. In fact, as the *Gainax Pages* review cited earlier maintains, "there's plenty of depth to *FLCL*. Like most Gainax shows, it's about a boy growing up and experiencing the turbulence of adolescence. Haruko represents sexual awakening in general, while the bizarre horns and robots that mysteriously pop out of Naota's forehead are the surprising desires first experienced by teenagers" ("*Gainax Pages* reviews: *FLCL*"). This review's sexual interpretation of Naota's outlandish condition is interesting. Nevertheless, it should be also noted that Tsurumaki himself has put forward quite a different explanation for the sprouting of *mecha* out of the boy's head: "I use a giant robot being created from the brain to represent *FLCL* coming from my brain. The robot ravages the town around him, and the more intensely I worked on *FLCL* the more I destroyed the peaceful atmosphere of Gainax" (Tsurumaki 2001).

The recurring image of *mecha* and aliens sprouting out of Naota's head (and, occasionally, out of other characters' heads, as well) may or may not symbolize erections. However, sexual innuendoes abound, as exemplified by the use of the phrase "swinging the bat" not simply as a reference to baseball but also as an action meant to mark the protagonist's progress beyond childhood. The scene in which Eri fondles the furry ears that protrude from Naota's skull in Episode 3 is also obliquely erotic, as signaled by Haruko's warning: "A young girl like you shouldn't touch it with your bare hands." (Eri indeed feels almost instantly nauseous.)[4] In Episode 4, the theme of psychosexual development is comically pursued by means of the Oedipal farce centered on Naota's apparent "murder" of Kamon. Guitars are also deployed as phallic symbols, most overtly in Episode 5 in which, following Haruko's extraction of the Flying V out of Naota's cranium, nosebleeds of portentous magnitude occur: The nosebleed is a classic anime metaphor for sexual arousal and even orgasm.

As for the OVA's Bildungsroman element — no less axial an ingredient in the context of Gainax's entire oeuvre than the theme of the absent or remiss parent — this is corroborated by Brandon W. Bollom's essay "*FLCL*: How Gainax Created the First Anime for the 21st Century": "Strip away the layers of sexual innuendo, parody, alien technology, self-reference, symbolism and so much more and you are left with a strong coming-of-age story starring a boy struggling with his liminality" (Bollom). Not only, therefore, does *FLCL* yield one of the most audacious formal experiments accomplished by the medium to date, it also provides an unsentimental yet touching exploration of the trials and tribulations besetting adolescence in its proverbial amalgam of inchoate desires and numbing insecurity, aggressiveness and depression, passion and apathy.

The injunction to grow up, with which Naota grapples from beginning to end, is made especially onerous by the ubiquitous ascendancy of selfish adults. Even when so-called grown-ups appear to adopt generous and liberal attitudes, their reasons for doing so remain dubious.

For example, when Naota elopes with Haruko and neglects school (Episode 6), and his teacher visits Kamon to ascertain what is going on, the boy's father claims that Naota has a right to his freedom. His words are not inspired by any lofty principles, however, but rather by total — and indeed pathologically immature — self-absorption. Naota's absence simply gives Kamon an excuse to draw attention to himself and to indulge unfettered in his self-dramatizing disposition — as borne out by his failure to discuss Naota's situation and expound instead on his own experience of being absent from school at some point in his childhood.

The callousness of adults is further thrown into relief by the vicious pleasure that Naota's seniors appear to derive from forcing sour drinks and spicy foodstuff upon the boy although he abhors them. It is as though their objective were to deny Naota's right to be a kid and accordingly harbor kiddy tastes. Eri is also the casualty of adults' egoistic conduct, being caught up not only in the thicket of a bitter parental dispute likely to result in divorce but also in the broader political implications of her father's affair with his secretary. Paradoxically, given Kamon's own suspect sexual ethics, it is Naota's father who is held responsible for divulging the illicit liaison through his magazine — an amateur tabloid he conceitedly describes as "investigative journalism." Eri puts on a brave face and claims that the uproar is "no big deal" but privately does feel bereft and deprived of a real "home" to return to. No amount of smart clothes allowed by her privileged social status can ultimately compensate for her lack.

The girl's sadness is also palpable in the scene in which she tells Naota that although taking part in school plays may be dull, the experience is positive for her because her parents come to see her together. In a separate scene, Mamimi communicates the same idea, recounting that she once participated in a school performance and felt terribly embarrassed, yet also happy because her father and mother had both turned up at the event. It should also be noted, in this context, that selfish grown-ups are not the sole source of abusive behavior: In fact, Episode 2 suggests that one of the causes of Mamimi's isolation is her being the victim of severe playground bullying. Naota himself remains suspicious of adults and does not even seem to believe in the empirical existence of adult standards of behavior. This brief exchange from Episode 5 concisely confirms the point:

> Haruko: You should start acting like an adult.
> Naota: You should talk!

The scene in Episode 2 in which Haruko crashes spectacularly into M.M. and Naota intervenes to rescue her, so to speak, foregrounds the bizarreness of the two characters' relationship with specific reference to the age issue as the alien girl announces to the guards that Naota is her "legal guardian."

Naota's psychology, albeit pivotal to the story, is not the sole instance of elaborate characterization. In fact, one of the OVA's most striking attributes is a stalwart dedication to the presentation of personae that manage to come across as palpably real, and hence provide a convincing study of humanity, even when they are invested with stereotypical facets for jocular purposes. Relatedly, all the characters are carefully constructed with a consistent emphasis on their plurality and inner dividedness. Fuyu Kimata cites Haruko as a primary illustration of multifaceted characterization: "When you take a good look at Haruko, she is pretty, but her wild behavior completely overpowers that beauty.... Once you get used to her wild and crazy personality, you realize she's actually a lovely girl. The thrill of seeing her speeding down the road on her Vespa is what makes her so exciting" (Kimata 2002, p. 24). Furthermore, much as she abuses Naota's physical and mental integrity, Haruko respects the boy's pride (and incipient virility), for instance, in the scene in which she states that she could never simply team up with Kamon and play along with his randy fantasies because Naota is the one she saw first. This assertion constitutes a tongue-in-cheek concession to an old-fashioned moral code that facetiously clashes with Haruko's—and indeed the entire show's—wacky iconoclasm but also lends the drama a gentle, even moving, note.

The voice actors (*seyuu*) were themselves baffled by the characters' ambiguous personalities, and they arrived gradually at an understanding of their proclivities and objectives, never quite taking anything for granted. When interviewed in the early phases of dubbing, the performers made a point of admitting to a scant knowledge of their characters' development. Mayumi Shintani (Haruko's *seyuu*), for example, observed: "Haruko is a pretty girl who's full of mysteries—I don't know why she obsesses over Naota.... I try my best to sound mature. But when I shout, I end up sounding young. It's a challenge for me to find the right balance" (quoted in Kimata 2002, p. 24). Jun Mikuki, Naota's voice, honestly conceded that not just his character but the show as a whole struck him as one big mystery: "I still don't quite understand the strange dialogue, setup and situations" (quoted in Kimata 2002, p. 24). Mamimi's *seyuu*, Izumi Kasagi, likewise described her initial understanding of the character as lacunary: "Mamimi seems to be seducing Naota, but I get the feeling there's actually something else to it. I still don't know her true motives" (quoted in Kimata 2002, p. 25). Kamon's character was, arguably, more easily readable from the outset but still posed a very challenging part. The scriptwriter, producer, essayist, novelist and actor Suzuki Matsuo, the *seyuu* behind Kamon's salacious antics and source of inspiration for the character, stated: "Kamon never says anything serious and he's very high strung. So if I don't play the role right, he'd turn out to be nothing more than an idiot" (quoted in Kimata 2002, p. 25).

Undeniably, what hits most viewers upon their first encounter with the series is not *FLCL*'s underlying thematic seriousness but its raw vigor, chaotic ambiguity and chafing lunacy. However, this ought not to discourage any genuine animation enthusiast from delving deeper into the OVA for its rewards are considerable. A tumult of visuals, music and concepts delivered at so swift a pace as to sometimes feel like a bombardment of the entire sensorium, *FLCL* is nonetheless capable of appealing to diverse sectors of the anime public. Much as it cultivates dynamism to hyperkinetic extremes, the show does not fail the comedy lover; conversely, while yielding jokes, puns and zany acrobatics in spades, it never loses sight of the action-oriented viewer.

A review of the OVA published in *AAW* indeed proposes that "*FLCL* encompasses almost everything in anime that its fans enjoy.... *Mecha*, love triangles, weirdness, voluptuous women, societal taboos, supernatural battles, cosplay fetish costumes, it's all in there" ("Animonster"). The *Anime Meta-Review* substantiates *FLCL*'s standing as a consummately satisfying accomplishment by underscoring the distinctiveness of Gainax's approach to the medium of animation: "There's some wonderful dialogue, which subtext hunters can go to town on, and potent character moments.... And over all this is the sense that there is a meaning that will become clear at any moment. This powerful sense of hidden meaning makes the anime fairly addictive" ("*Anime Meta-Review—FLCL*").

Crisp and fluid by turns, the animation itself incorporates—in full accordance with Gainax's established preferences—flashing and scrolling text rendered in various calligraphic styles, as well as SD caricatures. Most memorable, on the experimentation front, are the aforementioned sequences in which conventional animation stops altogether and the narrative is recorded by a camera seemingly bouncing across pages of black-and-white manga panels. Concurrently, the OVA offers lyrical natural backgrounds that serve to augment, by ironic contrast, the defamiliarizing uncanniness of many action sequences and domestic vignettes alike. Such scenarios tend to feature peacefully flowing rivers, glowing autumn skies, snow-capped mountains, glittering oceans and mournful rain.

Meticulously researched and planned throughout, art director Hiromasa Ogura's scenery reaches its crowning achievement in the harmonious orchestration of snippets of ordinary life, on the one hand, and overtly fantastical sci-fi elements, on the other. Mellow colors and fluid lines are generally predominant while the lighting relies by turns on the evocation of a pale, even melancholy, luminosity for the daytime sequences and on a mood of forbidding tenebrousness for the nocturnal ones. The lighting effects used in the scenes set in the hospital where Haruko in her nurse disguise subjects Naota to sadistic examination, as well as those set in the M.M. foyer, drastically depart from the realistic handling of light and shadow prevalent elsewhere. Indeed, they exude a frigid atmosphere of sterility consonant with the glacial ruthlessness of the activities taking place within those venues.

Some of the everyday locations are modeled on real places. The Nandaba family bakery, for example, actually exists in the Mitaka area of Tokyo. The town of Mabase as a whole, however, is based on Toyonaka (Aichi Prefecture). Ogura used pictures of the area as the foundation on which he could "create a generic-looking city, like what you'd see in a manga," thus complying with the director's desire for backgrounds that would come across as "very simple and abbreviated." Commenting on the challenges entailed by this task, the art director has noted: "It's actually more difficult to leave details out and to make the audience's imagination fill in the parts you don't draw. It's not about making something simple, like a short comic strip, but more like bringing a new and more realistic style to the audience" (quoted in Kimata 2002, p. 27).

A distinctive trait of the animational style used to choreograph the more frenzied moments in the action is the presentation of the affected characters as quasi-mechanical apparatuses, whereas the repercussions of violent physical traumas are conveyed by the grotesque contraction of their bodies into seemingly rubberized, drooling heaps or else their flattening into pancake-thin cutouts. This leaning toward extreme stylization is deftly counterbalanced by character designer Sadamoto's passionate attention to realistic details, especially in the depiction of the characters' garb, accessories and stylistic obsessions. Reflecting Japanese kids' legendary fetishization of designer brands, Naota's clothes and backpack are punctiliously represented as absurdly costly. The boy's addiction to stylishness, it should be noted, impacts on disparate aspects of his otherwise drab existence, including the humdrum reality of homework — a task Naota would rather undertake crouched on the riverbank than in the relative comfort of his bedroom because doing your homework at home, he avers, simply "isn't cool."

Moreover, Sadamoto's designs succeed admirably in capturing the protagonist's psychology — an aspect of the show that Kent Conrad has summed up as follows: Naota is "sullen, but not in [a] taciturn, gothic–Byronic way.... As Mike Toole ... points out, Naota is a 'pissed-off kid.' And he's right that 'we don't see enough pissed-off kids in anime' [Toole]. But Naota isn't pissed off in the awful, fake, pretend way you get from brats in Hollywood movies or cartoons. He's pissed off for real, and it works" (Conrad).

For all that, Naota is actually an unpretentious kid, made likeable not only by Sadamoto's gorgeous designs (his closest stylistic antecedent, incidentally, is undoubtedly *Evangelion*'s Shinji) but also by the almost incongruously poetic strain of his language, especially in the reflective voiceovers where he comments on his experiences and on the stubborn elusiveness of their possible meaning. This facet of the protagonist's characterization elliptically complements the lyrical beauty of the natural backgrounds discussed earlier. The expressive element inherent in both those scenarios and Naota's meditative discourse, moreover, provides a dialectical counterpoint for the action's cumulatively frantic tempo, dynamic exuberance, flurries of color and often perplexing cinematographical tricks. The mesmerizing alternative-rock music performed throughout by the Japanese punk band The Pillows, finally, contributes crucially to the series' cumulative aesthetic. (The "P" logo adorning Haruko's Vespa is actually the band's own distinctive emblem.)[5]

In evaluating the show's bizarrely surreal and deliberately illogical construction, it is worth engaging in some comparative analysis relating *FLCL* to the anime subgenre that fans affectionately refer to as "mindfuck." (Evidence for the intellectual legitimacy of this term despite its ostensible crudeness within the domain of film criticism is provided, among other sources, by the following entry and by the external links to which it gives access: http://en.wikipedia.org/wiki/Mindfuck.)

Characteristically idiosyncratic productions that deserve notice in the present context include:

- *Serial Experiments Lain* (TV series; dir. Ryutaro Nakamura, 1998);
- *Boogiepop Phantom* (TV series; dir. Takashi Watanabe, 2000);
- *Paranoia Agent* (TV series; dir. Satoshi Kon, 2004);
- *Elfen Lied* (TV series; dir. Mamoru Kanbe, 2004).

An eminently postmodern cinematographical experiment wherein narrative linearity is eschewed in favor of a circular or spiraling rhythm, *Serial Experiments Lain* mirrors thematically Gainax's ongoing fascination with the instability of the real — and, specifically, *FLCL*'s recurrent speculations about the impossibility of ascertaining where the lies end and the truth begins (to paraphrase Naota). However, Nakamura's show echoes Gainax's output most closely on the technical plane. The tendency to assault the eye with a barrage of hues and textures, in particular, features prominently among its recurrent ploys. *Boogiepop Phantom* blends disparate ingredients drawn from the classic ghost story, the psychological thriller, high school drama, the hospital chiller, teenage romance, horror and folklore to deliver one of the most challengingly nonlinear narratives ever embarked upon by an anime studio. Somber, brooding and so deliberate in its pace as to verge on the ponderous, the TV series derives its overwhelmingly enigmatic aura mainly from the adoption of a multiperspectival approach. *Boogiepop Phantom*'s uncanny flavor is maximized by the employment of cinematographical strategies of precisely the kind Gainax itself favors as ways of intensifying a scene's affective import: in particular, vignette-style framing, fish-lens effects, jarring flashbacks and desaturated color palettes.

Paranoia Agent yields a comparably intricate cinematic web that persistently redirects the viewer's attention from one set of events (and attendant emotional traumas) to another as the angle from which the action is perceived shifts at each turn. The show revolves around a bunch of varyingly freakish characters bound together by the simple fact that they all, at some juncture, get whacked on the head by a mysterious kid dubbed "Lil' Slugger," whose trademarks are a bent baseball bat and golden rollerblades. The young offender's possible motives are so inscrutable that his very existence becomes a bone of contention, and the viewer is accordingly prompted to wonder whether "Lil' Slugger" is a real kid, a perfidious ghost, a cover for other people's offenses or even an hallucinatory projection of their deep-seated fears. Apart from their shared references to baseball, *FLCL* and *Paranoia Agent* join forces in challenging the audience to reconstruct a cohesive logline out of a cryptic palimpsest of clues — or indeed of red herrings, as often turns out to be the case.

The split-reality effect evoked in *FLCL* by the juxtaposition of Naota's bland routine and the quirky world of aliens and *mecha* has a parallel in *Elfen Lied*'s likewise dual perspective. This facet of the series is evident from the start and finds an expressive vehicle in its very protagonist, Nyu (a.k.a. Lucy). The seemingly human girl is actually a "diclonius": a mutant endowed with formidable telekinetic powers. Like *FLCL*, moreover, *Elfen Lied* blends diverse styles, tones and generic formulae, proffering by turns insanely hyperdynamic action sequences and moments of gentle poetry. Elements of both comedy and romance are also occasionally incorporated into the cocktail. As seen in the course of this chapter, Naota's adventures veer toward ludic parody rather than intense psychodrama. Yet, the darkness is never entirely absent from its purview. This element is foregrounded in *Elfen Lied*, where prominence is accorded not only to physical violence but also — and more disturbingly still — to psychological abuse and sadistic instincts.

To say that *FLCL* is barmy is to state the obvious. To say that its barminess makes it impervious would, however, be grossly unfair. In fact, the OVA does lend itself to cogent analysis and the degree of depth one may be willing to accord to both its ludic moments and its engagement with serious science fiction depends entirely on how far one wishes to fathom it. One of the major challenges posed by *FLCL* is its deliberate withholding of background information of the kind one encounters in less adventurous anime. (In this respect, as in others, it echoes *Evangelion*.) In fact, the series leaps straight into the action, and goes on amassing complications at so swift a pace that even where it discloses the enigmas on which the plot thrives, one at first remains oblivious to the epiphanies on offer.

What is unremittingly captivating, even once the OVA's logline has been reconstructed (albeit tentatively) and its characters' motives have been approximately ascertained, is *FLCL*'s unpredictability. At any one point in the story, surprises sprout out of the screen in much the same way as *mecha* do out of the protagonist's head. A reflective scene bathed in soft hues and drizzle will unexpectedly give way to explosive battles inundated with lurid glows. A formal experiment in cinematography replacing fluid action with the staccato rhythm of comic-book panels will just as unforeseeably morph into a quiet take on a homely interior. Bodies moving at a realistic rate might suddenly begin to swirl so rapidly as to levitate and hover like helicopters, or else whiz about in circles upon imaginary wheels. Normal quotidian clothes might abruptly translate into flamboyant theatrical costumes. The scenery itself unpredictably switches from the idyllic to the baleful, and from the bleak to the sublime. However deeply we may choose to delve into *FLCL*'s narrative and structural puzzles, it is crucial to remember that its irreverent shifts of tone and non sequiturs cannot — and should not — ever be *ironed out*.

CHAPTER 10

Mahoromatic — Automatic Maiden (Mahoromatic)
Director: Hiroyuki Yamaga (2001–2002)

> *The obvious favorite of fans is Mahoro herself, who is a juxtaposition of cute and destructive power that is highly amusing. The bipolar nature of this anime is readily demonstrated in the opening animation, which depicts Mahoro doing various house chores on one hand and blowing away* mecha *on the other with a gentle love song playing in the background. This dual nature thrives in the characters, who at one moment will be very funny and at the next extremely serious, especially as the series draws to a close.*
> — Jason Bustard

Mahoro V1046 is a "Hyper Soldier": a combat android constructed to confront lethal alien invaders that threaten to annihilate the Earth unbeknownst to the vast majority of humans. Presented with this synoptic information, many prospective spectators might well respond with an exasperated "*again?*" Had the studio behind *Mahoromatic* been the kind of anime company (of which there are several in Japan) that aims for rapid returns without bothering inordinately about its work's enduring appeal, such a reaction would be perfectly justifiable. However, given that the production studio in question is Gainax, "*again?*" must surely be followed by "*and with what kind of quirky twist?*" Indeed, *Mahoromatic* is no less a genre-bending project than the previous works discussed in this book, using its *mecha* backdrop as merely a narrative prop in what is otherwise a sophisticated and often pensive coming-of-age tale suffused with somber allusions to an indelible legacy of loneliness and loss.

After lengthy and unflinchingly loyal service under the aegis of the secret agency Vesper as their most powerful soldier, Mahoro is finally allowed to retire and to have her remaining operating time extended to just about one year by living as an ordinary human instead of continuing in her martial mode to the bitter end. Accepting this option, Mahoro chooses to work as a maid for the orphaned high school student Suguru Misato, channeling her energy into looking after him, cooking gourmet food for Suguru and his mates, and keeping his residence fabulously clean and neat. This seemingly tranquil arrangement is darkened by two factors. First, Suguru happens to be the son of Mahoro's former commanding officer, whose demise she has been directly, albeit unwillingly, responsible for. Painful memories of the incident resurge to haunt the otherwise cheerful Mahoro with increasing frequency as the series progresses and its serious undertones intensify. Second, threats from the aliens little by little disrupt the maid's human routine, requiring her to take action as a combat android and thus both consume the precious operating power she has left and allow her secret identity to surface.

Heir to *Gunbuster* in its gloomier moments (Mahoro's inner turmoil often echoes Noriko's), *Mahoromatic* simultaneously perpetuates Gainax's tongue-in-cheek fascination with self-reflexivity. For example, when the heroine first describes herself as a "combat android," Suguru finds it hard to believe her since the image of the lovely maid is totally incongruous with the stereotypical concept of such an entity he harbors — a notion which he would seem to have derived entirely from classic *mecha* anime shows, as humorously suggested by the shot of the cartoony, metallic and clunky robot standing in a smoldering battlefield used to encapsulate the mental image that the phrase "combat android" instantly evokes in the boy's head (Episode 1, "In The Garden Where the Hydrangeas Bloom"). A further example of genre-specific self-reflexivity can be found in Episode 2, "Woman Teacher Saori, 25 Years Old," in which Suguru remarks that Mahoro has a voice worthy of "an anime actress."

The series' self-reflexive dimension does not only pertain to its generic tropes, however. In fact, it also extends no less effectively to the formal domain, giving rise to an animational approach that foregrounds the constructedness and material underpinnings of its images. This is borne out by the use of black-and-white manga panels (as in *FLCL*) to present climactic situations in a condensed and viscerally impactful fashion. The show also deploys to great dramatic effect marginal frame-within-a-frame drawings, often zipping across the screen, that serve to highlight a character's mien and emotions. In Episode 1, for instance, much of the comedy pervading Mahoro's first inspection of Suguru's abysmally untidy household revolves around icon-like snapshots of her face deteriorating gradually from a customarily composed expression, though mild aggravation, into farcical despair.

Like *Neon Genesis Evangelion*, *His and Her Circumstances* and *FLCL*, *Mahoromatic* concurrently brings typography into play, frequently to take the focus temporarily away from the action itself and draw attention instead to the thoughts and feelings affecting particular scenes. A paradigmatic example is provided by the sequence from the opening installment in which Suguru ponders the implications of hiring what appears to be a hypercute female teenager as a maid. The typographical techniques employed in the program deliver a wide variety of discordant effects, ranging from spectacular and even aggressive fonts traced in gaudy hues to monastically restrained brushstrokes executed in traditional black ink (*sumi*). An amusing instance of the show's use of text is supplied by the scene from Episode 6, "Moon Flower Design," in which the lustful schoolteacher Saori Shikijo fantasizes about Suguru, whom she fancies to obsessive extremes, and the action gives way to a bright pink screen bearing the cautionary caption "Sorry, this fantasy is too abnormal and dangerous to show."

In assessing *Mahoromatic*'s stylistic handling of all of its characters' more or less idiosyncratic fantasies (and not just Miss Shikijo's), Yamaga's employment of fan service can barely go unheeded. It is worth recalling that the phrase "fan service," as the relevant entry in the *Anime News Network* encyclopaedia explains, typically connotes

> the act of adding something with no direct relevance to the story or character development into an anime (or manga) for the purpose of pleasing fans. The most common form of fan service is the addition of scenes of scantily clothed, seductively posed, well-endowed women, or something similar (panty shots), also common in anime and especially manga aimed at female readers are similar situations involving male characters. However, fan service does not have to be sexual in nature. Other forms of fan service include gratuitous amounts of detailed *mecha* transformation scenes, mascot placings and so on ("Fan Service").

Miss Shikijo's freaky fantasies lead to fan-service gags so immoderate and extravagant that some viewers may unceremoniously dismiss them as low comedy. This is most pointedly the case with the scenes in Episode 4, "Shoot Me Straight through the Heart," in which — in preparation for a trip to the seaside that constitutes habitual fare in romantic comedies of this kind — the teacher seeks to allure Suguru by donning a nearly invisible bathing costume. The overall effect is grotesque rather than enticing or merely farcical. Audiences inclined to deem fan service acceptable as long as it utilizes innuendo or implied nudity but to condemn it as a gratuitous concession to vulgarity when it revels in splashy oversexed antics may decry such moments as undilutedly obscene. Yet, it could be argued that Gainax's overwrought use of fan service in *Mahoromatic* is part and parcel of the studio's genre-bending proclivities. Just as the show's solid sci-fi plot enables it to transcend the limitations of romantic yarns centered on a nerdy teenager's erotic dreams, so its approach to fan service helps *Mahoromatic* go beyond the established parameters and, in so doing, urges the spectator to ponder critically what exactly, if anything, is supposed to make that visual strategy legitimately enjoyable. As Sarcasm-hime's review of the series economically asserts, "This is a Gainax show, and as we've seen time and again they have a knack for making even the most bizarre or offensive premise fun and entertaining" (Sarcasm-hime).

On the whole, in *Mahoromatic* as in Gainax's oeuvre at large, the animation draws verve and poignance from the studio's juxtaposition of stylized character designs and cartoonish patterns of motion with exquisitely painterly backgrounds. Stylization reaches its comedic climax in the employment of *chibi*: infantilized caricatures of certain characters, intended to enhance a scene's humor. (The word translates literally as "little" but also stands as a contraction of "child body.") This strategy is deployed most effectively in Episode 3, "A Grave So Transient," in which *chibi* versions of Mahoro and of Miss Shikijo bickering in an overheated sauna are ironically contrasted with images of Suguru as he morosely observes that he has never lived as a son to the full. The action briefly returns to the sauna's zany antics, displaying a virtually sizzling Mahoro and a shriveled Miss Shikijo, and then switches once more to the serious mode, with a shot of the Misato family plot and a flashback in which Mahoro vividly recalls her part in Commander Misato's death. Stylization also abets considerably the more dramatic moments in Episode 5, "8–634 Is Doing Fine," in which Suguru and his mates engage in Summer School Activities requiring them to investigate "the nine mysteries of Hiryu School,'" including notorious rumors concerning vengeful ghosts. The characters' normal faces morph into minimalistic sketches in the scene highlighting their terror at the sight of a presumed ghost, offering a deft combination of equal measures of comedy and pathos.

Installments such as this play a key part in foregrounding the intersubjective network of relations unfolding around the protagonists. It would, of course, be preposterous to deny that the relationship between Mahoro and Suguru constitutes the show's affective fulcrum and that Mahoro, in particular, provides the catalyst through which *Mahoromatic*'s dynamic chemistry operates. Nonetheless, the supporting characters serve a vital function in enhancing the program's dramatic scope. Especially notable are the kindly and unpretentious tomboy Sakura Miyuki, the exquisitely feminine Rin Todoriki and the doll-like Chizuku Oe, the ultimate gourmet. Last but not least, Suguru's dog Guri-chan and the *mecha* support dispatched by Vesper named Slash, who is fashioned in the guise of a black panther, contribute both humor and drama to some of the show's most intense moments.

As mentioned earlier, the ominous spectre of loss — both past and impending — is never far from *Mahoromatic*'s diegesis. No pleasure that the comedy and its alternately romantic and slapstick variations offer is ever posited as unproblematic. On the technical plane, some of the more touching moments are constellated around elegantly simple line drawings — as in the relatively early scene in which Suguru takes a bath with Mahoro and bittersweet recollections of his departed mother flood his senses. The minimalistic pencil sketch of the little boy and his mother recalls analogous depictions of Shinji and Yui Ikari in *Evangelion*.

A haunting mood of imminent and inevitable loss pervades later episodes, as Mahoro slowly but surely nears her end. Episode 6 is especially memorable, in this regard. At the end of the Summer Festival in which Mahoro has played the pivotal role of "Dance Maiden," flawlessly and effortlessly performing a grueling routine, Suguru declares that they must revisit the celebration the following year at all costs. Understandably, the girl's response is a sad silence, graphically enhanced by the concomitant eruption into the night sky of glorious fireworks: a potent symbol for the ephemerality of joy, pleasure and life itself. Analogous chords are struck in Episode 8, "One Who Has a Perfect Heart," by the scene in which Mahoro reflects that Suguru will be forced to experience all over again the torment of separation when her functionality expires.

Even when *Mahoromatic* asserts most joyfully its lighthearted dimension, it remains capable of appealing to very human emotions with warming sincerity. A case in point is the opening part of Episode 4 in which Suguru and his friends embark on a trip to the beach and Mahoro supplies them with all manner of culinary treats, determined to stay behind in accordance with her subordinate role. (Mahoro has an extremely old-fashioned concept of "servitude.") The sheer passion with which each and every member of the gang insists on her joining them and proclaims an honest desire to befriend her as an equal is genuinely moving. The sequence in which Suguru's female friends engage in the selection and purchase of a bathing suit for the maid with a zeal one would expect of some momentous mission is also highly entertaining and prefigures similar sartorial exploits in the early installments of *This Ugly Yet Beautiful World*.

The show's serious import is also confirmed — as in other Gainax works examined earlier — by its unsentimental stress on adults' immaturity. In *Mahoromatic*, teachers are repeatedly portrayed as the principal target of this critique and although the bosom-centered jokes surrounding the character of the randy teacher Miss Shikijo occasionally become so insistent as to degenerate into shallow repetitiveness, the darker connotations of adults' irresponsible behavior never quite dissolve into vapid farce for its own sake.

As Teji Sarkin has noted, the show's darkness and its humor are inextricably intertwined and gain dramatic impact from their mutual support: "*Mahoromatic* is full of contrasts. From the first episode of *Mahoromatic* it is established that Mahoro will die, and soon. Her impending death is further accentuated by a little counter appearing at the end of each episode displaying her remaining time. This is put in direct conflict with the lightheartedness of the ordinary life of Misato and his friends" (Sarkin). John Huxley has analogously remarked upon *Mahoromatic*'s tonal variety in his review of the show's first DVD volume: "One minute you'll be tittering at Miss Saori's over exuberant attempts to unsettle Suguru's relationship with Mahoro (which mostly involves sticking her breasts into his face), the next you'll be encouraged to contemplate the fragility of life as Suguru mourns the untimely death of his parents" (Huxley).

The action gains unprecedented momentum with the advent of the character of Ryuga in Episode 7, "The Maid Chased by Her Past." Just as Mahoro is Vesper's most capable warrior, so Ryuga is introduced as the most powerful combat machine employed by the rival power Saint. Mahoro and Ryuga are supposed to have confronted each other many times, with each duel resulting in a draw. When Mahoro discovers that the Saint emissary has infiltrated her world, disguised as an athletic and handsome supply teacher at Suguru's school, she darkly ponders: "My past has finally caught up to me." This utterance marks *Mahoromatic*'s decisive shift toward a noncomedic modality. Ryuga, for his part, is at first convinced that Vesper intends to use Suguru as his dad's worthy successor and that Mahoro has been sent to protect him but rapidly realizes that the boy knows nothing about his father's past and professional obligations.

Members of Saint, we are told, have been roaming the universe for time immemorial, by and by losing all recollection of the planet where their quest began. Ryuga is an android designed solely for combat (not unlike Mahoro herself) but still bears vestiges of submerged memories related to his culture's origins and goals. The first generation of Saint travelers departed in search of cultures with which they could interact but found no civilizations or even signs of life until they reached Earth, the "blue planet." A voiceover preceding Mahoro and Ryuga's final duel recounts the outcome of the Saint culture's encounter with humans as follows: "Ironically, first contact with their long-sought culture was accidental, though it was through the most primitive method. War. The thus far unique, simple culture of Saint does not like war. However, the receiving race is so underdeveloped they continue to reject all contact besides war." Human civilization's refusal of nonbelligerent interaction with their visitors is precisely the reason behind Saint's construction of creatures like Ryuga.

The climactic fight presented in Episode 12, "To the Scenery I Once Dreamt Of," is *Mahoromatic*'s most sophisticated and complex sequence in terms of both choreography and psychology. As the *DVD Times* review of the series' third volume maintains, the sequence constitutes "an impressively directed bout, making full use of the setting at an abandoned high school to produce a tense stand-off.... When close-combat does kick in it's handled beautifully by some fluid animation, while the art design manages to keep a good sense of proportion and detail throughout" ("*Mahoromatic: Automatic Maiden Vol. 03*: Review").

Stylistically, the sequence echoes some of *Evangelion*'s most conspicuous battles in its ingenious fusion of the staple elements of both space opera and the western (Ryuga's armor, incidentally, is vividly redolent of Shinji's Eva-01). Among the numerous instances of intense drama communicated by the duel, one of the most epically resonant is the scene in which Ryuga emerges from the ruins despite having been hit by Mahoro with an antimatter cannon believed to be capable of annihilating him for good. No less memorable is the scene in which Ryuga hits Mahoro with preternatural vehemence and sends her flying backwards through space along a flight path that, through perspectival distortion and decelerated motion, appears to last for a truly interminable length of time.

This temporal suspension gives Yamaga's camera the opportunity to indulge in an imaginary, dreamlike flash-forward in which Mahoro fantasizes about what it would be like if she were to defeat Ryuga and go back to her ordinary domestic routine the following morning as though nothing extraordinary had ever come to pass. The sequence is bathed in a distinctively idyllic atmosphere, as Mahoro, Suguru and their friends are seen to enjoy a rural picnic, crowned by the scene in which the girls sit in a tree musing over their aspirations for the future — a dimension that for Mahoro herself, regardless of the duel's outcome, feels flimsier and flimsier by the instant.

Mahoro is forced back to reality by Ryuga's savage beating in a scene of heightened dramatic vigor, made all the more disturbing by being initially presented in the form of storyboard-style rough pencil sketches. Among the most effective cinematographical strategies brought to bear on this part of the sequence are the "zip pan," an effect based on backgrounds that consist entirely of lines instead of defined images to evoke a vibrant impression of movement, and the "image BG" technique, in which the backgrounds are flooded with vigorous palettes to convey extreme emotional states or to signal a shift to alternate reality levels. The zip pan is used effectively for the frames in which Mahoro takes the thrashing of her life, where the background is filled by starkly ominous black and white lines. The image BG technique, for its part, features in the shots where the heroine starts bleeding, and we are treated to a realistic portrait of her face in profile against a white background, with an explicitly spray-painted jet of scarlet dots issuing from the mouth.

Truly breathtaking is the shot of Ryuga as a hyper-stylized charcoal sketch with bright green eyes so passionately realistic as to appear endowed with an independent life of their own. (The Eva-01's charismatic eyes readily spring to mind.) At the end of the fight, when Mahoro has sacrificed part of her scanty life-span to beat Ryuga (satisfying his own desire for an ultimate, all-out confrontation against her own interest), the screen delivers the moving shot of a nocturnal sky embroidered with a splotchy yellow moon and stars, depicted in a childlike style through the medium of crayon. Gainax's undying dedication to the quintessentially artisanal qualities of anime has the last word.

It is worth noting, in this context, that the countdown toward Mahoro's inexorable termination will gain additional momentum in the show's second season, directed by Yamaga and aired in 2002–2003, namely, *Mahoromatic — Automatic Maiden: Something More Beautiful*. In this program, the drama surrounding the merciless ticking of the heroine's biological clock is enriched through the consistent use of flashbacks, introspective moments and déjà-vus that invite the viewer's own imagination to map out the actual passage of time. In *Mahoromatic*'s second season, the multiple relationships involving the android maid, Suguru and their friends are developed further and complicated by the appearance of another female android, Minawa, who becomes deeply attached to Mahoro. Any spectator with an interest in anime's handling of relational dynamics is highly likely to find the show's articulation of Mahoro and Minawa's interaction a veritable jewel in the field. (This same motif will be revamped in *This Ugly Yet Beautiful World*, in which the introduction of the principal supernatural agent, Hikari, is soon followed by the appearance of her alter ego Akari.)

Given the explicitly belligerent purposes underlying Mahoro's construction — not to mention her formidable martial assets — the android's disarming prettiness and deferential meekness may come as a surprise, or even appear incompatible with the character's intrinsic nature. However, it is precisely from this dialectical tension that Mahoro gains psychological and emotional depth, in both her gladiatorial exploits and in her gentle quotidian behavior. Thus, the show boldly challenges the stereotypical association of "cuteness" and "niceness" so proverbially endemic to fantasy fiction and cinema. Another intriguing instance of this trend is provided by the TV series *MoonPhase* (dir. Akiyuki Shinbo, 2004–2005), in which one of the cutest young females to have ever featured in anime, Hazuki/Luna, turns out to be an indomitable blood-drinker in the thrall of a baleful curse. (Alongside lacy doll-like accoutrements, the character occasionally vaunts a cat-eared headband — a staple of girlish daintiness in anime.) The idea that supercute girls can be lethal is also humorously conveyed by the TV show *Coyote Ragtime Show* (dir. Takuya Nonaka, 2006): The minions of the "Criminal Guild," known as the "Twelve Daughters," are absolutely adorable cuties decked out in frilly Loli-Goth apparel but also happen to be agents of death equipped with all manner of malefic weapons.[1]

Yamaga's generic experimentation does not only impact on *Mahoromatic*'s take on *mecha* but also on a further anime formula invoked by the series, namely, *moe*. A controversial and multiaccentual term, "*moe*" takes the Japanese passion for all things "*kawaii*" ("cute") to extremes by capitalizing on female characters that are so ardently cherished, yet respectfully worshipped from a discrete distance, as to acquire the status of fetishes. On the thematic plane, *moe* exhibits numerous affinities with the *shoujo* genre and accordingly tends to elaborate romantic yarns and melodramas pivoting on beautifully drawn young females. Like *shoujo*, however, *moe* does not unequivocally enthrone the sentimental dimension as its sole focus but actually provides plenty of scope for adventurous forays into the territories of historical drama and serious or semi-serious science fiction. Its axial personae, relatedly, are not automatically defined as huge-eyed teenagers exuding innocent charm amidst streams of flowers, hearts, stars and glowing lights. In fact, *shoujo* and *moe* heroines alike frequently reveal unexpected layers of psychological complexity that grow in accordance with their exposure to varyingly intense societal pressures. As argued in Chapter 1, nowhere is this trend more pithily and audaciously proclaimed than in Gainax's productions, in which even the cutest of girls may disclose turbulent drives and dark intentions. A seemingly naive mien does not unproblematically preclude the lurking presence of unsavory personality traits, such as acquisitiveness or cynicism.

Several critics and commentators have reacted unsympathetically to *moe* on the assumption that its penchant for fetishization lowers it to the level of genres eager to satisfy voyeuristic scopophilia and even paedophiliac propensities. Within Japan's entertainment industry, one such genre is the *lolicon* (an acronym forged from the fusion of "Lolita" and "complex"), in which the emphasis falls straight upon the satisfaction of an adult male's erotic fantasies by means of starkly reified *shoujo*esque idols. *Moe*'s supporters counter these accusations by claiming that in this genre, the idealized character is not presented as a passive object for active consumption by an avid male gaze but rather as an eminently fictional construct meant to invite protective and sympathetic responses without any overt notion of sexual titillation coming into play. Gainax's experiments with *moe* radically subvert the association of the genre with the masterful appropriation of nonthreatening, submissive or even downright vulnerable females by presenting their heroines as plucky, resourceful and capable of taking their fate into their stride, undesirable though this may be.

Architectural theorist Kaichiro Morikawa has succinctly summed up *moe*'s peculiar approach to the concept of attractiveness in his essay "Learning from Akihabara: The Birth of a Personaopolis," in which he maintains that *moe* fundamentally refers to a person's fascination with a certain character type or, more accurately, with "specific elements or characteristics" that single it out as desirable. A case in point is "'glasses *moe*,'" namely, "a taste that is taken with a character who wears glasses; ... this taste fetishizes the feature itself of glasses-wearing" (Morikawa). The character of Miss Shikijo in *Mahoromatic* is an eligible candidate, in this respect. So is the supporting character of Mune-Mune in *Magical Shopping Arcade Abenobashi*. No less cogent instances are provided by the TV series *Please Teacher!* (dir. Yasunori Ide, 2002)—whose female lead, Mizuho Kazami, is an extremely sexy bespectacled alien—and the OVA series *UFO Ultramaiden Valkyrie: Bride of Celestial Souls' Day* (dir. Shigeru Ueda, 2004). The latter, a vibrantly animated show laced throughout with attractive character designs, chronicles the amiable bathhouse manager Kazuko Tokino's befuddling interactions with a gaggle of zany Valhalla goddesses from outer space, and it devotes the whole of its opening installment to the alien princess Pharm's resolution to make every girl in sight wear glasses—and look cute in them.

In the case of Mahoro, Gainax's aversion to sexualized fetishization as an end in itself is intradiegetically consolidated by the android's unwaveringly censorious attitude toward porn, however "soft." (This theme will be accorded categorical centrality in the one-episode spin-off *Mahoromatic—Automatic Maiden: Summer Special*, directed by Shouji Saeki and aired in 2003, in which Mahoro and her female allies embark on a crusade to purge Suguru's house of any trace of dubious literature.) In the original show, Mahoro's ethical integrity is refreshingly enhanced by her unsullied conviction that there is nothing indecorous about her sharing a bath with Suguru, which demonstrates that her dislike of commercial erotica is not just conducive to puritanically stuffy prurience.

Thus, much as it retains the unmistakable traits of a romantic plot featuring cute girls and adoring male youths, peppered with a fairly bounteous portion of fan service, *Mahoromatic* never employs the conventions of *moe* as more than an ancillary diegetic ploy. In fact, it goes as far as subverting *moe*'s classic "division of labor," according to which the female cutie is the party requiring pampering and protection, by positing Mahoro as a capable, autonomous and generously supportive agent. (*Moe* will also be addressed in relation to *This Ugly Yet Beautiful World*.)

Mahoromatic's most explicitly *moe* aspect resides with its heroine's physical appearance and, specifically, with its interpretation of the visual conventions associated with the "maid" type. This, it is worth stressing, has become so popular in anime as to have affected pervasively both the world of cosplay and the ancillary-merchandise sector. Furthermore, the district of Akihabara in Tokyo, once renowned as the otaku paradise of electronic goods, has recently sprouted numerous "maid cafés" with a decidedly *moe* ambience. Amos Wong has commented on the venue "@home café" as an illustrative example: The place is run by "cute waitresses dressed in maid gear" and exudes a "warm, fuzzy atmosphere," complemented by a menu that includes "dainty desserts like cakes decorated with rabbits, bears and little Yorkshire terriers." The clientele, Wong adds, does not consist solely of "otaku types" but of "a varied bunch from both genders" (Wong 2006, p. 71).

On the "maid" front as on several others, Yamaga's show departs from the standardized formula to engage in some inspired generic experimentation. As Mark Clark points out, the show initially posits itself as just one more entry "into the 'boy meets cute robotic maid genre'" and does not, to this extent, constitute an especially challenging artistic intervention. Nevertheless when it transpires that "Mahoro actually has a good reason for being a maid and working for Suguru," the story acquires a depth that sets it apart from more simplistic treatments of the established formula: "those expecting another *Hand Maid May* are in for something a little different this time" (Clark, p. 154). In the TV series (directed by Shinichiro Kimura and broadcast in 2000), which Clark cites as an apposite point of comparison, the "maid" in question is actually a palm-sized cyberdoll (eventually upgraded to a model with real-life dimensions and proportions). The notion of the *moe* maid as an enticingly delicate projection of male fantasies is communicated, in Kimura's program, by the explicit equation of May to a quintessentially Barbie-like fetish.

An unusual take on the "Servant-Master" relationship, garnished with gentle hints at the maid type, is offered by the TV series *Fate/stay Night* (dir. Yuji Yamaguchi, 2006), in which powerful sorcerers known as "Masters" periodically engage in epic confrontations with the objective of gaining the "Holy Grail." They are aided, in their mission, by reincarnations of legendary souls named "Servants," who boast supernatural abilities and weapons. The protagonist, Shirou Emiya, is a would-be sorcerer hailed as "Master" by the "Servant" Saber — a loyal and powerful warrior garbed in a costume that blends elements of the mediaeval armor with motifs (such as the frilly hem) characteristically associated with traditional maids. Just as Suguru endeavors to hide Mahoro's very existence from his friends and teachers and, when he eventually has no choice but to introduce her, conceals her real identity, so Shirou does his best to prevent his tutor (and self-appointed guardian) Taiga and his school friend Sakura from finding out about the Saber. However, there comes a point when he must introduce her to his earthly acquaintances willy-nilly since he cannot simply keep her locked up. Nor can she assume the spiritual form that would be more appropriate to the status of a "Servant" of her caliber: Shirou's magical powers are not adequately developed and therefore do not provide the energy the Saber needs to absorb in order to achieve that aim.

A major point of contact between Mahoro and the Saber lies with their use of a deferential register whenever they address their employers. The combat android seems to find this code of conduct utterly natural, whereas *Fate/stay Night*'s heroine initially adopts it merely in accordance with tradition and an ingrained regard for hierarchy — and not without a marginal dose of resentment. This emotional conflict manifests itself in two ways. On the one hand, even though the Saber takes her duty toward her Master very seriously indeed, she gets irate when he treats her as though she were an ordinary, defenseless girl. On the other, while she is on the whole very respectful and obliging, she nonetheless objects persistently to what she perceives as Shirou's recklessness and gullibility. Hence, although the Master and the Servant are supposed to be pursuing a common goal, they often find themselves butting heads. It is not until the series is well under way that the Saber begins to feel that she is abetting a "boss" she can be truly proud of and not a bumbling neophyte.

Mahoromatic partakes of several of the codes and conventions typically associated with that branch of anime known as "Magical Girl"— or, where relevant, "Magical Girlfriend." This form tends to dramatize adolescent male wish-fulfillment fantasies and to feature an inept hero on whom fate suddenly smiles as a beautiful, sweet-tempered and utterly devoted female enters his existence. The girl in question is normally a supernatural or virtual entity endowed with special powers, whose abilities are inevitably conducive to dramatic irony: In helping the male lead discover true love, she also ends up giving him a bit of an inferiority complex. At the same time, paradoxically she feels clumsy, weak, unworthy of his affection and the cause of unpleasant complications (domestic or cosmic as the case may be).

The TV series unanimously hailed as the epitome of the "Magical Girl" typology is *Sailor Moon* (dirs. Junichi Sato et al., 1992–1997), the longest-running anime program of its kind (200 episodes). The heroine is Tsukino Usagi, a clumsy teenager prone to emotional outbursts who receives magical tools from a cat named Luna and gradually discovers that she possesses superpowers capable of affecting the entire cosmos. *Sailor Moon*'s admixture of humor and romance has become a defining trait of the genre that comes resplendently to the fore in *Mahoromatic*. *Oh My Goddess!* (OVA series; dir. Hiroaki Gouda, 1993) and subsequent productions in the same franchise up to *Ah! My Goddess: Flights of Fancy* (OVA series; dir. Hiroaki Gouda, 2006) also provide relevant points of historical reference.

This epoch-making saga chronicles the adventures of student Keiichi Morisato as his tedious routine is disrupted by the appearance on the scene of the goddess Belldandy — a stunningly beautiful and kindly creature who vows to live with Keiichi forever — and, as the plot unfolds, by the advent of Belldandy's sisters Urd and Skuld as further unexpected additions to the protagonist's unorthodox "family." As Keiichi and Belldandy become increasingly attached to each other, in spite of Urd's and Skuld's respective attempts to either consolidate or disrupt the relationship with equally disastrous outcomes, the familiar cocktail of comedic and romantic ingredients dominates the narrative's mood over the decades of its release history.

The web of relationships woven by Suguru's interaction not only with Mahoro but also his school friends and teachers at times recalls the atmosphere of the "harem comedy" *Love Hina* (dir. Yoshiaki Iwasaki, 2000), a TV series (complemented by two feature-length productions and an OVA) focusing on the hapless Keitaro Urashima and the bevy of hugely attractive — and no less idiosyncratic — women he is surrounded by as fate unexpectedly puts him in charge of an all-girl dorm. What makes *Love Hina* truly memorable over and above the formulaic trappings of the "harem" genre is its refreshing knack of infusing farcically absurd elements into an otherwise well-tested scenario (including *mecha* and ghosts quite incongruous with the main plot). In this respect, the show supplies an apt parallel to *Mahoromatic*'s tendency to sprinkle the action with barmy incidents — especially when it indulges in the depiction of the perverted Miss Shikijo's hot-blooded pranks.

Mahoromatic's drama at times echoes the mood of the TV show *Vampire Princess Miyu* (dir. Toshihiro Hirano, 1997–1998). Indeed, in both programs, the heroine's raison d'être is intertwined with the obligation to undertake an inescapable and unpalatable duty. In Miyu's case, the mission consists of hounding down and destroying a breed of bloodthirsty demons known as "Shinma," thus returning them to the "Darkness" whence they have unlawfully sprung. The vampiric princess has no more choice in the matter than Mahoro does on the issue of battling and vanquishing alien attackers. Like Mahoro, moreover, Miyu is painfully aware of the age-related gulf that separates her from humans. For example, when a classmate with an unhealthy appetite for the esoteric discovers the princess's true identity and begs her to transform him into a creature of her kind, Miyu's response unequivocally shows that she does not regard her fate as a blessing.

Additionally, when the schoolgirls who insist on befriending Miyu despite her reclusive attitude draw her into their innocent merry-go-round of blatantly girlish pursuits, she appears — and indeed *wants to* — play along but remains all the while aware of her irreducible alterity and of the prospective grief to which she makes herself vulnerable by participating in human activities. At the same time, although both *Mahoromatic* and *Vampire Princess Miyu* present angst-ridden situations and often intensely dynamic action, their pathos characteristically emanates from a subdued sense of melancholy — distinctively Japanese in flavor — and an unnervingly sustained, yet subtly modulated, evocation of the two heroines' bond to their respective destinies.

Furthermore, in both shows, considerable dramatic impact derives from the central characters' ageless status. In *Mahoromatic*, the protagonist is essentially designed as a construct unaffected by the passage of time as long as it is functional, and to simply cease to operate once its power has run out. Mahoro's programmed inability to grow old is ineluctably coterminous with her lack of a long-term future. Gainax's oeuvre exhibits an inveterate fascination with the dream of eternal youth (encapsulated by the "Peter Pan Syndrome" alluded to in Chapter 3 and to be revisited in Chapter 11). However, it concurrently intimates that exemption from ageing is not an unproblematic gift for it may also entail the prospect of premature termination. *Vampire Princess Miyu* provides a complementary perspective on the issue by overtly presenting endless adolescence as a burden. Insofar as she cannot either age or die, Miyu is plagued by what could — by oblique analogy — be described as the "Vampire Complex": a condition wherein agelessness is not synonymous with the absence of a practicable future but a condemnation to a forever deferred tomorrow.

The age theme is also pivotal to another recent Gainax production, the TV series *Petite Princess Yucie* (dir. Masahiko Otsuka, 2002–2003). A seventeen-year-old girl who looks as though she were barely ten, the heroine of this classic *shoujo* anime labors under a curse that impedes her physical development. While *Mahoromatic* contains elliptical references to magical fantasy, yet remains grounded in a contemporary urban environment throughout the majority of the action, *Petite Princess Yucie* indulges wholeheartedly in fairy tale. Its recurring symbolism and iconography — a multiturreted castle, dragons, gems and passionately mediaeval townscapes — fully attest to this graphic preference. Charmingly scatterbrained and prone to outbreaks of zany romantic lunacy, Yucie is nonetheless a character not to be taken with total levity. Otsuka's show indeed reverberates with *Gunbuster*'s ethical message in its emphasis on the protagonist's intrepid efforts to become the "Platinum Princess" through exacting training at the "Princess Academy," where ruthless competitors for the position abound, and reconstitute the "Eternal Tiara" whose fragments are scattered throughout the Human, Demon, Heaven, Spirit, and Fairy worlds. The jeweled headdress, according to legend, is capable of fulfilling any wish and would therefore enable Yucie to grow into a proper woman.

The character of Yucie brings to mind *Gunbuster*'s Noriko (while also adumbrating *Gunbuster 2*'s Nono) in her unflinching determination to succeed against seemingly impervious obstacles. This does not entail, of course, that she initially harbors the self-assuredness necessary to accomplish her quest any more than either Noriko or Nono does. This is borne out by the closing sequence of Episode 1, "A New Platinum Princess Candidate." In this foundational portion of the story, Queen Ercell (principal of the Princess Academy as well as appointed keeper of the Eternal Tiara) states that the quality Yucie must foster in order to embark on her trial is "confidence," and the girl concedes that she has not yet developed this strength. She adamantly adds, however, that she is determined to try to do her best. *Petite Princess Yucie* is also redolent of *Gunbuster* in the scenes dramatizing the heroine's cruel bullying at the hands of coetaneous girls scornful of her diminutive size and doll-like countenance.

Petite Princess Yucie recalls *FLCL* in its suggestion that no blessings automatically accrue to the state of "being a kid"— or being regarded as one for that matter. Concurrently, Otsuka's series anticipates *This Ugly Yet Beautiful World* in its deployment of supernatural imagery, particularly in the early sequence displaying the discovery of the baby Yucie in a forest amidst a halo of magical light. *Petite Princess Yucie* also foreshadows the later series in its dramatic treatment of psychological and emotional tensions that may seem incongruous with the story's fairy-tale dimension, yet gain poignancy precisely from their unexpected emergence within an ostensibly uncomplicated context.

Replicating a stylistic tendency to be found in virtually all of Gainax's animations, *Petite Princess Yucie* opens on a sunny and chirpy note, yet its tone progressively darkens to verge on tragic intensity in the climactic episodes. In these installments, it transpires that the heroine's achievement of her goal comes with a steep price, namely, the erasure of all the other competitors in the tournament, who have become Yucie's loyal friends in the course of her adventures. Should the candidate chosen by the Eternal Tiara to become the Platinum Princess reject the appointment, her world will be annihilated. The protagonist is initially protected from this sinister truth as the judge of the Magic World compassionately agrees to obliterate her memories of her erstwhile companions. However, these gradually begin to resurface in the form of a haunting sense of loss causing Yucie to feel that a very vital part of her is missing but utterly unable to pinpoint its significance. By and by, ghostly apparitions of the vanished girls also begin to punctuate the dusky streets. Eventually, Yucie pulls off the ultimate magical feat — though, it should be stressed, relying no more on magic per se than on sheer human guts — and brings the missing girls back. In spite of its fairy-tale ending, the sadness and daunting feeling of bereavement affecting the portion of the story in which Yucie is at her most miserable exactly when she ought to feel triumphant leaves lasting imprints in the viewer's memory.

Mahoromatic's sci-fi dimension and *Petite Princess Yucie*'s engagement with the domain of legend come together in *The Melody of Oblivion*, a 24-episode series directed by Hiroshi Nishikiori and originally broadcast in 2004, helmed by J. C. Staff with Gainax's contribution in the areas of planning and production. (The series, incidentally, also bears affinities with *Evangelion* in the handling of mythological motifs, and with *This Ugly Yet Beautiful World* in the deployment of cosmic imagery.) The story, set in the twenty-first century, proceeds from the premise that in the previous century, humans were involved in a momentous conflict with entities known simply as "Monsters," which resulted in their total subjugation to that breed. However, even though the Monsters dominate the Earth, they keep hidden from the public, thriving on a *Matrix*-like system that virtually effaces their existence.

The only people who are still aware of the rulers' presence and endeavor to vanquish them so as to restore humanity to its pristine liberty are the "Warriors of Melos." Allied to these valiant fighters' ability to perceive and combat the Monsters is their capacity to see and hear a phantom girl known as the "Melody of Oblivion" ("*Boukyaku no Senritsu*"): the spiritual force whose release would conclusively free the world. The protagonist, an ordinary teenager named Bocca, unexpectedly discovers his potential as a Warrior when, in witnessing a duel between a Melos and a Monster, he unexpectedly senses the melody. He thereby resolves to seek out and release the occluded *Boukyaku no Senritsu* at all costs, which draws him into a whirl of adventures involving legion demons and their agents, as well as new friends and companions.

As noted, Mahoro reveals considerable psychological complexity in spite of her surface association with the proverbially unponderous *shoujo*, *moe* and maid typologies. Yucie, likewise, discloses levels of affective richness one would not habitually expect of a standard fairytale heroine. Bocca harks back to both of those characters insofar as his ostensibly uncomplicated personality actually belies somber involutions. Assessing Bocca's attitude to life, producer Hiroki Sato has indeed stressed the importance of looking past appearances. Gainax's strength, it is intimated, does not merely lie with a flexible approach to generic classifications (although, as insistently observed in the present chapter as in previous ones, this is undoubtedly one of the studio's most distinctive attributes). In fact, it also resides with a no less supple take on the core elements of its characters' makeup. For instance, neither determination nor self-doubt, neither maturity nor infantilism, are uniformly portrayed. The same basic proclivity may actually lead to radically divergent manifestations. "Bocca," Sato states, "lives his life according to his own principles, which makes him less a child than Shinji. But that can be a sign of childishness, too!" (Interview in "Gainax turns 20!" p. 39). Furthermore, *Melody* copiously documents Gainax's penchant for intertextuality in that it draws inspiration from an astounding range of repertoires, from Zen Archery to the samurai code of *Bushido*, from Greek mythology to the Bible (and especially the Book of Revelations), from Satanic worship to the Chinese Zodiac.

Even though *Mahoromatic* is not, by any stretch of the imagination, Gainax's most acclaimed or most spectacular production, it does function effectively as something of a compendium of recurring generic and formal motifs characteristic of the studio's entire output. On one level, it echoes early works such as *Honneamise* and *Gunbuster* in its elaboration of a sophisticated sci-fi yarn and the latter, specifically, in its emphasis on female bravery. On another, it harks back to *Nadia* in dramatizing the vicissitudes of a heroine torn between a murky past and a potentially baleful future. At the same time, *Mahoromatic* joins forces with *Otaku no Video* by offering a critical approach to some of the more overtly formulaic facets of anime, especially in the areas of *mecha* and Magical-Girl entertainment. *Mahoromatic*'s exploration of a twisted romance, often by recourse to bold pictorial and calligraphic gestures, concomitantly brings it close to the visual universe of *His and Her Circumstances*, while its choreographing of sensational action sequences out of quiet situations relates it to *FLCL*. Additionally, Yamaga's series looks forward to *This Ugly Yet Beautiful World* in its deconstruction of *moe*, and to both the latter and *Gunbuster 2* in its enthroning as pivotal agents of apparently cute and acquiescent but intrinsically indomitable female protagonists.

In the elaboration of these multifarious elements, Gainax's iconographic preferences assiduously assert themselves. Particularly commendable, in this regard, are the characters' soft and realistic facial expressions and the punctiliously depicted natural and urban backgrounds. As far as the background art is specifically concerned, one of its most striking aspects is the deft alternation of the blue-green and red-orange ends of the spectrum to evoke clear dramatic contrasts. By recourse to this chromatic strategy, the animation sets up a dialectical tension between two contrasting sorts of scenarios: present-day scenes, generally characterized by an uplifting sense of airiness and spaciousness, and combat-centered flashbacks l.blighted by a sepulchral atmosphere, smoke-saturated gloom and doomful flares. It is also notable that the crisp and neat artwork devoted to the representation of the characters and settings is complemented throughout by highly detailed and studiously scaled mechanical designs for the sci-fi props, including both weapons of relatively modest dimensions (by anime standards, that is) and mammoth spaceships and robotic aliens. Through a subtle use of shading, especially in the rendition of light reflections and refractions, the peculiar attributes of diverse textures and materials are enabled to proclaim themselves to a palpable degree, and hence rise to the status of animated characters no less memorable than the human agents themselves.

CHAPTER 11

Magical Shopping Arcade Abenobashi (Abenobashi Mahou Shoutengai)
Director: Hiroyuki Yamaga (2002)

> Magical Shopping Arcade Abenobashi's *shining element is its drama.... Yes, you wouldn't expect the genre-per-episode format to feature much in the way of serious issues, but the manner in which the dramatic scenes convey far more than just the simple lives of real people is strongly reminiscent of* His and Her Circumstances.
> ... In part, this is all due to the concept [which], while not exactly original, provides a creative vehicle for the story and characters to expand.
> —Anime Academy *Review: Magical Shopping Arcade Abenobashi*

Sasshi Imamiya and his best friend Arumi Asahina are residents of the rundown Abenobashi Shoutengai (Abenobashi Shopping District) in Osaka. In Episode 1, "Mystery! Abenobashi Shopping Arcade," a summer day like countless others is suddenly disrupted by two related events. Arumi's grandfather, Grandpa Masa, falls from the roof of the Pelican Diner, the small restaurant he runs in conjunction with his Francophile son, in an attempt to shoo the obese family cat off the beak of a stone pelican situated above the restaurant, while the bird itself (one of the arcade's four linchpin statues) crashes spectacularly to the ground below. Grandpa Masa is conveyed to hospital, having sustained injuries so serious that his chances of survival are uncertain. At the end of the same day, the two kids are magically transported from their so-called real world to the alternate realm of Mahou Shoutengai (Magical Shopping Arcade). This is a bizarre parallel universe where common sense and logic appear to have been altogether suspended. Arumi and Sasshi repeatedly find themselves traversing a series of seemingly absurd worlds that consist of more or less explicit parodies of familiar media and genres, including video games, movies of both the animated and live-action varieties, and multifarious incarnations of the fantastic at its wackiest and most surreal.[1]

Insofar as this ever-shifting frame of reference spawns vastly different domains governed by context-specific rules, the protagonists are never in a position to take their environment for granted and must, in fact, struggle to identify the type of world they find themselves in at each turn of the narrative, grapple with its laws and requirements, and interpret it accordingly. The discourse of mediaeval role-playing games dominates Episode 2, "Adventure! Abenobashi Sword and Sorcery Shopping Arcade," whereas Episode 3, "Hook Up! Abenobashi Great Milky Way Shopping Arcade," accords generic centrality to science fiction of the *mecha* variety. In Episode 4, "Fire It Up! Abenobashi Hong Kong Combat Shopping Arcade," the formulae of the martial-arts movie come flamboyantly into play, to give way to the prehistoric-world cartoon style in Episode 5, "Extinction! Abenobashi Ancient Dinosaur Shopping Arcade."

A collage of film-noir tropes amalgamating the visual rhetoric of hard-boiled detective fiction, the gangster film and Sherlock-Holmes London is firmly enthroned in Episode 6, "In the Night Fog! Abenobashi Hard Boiled Shopping Arcade." Replete with popular anime characters, Episode 8, "Set Your Heart Aflutter! Abenobashi Campus Shopping Arcade," parodies the dating-sim genre (a type of adventure-oriented video game pivoting on romantic interactions between the player and anime girls). In Episode 10, "Fluffy, Bubbly! Abenobashi Fairy Tale Shopping Arcade," the stylistic lead is taken by the codes of fantasy fiction at its frilliest and tackiest. In stark contrast with this world of cute paper dolls and Magical Girls, the realm portrayed in Episode 11, "Resolution!! Abenobashi Battlefield Shopping Arcade," presents a dismal war-torn version of the arcade wherein painful feelings of remorse and dejection come to the foreground despite the abiding parodic tone in which the action is couched. The show's habitually comedic mood is ostentatiously restored in Episode 12, "Huge Reversal?! Abenobashi Hollywood Shopping Arcade," a tantalizing pastiche of Hollywood action movies of all kinds, including *Terminator 2*, *Titanic*, *Jaws*, the Indiana Jones films, and legion allusions to the horror genre, the musical and the plane-hijack yarn.

Intriguingly, each transition to a parallel universe signals a related alteration in the type of discourse used by the characters to negotiate its "reality," and an attendant exposure of the linguistic clichés that accrue to the register in hand. In Episode 2, for instance, the villain of the piece is referred to as an "honest-to-god Evil Lord," while in Episode 3, the injunction to take rapid action against Space Pirates is justified on the basis that failure to do so would result in the Earth doing the "annihilation thingy." The shopping arcade itself changes in accordance with the codes and conventions peculiar to the genre that each installment draws upon. Thus, in Episode 2, it exudes an unmistakably mediaeval aura and the merchandise on display accordingly encompasses suits of armor, chainmail, swords and talismans. In Episode 3, the action's *mecha*-oriented thrust is mirrored by the inclusion of robotic contraptions and futuristic layouts — with a *mecha* version of the crucial pelican statue mentioned earlier also making a cameo appearance, as though to intimate unobtrusively a sense of continuity despite the overall adventure's reeling evocation of an atmosphere of implacable flux.

Gainax's own oeuvre is repeatedly invoked for parodic purposes by means of both spectacular references to major productions such as *Gunbuster* and *Evangelion* (e.g., in Episode 3) and more discrete hints at relatively marginal works: In Episode 2, the wallpaper on Sasshi's mobile phone displays a Bunny Girl redolent of the character from the short animation produced for *Daicon 4*, while Arumi's metamorphosis into a Magical Girl in Episode 8 vividly recalls the persona of Misty May from *Otaku no Video*.

The parodic element found in the anime is also conspicuous in the *Abenobashi* manga (produced by Gainax in the wake of the animation), as underscored by Justin Kovalsky in a review of the first volume. His comments apply no less fittingly to the TV show than to the printed series: "It's a great example of Gainax's twisted sense of humor. The corporate invaders who show up to take over Abenobashi look a lot like *Zaku* (enemy mechs from *Gundam*), so much so that a character jokes about copyright infringement. But the heartiest chuckle came when Abenobashi's ultimate counterattack is revealed — the *Banangelion*.... If you're an *Evangelion* or *Nuku Nuku* [i.e., *All Purpose Cultural Cat Girl Nuku Nuku*, dir. Yoshitaka Fujimoto, 1998] fan, you'll get the joke" (Kovalsky). Through both the anime and the manga versions of *Abenobashi*'s prismatic adventure, with its virtually innumerable forays into generic and stylistic pastiche, the series demonstrates that Gainax is not in the least scared of taking chances when it comes to experimentation.

Formal diversity makes the program deliberately discontinuous (the episodes are markedly disparate, especially at the level of genre), which contributes vitally to the defamiliarizing effect steadily pursued by Yamaga throughout. This may make *Abenobashi* a bit hard to get into for audiences new to Gainax's tricks, and even induce them to find the series inconsistent. These reservations are bound to evaporate, however, as the intentionality with which *Abenobashi*'s non sequiturs are engineered becomes patent, and one recognizes the ingeniousness with which the various pieces are linked closely together as by dovetailing. It must also be stressed, at this juncture, that cultural allusions to legion aspects of Japanese popular culture, stereotypes, dialects and idiolects abound, and that some of these might at first impede undiluted enjoyment for the average Western viewer.

As documented by Arata Kanoh in the "Guided Tour" to *Abenobashi* provided by *Newtype USA*, one of the show's most salient cultural references and recurring thematic concerns lies with "*Onmyou* mysticism," namely, the ability to "solve all your problems by hopping from world to world." *Onmyou* is indeed mentioned right from the start — in the preamble to the first installment, to be precise — and visually associated with the pentagram (or pentacle): the series' logo and arguably the most ubiquitous symbol for esoteric practices the world over. Also significant, according to Kanoh, is *Abenobashi*'s assiduous employment of a "narrative style" specifically redolent of "a comic storytelling style that's popular in the Tokyo area." This relies on the accumulation of a plethora of loosely connected jokes rather than on single punch lines (Kanoh, p. 61).

Moreover, even as it delivers a series as jam-packed with clownish comedy as *Abenobashi* unquestionably is, the studio is still capable of offering a sensitive look at life through the eyes of tentatively developing kids. In its treatment of cross-generational interactions, *Abenobashi*'s critique of adults is certainly not as vitriolic as *Evangelion*'s — or even as nostalgic as *Gunbuster*'s or *Mahoromatic*'s. It does, however, work in a distinctively Gainaxian fashion in its uncompromising emphasis on the immaturity, duplicity and selfishness of grown-ups even if these unsavory traits are predicated upon eccentricity instead of downright malice.

The characters' pervasive childishness is concurrently highlighted, which serves to remind us that if one of Gainax's staple themes is the maturation process painfully and ineluctably undertaken by its many young heroes and heroines, the studio's artists remain deeply fascinated with the diametrically opposite option: staying young forever. This tendency is arguably more explicitly accentuated in *Abenobashi* than anywhere else within Gainax's megaverse. The show indeed evokes, albeit obliquely, the aforementioned "Peter Pan Syndrome," namely, the concept formulated by Dan Kiley to describe the desire (potentially but not necessarily pathological) to remain anchored to a preadult world. The age issue will be examined in greater depth in the analysis of the show's closing installment.

As the show's story unfolds, it gradually transpires that Sasshi has no desire to go back and is, in fact, the cause of his and Arumi's wandering between worlds. The reason behind his aberrant behavior, it is suggested, is that he knows that if they return to normality, Arumi will have to witness her grandfather's death, does not wish to expose her to this harsh reality, and would therefore rather retreat into sheer fantasy than face the unpalatable truth. However, Sasshi also has personal reasons for not wishing to return to the real Abenobashi since, just prior to the pelican-related accident, he has been informed that Arumi's family is just about to relocate to Hokkaido (where her dad hopes to fulfill his dream of becoming a high-class restaurateur), which would deprive Sasshi of the most meaningful relationship in his young life. Additionally, the boy is anxious about the future of the real shopping district in which he has grown up as a result of rampant evidence for ruthless redevelopment schemes entailing the demolition of vast portions of the area: a practice to which Sasshi's original family home is seen to have fallen victim in the program's very opening. Arumi, conversely, wishes to reenter her home world come hell or high water. This tension sustains the action throughout, providing a dramatically powerful connective tissue for a profusion of ostensibly incongruent yet subtly interlaced vignettes, incidents and digressions.

The protagonists' quest to either recover or forsake, by turns, their original world offers something of a Bildungsroman requiring them to learn about their origins, their family histories, and ultimately themselves. This element is reinforced by the introduction, within the various alternate dimensions, of characters that are not entirely imaginary but actually replicate, albeit in a preposterously distorted fashion, Arumi's and Sasshi's real-life relatives and friends. Kanoh corroborates the reading of the series as an exploration of the characters' growth from childhood to maturity, maintaining that *Abenobashi* is primarily a "coming-of-age" adventure: "coming-of-age experiences are often triggered by a journey into a world of unknowns.... We assume Arumi and Sasshi will travel around chasing after some goal, and when they finally find what they're looking for, we'll likely discover that the two of them know a bit more about life than they did when they set out" (Kanoh, p. 58).

A key figure recurrently encountered by Arumi and Sasshi as they travel across Abenobashi Mahou Shoutengai's sophisticated hobby worlds is the renowned *Onmyou* mystic Abeno Seimei (a.k.a. Eutus), the very founder of the arcade. For the sake of historical accuracy, it must be noted that Abeno Seimei (a.k.a. Abe no Seimei) was a real-life *Onmyou* master reputed to have lived during the Heian Period (the last phase of classical Japanese history spanning 794 to 1185) and to have excelled at the handling of yin-yang wizardry (which is really *Onmyou*'s ultimate objective). No less prominent in the areas of legend and popular entertainment than in the realm of lived history, Abe no Seimei features in countless tales and films. The TV series *Shounen Onmyouji* (dir. Kunihiro Mori, 2006–2007) exhibits some intriguing points of contact with *Abenobashi*, especially in its vibrant articulation of the Bildungsroman element. The show's protagonist is Abe no Masahiro, Abe no Seimei's grandson, and his principal aim is to regain the preternatural power to perceive demons and spirits that his grandfather has sealed away for his own safety. Although the boy's initial shots at magic deliver modest results, Masahiro's authentic abilities are gradually revealed as the adventure progresses and he becomes increasingly determined to surpass his ancestor's competence and reputation.

In order to grasp the full import of *Abenobashi*'s seemingly chaotic but actually carefully orchestrated plot, it is important to acknowledge its mythical infrastructure and, specifically, its slick adaptation of a notion deeply embedded in numerous Eastern traditions and their perception of temporality, namely, recurrence. No less axial to the plot's organization is its employment of a key topos drawn from classic Japanese folktales: the concept of interpenetrating worlds. This phrase designates everyday situations, non-quotidian domains and liminal fissures between those two dimensions, across which characters transmigrate either of their own design or as a result of enchantments. *Abenobashi* provides a paradigmatic illustration of this motif by rendering the membrane that putatively separates inner and outer levels of being perplexingly flimsy.

The present-day action can be grasped, ultimately, only in relation to ancient events, which it both echoes and intermingles with. Those events go back to the Heian Era, and specifically to the intrigues surrounding the characters of Abeno Seimei, his noble friend Masayuki and Masayuki's wife, Mune. A romantic liaison between Abeno and Mune, which Masayuki has unwittingly encouraged by asking his friend to keep Mune company during his own prolonged absences from the palace, eventually results in Masayuki murdering Mune and committing suicide. Overwhelmed by guilt, Abeno resolves to perform the forbidden *Onmyou* ritual that will enable him to resuscitate the dead by placing himself in an alternate world in which they are still alive. As a corollary, Abeno finds himself as "Mr. Abe" in twentieth-century Osaka, a world that Mune Imamiya (Sasshi's grandmother) and Masayuki Asahina (Arumi's grandfather) already inhabit. Masayuki is deeply in love with Mune but the girl herself only appears to have eyes for Abe, who eventually yields to her advances and makes love with her. When Masayuki accidentally discovers this unpalatable truth, he plans to murder Abe but the latter — being smarter than his rival — preempts the acts by vanishing and returning to his Heian-Era persona, leaving a pregnant Mune behind. Her child will be Sasshi's dad. The original affair bringing Abeno and Mune together in the Heian period occurs in Episode 9, "It Cries! The Bush Warbler Heiankyo." The 1950s version of the liaison involving Mr. Abe and Mune is presented in Episode 7, "Flashback! Magical Shopping Arcade Birth." This temporal scrambling at the level of the diegesis itself felicitously contributes to the show's passion for convoluted editing.

Abenobashi's most sensational revelation is that Sasshi, when faced with the prospective death of Grandpa Masa, unintentionally triggered a spell analogous to the one originally employed by Abeno, transforming his familiar environment into something of a portal to a series of parallel existences and thereby sending reality on indefinite vacation. This explains his and Arumi's shift to a spate of increasingly bizarre and intricate worlds, as well as the existence of Masayuki, Abe and Mune in both Sasshi's original dimension and the alternate ones. Episode 13, "Return to Life! The Legendary Onmyou Mystic," supplies several snippets of explanatory material, thereby offering not only the show's denouement but also a partially serious reflection on the joys and afflictions of both childhood and the inexorable transition to adulthood.

Arumi cannot quite comprehend why Sasshi is so profoundly reluctant to return to reality: The girl's perception of this dimension is still innocently optimistic and leads her to believe that the real Abenobashi world has much to offer despite people's failings and foibles. Eventually, however, Arumi does realize why Sasshi has kept the two of them wandering from one fantasy world to the other, and tearfully expresses her acknowledgment in an intense moment of wordless pathos. As for Sasshi, after lengthy and tortuous reflection, he hesitantly agrees to go back at last. The obligation to come to terms with the inevitability of a return to reality becomes unnegotiable once his father unexpectedly infiltrates the scene and unsentimentally presents the boy with the naked truth. Constructing yet another fictitious realm, the older man states, will leave reality itself utterly unaffected: "The only thing that'll change is what's in your head. Only your imaginary world.... In the end, you're just a kid out even after the sun's gone down." Although Sasshi realizes that he can no longer indulge in his escapist dream, just as he and Arumi are about to reaccess their original world, he regrets the decision and breaks the spell intended to guarantee a successful return, which causes his father to remark sternly upon his stubbornness, aggravation etched across his countenance.

It is at this point that the adventure's true magic asserts itself most potently: Sasshi assumes what will be his adult form — thereby revealing his self-sacrificing preparedness to leave childhood behind for the sake of his friend — and casts a spell of formidable magnitude capable of reconfiguring drastically the course of events. (This ability, it is intimated, results from his caliber as the ultimate god of Onmyou art.) We see Grandpa Masa attempting to dislodge the cat from the bird statue on the roof of the Pelican Diner once again but this time around the old man does not fall to his death. Moreover, a last-minute revocation of the Asahinas' business deal implies that Arumi and Sasshi will not, in this alternative dimension, be separated. The shopping district itself is granted a rosier fate in this magnanimously edited version of the story, having been designated as the target of massive redevelopment likely to benefit its original inhabitants.

In this sequence, Gainax's ambivalent take on the age issue comes dramatically to the fore. On the one hand, the sequence suggests that Sasshi's father is absolutely right in urging his son to confront reality and the ineluctability of growing up. On the other hand, it irreverently celebrates Sasshi's rebellious personality in enabling the boy to cock a snook at his parent's ethical lesson, and have it his own way after all. Sasshi's and Arumi's return to the real Abenobashi effectively constitutes a relinquishing of the "Pleasure Principle" (in Freudian parlance) and concomitant acceptance of the "Reality Principle." Relatedly, the move could be said to signal the boy's transcendence of the Peter Pan Syndrome that appears to have affected his conduct throughout the preceding episodes. Yet, the Abenobashi that Sasshi and Arumi reenter is a happier version of the place than the one they would have encountered if the incidents dramatized in the opening installments had not been magically altered and their outcome inversed. This would seem to indicate that the protagonists' point of arrival at the end of the series is still an idealized fantasy world in spite of its ostensible connection with reality.

In keeping with Gainax's distinctive cachet, these developments show that even a series that could have amounted to a gleefully unrestrained celebration of the carnivalesque spirit is actually capable of accommodating darker preoccupations. Also entirely consonant with the stylistic preferences exhibited by the studio practically from inception, the reality level (and hence credibility) of the world depicted in the closing episode remains open to debate: neither the characters nor the audience can be conclusively certain that they are not still ensnared in ludic territory.

CHAPTER 12

This Ugly Yet Beautiful World (Kono Minikuku Mo Utsukushii Sekai)
Director: Shouji Saeki (2004)

> *... the deepest darkest woods are still ahead—where the trees are thick and their smell is sweet and the past is still happening.*
> — Stephen King

High school student Takeru Takemoto, employed on a part-time basis by his uncle's courier service, is in search of something to aim for, something to dream about—but has no clue whatsoever as to where he should even begin to look for such an object. Much as he aches for some exciting new direction to reveal itself, Takeru feels that he inhabits an incurably stagnant world in which wars and crimes will continue unabated as long as humankind endures and that none of his actions will ever carry the slightest weight in the larger scheme of things. Therefore, even though the adolescent's intrinsic disposition leans toward dynamic change, his prevailing attitude is one of inertia. Unsurprisingly, his friends and relatives—and, most notably, his cousin Mari—do not miss any opportunities to remind him what a lazy bloke he is, thus delivering some sparkling gems of humor in the process.

Takeru's fate takes a sudden turn in the opening episode ("Dawn Is the Dividing Line between Light and Darkness") with the dramatic appearance of an ethereal girl amidst glorious emanations of light in a local forest. The event is accompanied, alas, by the concomitant emergence of a colossal dragon-like enemy in pursuit of the creature and, no less disturbingly, by Takeru's discovery of his hitherto unsuspected ability to morph into no less formidable a prodigy. The monster is the first instance of a series of baleful life forms eager to destroy the mysterious girl, while Takeru's transformation is likewise the first manifestation of his hidden power in a chain of analogue metamorphoses.[1] The teenager's entire outlook on life changes drastically as he commits himself to the protection of the girl, for the first time ever appreciating the value of responsibility toward another being and the strength to stand up for what he believes in. Nonetheless, this chivalric mission is embarked upon at great risk, for the girl's origins and aims are utterly unfathomable and although neither Takeru nor his best friend Ryou Ninomiya (who witnesses the initial epiphany) knows this, the discovery actually holds Earth-shattering implications.

What is, however, quite clear about the girl—whom Takeru names Hikari (the Japanese word for "light") due to the circumstances of her advent amidst wondrous radiance—is that she is herself ignorant of her background and all she knows (or appears to know) is a result of her having absorbed Takeru's own memories. Invited to explain the reason for her coming to Earth, Hikari simply says: "I think I was lonely." The creature's past is indeed associated throughout the adventure with hazy sensations of loneliness and emptiness. These very feelings have been both the *cause* of Hikari's initial attraction to Takeru, a human with an intimate knowledge of their grievous influence from an early age, and an *effect* of her assimilation of the boy's mnemonic baggage. This idea is succinctly captured by the recurring image of the toppling toy car: a recollection that captures the moment when Takeru finally discovered that his mother had no time for him. This visual refrain seems to emanate from Hikari herself no less than from Takeru, thus consolidating the strength of the bond uniting the two characters.

No less importantly, Hikari's feelings are repeatedly invoked to communicate a potent sense of the transience of things (*mono no aware*), and graphically complemented by a plethora of images saturated with nostalgia and bittersweet longing — most memorably, that of Hikari sitting in a tree as shooting stars cascade across the sky above her (Episode 6, "Lingering by the Water's Edge"); that of a dead bell cricket treasured by Hikari as a pet (this is her first direct experience of what Earthlings call "death") juxtaposed with a flurry of Bon-Festival fireworks (Episode 8, "This Wonderful World"); those of autumn leaves and cherry blossom (Episode 12, "My Heart's Song"). These visual motifs alluding to the ephemerality of life and beauty are among Japanese culture's most abiding symbols of unanchorable pleasure.

At no point, irrespective of the moments of humor often yielded by the anime, can one stop wondering how soon and with what consequences Hikari's past will catch up with her. The girl's depiction as a character whose personality is traversed by streaks of darkness in spite of an endearing appearance consistently reinforces these haunting admonitions. This portrayal is bolstered by the pseudoscientific hypothesis from which the adventure proceeds. This is formulated suspensefully throughout the show, with Episode 8 providing some of the more telling snippets of information. The Earth, we are told in this installment, has undergone periodical (though by no means predictable) mass extinctions over the millennia, and the sudden emergence of both the monsters seeking to pulverize Hikari and the metamorphic version of Takeru intent on protecting her indicate that a seventh occurrence of the phenomenon is imminent. Both, as the scientists investigating the case maintain, consist of "E.D." ("Extended-Definition" or "Extended-Domain") creatures that are endowed with the characteristics of diverse species from bygone eras and are supposed to prevent the agent of extinction — the cosmic force from which Hikari ensues — from achieving its goal. In the case of the attacking monsters, the theory unquestionably holds.

Takeru, however, is something of a wild card in the game, insofar as he is inexplicably keen on "protecting what he ought to be destroying." It is suggested that in resisting what would logically be expected to constitute his ruling instinct, Takeru is the first E.D. specimen ever encountered by science to be able to control his powers. As to the cause of this anomaly, it is opined that this lies with the boy's possession of a "heart," and hence of affects that transcend instinctive behavior. As for Hikari herself, her core consists of an amorphous energy that merely happens to acquire the shape of a pretty teenage girl as a result of its coming into contact with Takeru (she indeed closely resembles the boy's notion of the ideal woman, as sketched out in pencil by Ryou early in the series). She could, however, have taken any other imaginable guise depending on the circumstances of her materialization.

The force in question, given its penchant for triggering massive waves of extinction intended to secure biological evolution, is inherently destructive. Yet, this does not make it evil in a conventional ethical sense, since in pursuing destruction, it simply operates in compliance with its cosmogonical raison d'être. Despite appearances, therefore, Hikari harbors a capacity to annihilate the human race — alongside all the living species that coexist with humans within that particular evolutionary stage. As the girl herself puts it in Episode 10, "False Heart," she is the "bringer of destruction ... responsible for all the mass extinctions that have happened on Earth in the past," and hence "a bottomless darkness," a "goddess of death." (Hikari is attacked by formidable E.D. creatures in Episode 1, as seen earlier, and again in Episode 7, "Prelude to a Kiss," and both are vanquished by Takeru in his own E.D. configuration. A third monster materializes in Episode 10: On this occasion, the entity is destroyed by Hikari herself, who has by now owned up to the darkness governing her intent.)

Upon reaching Earth, the intergalactic energy at the core of Hikari has actually split into two separate beings: Besides the catastrophe-driven Hikari, it has also engendered the stability-seeking Akari. If Takeru's deviant conduct as an E.D. creature muddles the situation in ways as yet to be recorded by science, the cosmic force's bifurcation poses no less of a conundrum. Hikari's own behavior complicates matters to unprecedented extremes when, in the adventure's climactic moments, she contravenes her appointed role by choosing to save the Earth and, by joining forces with Akari, to "lock the door against extinction."

However, the quasi-scientific dimension was not director Shouji Saeki's principal aim in the execution of *This Ugly Yet Beautiful World*. In fact, his objective was to transgress the standard formulae associated with romantic anime. In this respect, the show's hypothetical frame of reference was useful insofar as it provided a valid and cogent pretext for depicting its romantic heroine as an untypical member of that species and hence abet the artist's deconstructive purpose. As Saeki explains in a "Creator Profile" feature published in *Newtype USA*, "in many [shows], the main character has incredible luck; girls just automatically like him. We wondered if we could start where everyone else does and go someplace that no one else had" (Saeki 2006a, p. 51). The director's primary targets were the concept of *moe* and the erotic mores underlying its narrative deployment: "What caught my attention about *moe*," he remarks, "is that it makes the sex so vague — *moe* is used to hide our embarrassment about sex" (pp. 52–53).

As argued earlier in this study, Gainax's creators seek to undermine *moe*'s canonical polarization of male and female roles that usually idolizes the beloved as a passive and helpless fetish. They do so by instilling discordant dispositions into their characters and thus rendering them unstereotypically multifaceted. Gainax's seemingly orthodox *moe* heroines, in particular, are wont to disclose murky depths quite at odds with the formulaic depiction of the type. *This Ugly Yet Beautiful World* marks the apotheosis of this aesthetic trend to date.

Saeki's handling of *moe* exposes the fundamental weakness at the core of not only that particular romantic convention but practically any idealization of love founded upon chivalric values — and especially upon the notion that the object of desire is defined by unmarred superiority. In classic versions of courtly infatuation, the beloved is characteristically placed upon a pedestal that declares at once her desirability and her eminence. *Moe*, too, fosters these principles by presenting its heroines' affection as analogous to "a mother's love ... one-sided" (p. 53). What is evident in both instances is a denial of reciprocity and equality bound to impact on perceptions of the erotic, sexual and broadly emotional connotations of the relationship in hand.

By portraying Hikari as capable of cynicism and destructiveness — and therefore as neither *kawaii* ("cute") nor *yasashii* ("meek," "kindly") in the classic *shoujo* vein — the series irreverently dismantles its generic basis. Its ultimate goal is to lay bare the internal contradictions of romantic anime at its most orthodox as a genre that is only able to satisfy the spectator's desire for unfractured affective wholeness as long as it resolutely excises all traces of an unsavory disposition from the loved object but, in so doing, reveals that such an object is a synthetic icon—a construct dependent for its aura of perfection upon the implicit, yet disavowed, existence of quite contrasting features. In other words, the *moe* heroine is only exemplary insofar as her perfection is erected upon the repression of flaws that actually define her no less vitally than her virtues. The classic *moe* heroine, in this respect, is not *inherently* pure but *ideologically* sanitized. Hikari's explicit multifacetedness presents us with a refreshing subversion of the sanctioned treatment of her cinematic breed.

While darkening the show's overall tone by transgressing the codes and conventions of romantic comedy and of both *shoujo-* and *moe-*centered stereotypes, Saeki was also eager to engage with satellite themes likewise allusive to emotive and psychological darkness. What is most effective about *This Ugly Yet Beautiful World* is the sheer pace at which it stokes and then intrepidly subverts the viewer's expectations. Whereas *Evangelion*—although it unquestionably gets darker and more apocalyptic as the series unfolds—emanates ominous vibes right from the start, Saeki's show works its way toward potential catastrophe with almost deceptive circuitousness. The cocktail of rapid action, domestic comedy, romance and fan service-oriented romp delivered by the early episodes almost conceals any prospects of unrest—almost. On close inspection, it becomes clear that hints at the darkness to come are dropped unobtrusively from the very beginning.

Theron Martin highlights the show's departure from established formulae in favor of a degree of profundity one would not automatically expect to find in such a generic mix: "Cute/sexy alien girls/women who wind up cohabitating with boys/young men that they have fallen in love with has been a common anime plot device at least since *Urusei Yatsura* in the early '80s, and at first glance this series seems to be just another installment of that tried-and-true theme.... But this is a Gainax series ... so things aren't as simple as they look. More depth is present here than may be initially apparent" (Martin 2006a). The potential darkness intimated by the first four episodes steadily intensifies in the course of Episode 5 ("School Days") to Episode 8. As Martin observes, these at first appear "intent on packing into *TUYBW* all the stereotypical elements that anime romantic action-comedies should have.... But again, this is a Gainax series, and Gainax series never let their characters off so easily" (Martin 2006b).

Moreover, it is made clear from the very first installment that Takeru has no adult to guide him: His endearingly disheveled uncle and pragmatic aunt are kind enough to supply him with accommodation and food, and accept with genuine generosity the boy's wish to house Hikari within their walls. Yet, the fact remains that Takeru's actual mother is seen in some deeply unsettling flashbacks to have deserted him when he was only a little kid. Clues to Takeru's checkered past are offered from the story's early stages to gain darkness and momentum as the plot takes a decisive turn toward serious drama. In the second installment, "You're My First," the boy's dread of abandonment and loneliness is poignantly conveyed by the scene in which he fails, at least initially, to go looking for the missing Hikari on the basis that it is always his fate to be left behind. Flashbacks alluding to his mother's callous departure punctuate this and numerous subsequent scenes. The absent-parent topos so assiduously revisited by Gainax throughout its evolution is also foregrounded through the character of Ryou, who fares no better than Takeru on the familial front having lost both of his parents and having been therefore left to fend for himself and his younger sister Kimi.

FLCL's Naota is eager to present himself as older and wiser than he actually is since, as a kid, he does not feel he is taken seriously enough. Nevertheless, his behavior concurrently suggests that Naota, aware that becoming a grown-up might well mean becoming somebody like his father or even Haruko, does not seem to be in any real hurry to enter adulthood. *Abenobashi*'s Sasshi harbors a more monolithic aversion to growing up insofar as he equates adulthood with a realm of dire responsibilities, on the one hand, and whimsical attitudes, on the other. The adolescents portrayed in *This Ugly Yet Beautiful World* typify a third possible take on the maturation process. Although they lack desirable role models they could consider emulating, they are nonetheless determined (though this determination develops at different rates for different characters) to develop into autonomous individuals. This message is most vigorously communicated through the character of Ryou. When Takeru anxiously wonders whether kids that have been abandoned have any chance of growing up, his mate declares: "Try and stop them!" (Episode 9, "Wish Upon a Star").

Ryou's sister Kimi, even though she is the youngest member of the cast, likewise exhibits remarkable pluck and inner strength, especially in her determination not to wallow in self-pity. In Episode 4, "Life from Now On," she tells Akari that she deeply resents people who address her as a "poor little thing" on account of her orphaned status, stating that if she lacks parental support, those people lack no less crucial an asset: "an imagination."

The show's synthesis of humor and darkness is conveyed most effectively by the topos of otherness with which Hikari is persistently associated. A source of simultaneous amusement and puzzlement is Hikari's ability to absorb the Japanese language from one day to the next, allied to her seemingly innate knowledge of Takeru's life, family and friends. The funniest moments in the early portion of the series lie with Takeru's friends' tentative speculations regarding Hikari's true nature. In a characteristic flourish of Gainaxian intertextual self-reflexivity invoking the world of Japanese animation at large, the young company's fantasies are visualized by means of references to classic shows featuring otherworldly beauties, including the Oni princess Lum clad in a tiger-skin bikini from *Urusei Yatsura* (dirs. Mamoru Oshii, Kazuo Yamazaki, Satoshi Dezaki and Katsuhisa Yamada, 1981–1991) and the alien cutie from *Please Teacher!* (dir. Yasunori Ide, 2002). While *Urusei Yatsura* could be seen as the foundational anime in the emplacement of the alien-girl-lives-with-human-family theme, *Please Teacher!* experiments with the integration of a female creature from outer space into human society with arguably unprecedented daring and visual imagery that overtly foreshadows *This Ugly Yet Beautiful World*.

In Ide's series, high school student Kei Kusanagi is busy fantasizing about his ideal girl when, one night, a blinding light descends into a nearby forest. Intrigued, the boy investigates its cause and discovers a woman floating on a lake. He flees the baffling scene only to discover, the following day, that the enigmatic female has been appointed as his new homeroom teacher. As though having an extraterrestrial beauty as a tutor were not a sufficiently tough challenge for Kei, his life is further thrown into disarray when he is virtually forced to marry her in order to protect her true identity as a surveillance officer from the "Galaxy Federation." In Saeki's show, the gorgeous alien from Ide's program is explicitly referred to as a "candy-loving, pink-haired teacher in glasses who pressures you into marrying her."

While alluding intertextually to other shows, *This Ugly Yet Beautiful World* also invokes the broader domain of anime fandom and ancillary activities, notably in the scene from Episode 2 devoted to the selection of Hikari's human wardrobe. When Takeru's aunt, Sumie, suggests that her daughter Mari could give Hikari one of the many dresses she has made for her that the girl has never deigned to wear, a gallery of outfits varyingly reminiscent of classic cosplay numbers flashes past the viewer's eye. Among them is the iconic blue-and-white maid's uniform immortalized by *Mahoromatic*, Saeki's show's most direct predecessor. Also highly entertaining, on the self-referential front, is the human girls' eventual decision to deck Hikari out in overtly stylish — and gloriously outmoded — clothes that echo the aristocratic French vogue and hence bring to mind cosplay at its most flamboyant. (The chosen period is one of anime's favorite epochs.)

Gainax's passion for intertextuality is likewise communicated by the scene in which Takeru's friends discuss his metamorphic abilities and the boys, already besotted with Hikari, claim that they do not care in the slightest about their mate's powers but would be very interested indeed in witnessing the extraterrestrial girl's own transformation. These fantasies are accompanied by a shot of Hikari in typical Magical-Girl garb that is overtly inspired by the character of Tsukino Usagi from *Sailor Moon* (TV series; dirs. Junichi Sato et al., 1992–1997). The scene is also deeply ironical, since the transformational powers Hikari will eventually exhibit are nowhere near resembling the gratifying visions conjured up by the boys' stereotypical imaginations but rather apocalyptic harbingers of a drastic evolutionary phenomenon.

Hikari's ineliminable alterity — encapsulated by the proposition that she is "different, yet the same," and "the same, yet different" — is not only conveyed through superficial markers such as her vestimentary attributes but also, more crucially, by her outlandish linguistic and ethical standards. The unearthly girl's perception of Earthlings and their mores is, by and large, idiosyncratic and this renders her overall perspective on human life naive, touching and pathetic by turns. At times, however, it comes across as just downright funny. This is clearly demonstrated by the scene in Episode 2 in which she introduces herself to Jennifer Portman as a being from outer space and responds to the scientist's quizzical reaction with the words: "Is it rare to meet someone who's from outer space?"

Analogously humorous is the sequence in Episode 7 in which Takeru's uncle, Itchou, requires his daughter Mari, Hikari and their female friends to don scanty bikini outfits to work as maids in his seaside restaurant. Mari, the quintessential anime puritan, finds her uniform excessively "revealing" and the other human girls appear at least baffled, if not actually troubled, by their employer's demand. Hikari, conversely, cannot understand what the fuss is about and innocently points out that the customers (predominantly male ones, it has to be said) like to see them dressed that way. It should also be noted that Hikari is not here exploited as a vehicle for cheap fan service or as a jolly justification thereof. In fact, it is ingrained in the extraterrestrial's intrinsic nature — when she is not intent on erasing humanity, that is — to like and wish to please everybody around her.

The idea that Hikari does not quite belong in the restaurant context — let alone share her coworkers' ethics — is reinforced by the fact that she is incapable of going anywhere near an order without frazzling it into charcoal, lethally overseasoning it or simply spilling it all over a hapless (and regrettably bare-skinned) patron. Akari partakes of this proclivity to a lesser extent, which is consonant with her intrinsic role as an agent of peace: when mayonnaise ends up covering her entire face due to lavish application of said condiment, she simply slurps it up in one effortless motion. The trope of the accident-prone waitress is prominent in anime comedy. This is demonstrated, for example, by the characters of Ayu and Mayu in the rare moments of ludic relief offered by the TV series *Rumbling Hearts* (dir. Tetsuya Watanabe, 2003–2004). As shown in the next chapter, *Gunbuster 2* revisits the topos to memorable dramatic effect.

On several occasions, Hikari's alterity is conveyed by the dialogue's emphasis on her possession of moral values that are, quite simply, unaffected by conventional human ethics. This is borne out by the scene from Episode 8 in which Mari defiantly announces that she, too, likes Takeru and is not prepared to give in to Hikari. Far from taking the words as a declaration of war, the unworldly girl responds enthusiastically to the revelation, pointing out that her and Mari's shared feelings toward the boy demonstrate that they are "birds of a feather." Moreover, although Takeru's cousin cannot help regarding Hikari as serious competition in her quest for the boy's heart, she is at a loss when the alien states that she likes Mari as deeply as she appreciates and cares for all of her human friends (Episode 10). At one level, Hikari is not really differentiating between Mari and Takeru himself—the only ineradicable factor that makes him unique is that he is the person who summoned and named Hikari in the first place, thus investing her with a human appearance and a place in human society.

A further strategy deployed to communicate Hikari's irreducible otherness consists of her association with an idiosyncratic and, on occasion, overly formal register. In Episode 5, it is suggested that the girl's unorthodox discourse emanates from a no less eccentric perception of her environment at the sensory level. Walking to school with Takeru and Mari, for example, she remarks: "I like walking because I see so many colors." Hikari's singular grasp of her surroundings impacts on her human friends insofar as it powerfully (and often amusingly) defamiliarizes their own habitual perceptions. In Episode 6, the alien's linguistic eccentricity strikes its most exhilarating chords when she enters a shallow pool in the woods and is delighted to discover that the water "slippers" in different ways on different parts of her body: The human girls in her company are understandably baffled, and Sakurako and Amika indeed wonder in unison whether this is "space language." In Episode 8, Hikari's use of language indicates that her sensorium operates in a fundamentally synaesthetic mode when she gleefully declares that the very sound produced by the bell cricket is "sparkling."

This pervasive emphasis on Hikari's otherness serves to remind the audience that even at her most human, the girl never quite fits into the world she has entered in an unproblematic fashion. The exact extent of Hikari's difference is progressively revealed as her ominous role in the fate of the human planet becomes increasingly obvious. Although Hikari's darkness does not come fully into view until later in the series, this is alluded to in the opening installment by the scene where her innocent mien gives way to a malicious grin, the color of her eyes changes from emerald green to dusky pink, her glossy tangerine locks likewise shift to an eerily matte pink, and she declares that she loves the smell of the monster's blood, a clear indication that the creature is dying.

Having made a brief appearance in Episode 1, Dark Hikari assumes quite a central role in Episode 5, in which the alien's pink-haired and cynical incarnation causes the collapse of the entire school compound and, at the end, reminds her gentle counterpart that everything pleasurable and beautiful is destined to end, swamped by monotonous repetitiveness. Dark Hikari comes even more prominently to the fore in Episode 7, in which her callousness combines with a total lack of the stereotypically feminine sense of modesty normally associated with the meek Hikari, inducing her to adopt an overtly provocative attitude toward the timid Takeru. In Episode 8, Dark Hikari becomes so powerful as to assume a separate body and openly confront the *yasashii* version in a nightmare in which she endeavors to "awaken the destroyer" in her. As Hikari literally splits into two adversarial personae, the dark side's personality is encapsulated by her disdainful crushing of the bell cricket's wooden cage, while the gentle version of the character finds herself holding the pathetic wreck in her hands. Dark Hikari's heartlessness is not without a humorous edge, however. When the amiable Hikari is literally devastated by the discovery of her pet's death, her marble-hearted counterpart sardonically observes: "there's no need to cry. After all you're going to bring a lot more death to this world than that."[2]

The situation presented at the beginning of the program is complicated, after some respite provided by domestic scenes focusing on the developing relationship between Takeru and Hikari, as Ryou discovers another girl very much akin to Hikari in the nearby woods: the aforementioned Nature-loving Akari. Parallels between Takeru's and Ryou's experiences result largely from the principle of complementarity on the basis of which they were conceived. Indeed, the director has openly stated that he regards the two male characters as embodiments of two different aspects of himself: "Takeru wants to do all sorts of things, so he's always floundering bout, struggling to succeed.... Ryou, on the other hand, likes things the way they are just fine, so he figures he might as well relax" (Saeki 2006a, p. 52).

Takeru's and Ryou's attitudes toward life in general encapsulate ostensibly contrasting, yet mutually sustaining, personality traits in much the same way as Hikari and Akari are two halves of a single entity or life force. The two pairs of characters are accordingly woven together in a subtly balanced pattern of intersubjective positions. Takeru longs for change and it is therefore quite apposite that he should be responsible for summoning Hikari, the agent of radical transformation. Ryou, conversely, longs for stability and hence invokes a power that seeks to maintain the planet's existing equilibrium in the shape of Akari. Mirroring the narrative trajectory traced by the first two installments in their depiction of Hikari's epiphany and of her introduction into the human community, Episode 3 ("Two in the Shade of a Tree") and Episode 4 delineate Ryou's discovery of Akari and the girl's subsequent emplacement within the Ninomiya household.

The first speculative explanation of the relationship between Hikari and Akari is supplied in Episode 4 by Jennifer, who is investigating the phenomenon of mass extinction and residing as a lodger in the Takemoto household. Jennifer is a tantalizingly multifaceted character, incidentally. Like *Evangelion*'s Misato, she presents herself as a sensual, carefree and boisterous woman with a hearty appetite for beer (and indeed anything alcoholic) in her domestic configuration but displays unequivocal professionalism while on the job. In the scenes in which Jennifer dons her white coat and discusses mass extinction with her boss, her demeanor is indeed more overtly redolent of Ritsuko's restraint and absolute dedication to her mission.

Addressing the extraterrestrial girls, Jennifer opines: "Maybe the two of you were originally one being and you split up." The researcher's hypothesis is that Hikari and Akari derive from "Some kind of psychic unit that didn't have a physical body to speak of until [it] came to Earth and split apart." To corroborate the proposition that the two creatures did not possess corporeal attributes prior to their arrival on the planet, Jennifer maintains: "Something with a physical metabolism wouldn't be able to survive a trip across the universe. The trip would take millions of years, maybe even trillions, so there's no way a flesh-and-blood human body could ever make it."[3]

An important addition to the show's cast made in Episode 5 that also serves to shed some light on Hikari's cryptic past is Ioneos, a *mecha* materializing from the ruins of the school building when Dark Hikari's advent occasions the edifice's sensational destruction. While functioning as something of a "bodyguard," Ioneos also complements Hikari's personality and power in vital ways. Akari's own existence, it should be noted, is itself virtually inextricable from that of the enigmatic Kuon — a creature redolent of a small sack endowed with formidable strength and cunning, and capable of inflicting a mighty blow to Ioneos's head by merely touching it while, by landing squarely on Akari's skull, it causes her no discomfort whatever. (Kuon will be returned to in a later assessment of the show's generic affiliates.)

Although Ioneos's intervention delivers some crucial clues to Hikari's true nature, his presence also contributes memorable comedic notes to the program's overall mood. Ioneos is characterized by a wry sense of humor right from his first appearance. When Takeru, still traumatized by his fight against the dragon-like creature in Episode 1, wonders whether he is facing yet "another monster," Ioneos crisply observes: "Well, that wasn't a very nice thing to say." The comedy escalates in the conversation involving the *mecha*, Takeru and the boy's friends:

Takeru: You're the one who destroyed our school?
Ioneos: That was pretty much it.
Takeru: Well, I think you need to explain yourself.
Ioneos: No, don't wanna.

Takeru: What?
Ioneos: It'd be a pain in the ass to explain, so I won't.
[At which point the *mecha* rests on his elbow as though to relax.]
Shinichi: What kind of robot is that anyway?
Amika: The *Lazy Bum 2000*?

Hikari insists that Ioneos owes her human friends some sort of explanation, which causes his attitude to alter drastically: Hikari, whom he considers his "mistress," appears to have an automatic right to his full acquiescence. He thereby launches into full-fledged rhetoric:

Ioneos: Let me tell you what happened. At the core of my body is a brilliant blue crystal. All of my memories and intelligence are contained within it, everything I know or have known. It can operate on any and all matter to create the body I now have. However, while I was in the middle of a long long sleep, that crystal was, well...

Takeru interrupts him, urging Ioneos to "skip the bedtime stories," get to the point and simply tell them why he "wrecked the school" but Ryou suggests that perhaps the robot did not consciously intend to perpetrate a destructive act but triggered the calamity inadvertently by awakening. Ioneos nonchalantly confirms this hypothesis: "Yep. That's about the size of it." The creature's essence woke up upon hearing Hikari's voice and sensing her "presence" and, in so doing, caused the building to crumble. Shinichi mordantly comments: "You sure picked a hell of a way to wake up, buddy" while Daijirou, no less sarcastically, points out: "Maybe you should have snoozed for a little." Ioneos, who appears to have no interest whatever in such speculations, tersely ripostes: "Not possible."

Episode 6 provides a further clue to Hikari's (and, by implication, Akari's) background by means of an exchange between Takeru and Hikari taking place while they are engaged in a "test of courage" (deemed "an absolute summer vacation 'must'" by the boy's friends) and walking through a forest at night.

Takeru: Hikari...?
Hikari: What is it?
Takeru: You said before that you were wandering through empty space. Was it kind of like this?
Hikari: Oh, not at all. It was completely different.
Takeru: There is a *different* kind of nothing?
Hikari: It's hard to explain, but there wasn't anything there. A world was something that I looked at from afar, and then one moment later it was so far behind me that I barely remembered it.

The phenomenon described by Hikari recalls the time warps hypothesized in *Gunbuster*.

Episode 9 dramatizes Hikari's mounting awareness of her mission: a truth she has endeavored to repress in favor of a peaceful existence among humans. It is ironical that Akari, the peace-loving member of the dyad, should be responsible for reminding her alter ego of the destructive reason for which they came to Earth in the first place. Yet, this is fully consonant with the logic of the series, since Akari is ultimately fulfilling a cosmic imperative and therefore has no more choice on the matter than Hikari herself does.

Episode 10 deploys the mythological trope of the "River of Three Crossings," the Japanese Buddhist equivalent of the River Styx in the Graeco-Roman tradition. The dead are supposed to cross the stream seven days after their demise, treading a gorgeous bridge adorned with precious materials if they have led virtuous lives or wading through serpent-infested whirlpools if they have performed evil acts. The female demon Datsueba is said to lurk on its banks to steal their clothes as they are about to cross, while her male companion hangs them on a tree in order to gauge the magnitude of their sins. The clothing hung on trees in the installment's opening frames is an explicit reference to this legend and suggests that Hikari and Takeru are on the verge of traversing the grim waters. One of the last images presented in the montage at the end of the final episode, incidentally, is that of Hikari's and Akari's empty costumes floating through the vastness of space like two discarded husks.

Episode 10 also contains one of the entire show's most touching moments in the scene in which Akari is surprised to hear that summer must end and disappointed by the realization that the four seasons cannot coexist. Ryou comforts her by admitting that he, too, found this sad when he was little but gradually understood not just the necessity but even the desirability of change. It is most likely, however, that this is the kind of change the boy can accept insofar as it is regular and more or less foreseeable. (The repercussions of global warming do not seem to come into play in the universe of *This Ugly Yet Beautiful World*.) Drastic commotions are no more to Ryou's liking than they are to Akari's.

The opposite message is articulated by Hikari in the sequence from Episode 12 in which she and Takeru are floating through space and she states that everything must at some point cease in order to make room for something else. This is her terse explanation for the inexorability of extinction. An analogous message is conveyed by the climax of Goro Miyazaki's *Tales from Earthsea* (2006), in which the character of Sparrowhawk states that "Life without death is not life." Denying death, the story proclaims, is tantamount to denying life itself.

Episode 11, "Flowing Along with Time," poignantly shows that Takeru is terrified of not deserving another creature's love and of being once more abandoned as he was by his mother — a person he loved and yet feared. In this episode, we also discover that the reason behind the woman's seemingly callous act was that the shock caused by her husband's premature death had scrambled her psyche. (The theme of parental neglect is further reinforced, in the course of the same installment, by Ryou's revelation that his and Kimi's parents have not perished in a car crash as stated earlier in the show but actually run away.) Takeru's memories are brutally reawakened by Hikari herself much against his determination to bury the past. In rekindling that submerged reality, Hikari-the-Destroyer is partly aiming to provoke the final chapter of the extinction program by stoking Takeru's instinctive urge to annihilate her and thus fulfill his appointed role as an E.D. life form. At the same time, however, she is also unsentimentally showing that as long as the boy keeps disavowing his background and refusing to negotiate the raw pain it entailed, he will not be truly able to love another being. The subliminal fear of his affection not being reciprocated and of being deserted again will make him forever incapable of opening up to others and cause him merely to flounder between timidity and obsequiousness.

Indeed, the fear of losing Hikari and having to endure all over again the torments of loneliness and failure experienced in childhood at first compels Takeru to give up on her. Cruel as Dark Hikari's intervention in his affective and psychological development may seem, it has a therapeutic effect insofar as it enables Takeru to emerge from his self-imposed emotional cage and, with Ryou's support, to act at last in conformity with his own free will and not just in accordance with other people's demands, whims or expectations. Ryou plays a key part in Takeru's rite of passage by warning his friend that Hikari, too, is intimately acquainted with loneliness (indeed with Takeru's *own* loneliness) and does not deserve to be abandoned any more that a human being ever does: Hikari "was born from your heart," Ryou reminds him. "What would happen to Hikari if you abandoned her?"

Ultimately, it is precisely the possession of feelings that prevents Takeru from destroying Hikari even though, as we have seen, his E.D. powers ought to be pursuing that very aim. In resisting his visceral drive and choosing to follow Hikari even as she recedes into infinity—

until she will own up to her own genuine affection toward both him and the planet at large — Takeru accomplishes the ultimate existential task: He confronts and takes responsibility for his destiny rather than continue hiding in a limbo of hazy delusions and amorphous ambitions.

Episode 11 also serves an important narrative function in its treatment of Ryou's preternatural abilities. Whereas Takeru's superpowers are overtly spectacular from the start, Ryou's are subdued. They can first be glimpsed in a shot from Episode 4 in which he assures Akari that there will be no rain on the morrow, and gleaming patterns of silvery light appear on the palms of his hands, unseen by anybody except the boy himself and the audience. Ryou's powers, when he establishes that they chiefly amount to the instant fulfillment of his wishes, do not come across as any more momentous. To begin with, in fact, all they grant him is paltry rewards such as miniature toys, free popsicles and extra-large helpings of meat at the dinner table (Episode 9).

A hint at the true, and much greater, amplitude of Ryou's faculties is supplied in Episode 7, in which there are unvoiced indications (left intentionally vague by the director) that he plays a part from a distance in the vanquishing of the sea monster just as this is about to swallow Akari. Ryou's superior energy finally manifests itself in its full import in the climactic conflict presented in Episode 11 when he stops Akari from attempting to destroy Hikari by neutralizing her weapon and turning it into a rhinoceros beetle. The cosmic will's stability-loving component is thus hindered from betraying its true nature by becoming itself an agent of death. The image of the insect, moreover, reactivates memories of Akari's and Ryou's first encounter, when the girl was still living in the woods like a dryad and the boy told her about the species and the possibility of one of its members appearing out of season, impatient to make her acquaintance.

Although Ryou's powers are, on the whole, understated and hence more subtle than Takeru's, the latter also hold fine psychological nuances that prevent them from descending to the level of outbursts of mindless anger. This is already evident in Episode 1 in the scene in which Takeru in E.D. guise, having injured Hikari's attacker to death, is about to inflict one more lethal blow by means of a multipronged arm but checks himself in the nick of time, reckoning that he has perpetrated sufficient damage and that indulging in additional violence would amount to sheer brutality. The pathetic expression evinced by the creature beneath its façade of scaly monstrosity would seem to have touched the heart of the beast within Takeru, just as it cannot fail to move the sensitive viewer.

Saeki's ingenious handling of diegetic details that, though marginal, actually add both pathos and verve to the cumulative action is attested to by Episode 11 with the scene in which Ioneos expresses his gratitude to Takeru's guardians for their hospitality. This brief but beautifully choreographed scene serves to intensify the sense of things winding down to a close that pervades the closing installments. Hints at a romantic liaison between the *mecha* and Jennifer, who has always admired his willingness to join her for a drink (or a few dozen), concurrently contribute to the richness of the show's narrative infrastructure in the conclusive segments.

The sequences exhibiting the show's climactic confrontation deliver a spectacle so intense and viscerally engaging as to recall onstage theatrical performance even more pointedly than live-action cinema. Their poignance, notably, does not stem exclusively from the explicitly dramatic dimension but also from Saeki's meticulous attention to details. One particular instance of this artistic proclivity deserves close attention in the context of Episode 10. The director, aware of the importance of foregrounding the younger generation so as to underscore the story's coming-of-age dimension, deemed it vital to remove temporarily Takeru's guardians from the scene. This move would have felt awkwardly gratuitous had no reason been given for the aunt and uncle, normally ever-present in the scenes set in or near the Takemoto residence, suddenly disappearing. Saeki was sensitive to this possible incongruity and subtly inserted a snippet of dialogue in which Sumie informs Mari early on in the installment that she and Itchou will be going out that afternoon.

In Episode 12, Ioneos tells Jennifer that what matters most to the cosmic force that he and Hikari embody is "the future": their instinctive tendency is always to look forward. "Things that have fulfilled their function," the *mecha* continues, "or have lost their function will disappear. It's one of life's inevitabilities." Jennifer responds in a characteristically insouciant fashion: "It's kind of disappointing that the world's going to end because of such a simple concept." The scientist's deflating remarks on the rather simplistic nature of the phenomena she is observing are not only perfectly consistent with her consummately pragmatic and unsentimental outlook. In fact, they also serve to remind us that Saeki was not aiming to promulgate a sophisticated and scientifically cogent evolutionary theory but to deploy the mock-academic hypotheses from which the adventure proceeds as diegetic underpinnings of entertainment value. Jennifer also humorously notes that even though she has been determined from the start to write and publish a conclusive report on the phenomenon of extinction, she is quite at a loss as to where to start: "How in the world am I supposed to explain this kind of crazy shit?"

The editing of the action's crowning moments is flawless, deftly intercutting portions of this dialogue involving Jennifer and Ioneos with a parallel exchange between Hikari and Takeru concerning extinction, evolution and their roles in these waves of birth, death and rebirth. An impressive piece of cinematography, the sequences concerned also enable the denouement to come across as a dynamic event, whereas the explanations they provide would have smacked of static deus-ex-machina lecturing had they issued from a single source.

On the mythological and cosmological planes, the key concept invoked in the final installment is that of "*anastasis*"—resurrection, redemption. From a strictly visual point of view, the action is here dominated by the portentous swarm of red butterflies from which the show's memorable logo derives. (The swarm makes its first spectacular entry in Episode 10.) The creatures, engendered by the phenomenon of *anastasis* itself, are said to connote the temporary shapes taken by life "shards" that have not yet been born but might. Ultimately, Hikari and Akari relinquish their human bodies and go in search of a place in the cosmos in which the shards may be born. Takeru, who has lost his physical shape in the course of the climax, regains it through Hikari, who chooses to endow him with a body in the same way as he bestowed one upon her on that fateful full-moon night when it all started.

Before letting go for good, Takeru wishes to give Hikari one last present: mental images of the different seasons (which she would not have exhaustively experienced in the course of her life on Earth as a human), captured in an imaginary journey on his bike. Breathtaking pictures of glowing autumnal landscapes, snowy scenery (inclusive of a snowman redolent of Ioneos), and cherry blossom successively fill the screen as a crowning hymn to the spirit of *mono no aware* at is purest. At the close of this mental excursion, Hikari asks Takeru to take her "home" one last time, where the characters catch a glimpse of their own adult incarnations.

A major challenge for character designer Kazuhiro Takamura (also chief animation director on *Mahoromatic* and episode director on *His and Her Circumstances*) resulted from the show being "completely original work." "I felt like I was really groping around in the dark," Takamura continues. "...For Hikari I could simply draw what I thought was 'cute,' but the other girls also absolutely had to be 'cute.' I had a bit of a hard time drawing variations of 'cute.' If I'd been drawing non-cute characters, there'd be all kinds of easy variations, but if the condition is 'They all have to be cute,' it's difficult" (Takamura).

At the level of character presentation, *This Ugly Yet Beautiful World* may not seem to signal an especially adventurous departure from the popular anime formula favored today (largely due to the impact of digital technology on the design and production processes). It indeed offers a cornucopian abundance of frames dominated by beautiful females endowed with lustrous skin and liquid eyes. What does distinguish Saeki's series from many programs of a germane nature is that the glossy effects are extremely varied and hence disclose a wide range of both visual and tactile impressions. Recalling, by turns, the translucence of porcelain, the satin sheen of eggshell and the elegant glow of silk, those effects aim consistently at the evocation of softness. However, although this is a sensory attribute that is assiduously invoked, notably in the rendition of the various girls, it is also diversified and therefore never descends to the level of a generalized puppyish look. Delicate and tastefully refined, the palpable smoothness of many enticing frames owes much to the careful orchestration of lighting and coloring strategies with texture-imparting techniques.

Takamura and his associates alternate between stark contrasts of light and dark colors (to suggest emotive or dynamic conflict) and gracefully graded or smudged chromatic combinations (to mellow out the look of the more lyrical and dreamlike scenes). Textures play a pivotal role, infusing the images with degrees of aliveness that brightness and color balance alone could not be expected to achieve. Blending a separately created texture with the underlying hues is a major challenge for animators, yet the rewards in store if the operation if proficiently and imaginatively handled are also considerable. No less central to the accomplishment of a comprehensively vivid picture, however, is the final balancing of its multiple components: a task that is often abetted by the inclusion of ancillary details such as a light flare, a floating petal or feather, a dewdrop or a tear.

The unparalleled level of sophistication achieved by Takamura's team in the execution of the character designs by means of stylish diversification is eloquently borne out by the portrayal of Hikari and Akari. The two girls do not merely represent superficial variations of the same basic matrix, as is often the case with anime productions featuring various personae bound by a common origin or function. In fact, several strategies are deployed in order to throw into relief their individuality and distinctiveness, even as the complementarity of their roles is underscored. The textures brought to bear on the rendition of their somatic traits, hairstyles and clothes — allied to defining palettes that tend to associate Hikari with the elemental qualities of air and fire and Akari with those of water and earth — mark them as distinct beings, thus adding a satisfyingly realistic factor to the show's fantasy base.

The sensory attribute of softness discussed above permeates the program's aesthetic ethos in its entirety, not only the representation of its alluring female characters. This is attested to by Saeki's consistent tendency to tone down the animation's more sensational moments, prioritizing fluidly choreographed and balanced compositions over showy effects. On numerous occasions, and most strikingly in the closing episodes, marked chromatic contrasts (primarily of red and blue hues) are employed to convey a situation's affective intensity without recourse to explicitly theatrical action, and this invests the overall visuals with restrained sensuous elegance. The juxtaposition of swarms of red butterflies and azure skies in the climactic sequences sums up this aesthetic preference for posterity.

On the thematic plane, *This Ugly Yet Beautiful World* is not merely complemented but positively enhanced by a musical score that matches the atmosphere of specific sequences and accordingly ranges from placid harmonies for the quieter and more introspective moments to jarringly discordant effects for scenes of emotional turmoil, retaining throughout a penchant for melodic ornamentation and chromaticism. Especially notable is the opening song — performed by Yoko Takahashi, the singer rendered famous the world over by "Cruel Angel's Thesis," *Evangelion*'s epoch-making opener. Titled "Metamorphose," the song accompanying the inaugural segment of *This Ugly Yet Beautiful World* might at first appear to have little to do with the show's content. Nevertheless, as the series gradually unfolds and moves into dark territory, the relevance to its key themes of Takahashi's lyrics becomes patent.

The opening line — "We whisper good-bye to the ugly world" — sums up Hikari's quest, namely, the discarding of an ecosystem considered undesirable. The word "ugly" does not here indicate that the world under attack is aesthetically displeasing *as such* but, quite simply, that it has become obsolete. The ethical ambiguity pervading the story (and mirrored by the psychological characterization of each of the key personae) is later conveyed by the lyrics with the lines "The more I hate you, the more I want to hold you in my arms." The extent to which discordant emotions are woven into an intersubjective tapestry is confirmed by the following line: "I'm standing in front of the mirror staring at another me."

As we have seen, specular correspondences abound throughout the whole fabric of *This Ugly Yet Beautiful World* — not only in the depiction of Hikari and Akari as inseparable components in a doublet of intergalactic proportions but also in the portrayal of Takeru and Ryou as complementary personalities. Hikari and Takeru are likewise presented as mirror images of each other insofar as the girl's physical appearance and mnemonic storehouse reflect directly the male lead's preferences and experiences. Similarly, Ryou and Akari are bound by a shared heritage insofar as Akari embodies Ryou's aspirations and fears in much the same way as Hikari incarnates Takeru's. The supporting characters, concurrently, are brought together by several mirroring equivalences: Mari and Kimi in their proprietorial attitudes toward their cousin and brother, respectively; Sakurako and Amika in their encapsulation of alternative facets of femininity; Ioneos and Kuon in their inherently identical functions as key aspects of Hikari's and Akari's identities in spite of stark external differences. Even absent characters are specularly related, as suggested by parallels between Takeru's mother and Ryou's parents.

The closing line, "You can change once again," finally, encapsulates the ubiquity of transformation in the narrative universe of *This Ugly Yet Beautiful World*, alluding at once to planetary metamorphosis and to the individual's ability to intervene in a preordained course of action — no matter whether the individual involved is a human being, an alien visitor or an E.D. entity.

The music video containing Takahashi's execution of the song to the accompaniment of a string quartet in the setting of a Western-style church provides an intriguing companion piece to both the show's opening animation and its narrative and symbolic import at large. (In the DVD set released by ADV Films in 2006, the video footage features in the "Extras" submenu included in the second volume, "Eye of the Beholder.") The ecclesiastical architecture and decor — replete with magnificent stained-glass windows, organ pipes, an altar adorned with a gold crucifix and candelabra, a carved-wood pulpit, mosaic-laced pillars, intricate stonework of Gothic inspiration for the interior and sober, almost classical lines for the exterior — conjure up a ceremonial atmosphere of luminous solemnity. This aptly echoes the story's implicit emphasis on the world's ongoing transformation as a ritual of cosmic proportions. Concomitantly, the setting's richness replicates the sumptuous profusion of details that proclaims itself throughout the series as one of its most distinctive visual markers.

The exquisitely simple, uniform-like outfits donned by the four players complements the surrounding architecture's more austere aspects. Takahashi's own costume and makeup, for their part, succinctly encapsulate three of the program's most prominent visual ingredients: the butterfly motif (in the form of a tattoo located on the artist's upper left arm); the color red (used for the main dress); and the ever-changing sky (captured in the external shots in which fleecy clouds race against a sapphire background). Takahashi's costume is also important by virtue of its integration of ornamental elements that evoke quite a distinct ritual legacy from the one alluded to by the church. The feather tunic and accessories worn by the singer, specifically, point to a symbolic heritage of non–Western derivation that is immediately relevant to the message conveyed by *This Ugly Yet Beautiful World*.

Feathers play a vital ceremonial part in countless traditions and cultures, and are frequently deployed as healing instruments invested with talismanic powers and symbolic connections with the spirit realm. The relevance of the feather motif to *This Ugly Yet Beautiful World* is unequivocal when one reflects on the story's emphasis on the concept of evolutionary change as a regenerative phenomenon tied up with otherworldly imperatives. In the specific context of Japanese lore, feathers feature most emphatically in the tale "The Robe of Feathers," a lovely variant of a legend also found in Native American and Celtic mythologies. The story explicitly points to the supernatural qualities of feather garments. A fisherman finds a splendid robe of feathers and is determined to keep is at all costs. Confronted by the celestial maiden to whom the array once belonged, and without which she is unable to reenter the heavens, the man eventually agrees to surrender his treasure on condition that she will dance for him. The deity performs as requested, thereby soaring into the dawn amid the rainbow-hued halo emitted by her gleaming robe. Hikari's and Akari's evaporation into cosmic infinity tangentially echoes this mythical scene.

This Ugly Yet Beautiful World bears numerous affinities to *Mahoromatic*, especially in its ingenious integration of science fiction and romantic comedy allied to a serious psychodrama replete with contorted personalities. On a more facetious note, it is also notable that both *This Ugly Yet Beautiful World* and *Mahoromatic* place consistent emphasis on enticing curves so as to furnish their plots with generous doses of fan service, on the one hand, and offer genuine paeans to female beauty, on the other. Most importantly, the two shows share a truly inspired ability to handle set pieces commonly associated with romantic comedy in ways that refreshingly transcend generic shackles and formulaic portrayals. The following pattern of correspondences can be observed:

i. Beach drama
Mahoromatic
Episode 4

This Ugly Yet Beautiful World
Episode 7

ii. School adventure
Mahoromatic
Episode 5

This Ugly Yet Beautiful World
Episode 5

iii. Festival celebrations
Mahoromatic
Episode 6

This Ugly Yet Beautiful World
Episode 8

iv. Sylvan expedition
Mahoromatic
Episode 12

This Ugly Yet Beautiful World
Episode 6

Similarities between the two programs are not surprising when one considers that prior to the 2004 series, Saeki's major works in a directing capacity had included *Mahoromatic: Automatic Maiden—Something More Beautiful* (2002) and the TV special *Mahoromatic: Summer Special* (2003). (Saeki had reached this stage in his career having already been an episode director on *Mahoromatic*'s first season — the TV series discussed in detail in this book — and storyboarded five of its twelve episodes.)

This Ugly Yet Beautiful World exhibits thematic and iconographic affinities with further anime titles. As far as the ideation of mascots is concerned, Akari's Kuon finds a motley crew of illustrious peers in the semiorganic program Marie from *Please Teacher!*; the blobby pet Gulliver from *Eureka 7* (TV series; dir. Tomoki Kyouda, 2005–2006); the plethora of entities, comparable to humorous versions of Shinto deities, that populate *Kamichu!* (TV series; dir. Koji Masunari, 2005); and the hand-held puppet Pucchan from *Best Student Council* (TV series; dir. Yoshiaki Iwasaki, 2005). In its handling of the narrative ploy of chance encounters, Saeki's show echoes the TV series *Chobits* (dir. Morio Asaka, 2002), in which the protagonist finds a "Persocom" (a synthetic human meant to serve as a PC) in the shape of a lovely and senseless girl. The accidental discovery by a human boy of an ultramundane female is also axial to the TV shows *Yumeria* (dir. Keitaro Motonaga, 2004) and *Elemental Gelade* (dir. Shigeru Ueda, 2005), while the trope of the enigmatic female dropping out of the sky is memorably dramatized by the TV series *Solty Rei* (dir. Yoshimasa Hiraike, 2005–2006).

In its most playful romantic moments, *This Ugly Yet Beautiful World* recalls the "harem" comedies *Negima!* (TV series; dir. Nagisa Miyazaki, 2005) and *Tenchi Muyo! Ryououki* (OVA series; dir. Masaki Kajishima, 1992–1993). Although Saeki's show does not embrace the genre in an overt sense, it does adopt two of its main conventions: a preponderance of female characters and an emphasis on the centrality of their aims to the plot as a whole. Where Saeki's series and *Negima!*, specifically, come more closely together is in the incremental darkening of their plots. If *This Ugly Yet Beautiful World*, though invested with ominous premonitions from the start, sets out as a gentle and jovial romance, *Negima!* likewise exhibits a light complexion at its outset by integrating the ingredients of harem comedy with hints at classic fantasy yarns. Nevertheless, just as the mood of the Gainax show grows increasingly somber, so *Negima!* gradually drops the farcical tone ensuing from its male protagonist's dealings with the aberrant females around him. In the process, the adventure advances toward a potentially baleful climax. In the handling of romance in tandem with coming-of-age motifs, finally, *This Ugly Yet Beautiful World* at times recalls the TV series *Happy Lesson* (dirs. Akira Suzuki and Takeshi Yamaguchi, 2002), whose parentless hero finds himself at the mercy of five overenthusiastic surrogate mothers. Like Saeki's series, *Happy Lesson* intimates that even the most benevolent intentions are capable of unleashing disastrous consequences.

In gradually ascertaining the parameters of his directorial responsibilities, Saeki did not only come to refine his personal artistic skills but he also developed a full-rounded understanding of Gainax's singular modus operandi. "At Gainax," he explains, "even novices can end up in charge [of big projects]. If they think you can do it, they give you the chance. It ends up getting pretty out of control — there are both good and bad sides to it" (Saeki 2006a, p. 52). Allowing its members to learn empirically, through an ongoing trial-and-error process, the magnitude of the tasks laid before them, instead of inculcating pre-packaged *how-to* tenets into its animators, is axial to Gainax's policies. In the execution of the 2004 series, Saeki could rely on the support of several budding talents but also, importantly, on veteran Hiroyuki Yamaga's decade-long expertise. "It was Yamaga," in fact, "who refined the show's concept of duality; Saeki was instantly captivated and decided to use it for the title" (p. 53). Martin's comments on the show's title are useful, in this regard: "Calling the series *This Ugly Yet Beautiful World* was a brilliant stroke of marketing by Gainax, as it's not only one of the all-time great names for an anime.... The name isn't idly chosen, either" (Martin 2006a).

Most importantly, in problematizing the relationship between beauty and ugliness in ways that defy crude binary oppositions, the series focuses on the characters' inner worlds and their precarious suspension between the ideal and the real. In negotiating the tension between what is "ugly" and what "beautiful" about the world he depicts, Saeki dramatizes the characters' own coming to terms with the darkness lurking within apparent radiance, and concurrent development of a commodious disposition toward the direful as the potential messenger of uplifting discoveries.

What enables *This Ugly Yet Beautiful World* to yield a memorable anime experience is the impeccable timing of its shift toward the ominous. This move affects all the characters, as Takeru must confront the truth behind his supernatural powers, and hence behind Hikari, and Hikari herself becomes prey to sinister dreams. The emotional awakening in which the various personae are, one by one, implicated is summed up by the attitude evinced by the rowdy Jennifer at the end of the adventure, in which she appears to sense that she may have to start taking things a bit more seriously than she has been wont to do thus far. If *even* Jennifer is compelled to reach this sobering realization, there can be little doubt as to the other characters' recognition that retreating into the old familiar world they once knew — or thought they knew — is simply not an option. Emotional turmoil and the unforeseeable insights this state inaugurates are what the series is fundamentally about: "Humans," Saeki proposes, "try to achieve perfection, and as they reach for it, they themselves change. That's what's most important" (Saeki 2006a, p. 52).

At the same time, the director was eager to emphasize the "plurality of life," a facet of the series that the title itself poetically epitomizes, and the prismatic open-endedness of his characters' existential quest: "I really like it," Saeki maintains, "when one thing has many aspects to it ... and in some way you can't say anything definite about it." Commenting specifically on the show's ending, the director has stressed that this entails a "variety of meanings" and that even though he personally views it as intrinsically "happy," he is more concerned with entrusting chance to "bring interesting things out of even obvious, ordinary things" (Saeki 2006b).

The unpredictability of the action's outcomes, and hence of its impact on a character's mental and emotional development, emplaces chance and contingency as the show's governing forces. Additionally, the director's own openness to multiple and even discordant interpretations of his work's cumulative message eschews any deterministic preclusion of the story's destination. In conjunction, these factors bear witness to the axial importance of the principle of randomness in *This Ugly Yet Beautiful World*. This is confirmed by the fortuitous adoption of the butterfly motif not only as the program's emblem but also as a potent graphic and diegetic component of the adventure.[4] Saeki has indeed noted that butterflies ended up becoming central to the story by sheer "coincidence," simply because the designer appointed to produce the logo for the series happened to have some "butterfly materials" available on his computer. Intriguingly, the phrase "butterfly effect" is pivotal to chaos theory and its investigation of random systems, designating the ways in which seemingly infinitesimal variations of the initial condition of a system (such as the flutter of a butterfly's wings) may trigger momentous and hugely disruptive variations in the system's long-term behavior.

While epitomizing the story's implication with the principle of randomness, the butterfly also resonates with multiaccentual symbolic connotations. Butterflies have been utilized as emblems of transformation and rebirth all over the world for time immemorial. Simultaneously, the image has often been invoked to connote the ephemerality of beauty — a theme, as noted earlier in this chapter, central to the Japanese perception of the phenomenal world. (Unlike the phoenix, whose metamorphosis and successive phases of death and resurrection are posited as never-ending processes, the butterfly typifies the uncompromising transitoriness of the fleeting moment.) Rendered in ancient Greek with the word also used for "soul," namely "*psyche*," the butterfly may also symbolize the transformations undergone by the spiritual essence of humans (and indeed other species). The creature's flighty transience can also be associated with the impalpable realm of the daemonic: fairies, elves, pixies and mythical creatures such as the Greek Hypnos, the god of Sleep, are frequently equipped with butterfly wings. In Aztec lore, the insect was linked to the supreme power of the Sun, on the one hand, and with the dazzling light of stars, on the other.

All of these meanings are relevant to *This Ugly Yet Beautiful World* at various levels. Quite apart from the obvious link between transformation and evolution dramatized by the series, the butterfly alludes to the spiritual, psychological and even physical metamorphoses undergone by the characters — both human and alien — in the course of the adventure. The creature's connection with otherworldly figures and occurrences is also summoned — most remarkably, in the representation of Dark Hikari as a haunting spectre that challenges with increasing insistence her meek counterpart's obliviousness to her true nature through unsettling dreams and hallucinations. Sun- and star-related imagery also abounds throughout the show, echoing its traditional connection with the ubiquitous butterfly motif.

In the specific context of Japan, the butterfly has often signified young womanhood, and pairs of dancing butterflies have been used as metaphors for marital harmony. The image also plays a key role in one of Japan's most cherished fairy tales. Titled "The White Butterfly," this pivots on an ancient and dying man named Takahama, who has devoted his life to the memory of his former betrothed Akiko, killed by consumption shortly before the wedding. As Takahama approaches his final hour, Akiko returns to him in the guise of a white butterfly symbolizing her unwaveringly loyal soul. Hikari's desire to be remembered by Takeru forever and promise, in return, to revisit Earth some day reverberates with an analogous message.

Most crucially, and in accordance with the ethos of *mono no aware* that pervades *This Ugly Yet Beautiful World*, Japanese poetry has persistently deployed the butterfly trope as a pithy symbol for the past's irretrievable pleasures. As Chris Eisenbraun observes in the entry of his online dictionary of symbols devoted to butterflies, "There is a line of Japanese poetry expressing sorrow over the lost pleasures of the past, a response to the maxim, 'The fallen blossom never returns to the branch'; 'I thought that the blossom had returned to the branch — alas, it was only a butterfly'" (Eisenbraun).

Defying simple categorization, *This Ugly Yet Beautiful World* does not merely constitute one of the most recent chapters in Gainax's established reputation as a mold-breaking enterprise but also a recapitulation of the studio's artistic mission insofar as it marks its twentieth anniversary. In this respect, while inaugurating novel opportunities for experimentation, the series also brings together pivotal aspects of Gainax's whole history. Few programs created to commemorate a significant stage in the evolution of an anime venture could be deemed more holistically satisfying.

CHAPTER 13

The *Diebuster* Saga

> Gunbuster 2 ... takes elements from the original series [and] adds the modern Gainax flair without losing the charm of the classic series.... Gorgeous animation, colourful characters, a little fan service and a fresh new story line that continues a classic tale makes Gunbuster 2 ... a bold declaration of Gainax's continuing dedication and love of anime and otaku culture.
> — Gail

Gunbuster 2 (Diebuster)
Director: Kazuya Tsurumaki (2004–2006)

Sixteen years after the release of Hideaki Anno's epoch-making 1988 OVA, Gainax produced its long-awaited sequel *Gunbuster 2* (a.k.a. *Diebuster*) under the direction of Kazuya Tsurumaki of *Evangelion* and *FLCL* fame. *Gunbuster 2*'s heroine, Nono, shares with Noriko the determination to become a top-notch space pilot: a goal she pursues with a naivety that at times verges on simplemindedness. Concurrently, a total commitment to the task in hand and a firm belief in the notion that doing her best will get her through successfully animate Nono's adventure no less ardently than Noriko's. The two girls' stories, we eventually discover, are so intimately interwoven as to amount to two strands of one and the same story.[1]

When we first encounter Nono in Episode 1, "Please Let Me Call You Oné-sama," the prospect of her becoming a space pilot could barely seem more remote. Maintaining her balance on the treacherous coat of ice surrounding the home from which she is about to run away poses a herculean challenge unto itself. Yet, vestigial hints at her mettle are offered by Nono's resolute treatment of the family dog determined to be taken for a walk at such an inconvenient time. The action does not suggest any propensity for premeditated brutality, for Nono is clearly fond of the animal and wishes him a long and happy life in the fondest and most ceremonious of tones, and this serves to reinforce the honest sense of determination underpinning her attitude.

The opening is also remarkable, in animational terms, due to its ability to communicate wordlessly the tension between Nono's lowly background and the grandiosity of her ambitions. Overtly inspired by real-life locations, the algidly immaculate nocturnal scenery exudes an atmosphere of hushed provincial domesticity that echoes the heroine's more innocent and delicate side. The sublimity of the silently descending flakes, crowned by the shot of a gigantic star within a breathtakingly nuanced sky (symbolic of Nono's dream), conversely, reflect the epic scale of the quest upon which she is just about to embark. The setting presented in the show's inaugural portion is important since, as scriptwriter Yoji Enokido emphasizes, although the bulk of the "story is set in outer space," Tsurumaki's troupe "still wanted to start it off as a more normal depiction of everyday life, following in the tradition of the previous *Gunbuster*. For example, in the original *Gunbuster*, the girls' pilot school is located in rural Okinawa. Similarly, *Gunbuster 2* starts off with a typical snowy landscape in the north of Japan where you see trains passing through at night and that sort of thing" (Enokido 2007a, p. 42).

Although technology tends to hold center stage in much of *Gunbuster 2*'s principal sequences, scenes (such as those offered in the opening installment) in which the natural environment is prioritized are important indicators of Tsurumaki's vision. Indeed, the director has stated that he harbors no unproblematic faith in "almighty science," and is reluctant to allow fully urbanized settings packed with "white skyscrapers" to dominate space (Tsurumaki 2007a). In fact, he believes that Nature is immensely resilient and will never be totally subjugated to technoscientific agendas. Tsurumaki thus cultivates a preference for locations wherein Nature and science coalesce. The presence of lush vegetation within the HQ of the cutting-edge organization known as the "Fraternity" epitomizes this idea.

Furthermore, Tsurumaki felt that opening *Gunbuster 2* in a remote village deep in the snow would provide an ironic contrast with the ending of *Gunbuster*, in which the emphasis falls on the intergalactic dimension of the adventure. The opening, the director maintains, is "meant to throw you off a bit." Additionally, the early sequences gave him a precious opportunity to experiment with "story-telling" at its purest since the "most important thing in a *story*," he believes, "is up to the point where the action begins" (Tsurumaki 2007b, p. 8). Equally crucial, in this respect, is the diner scene in which Lal'C makes her first appearance. From this point onwards, "the tempo speeds up and up and up" (p. 9), replicating a proclivity already witnessed in *FLCL*.

In *Gunbuster 2*, humans are still busy fending off a breed of Space Monsters, seemingly keen on invading the Sol System, by means of giant robots piloted by psychic children known as "Topless." The strongest of them all is the snobbish Lal'C, who does not initially believe in hard work and guts but is deeply convinced that special abilities are innate. Not surprisingly, Lal'C at first shuns Nono as intrepid but essentially klutzy. However, she has no choice but to recognize that the girl's underlying talent is real, though as yet unrefined, when a Space Monster makes an unexpected landing on Mars and Nono impressively saves the day — and Lal'C's own life — in response.

Ironically, Nono's guilelessness comes to militate in her favor since the kids responsible for piloting the Buster Machines — all members of the Fraternity — derive their strength precisely from their possession of what Fuyu Kimata describes as "a childlike innocence" (Kimata 2007, p. 27). At times, one even senses that the magnitude of the Topless fighters' powers actually depends on the degree of their immaturity: the further from childhood they have advanced, the less effective they are bound to have become. Accordingly, physical prowess per se is not sufficient. As to what particular abilities make the Topless superior, these disclose themselves gradually and subtly as the series unfolds. This diegetic factor is undoubtedly one of director Tsurumaki's most impressive talents — as already demonstrated, though with a plethora of surreal jolts into which *Gunbuster 2* deliberately does not venture, in *FLCL*.[2]

The representation of *FLCL*'s protagonist, Naota, as a character who lacks a physical brain foreshadows Tsurumaki's initial depiction of Nono as a dimwitted bimbo. Nevertheless, in *FLCL* as in *Gunbuster*, it is simultaneously proposed that so-called brainlessness does not automatically equate to asininity but actually functions as an effective metaphor for innocence, and hence the faculties to which innocence might give rise. As Enokido points out, "an empty head can be an advantage." The quest he undertook with Tsurumaki in the ideation of *Gunbuster 2* was essentially to discover "what that kind of advantage is all about" (Enokido 2007a, p. 42).

FLCL and *Gunbuster 2*, therefore, could be approached as companion pieces. However, as Enokido emphasizes in a joint interview with Tsurumaki, *Gunbuster 2* departs significantly from *FLCL* insofar as the latter adopts a relatively pragmatic worldview, whereas the former favors idealism. "*FLCL*," the scriptwriter explains, "is about losing something important and becoming an adult without getting it back. I think that's a case where 'everyone could have an experience like that sometime.' But in *Gunbuster 2*, Lal'C has lost Nono, but Nono-Riri comes back to her. This is a romanticism of a kind that does not normally happen." The difference, Enokido adds, springs from the later show's incorporation of an element of "SF-style romance" (Tsurumaki and Enokido, pp. 14–15).

Although the dose of fan service dispensed by Tsurumaki over the course of the adventure is relatively generous, this classic anime trope is intelligently employed. Various scenes in which it occurs are not merely concessions to scopophilia but serve to offer deeper insights into a character's psychology and status. A paradigmatic illustration is provided by the sequence from Episode 1 in which Nono's delicate body is ungallantly handled by massive *mecha* piloted by lecherous types who visit the diner at which she is employed in the show's early segments. While the sequence indulges in some salacious frames and lines of dialogue, its main purpose is to draw attention to the naive maid's physical and emotional vulnerability and exposure to the possibility of unscrupulous abuse. A later shot economically captures Nono's defenselessness through a close-up of her shoeless left foot, only partially encased in a torn and soiled stocking from which a sad-looking big toe shamefully protrudes.[3]

A further instance of fan service utilized in order to throw into relief the heroine's lack of experience is supplied by a later sequence from the same installment in which she prepares to attack a Space Monster by tearing away the corset of her waitressing uniform and hence baring her breasts: unaware that the term "Topless" elliptically refers to brain functions associated with the members of the team thus designated, Nono is assuming that a literal exposure of the upper torso is expected of a Topless fighter. In Episode 2, "I Don't Want to Be an Oné-sama," more fan service is generated by the sequence in which the technician Casio gives full vent to his voyeuristic impulses, gleaning evident erotic gratification in the process, by surreptitiously watching on a surveillance monitor Nono's thorough cleansing at Lal'C's hands.

Once again, the trope is not here used as an end in itself but as a means of exploring Nono's nature. It is indeed in these scenes that Lal'C and Nono address for the first time the topic of the latter's robotic constitution. Even though Lal'C treats Nono in a comradely fashion, there are suggestions that she also regards the new arrival as something of an amusing plaything—as attested to by her unceremonious twisting and bending of Nono's limbs and joints: a procedure, the alien girl politely observes in the course of a particularly bold manipulation of her left knee, that actually "hurts a little."

Complementing fan service, *Gunbuster 2* also alludes to the aesthetic of *moe*. Nono herself is overawed by Lal'C's combination of putatively unmatched martial skills and a *moe* appearance. The term is also used in the aforementioned scene in which Casio indulges in his sexual fantasies and attempts to justify a behavior that some may consider perverse on the grounds that Nono is, after all, a non-human entity. The Topless pilot Nicola wonders whether the eye's fetishistic consumption of a robotic *moe* girl differs substantially from analogous treatment of a flesh-and-blood Lolita type, thus inviting us to reflect on the broader issue of Nono's fundamental otherness and on its plausible repercussions on the intersubjective network to which she is being—at least partially—admitted.

According to character designer Yoshiyuki Sadamoto, it is also important to remember that Japanese popular culture offers two distinct approaches to *moe* (as seen in Chapter 1). Invited to comment on what both Tsurumaki's series and Anno's prequel mean to him, the artist has stated: "A happily embarrassing beautiful girl robot anime! But with a 'passion' that requires no explanation is what the *Gunbuster* series is all about. No matter what anybody may say, this is 'moe 燃' (the blazing passion of the heart), and not 'moe 萌え' (the affection toward anime girls)" (Sadamoto, p. 11).

Gunbuster 2 simultaneously engages with a topos that is absolutely pivotal, as argued in the preceding chapters, to Gainax's thematic cachet: the depiction of adults as obstacles to kids' self-realization. This trend is epitomized, in Episode 1, by the manager of the diner where Nono works, a lucre-driven woman callously disparaging of youth's dreams and ambitions. It should be noted, however, that when the lady recognizes that Nono's life is in danger, she does not hesitate to put her own safety on the line to come to her aid and is literally overwhelmed by her humble employee's heroic performance in the confrontation with the Space Monster. The shot in which the manager dumbfoundedly stares at Nono after the latter has released her from the wreck of her vehicle indeed carries epiphanic connotations. The Sistine Chapel mood imparted on the *mise-en-cadre* makes the moment a true gem of anime cinematography.

The underlying generational tension comes to the fore in the second installment with the sequence in which Captain Hatori, a powerful officer in the "First Inspection Squadron," summons Lal'C to his spaceship, the Lalahcharn, to investigate the circumstances surrounding the emergence of the Space Monster seen in Episode 1. No sooner has the girl settled in his office than he proceeds to handcuff her on the pretext that the Topless must be prevented from deploying their powers aboard the Lalahcharn. The valiant pilot acerbically dismisses Hatori's explanation by pointing out that it is "a pathetic excuse for an adult." Unlike Nono's boss, the captain does not exhibit any redeeming features whatsoever. Additionally, he is keen on promulgating the hypothesis that the Topless, like the Space Monsters themselves, are humankind's enemies and corroborates his view by pointing out that the alien attackers' resurgence coincided with the advent of the Topless. However, his callousness and basic lack of manners — largely bred by resentment against children who still possess the faculties he once also held but has inexorably lost upon growing up — make one wonder whether adults themselves might actually constitute the most sinister adversary.

The generational conflict is symbolically replicated by the discrepancy between the technologies at the Topless' disposal and those associated with the military personnel. The *mecha* piloted by the kids are by and large invested with an aura of playfulness, while the figure-eight-shape Fraternity space station orbiting Mars dubbed "Meganebula" resembles an infant's toy despite its commanding dimensions. The Space Force, conversely, resorts to forbidding equipment. As Ryusuke Hikawa comments, "In contrast to the bright, shining optimism of the far-off-future technology seen in the Buster Machines, the armed units of the Space Force — most strongly typified by the dour bellicosity of the space cruiser Lalahcharn — stand as examples of the kind of fatalistic warmongering we're all too familiar with" (Hikawa 2007b, p. 43). Paradoxically, it is as a result of an alien attack and of the resulting appearance on the scene of Nicola's Buster Machine — the *Vingt-Sept*— that Hatori's austere vessel loses its original configuration and morphs into a ludicrously toylike entity.[4]

Tsurumaki has clarified his personal take on the generational issue by pointing out that neither *Gunbuster 2* nor *FLCL* feature responsible grown-ups such as *Gunbuster*'s Coach Ohta because he does not "expect that much from adult characters" — in much the same way as his "generation" at large "doesn't tend to expect much from adults." Hence, Coach Ohta's role is taken over by the Buster Machines, who act "like teachers, in some ways" by inculcating principles through actions instead of words (Tsurumaki 2007a).

Whereas Hatori's crude antagonism compels him to view children and adults in uncompromisingly manichean terms, Casio — who was also a Topless in his youth — seems to have retained a refreshingly childlike ability to behave spontaneously and in accordance with the Pleasure Principle rather than in the service of the stolid rationalism cultivated by the captain and his associates. However, Casio himself is haunted by undying recollections of his days as a Topless fighter. "Once you pilot a Buster Machine," he glumly states in Episode 4 ("Resurrection! The Legendary Buster Machine"), "your heart is captivated by it." He later adds: "When we [the Topless] lose that power, we can't find any other point in living." In the course of the fourth installment, Casio's obsession escalates to the point that he becomes hellbent on reawakening his lost abilities and obtaining the machine Nono is in search of for himself. Needless to say, he fails to achieve his goal most pathetically: the seal worn by the Topless on their foreheads to contain their powers when these are not required resolutely refuses to stick to his brow in spite of a profligate application of tape.

The extent to which the relinquishment of Topless capabilities is perceived as a scourge of soul-shattering proportions is borne out by the preposterous lengths to which the characters of the Serpentine Twins — who rank among the most high-esteemed of their kind — are prepared to go so as to retain their powers. The Twins (the sisters Piaget and LeCoultre) claim to be eighteen years old but hide their actual age behind thickly applied coats of makeup and Goth-style masks. At one point, a close-up of their lips irreverently exposes some telltale wrinkles. Moreover, the sisters are restricted by the obligation to act in perfect unison as a precondition of their emission of Topless energy. (This plot strand will be returned to in the discussion of Episode 4.)

The idea that Topless powers amount to something of a curse if one is unable to accept their ineluctable demise is most graphically conveyed by the sequence from Episode 5, "Mover of Planets," in which Nicola, fearful that his "expiration" is approaching, attempts to rape Nono in the hope of absorbing her superior vigor. Nicola's bestial conduct is particularly disturbing in light of his exceptional skills and flair for performing sensational maneuvers effortlessly and even, at times, flamboyantly — qualities that frequently earn him a leadership role even though, strictly speaking, conventional military hierarchies do not obtain within the squadron. Not even the ingenious Nicola, however, can escape the fate ultimately awaiting all Topless. Although he hopes to partake of the Twins' recipe for eternal strength — should they be successful in eventually conquering it — he feels persecuted by the phantom of futility to which he knows he might fall prey after his retirement from the Fraternity. In the end, Nicola chooses to follow in Hatori's steps by joining the military forces. According to Enokido, the theme discussed above evolved out of the director's belief that "'today's society overflows with pleasures that can only be enjoyed when you are young.' ... However, nobody is young forever. I thought, if you know that you will lose all that power, authority and fun, that is just scary" (Enokido 2007c, p. 14).

Returning to the show's narrative focus, namely Nono's struggle to demonstrate her worth, it must be noted that this does not come to a close once the Fraternity has accepted her as one of its marginal members. In fact — as shown in Episode 3, "I Hate the Topless" — she now has to obtain her own Buster Machine and this draws her into an emotionally charged competition with the character of Tycho. Its object is the *Quatre-Vingt-Dix* — one of the most recently developed, martially effective and aesthetically fetching *mecha* available to the squadron that is, however, as yet to awake. In its design, this machine does not have much in common with the classic giant robot, replete though it is with lethal equipment and formidable energy sources capable of bending the laws of physics. On the contrary, it replicates the graceful curves of the female pilots' own blossoming bodies. Its lissome frame, Barbie-doll waistline and shapely legs, in particular, vividly mirror Nono's own constitution, while its attire adopts the contours and palettes characteristically associated with Nono's costumes (of both the waitressing-uniform and the training varieties).

The modelly element is reinforced by the fact that as it awaits arousal, the new *mecha* is stored in a giant blister pack adorned with cute megastickers akin to the type of container used for collectibles. Gainax is here engaging once again with self-reflexive allusions to the anime industry at large and, specifically, to the realm of ancillary merchandise in which the company's early history is firmly rooted. The girlishness of the decorative motifs accompanying the *Quatre-Vingt-Dix* contrasts ironically with the *mecha*'s tremendous powers — just as Nono's *moe* appearance belies her unique abilities. Through these paradoxes, Gainax encourages the audience not to attach inordinate value to surfaces, while also deconstructing mainstream generic conventions.

Having made just a couple of fleeting appearances in the course of the preceding installments, Tycho is firmly emplaced as a major character in Episode 3. Though ostensibly cheerful, addicted to candy and fizzy drinks, keen on girly language, and driven purely by the desire to be recognized as the most competent of the Topless pilots, Tycho carries a tragic legacy that often causes her determination to deteriorate into unforgiving harshness. At times, the girl's passionate commitment to the achievement of her goal even induces her to behave downright foolishly. This is borne out by the pre-credit segment of Episode 3 when, during a battle against a fleet of Space Monsters dubbed the "Jupiter Express," Tycho becomes so possessed by the desire to outshine Lal'C that she loses her own *Soixante-Six* and is forced to eject into space.

Tycho's checkered past also makes her deeply suspicious of the pursuit of happiness and indeed hostile to any form of charitable conduct. This is explicitly attested to by the sequence in which some kids she meets in the Jupiter hospital (where she is undergoing tests meant to establish whether her exposure to space has led to contamination) beg Tycho to use her Topless powers to bring snow to their city. The pilot sternly refuses to fulfill this wish in the conviction that it would amount to useless generosity. To the optimistic Nono, Tycho's attitude is anathema and this only serves to exacerbate the antagonism between the two girls. Importantly, although Tycho claims the *Quatre-Vingt-Dix* as legitimately her own and indeed ends up piloting it, Nono is the one who is actually able to awaken it. This is because she cares deeply for other people's welfare, whereas her colleague is locked in a dismal cage of resentment. While Nono trusts her instincts and flair for spontaneous tactical initiative over and above strategic planning, Tycho's natural faculties are marred by a paralyzing skepticism. Her tremendous potential, accordingly, cannot be adequately maximized.

It gradually transpires that at the root of Tycho's seemingly callous attitude there lies a deeply traumatic experience: the loss of a loved one, mercilessly eaten away by space-radiation sickness. Embittered by the realization that none of her famous powers could ever have saved the boy's life, Tycho is adamantly convinced that the Topless are incapable of bringing happiness to the world and that fighting, therefore, is merely an egotistical power game. The boy so deeply loved by Tycho carved the objects she now wears as mismatch earrings — a token of her undying affection but also, regrettably, of her inability to let go. The powers of these latently sinister amulets are exorcised when Tycho throws them away in a fit of chagrin and Nono promptly rescues them, turning them into the eyes and mouth of a miniature snowman she has made for the kids' benefit. The innocent creatures' wish is thus eventually fulfilled and Tycho's own heart purged by the recognition of dispassionate benevolence. Therefore, even though this portion of the show abounds with adrenaline-pumping action sequences, its reflective strain plays no less vital a role in steering the adventure toward grave psychodrama. (This portion of the action will be examined in further detail at a later stage.)

In Episode 4, Nono, spurned by the Topless, reaches the conclusion that her only chance of them acknowledging her and becoming her friends is to obtain her own Buster Machine. She therefore enters the "Fluctuating Gravity Well Excavation Site" on Titan, where the squadron is currently deployed, in the hope of unearthing the legendary Buster Machine believed to be hosted therein. Her violation of the top-secret zone is instantly detected, however, and Nono finds herself trapped in a computer-generated cage made of towering columns of fluorescent light. Expulsion (or worse) is the fate Nono should meet in the circumstances but the Twins, who form the Topless committee behind the Titan operation, leniently advise her to journey to Pluto, where another secluded machine thought to have been sunk in battle some twenty years earlier — the *Trente-Trois* — is rumored to be buried.

In actual fact, the scheming sisters simply wish Nono out of the way because they have recognized the Space Monsters' attraction to the alien girl, and hence believe that if she is absent from the scene, the Space Monsters will likewise be averted. As for their reason for wanting the putative enemy removed from the action at this particular juncture, this is that they have also established that the Space Monsters seek to keep humanity insulated from the Fluctuating Gravity Well, whereas their own objective is to awaken the entity as a means of achieving eternal life and enduring Topless powers. The Twins are indeed convinced, as Piaget puts it, that the Titan Well is the "Topless that has lived for over ten thousand years" and seek to absorb its strength: their tireless consumption of meat extracted from the site, which they dub "Titan crab," gruesomely attests to their fixation.

Aesthetically, the Well provides one of the entire show's most deeply satisfying sensory experiences, combining intensely dynamic curves with gorgeous chromatic modulations and gradations. These utilize a wide range of colors at the softer ends of both the warm-hue and the cool-hue spectrums — purple, lilac and pink, on the one hand, and turquoise, jade and aquamarine, on the other. It is profoundly ironical that so pleasing an ensemble should coincide with one of the adventure's most ominous presences. In its design, the Well echoes the aliens depicted in the original *Gunbuster*, which serves to corroborate the hypothesis that the enemy currently faced by humanity is of the same fundamental nature as the old one. Enokido equates the Space Monsters depicted in the original *Gunbuster* to eternal Topless specimens, thus echoing the Twins' own perception of the Titan Well: They "are basically children with superpowers who can't grow up. A form taken by immortal, never-ageing children with superpowers" (Enokido 2007b).

The Space Monsters indigenous to the sequel, for their part, are more akin to the "E.D." creatures depicted in *This Ugly Yet Beautiful World* in their commingling of characteristics from various bygone species. At times, they display overtly organic elements such as wings, carapaces and arachnoid appendages (as in the case of the "Reconnaissance Type" seen in Episode 1). At others, as in the case of the "Beastron-Class" specimen presented in the second installment, they evince more overtly robotic and angular constitutions.

The Twins' plan boomerangs when the Well stubbornly resists them by rejecting every single access code they attempt. The ensuing debacle is the most momentous disaster recorded by the adventure up until now and results not only in the horrific death of many dauntless fighters but also in the realization, as Lal'C states, that the Well is the real enemy and the so-called Space Monsters have actually been operating on humankind's behalf all along. "What the hell have we been fighting up to this point?" she anxiously wonders. The scene echoes the moments in *Neon Genesis Evangelion* in which the NERV staff come face to face with the Units' true, and inherently bestial, disposition and are therefore forced to ask themselves whether their weapons are really under their control after all.

Nono, meanwhile, discovers her Buster Machine in the form not of a *mecha* she can pilot by simply occupying its body as though it were a giant armor but of a force with which she is actually capable of merging. She thereby engenders the Buster Machine # 7, a composite of her original android self and the newly resurrected machine. According to Tsurumaki, it was Anno that first suggested, in the planning stages, the idea of making the heroine into a robot (Tsurumaki 2007a). Perhaps Anno was seeking to replicate, with a variation, the successful formula adopted in *Evangelion*: the cooperation of organic and synthetic pilots. Nono's transformation is physically signaled by the acquisition of a more imposing physique clad in a white spacesuit equipped with a physical reactor, Buster Missiles and heat-release vents. Her mane concurrently gains awesomely fiery tinges and her resolute mien is enhanced by the inclusion of glowing goggles.

This sequence features a direct intertextual allusion to Anno's 1988 show: as Nono discovers her powers as Buster Machine # 7, the original *Gunbuster* emblem fills her irises, as a flotilla of miniature Buster Machines gather around her in a formation that also recalls the iconic 1988 logo. By deploying space-time warp, the Buster Machine # 7 reaches Titan, rescues the depleted Topless ranks by corralling the Space Monsters so keen on obeying Nono's will, and thus quashes the Well's cataclysmic fury. (As we will see, the Titan Well incident is replicated, on a considerably larger scale, in Episode 5.) The epiphanic disclosures seen in Episode 4 occasion a significant reorientation in the viewer's grasp of the overall plot. They also played a key role in guiding both the director and the scriptwriter along the way, insofar as "the story development in the fourth episode" was the only part of *Gunbuster 2*—besides "the epilogue of the final episode"—that "were decided from the start" (Tsurumaki and Enokido, p. 14).

As the plot unravels in the course of the fifth installment, it is incrementally revealed that humanity's most lethal enemy is yet another Fluctuating Gravity Well more formidable still than the one encountered on Titan. This cosmic entity initially filled and eventually engulfed the black hole produced by Noriko and Kazumi at the end of *Gunbuster*, which humans now refer to as "Exelio." (This is the black hole created in *Gunbuster*'s Episode 5 by using the ship *Exelion*.) Following the generation of the black hole and the appearance of the Well, humanity was insulated from that threat by a defense system that gradually evolved into the alleged Space Monsters. The supposed foes, therefore, are actually humanity's keenest protectors. This realization turns the Topless into a cause of severe anxiety: If, in fighting the Space Monsters, they automatically advance the Well's deleterious design, they are implicitly working not in favor of but *against* humanity.

The pilots are accordingly banned from fighting by means of cumbersome headgear intended to block their brain waves. The official reason behind this drastic measure is that it is feared that they might actually degenerate into humankind's final bane if their powers were to get out of control. The hypothesis put forward by Captain Hatori in Episode 2 regarding the Topless' pernicious potential comes to sound unpalatably tenable. It is typical of Gainax, after all, not to apportion praise and blame unequivocally in accordance with a character's dominant drives, and hence allow at all times for an element of truthfulness to inhabit the intent of even the least attractive persona. Hatori may be unpleasant but this does not automatically render him utterly mendacious or undependable.

In order to grasp the interrelations among Space Monsters, Fluctuating Gravity Wells and the Topless, the following factors therefore have to be taken into account:

- the Space Monsters presented in *Gunbuster 2* are actually humanity's protectors against the lethal threat of Fluctuating Gravity Wells;
- Fluctuating Gravity Wells, accordingly, are the ultimate enemy;
- the Space Monsters presented in *Gunbuster* are real opponents seeking to annihilate humanity and are analogous in nature to Fluctuating Gravity Wells;
- the Topless' powers resemble those of Fluctuating Gravity Wells and of the Space Monsters from *Gunbuster*, which makes the pilots latently nefarious and explains why the "good" Space Monsters from *Gunbuster 2* fight them unrelentingly, and why the Serpentine Twins eat matter extracted from a Fluctuating Gravity Well to preserve their vigor.

The very concept of monstrosity is thereby called into question. However, *Gunbuster 2* does not merely undermine the stereotypical assumption that a monster unproblematically constitutes a malevolent force. In fact, it also proposes that Space Monsters are not so much fictional entities pure and simple as metaphors for social reality. According to Enokido, this invests the series with topical relevance despite its obvious affiliation to the imaginary. "In the last *Gunbuster*," the scriptwriter observes, "the space monsters were creatures that were aware of humans and came and attacked them.... [I]f you define 'space monsters' as 'creatures who become irritated by other people and attack them,' then in fact there are quite a lot of space monsters in our actual society.... People who refuse communication.... Isn't that what a space monster is?" (Enokido 2007c, p. 15).

Episode 5 conveys the action's inexorable descent into darkness with great subtlety, depicting the retired Topless' dejection and anger in all their poignance, yet also showing that Nono is not altogether exempt from the burden of sadness. Although she would seem to have every reason to feel undilutedly proud of her achievement and acknowledgment as humanity's sole hope, she actually tends to dwell on thoughts of loss. In recounting the story of the last bird ever seen on Mars, said to have lingered on the shore until the day when she could fly and to have then departed never to return, Nono's words communicate an overwhelming sense of nostalgia, and a keen apprehension of missed opportunities.

Relatedly, Episode 5 offers precious insights into the heroine's origins. Nono, we find out, is not a robot pure and simple but a life force discovered by a retired scientist (and his dog) in the middle of a comet and adopted by the man. In this regard, Nono resembles Hikari and Akari from *This Ugly Yet Beautiful World*. Like the latter, moreover, Nono acquires a humanoid physique and humanoid affects upon coming into contact with a human — specifically, by perceiving the existence of Noriko, whom she thereafter idealizes as "Nono-Riri." The appellation "Nono-Riri" derives from Nono's primal utterance upon awakening, which entails the tentative repetition of the first two syllables of the earlier heroine's name: "No ... no ... ri ... ri ... ko." Like Hikari and Akari, Nono has been floating about in outer space for an unimaginably lengthy period of time, in a state of absolute and impenetrable loneliness: capturing a vague awareness of Noriko has broken the spell.

At the same time, the show's fifth installment delves further into the true nature of Nono's powers, revealing that they exceed by far those of the Topless and indeed make her the ultimate defense system available to humanity. Sadly, as the android maid rises to epic stature, she thereby becomes painfully disconnected from her comrades. If Nono was initially singled out by her alterity as both a robot and an untrained combatant, now she finds herself once more framed as indomitably other by her superior strength. The intimation that her companions might feel not only dwarfed by her special status but also stigmatized as lethal threats to the fate of the human race puts Nono in a paradoxical position: The non-human creature is erected as the final protection against aliens. This situation echoes the ending of *This Ugly Yet Beautiful World*, in which a non-human entity is likewise responsible for preserving humankind in the face of certain extinction. Nono's primary task, in this respect, is to enlist the protective powers of the Space Monsters against the portentous Well. Banned from action, Lal'C realizes that right from the start, namely, her first encounter with Nono on Mars in Episode 1, the Space Monsters have been seeking out Nono as their legitimate "master" and endeavoring to bring her home.

However, although Nono's Buster Machine # 7 is meant to replace the Topless altogether, Episode 5 shows that Lal'C's powers are still needed at the point where it becomes clear that Nono is incapable of annihilating the Titan Gravity Well by herself and that the assistance of her *Oné-sama* is urgently required. Nono accordingly releases Lal'C from her restraints by recourse to a gorgeously forged — and uncannily magical-looking — key, enabling her to rejoin the fray and her trusted *Dix-Neuf*.

As the last resort against the Titan Well, Lal'C and the *Dix-Neuf* use the planet "Jupiter 2" to attack it, which gains the Topless pilot her semi-mythical reputation as the "mover of planets." Yet, the weapon does not succeed in destroying the enemy and it is decided that the Buster Machine # 7 must engage in a kamikaze mission by advancing inside Jupiter 2's extant core, turning it into a black hole and thus generating an "ultragravitational collapse" capable of annihilating the Well. Lal'C is determined to follow Nono to the bitter end but a dense barrier of Space Monsters blocks her and the *Dix-Neuf* conclusively off the battlefield. Once the Buster Machine # 7 has disappeared behind the wall's stylish tiling and no sign of further martial engagement can be detected, the humans simply assume that Nono has withdrawn from battle and dissolved into the ether.

Enokido explains the significance of this scene in relation to Nono's ethical stance — an attitude that demonstrates levels of intelligence and sensitivity lots of humans would greatly benefit from. Nono "pushes Lal'C away," the scriptwriter maintains, because she "actually sees that Noriko, who is forced to select the path of sacrificing herself for humanity, and Lal'C, who is intoxicated with the idea of self-sacrificial heroism, are the exact opposites" (Tsurumaki and Enokido, p. 15). Nono values selfless behavior highly but has no time for vapid quasi-militaristic propaganda. Much as she admires her *Oné-sama*, therefore, she simply refuses to absorb the Topless pilot's agenda uncritically and chooses instead to honor genuine altruism. In so doing, the heroine yields the entire adventure's most uplifting message. A tongue-in-cheek commentary on Nono's ethics is offered by the phrase "stupid sacrifice of life" adorning the box of "Top Sweets," which featured as the selected "Toppage" art piece for the official Gainax website in the closing week of August 2007. This is one of the many items surrounding the OVA through which its unique reality has been meticulously built by both Gainax staff and, as in this case, guest artists.

Episode 6, "Final Episode: The Story of Your Life," dramatizes the beleaguered humans' terminal task: the eradication of the Well occupying the black hole Exelio, which is reputed to be the most pernicious of its breed. For this purpose, the human fighters deploy Lal'C and her *mecha*, in charge of a colossal machine known as the *Douze-Mille*, under instruction to bombard the Well with the very last weapon at their disposal: an evacuated planet Earth. As the assault reaches its climax, it is revealed that Nono has not, after all, abandoned the conflict. The Buster Machine # 7 indeed resurges in stupendous form and size as the "Diebuster." Lal'C's Topless powers finally extinguish at this least appropriate of times but she bravely resists defeat by accessing the *Dix-Neuf*'s brain, where the machine's autonomous force resides and where the spacesuit worn by Noriko in the 1988 OVA is talismanically stowed. It is thus suggested that the venerable *Dix-Neuf* was once the very Gunbuster activated by Noriko before undergoing several physical and mechanical modifications and as many changes of pilot. This scene clearly shows that Lal'C's story is as intimately interwoven with Noriko's adventure as Nono's is.

Although Lal'C is at first determined to complete the mission to which she has been assigned according to the stipulated plan, the Diebuster earnestly prevents the *Douze-Mille* from reaching the Exelio and firing its final ammunition, thus saving the planet Nono has never set foot upon but has fondly speculated about from the instant of her awakening. The Diebuster's action echoes the sequence from Episode 2 in which Nono diverts Lal'C from her pursuit of a Space Monster in order to rescue the disempowered Lalahcharn, headed toward collision with Mars, as well as the sequence from Episode 3 in which she courageously guards the fate of defenseless humans based in the Residential Sector of the city-planet of Jupiter as the battle between Space Monsters and the Topless rages above them.

Donning Noriko's suit as though in homage to her valorous predecessor and enacting a strategic move redolent of the one employed by the previous heroine in *Gunbuster*'s climax, Lal'C joins forces with the Diebuster, which then reverts to the more Nono-like Buster Machine # 7 incarnation, and the two eventually succeed in annihilating the nefarious Well. The destruction of the Well unleashes an upheaval of a magnitude that seemingly exceeds any phenomenon that physics has ever known or even theorized. Lal'C is resolved to remain by Nono's side, loath to consign her once more to abysmal solitude but Nono is aware that this is not the way to proceed. She therefore bestows her "singularity" upon Lal'C and returns to the infinity whence she came.[5] Lal'C, for her part, is miraculously reunited with her human companions, unconscious but alive.

As she wakes up, it is disclosed that Nono's singularity has the shape of a crumpled origami crane: This is redolent of the *tsuru* given to Nono by Lal'C herself after the Topless' withdrawal from service. The whole sequence is strongly reminiscent of the denouement provided by *This Ugly Yet Beautiful World*. The scenes in Saeki's show in which Takeru endeavors to give Hikari one final gift in the form of visions of the places and seasons she has never experienced are mirrored, in *Gunbuster 2*, by those in which Nono imagines her and Lal'C's visit to the Topless girl's original home: a fantasy they shared in their days as roommates within the Fraternity HQ.

While the concluding installment derives much of its dramatic impact from the human fighters' last desperate attempt to withstand and eventually neutralize the Well's overwhelming power, a considerable proportion of its mounting suspense issues from the episode's dexterous unraveling of the underlying connections between Nono's and Noriko's respective quests.[6] This is fully corroborated by the epilogue, which takes place ten years after the climax of the main adventure. The sequence shows a considerably mellowed version of Lal'C, who has channeled her passion for birds (a leitmotif throughout the series) into a professional commitment. While observing the rare "Okinawa rail" flying through the sunset, Lal'C talks with Tycho over the phone, which endearingly suggests that the two girls have remained friends beyond the exhaustion of their special powers. Just as Lal'C reaches a summit and extinguishes her lantern, the lights go out one after the other for miles and miles around her in anticipation of an impending event that the "Hawaii Gravitational Observatory" has recently confirmed. "That night," the caption tells us, "the Buster Machines # 1 and # 2 returned, along with their pilots." The "Welcome Back" sign with the reversed final character once again fills the screen as it did at the close of *Gunbuster*.

Enokido has helpfully elucidated the nature of the interconnections among Nono, Lal'C and Noriko/Nono-Riri as follows: "The entire six episodes are about Lal'C looking back while waiting for Nono-Riri." The story's overarching structure, therefore, is a "look back over everything through Lal'C's feelings" (Tsurumaki and Enokido, p. 16). This explains why the offstage narration is in Lal'C's voice even at times, as in the opening part of Episode 1, when the monologue appears to issue from Nono. Tsurumaki came up with the idea of making the Topless pilot's perceptions and experiences the leading thread because he thought that the likelihood of Jung Freud being still alive and waiting for Noriko and Kazumi was practically nil and that this "was very sad." Hence, he settled for the idea that "there was a girl who was aiming to be like Noriko, and Lal'C is wondering who this Noriko is like." By recourse to this narrative formula, it became plausible to "have a story with someone who wants to meet Noriko the person, even though she doesn't know anything about Noriko" (Tsurumaki and Enokido, p. 17).

The end of *Gunbuster 2* thus coincides with the end of *Gunbuster*, which means that the year is A.D. 14,292 and the day the 6th of July. In *Gunbuster*, this is explicitly revealed by the dial on the dashboard of the homing pilots, whereas in *Gunbuster 2*, it is intimated by Tycho's allusion to the upcoming Tanabata Festival, which is customarily held on the 7th of July. Given the symbolic significance of this occurrence, it is hard to think of more apposite a choice of date. Also known as the "Star Festival," Tanabata celebrates the annual meeting of Orihime (Vega) and Hikoboshi (Altair), lovers normally separated by the river of stars forming the Milky Way. The tropes of separation, reunion and temporality bring this myth and the world of both *Gunbuster* shows intimately together.

Whereas *Gunbuster*'s finale gave no clear information as to the kind of planet Noriko and Kazumi were returning to, the sequel suggests that the Earth, though no doubt affected by its radical displacement in the *Douze-Mille* operation, is now a positively recovering body. Technology has clearly evolved exponentially, as shown by the fact that Lal'C is able to converse with Tycho, who is stationed on Pluto, in real time even though their respective locations are over four million kilometers apart. However, the planet portrayed in the closing scenes of Tsurumaki's OVA still bears traces of the ancient past (namely, our present time). Lal'C's classic birdwatcher outfit succinctly encapsulates this idea. Whether Gainax is here paying homage to Japanese culture's inveterate commitment to tradition or ironically suggesting that *plus ça change, plus c'est la même chose*, it is up to the individual viewer to decide.

In the handling of its scientific framework, *Gunbuster 2* departs radically from the 1988 series in the representation of the impact of space travel on its characters. In *Gunbuster*, as shown in Chapter 3, the characters traveling at a rate close to the speed of light experience time dilation, whereas those remaining on Earth do not. This results in a temporal discrepancy whereby the former age far less rapidly than the latter. In this respect, *Gunbuster* follows Einstein — and, specifically, his Special (or Restricted) Theory of Relativity of 1905 — in proposing that time passes more slowly for a body moving at sub-light speed than it does for a body at rest.

Einstein, it is worth recalling, reached this formulation by exploring how the physical laws governing the motion of a body are affected by the motions of its observers. The Special Theory of Relativity focuses on frames of reference moving relatively to one another. The General Theory of 1916 moves on to consider any number of viewpoints with mutual acceleration, namely, the rate at which a body's velocity (speed and direction) changes. Most importantly, and most relevantly to Gainax's outlook, Einstein's discovery that the position and time of an event viewed by different moving observers vary indicates that there cannot be an absolute space or an absolute time. In fact, the notion of a space-time continuum seems far more tenable. Concurrently, matter and energy are seen as inseparable. This fundamentally relativistic message is utterly consonant with the studio's distinctive worldview. Enokido openly admits to having assimilated Einstein's lesson: "We learned that matter and energy are one and the same and also that time and space are ultimately the same thing. So thoughts can be converted into matter or energy" (Enokido 2007b).

(A jocular allusion to pre–Einsteinian physics, incidentally, is made in the opening episode when Nono blames her unfortunate proclivity to be defied by gravity and, as a result, split everything in half, including a bulky refrigerator, on Newton himself. As to the barmy logic underlying the presence of a portrait of Sir Isaac behind the diner's counter, this is of a kind that only Gainax at its most gleefully unrestrained could conceive of.)

In Tsurumaki's sequel, all the characters occupy the same time frame and no disparities in the ageing process therefore occur. According to the *vissiOne* review of the OVA, time dilation in *Gunbuster* occurs because the characters moving at sub-light speed have to travel through ether much faster than bodies moving through the same medium at regular speed. This requires them to generate larger "amounts of energy" than would normally be necessary in order to counteract the "viscosity of ether" ("Beyond the Review: *Gunbuster* vs. *Diebuster*"). As a "material diffused across space," ether indeed "provides resistance in both space and atmosphere" ("Encyclopaedia of *Gunbuster 2*," p. 8). The greater the speed required of a moving body, the greater the degree of energy needed to negotiate that resistance, which causes the passage of time to slow down. In order to increase their speed without incurring time dilation, the Topless invoke their innate ability to bend the laws of physics by "controlling the ether," specifically, by transforming it into "plasma" ("Beyond the Review: *Gunbuster* vs. *Diebuster*").

Nowadays, physicists use the term ether (or, more accurately, "Luminiferous Aether") to describe not a material substance but a hypothetical medium enabling the propagation of light waves and particles. Thus, the viscosity of ether does not designate a material attribute but the conceptual property to resist flow. As for plasma, this denotes the fourth state of matter (besides the solid, liquid and gaseous states) and consists of a highly ionized gas, that is, a substance in which some atoms are positively or negatively charged as a result of losing or gaining electrons. A total of 99 percent of matter in the cosmos is held to be in plasma state. Unlike ordinary gas, plasma is capable of conducting electrical current and of being greatly affected by magnetic forces. These properties presumably make it a more congenial medium for the Topless to travel through than ether.

The crux of *Gunbuster 2*'s science-fictional infrastructure consists of the Topless' special powers: an inspired synthesis of fictitious ideas indigenous solely to the world of the series and snippets of genuinely scientific theories, both proven and hypothetical. According to a mock-explanatory "Science Lesson," the Topless' "brain is like a black hole, acting as the event horizon where events occur in the skull" ("*Gunbuster 2* Science Lesson — Chapter 1," p. 16). Of course, this may be a classic case of Gainax just reveling in pseudotechnical mumbo jumbo. Yet, black holes undeniably play a key diegetic part in both of the *Gunbuster* shows and therefore deserve some consideration in the present context.

A black hole is supposed to occur when a large star near the end of its life contracts and collapses into itself (or implodes). As the star's density increases exponentially, light becomes incapable of escaping from its boundary and from this moment, the star becomes unobservable. A black hole's boundary marking this "point of no return" is known as the *event horizon*. If a black hole were to collapse to one single dimensionless point of infinite density and temperature, this would constitute a *singularity* where the laws of physics simply do not apply. Such a point could not, of course, be observed because it would be blocked off by the event horizon. If, however, this boundary were to disappear, the singularity would become observable, or "naked." Accordingly, it would be theoretically possible to move in and out of it, defy all physical laws, and even travel across time or into parallel universes.

Episode 3 offers an example of such a phenomenon in the sequence in which Tycho finds herself "crossing time" and revisits the past. The experience, it is intimated, is both cathartic and strengthening in that it enables the girl to come to terms with her grief and to channel her Topless powers into her most challenging mission to date. In operating the *Quatre-Vingt-Dix*, Tycho is indeed able to deploy a weapon, the "Buster Smash," that has thus far been merely speculated about. The weapon is capable of freezing enormous numbers of opponents, as Casio points out, at the preposterous temperature of "negative one trillion, twenty million degrees"—a datum that would probably come across as unacceptably absurd even in Tsurumaki's outlandish universe were it not followed by Nicola's sobering remark: "Such temperatures do not physically exist...." The temporal displacement triggered by Tycho's movement through a singularity also enables snow to fall as it had done on the day of her separation from her precious friend, thus bringing a flicker of joy into the desolate lives of Jupiter's children. The exploration of a parallel reality is plausibly what Nono herself accomplishes in *Gunbuster 2*'s climax when she takes the singularity exposed by the Black Hole Exelio and gives Lal'C her own, in the process journeying into a purely hypothetical time zone.

In stylistic terms, *Gunbuster 2*'s most remarkable accomplishment consists of its integration of character designs of palpable texture, executed with a meticulous care for the minutest detail, and sublime cosmic vistas. At the same time, the *mecha*—combining established robotic features typical of Gainax's earlier oeuvre and motifs drawn from folklore, mythology and classic action-adventure—persistingly enhance the story's rhythm through a cornucopian variety of visual and special effects. Through the collusion of these elements, the viewer's attention is assiduously riveted by the intensity of the battles, on the one hand, and by the pathos of interpersonal relationships (both among peers and across diverse generations), on the other. And then there's Nono's streaming pink hair: a living prop whose sheer dynamism is sufficient unto itself to keep the eye glued to the screen. Gainax's commitment to the loving rendition of animational minutiae is economically encapsulated by the shot from Episode 1 in which Nono is recovering from some severe bashing about, courtesy of a Space Monster, and the first sign of life emitted by her body is the springing up of the distinctively untameable curl atop her head, as though this were endowed with autonomous motility.

At the level of character design, *Gunbuster 2*'s handling of an extremely varied range of facial expressions deserves attention. Nono is especially notable, in this regard, due to her ability to communicate a whole slew of contrasting emotions with equal intensity. Even though her attitude is pervasively positive, it is not uncommon for cheerful expressions to give way to moroseness, disappointment or even indignation. Subtle modulations in the rendition of her mien effectively evoke these mood swings even in the absence of verbal language to underpin or explain them. Sadamoto has commented as follows on the aesthetic principles underlying the execution of his designs for Nono's character: "I exaggerated Nono's cheeriness in order to convey her wonderfully uncomplicated personality" (quoted in Hikawa 2007a, p.105).

Lal'C's expressions, by contrast, tend to communicate a coolly collected disposition. Yet, this typical demeanor is capable of softening to deliver a very engaging smile. Tycho's expressions are stable at first, optimism being their leading quality on the surface. Deep down, however, the girl harbors a scarred and disillusioned personality and her childishly beaming countenance is not seldom superseded by a sour pout, especially when her ongoing competition with Lal'C does not quite deliver the hoped-for outcome. As the gravity of her trauma becomes patent, sullenness, despondency or even downright ire become accordingly dominant. With Nicola, the emphasis initially falls on carefree juvenility—a trait that his latent similarity to Peter Pan both underlines and complicates. Indeed, Nicola cannot partake of his fairy-tale analogue's eternal youthfulness and the recognition that his Topless faculties are therefore ephemeral incrementally causes his mien to acquire more aggressive and, occasionally, crazed undertones. As the epitome of an ostensibly self-possessed grown-up eager to proclaim his inviolability, Hatori typically shields his expressions, and hence his feelings, behind impenetrable sunshades, thus recalling both Coach Ohta from *Gunbuster* and Gendou Ikari from *Evangelion*.

Sadamoto's painstaking dedication to the portrayal of each of the characters' distinctive traits is not only eloquently demonstrated by the design of the principal personae, which could conceivably be expected of a sensitive and seasoned artist. In fact, it is also conveyed by the dexterity with which he seeks to capture the individuating facets of marginal actors by means of specific somatic features and vestimentary attributes. Captain Hatori, for instance, could hardly need anything other than his spiky accessories — an acuminate hat, cusp-shaped shoulder pads and sharp-pointed boots — to express his belligerently penetrative stance.

Yoshitsune Izuna's machine designs bear witness to representational skills on a par with Sadamoto's: not only is each of the Buster Machines subtly differentiated at the levels of size, equipment, attire and attitude but the more overtly functional machines are also endowed with individualizing attributes that enable them to transcend the boundaries of the purely serviceable and yield aesthetic polyphony. Izuna himself maintains that the "base" of his drawings "was the concept of 'uncool-cool.' Overall, they might look uncool, but as you get used to the design, cool oozes out" (Izuna, pp. 11–12). The most charismatic *mecha* is undoubtedly the *Dix-Neuf*. This giant robot's countenance brings to mind the image of an awe-inspiring warrior or even a demonic force (such as the indigenous *oni*), on the one hand, and that of a captivating rogue, on the other. Tsurumaki has stated that the main sources of inspiration behind the *Dix-Neuf* were the actor Ken Takakura, the epitome of the streetwise tough guy within Japanese cinema also known as the Clint Eastwood of Japan, and Lord Yupa from Hayao Miyazaki's *Nausicaä of the Valley of Wind*, the indefatigable traveler seeking vestiges of life across a depleted environment (Tsurumaki 2007a).

Furthermore, as Kimata points out, the "eye patch gives the impression that the *Dix-Neuf* is a hardened veteran of battle, and in conjunction with the cape, it helps provide the robot with a sense of personality" (Kimata 2007, p. 28). Both elements also serve to invest the principal *mecha* with legendary iconographic connotations redolent of pirates and knights of old. Providing a striking point of contrast with the thuggish *Dix-Neuf*, the *Vingt-Sept* exhibits stately characteristics. These are explicitly conveyed by its winglike supplementary arms and by the aura of Apollonian composure exuded by its robotic mask. On the whole, a predilection for curvy rather than angular lines distinguishes *Gunbuster 2*'s Buster Machines from many stereotypical anime *mecha*. This lends them a quasi-organic feel that matches the rhythm of the pilots' moves and thoughts.

The coalescence of the mechanical and the organic is also borne out by the Topless spacesuit donned to travel between stations: an armor rigged out with puppy-like floppy ears and a pear-shaped belly replete with navel. The Twins' pet, a stuffed animal named Hoehoe combining feline and canine attributes and mysteriously speaking with Nicola's voice, is one more charismatic member of *Gunbuster 2*'s outlandish menagerie. Hoehoe, notably, was designed by Nono's voice actress, Yukari Fukui. The Channeling Cat, a black kitten equipped with a smart collar and tail jewelry that allows Lal'C and Tycho to communicate telepathically, aptly complements the series' pantheon.

Stylistically, *Gunbuster 2* also marks the apotheosis of Gainax's proficient orchestration of explicitly hand-drawn visuals soaked in gleefully cartoony chromatic palettes and exacting photorealism. The latter modality is brought most emphatically to bear on the portrayal of the show's futuristic settings, vehicles and *mecha*. On occasion, the style is also applied to the representation of natural scenery, as evinced by the shots from Episode 1 depicting the shimmering bay flooded with golden, ochre and coppery reflections.

In designing the interiors of *Gunbuster 2*'s futuristic locations, Tsurumaki's team endeavored to integrate the visual conventions associated with the digital age, such as fluorescent green maps and diagrams, and an audacious handling of distance, elevation and depth by means of exaggerated or distorted perspectives. This strategy enables *Gunbuster 2* to evoke the impression of limitless and weightless space and to intimate a world's unrelenting transformation into other worlds. The spectator's eye can often follow the mutations as they unfold and indeed believe them, even though reason intimates that they are empirically unfeasible. Defying both gravity and logic through a drastic decentralization of space, the show thus demonstrates that its creators are unfettered by the constraints of everyday geometry and architecture in the belief that real-life configurations of built space are ultimately irrelevant to the realm of cinema and especially animation. What matters is the internal consistency of the coordinates ideated in order to further a story's immediate objectives.

In Tsurumaki's series, this aesthetic goal is proclaimed by the sequences (of which there are many) in which the camera plumbs space's quaquaversal surfaces and paths from multiple angles, at times in the course of just a single scene. A good example is supplied, in Episode 2, by the sequence in which Hatori's fleet is attacked by a Space Monster and, much as the officer trusts his "state-of-the-art" fleet to be capable of vanquishing the enemy no less effectively than Topless fighters, the ships are severely damaged and their "cyber-whale" brains are hacked into. The damage inflicted on the main cruiser is communicated by the distortion of its internal structure in an inflated version of a disorienting fairground ride, whereby rigid metal frames bend and undulate and the vehicle's entire body mutates into a mercurial creature redolent of a mythical sea beast.

Where high-tech locations are concerned, one of the show's most impressive accomplishments lies with the structure housing the Fraternity's lounge: a glass-walled tower in the guise of a gigantic bullet encasing multiple levels of indoor gardens. Whereas the martial connotations carried by the shape of the edifice invest it with an aura of forbidding austerity, the ubiquitous trees, bushes and clumps of ivy lend it a benevolent and almost pastoral feel.

Episode 5 offers a prime instance of ultramodern technology as the Chief of Staff Niigo explains some of the mysteries underlying the Sol System, its defensive apparatus, Fluctuating Gravity Wells and Space Monsters. The setting is dominated by an array of circular monitors illustrating Niigo's argument by recourse to multidimensional graphs, still images of relevant portions of outer space, holograms and animated documentary-style footage. Especially notable is the sequence charting the evolution of humankind's defense system from a shape reminiscent of a single spermatozoon into a proliferation of shapes that both allude to micro-organisms consonant with real-life specimens and blend imaginatively disparate aesthetic trends. These include the passion for stylized ornamentation characteristic of traditional Japanese art, the decorative motifs cultivated by the postmodern Japanese movement known as Superflat, and Joan Miró's creepy amoebas and bizarre doodles.

Tsurumaki's imaginary biology also bears affinities with the peculiar spirits central to the TV series *Mushi-Shi* (dir. Hiroshi Nagahama, 2006) — a breed of ethereal beings that "dwell, unseen, in the shadows — a host of creatures completely different from the flora and fauna familiar to us, an invisible world of life within our own." Both Nagahama's *mushi* and Tsurumaki's creatures could be said to represent life at its purest and are, therefore, amorphous and polymorphic at once. It is also noteworthy that *Mushi-Shi* mirrors Gainax's tendency to underscore the materiality and inherent aliveness of language in its rendition of pictographs that are actually capable of detaching themselves from the page and acquiring animate existence.

The notion that typographic characters are intrinsically endowed with vitality functions as a potent metaphor for the power of animation as an art to bring inert matter to life.

Retrofuturistic elements are assiduously utilized in various aspects of *Gunbuster 2*'s architecture and furnishings. These provide charming points of contrast with the highly advanced technologies that surround them on all sides. A case in point is provided, in Episode 1, by the restaurant situated in the vicinity of a Martian spaceport where Nono works for a while prior to her adoption by the Fraternity. So spacious as to allow several *mecha*-clad customers to sit comfortably within its walls without even having to leave their robotic suits, the edifice is adapted from the shell of an old spaceship. The signals, pylons, cables and monorail tracks that crowd the diner's surroundings enhance the steampunk mood of the scenery. These antiquarian touches contrast sharply with the more decidedly sci-fi look of numerous settings introduced in the following installments.

As for props, the equipment in Captain Hatori's office offers some of the most playfully incongruous dashes of retrofuturistic decor: The old-fashioned filter coffee maker and the rotary dial telephone are especially memorable in their exactingly realistic depiction. The notion that Hatori should need an ancient piece of technology to be informed of the advent of a Space Monster while he is busy boasting the unsurpassable technological sophistication of his fleet exudes with Gainaxian irony. Overtly futuristic and retro elements tantalizingly coalesce in the representation of Jupiter in Episode 3. This is one of the most ancient cities within humankind's reach and consists of a conglomerate of spaceship debris, portions of which are still identifiable. The urbanscape provides a mesmerizing blend of futuristic edifices of classic sci-fi orientation, Oriental canals teeming with old-fashioned produce-laden barges and crumbling buildings that nostalgically hark back to neoclassical magnificence of overtly European derivation.

Tsurumaki's fascination with the retro element is complemented by the director's desire to look back on the *mecha* tradition with deliberate "nostalgia." This is borne out by architectural motifs, such as those presented in the sequence in which Nono first perceives the main Martian conglomerate, that are patently indebted to the sci-fi style of the 1960s. An important source of inspiration behind these designs is the work of the science-fiction writer Ryu Mitsuse. Tsurumaki feels instinctively drawn to Mitsuse's work because it communicates a vision deeply akin to his own. In the author's stories, he notes, "Nature is very powerful. It's absolute. So even as science progresses, nature will never be displaced by science." Hence, central to Mitsuse's take on science is the use of ironical situations: "Like emigrating to an unknown star only to be decimated because of severe natural conditions" (Tsurumaki 2007a).

Both the hypermodern and the nostalgic settings emanate from the fertile imagination of the internationally acclaimed artist and illustrator okama (the lower-case spelling is intentional), who played a major role in the ideation of the OVA's world in his capacity as future visual creator. As producer Hiroki Sato explains, okama's task required him to produce "a kind of 'mental picture' of the future" that would encompass not only the macrocosmic dimension of the adventure and related large-scale structures but also "the clothing and customs of the people, the buildings, the plants, down to the popular sweets, fashions, all of this stuff together" (Sato 2007, p. 13). The punctilious care for details taken by okama, allied to a knack of executing intricate drawings oozing with unparalleled luminosity, chromatic vibrance and sinuous elegance, contributed vitally to that massive exercise in world building. *Gunbuster 2*'s ambience is imbued throughout with all of okama's distinctive trademarks, as also seen in other major projects in which he has been involved. These include the illustrations for the manga *Cloth Road* (Hideyuki Kurata, 2004–Present), the Magical-Girl TV series *Kamichu!* (dir. Koji Masunari, 2005), the space saga *The Wings of Rean* (OVA series; dir. Yoshiyuki

Tomino, 2005–2006) and the ninja comedy *Himawari!* (TV series; dir. Shigenori Kageyama, 2006).

One of okama's most appealing contributions to *Gunbuster 2* consists of the drawings for the closing credits. In finalizing their content, the artist followed one basic principle: "It was '*Top*' so I thought I should give it a 'pop-ish' feeling. I always tend to do things as I think of them, so I didn't pay attention to anything special in particular" (okama, p. 13). The images emphasize the show's more light-hearted angle, foregrounding its *shoujo* and *moe* undercurrents. Portraits of Nono in a variety of poses and outfits are predominant, and are displayed both as discrete visuals and in montages. Gainax's appetite for pictorial ensembles is also evinced by collage-like composites of various characters and ornamental motifs—down to minutiae such as the Topless' seal, the Fraternity's logo and Nono's hairclip.

Also notable is the use of the four-panel manga format as a means of economically depicting the relationship between Nono and Lal'C. Although the tone is jocular and the emotional tension pervading the series is therefore mellowed down, the panels effectively capture the two girls' personalities in a fashion that is entirely congruous with the story's import. Pictures in which Nono engages in cosplay with the *Dix-Neuf*, at one point treating the *mecha* to a provocative wink, stand out as delightful forays into self-reflexivity. That such images should carry slightly risqué connotations is not surprising, given okama's background in *hentai*, namely, manga with explicit erotic content. The visuals discussed above are beautifully reproduced in the volume *Top 2! Perfect Book*, an invaluable companion piece to the OVA. While it is not uncommon for art books supplementing popular productions to make claims to "perfection" in their titles, it is no less rare to discover that this amounts to an advertising cliché. In the case of *Top 2!*, however, the title truly reflects the work's standing as a gold mine of insightful information.

Gunbuster vs. Diebuster: Aim for the Top Gattai Movie
Director: Kazuya Tsurumaki (2006)

The *Gunbuster* and the *Gunbuster 2* OVA's have been recently complemented by the release of *Gunbuster vs. Diebuster: Aim for the Top Gattai Movie* (2006), which includes the theatrical versions of the two series. These consist of two feature-length films separated by a brief intermission. This production signals an important moment in Gainax's ongoing commitment to formal adventurousness, offering an enterprising experiment with two of the techniques most assiduously and passionately cultivated by the studio throughout its history: the montage and the collage. The word "*gattai*," which approximately translates as "combination," is of paramount importance to this production's aesthetic and compositional priorities. On the one hand, it aptly describes the cinematographical approach to cutting and editing that underpins its overall structure and therefore functions as a preeminently technical term. On the other hand, it echoes a narrative motif pivotal to both *Gunbuster* programs, namely, the advancement of the action by recourse to spectacular syntheses of discrete robotic apparatuses. The term *gattai* is indeed used in the domain of anime at large, and in the category of *mecha* anime specifically, to designate mechanical transmutations founded upon the criterion of combinatorial play.

A *mecha*'s actual "transformation" (*henkei*) into a different entity does not require the initial body to assimilate separate components in order to change but actually results from the creature's inbuilt capacities. With *gattai*, conversely, two or more bodies coalesce to engender a composite entity endowed with novel capabilities. The *Dix-Neuf*'s metamorphosis from a rocket-like vehicle into an actual fighting machine of humanoid form in Episode 1 of

Gunbuster 2 is a classic instance of *henkei*. So are the modifications undergone by the *Gratan* and the *Nautilus* in *Nadia* and by the Eva Mass Production Models 05–13 in *Evangelion*. The fusion of the Buster Machine # 1 piloted by Noriko and the Buster Machine # 2 piloted by Kazumi in *Gunbuster*'s Episode 5, for its part, exemplifies the *gattai* modality. So do numerous key sequences in *Making Breakthrough Gurren Lagann*. Nono's Diebuster partakes of both typologies insofar as it is a development of the Buster Machine # 7, which is itself a composite of sorts, yet also evinces metamorphic properties. While *henkei* supplies Gainax with precious opportunities to dramatize its vision of a protean universe in a state of continual becoming, *gattai* satisfies the studio's fascination with all manner of compositing, both analogue and digital.

Especially worthy of consideration, in examining *Gunbuster vs. Diebuster*'s contribution to the saga as a whole, are the stylistic and structural differences entailed by the OVA and feature-length formats. The *Gattai* does not simply deliver an alternate editing of the two shows but a cinematographical and dramatic accomplishment of autonomous stature, in much the same way as *Death* is not simply a cosmetic cut-and-paste job but a novel reimagining of the *Evangelion* TV series. The *Gattai*, therefore, constitutes a stylistically and structurally freestanding work that deftly prioritizes the principles of compression, condensation and telescoping in which the episodic programs can afford to dole out their dramatic substance at greater leisure. In the ensuing paragraphs, the former component in the *Gattai* is referred to as *Gunbuster*, the latter as *Diebuster*.

The constellation of scenes from the original series within the *Gattai* imparts the action with a distinctive rhythm and tempo. For example, sequences, which in their original presentation lay emphasis on rapidly paced dynamism, are at times reconfigured so as to reduce the action level and focus instead on the narrative's reflective dimension, as indicated by the first part of *Diebuster*. Conversely, dialogue-oriented scenes are occasionally clipped or exscinded altogether, as in *Gunbuster*'s early segment, in order to let the action factor gain the upper hand. These shifts impact on the audience by recharting the routes through which information is absorbed. Concurrently, they affect the characters' presentation at both the synchronic level of discrete scenes and the diachronic level of the overarching storyline.

The section of the *Gunbuster* feature preceding the opening credits portrays the *Luxion*'s final instants as dramatized in the preamble to the show's second installment. This emotionally fraught sequence is ironically contrasted with the following shots, in which images of the RX-7 training machines engaged in ludicrous gymnastics dominate the screen. We are next introduced to Noriko and Kimiko, to Coach Ohta as he instructs his pupils to achieve maximum control over their *mecha* and, in the wake of Noriko's shock at being selected as space pilot alongside Kazumi, to the show's axial message: the importance of hard work, guts and determination. These scenes are drawn entirely from Episode 1.

Following the credit sequence, the action shifts to the Silver Star Station and to a distinctively sci-fi tenor. Noriko and Kazumi's reconnaissance mission to the *Luxion*'s wreck (as seen in Episode 2) and Noriko and Toren Smith's doomed partnership (as seen in Episode 3) constitute the key elements in this portion of the movie. As this summary indicates, *Gunbuster* prioritizes action, eliminating the more methodically paced and primarily dialogical portions of the OVA's early installments and concentrating instead on the dynamic component of the story. From the rise of the Gunbuster — as seen in the OVA's fourth installment — to the end, the feature is extremely faithful to the parent show. Yet, in foregrounding the humans' desperate struggle, the film communicates an altogether more somber mood than the series.

A few instances of elision of the original OVA's contents deserve particular attention. In the series' first episode, when Ohta realizes that Noriko's coordination skills are appalling, he requires her to cover on foot the fifty laps in which the other pupils are negotiating aboard their RX-7s. Her pluck in the circumstances gives Ohta reason to believe that Noriko is capable of stoical determination, and hence explains (at least partially) his subsequent choice of the girl as space pilot. In the film, the heroine's punishment is alluded to but the actual spectacle of her exertions is left out: this omission greatly enhances the dramatic force of the scene that follows her humiliating performance, in which Noriko learns from Kimiko that she has indeed been selected.

Another important curtailment is that of the sequence from Episode 1 in which Kazumi intervenes to stop Noriko's classmates' ruthless bludgeoning of the inept pupil, urges Noriko to believe in herself and seals their friendship by giving the younger girl an emblematic bandanna. In the movie, we merely catch a glimpse of Kazumi in the cockpit of her RX-7 during Ohta's training session and next see her engaged in an intensive workout. Aboard the *Exelion*, Kazumi's relationship with Noriko is likewise understated: The older woman seems primarily concerned with having her partnership with the tentative young pilot revoked. It is not until the climax of the Gunbuster's first sortie that a clear sense of the connection between the two characters, bound to become pivotal to the adventure as a whole, is explicitly conveyed. In this way, the film consolidates the proposition that Noriko must depend on herself above all else.

Jung Freud, for her part, plays a much more marginal role in the feature than she does in the series. It is in the finale, as she passionately commits herself to welcoming Noriko and Kazumi back when they eventually return to Earth, that her role is accorded full standing. It is the encapsulation of Jung's presence within a single poignant scene that makes her contribution to the movie memorable. A remarkable case of subtle editing can be found in the employment of the character of Kashiwara. Since the duel sequence from the OVA's Episode 1 is not included in the film, Kashiwara is not seen until Noriko returns to Okinawa for her graduation in 2032, by which time the heroine's former rival is employed as the academy's top trainer. The inclusion of this detail might seem unnecessary at the time of its occurrence but becomes totally justified when the action reaches the climactic scene set in the year 2048 in which it is absolutely vital that Kashiwara (now an elderly lady) should feature.

Diebuster's opening part follows the events portrayed in the OVA's Episode 1 almost frame by frame (with some minor abridgements in the restaurant sequence) up until the climax of Lal'C's fight against the Space Monster and then abruptly diverges from the original. In the movie, Nono does not contribute to the enemy's defeat in any explicit fashion but is seen floating through space, eager to join her *Oné-sama*. This change impacts significantly on the movie's overall diegesis insofar as it serves to understate Nono's capacities: Although she is clearly endowed with unusual skills, the full extent of her superhuman powers does not become patent until much later. Following a brand-new scene in which the *Dix-Neuf* lands within the Fraternity HQ with Nono perched on its left hand, the film immediately proceeds to introduce the strand of the plot based on the Serpentine Twins' hideous plan and their use of Nicola as something of an informer from within the Fraternity. The sisters' unhealthy interest in "Titan crab," on the one hand, and in Nono's enigmatic origins and aims, on the other, is accordingly revealed in snippets of conversation between Nicola and the Twins drawn from Episodes 2 and 3 of the show. This strategy emplaces the story's expressly harrowing component as the film's narrative priority.

The action leaves out the main events included in the original Episodes 2 and 3, focusing at an early stage on the 'Topless' expedition to Titan and on the resulting upheaval. The sequence depicting the interplanetary journey (utilizing the plane used in the series' third installment for the trip to Jupiter) is a fresh addition to the diegesis and focuses on Nono as she writes a detailed letter to her adopter, which explains how he got the snapshot of her and Lal'C seen toward the end of the OVA. A conversation involving various Topless members provides useful background information concerning Titan. Just as Jung Freud plays a peripheral role in *Gunbuster* until the denouement, so Tycho is substantially marginalized in *Diebuster* and greater emphasis is accordingly placed on the Topless as a group.

Cinematographically, one of the most effective techniques used in this segment of the film is the smooth intercutting of shots from a conversation between Nicola and the Twins and scenes from Nono's infiltration of the Excavation Site in search of the Buster Machine reputed to be buried therein. Both sets of images are drawn from Episode 4. The same technique is utilized later in the action to alternate between shots of the Titan Well's fateful power and of Nono and Casio on Pluto. In Episode 4 of the OVA, Casio is sent to Pluto as a punishment for making a disrespectful remark about the Twins' age, and meets Nono when she has already reached the planet by her own means. Meanwhile, he has also found out about the Buster Machine that Nono is after and resolved to appropriate the *mecha* for himself. In the movie, by contrast, the technician's plan is rendered more unsavory by his deliberate decision to accompany the girl on her expedition. This change infuses an element of deviousness into Casio's habitually jovial character, which the shifty look in his eyes economically reinforces. Yet, the variation also intensifies the levels of insanity to which ex–Topless are pushed if they cannot come to terms with the loss of their powers.

From the emergence of the Buster Machine # 7 and the Titan Well's vanquishing (as seen in Episode 4) to the completion of Nono and Lal'C's climactic mission in Episode 6, the film follows closely the original series. The one impactful difference consists of the repositioning of the scene in which the elderly scientist and his alacritous pooch chance upon Nono. In the OVA's fifth installment, the scene is presented just prior to Niigo's meticulously documented spiel about defense systems and evolution. This forges an implicit connection between Nono's appearance and the broader cosmic events portrayed in the story, making the girl's discovery come across as akin to a scientific phenomenon. In the film, conversely, the scientist recounts the event to Lal'C when the latter visits him in Marineris, wishing to see Nono's human home. This invests the occurrence with infinitely more intimate and moving connotations, magisterially intensified by the melancholy beauty of the old-fashioned abode and its snowy surroundings.

The placing of the *Diebuster* portion of the compilation directly after the *Gunbuster* component would seem to indicate that the *Gattai* adopts a straightforwardly paratactic structure of a sequential stamp. However, once the viewer concentrates on the logic guiding the selection of particular scenes from each show and their constellation within each feature, it becomes clear that *Gunbuster* and *Diebuster* are conceived as intercomplementary narratives diffused with hypotactic connections. This is not to say that the work explicitly highlights causal links between the two diegeses. In fact, it is ultimately up to individual spectators to establish which aspects of each film mirror aspects of the other, and which perceived connections strike affective chords in their personal purview of the saga. Therefore, in watching the two films as autonomously worthy pieces of anime, it is also important to inspect them relationally on the basis of implied parallelisms, harmonies and discordances.

The two aspects of the original OVAs that the *Gattai* captures most effectively are the topos of friendship and the orchestration of scientific concepts. Whereas in *Gunbuster* the value of friendship is foregrounded from the start by means of Noriko's and Kimiko's interaction, in *Diebuster* it develops gradually and almost surreptitiously. In both stories, however, it is triumphantly enthroned in the climactic moments, extrapolated from the final installments of the two series. The key shots from *Gunbuster* are the ones in which Noriko realizes that she will be unable to return to Earth for an immeasurable length of time (if at all) and cries out a farewell to Kimiko. At that very moment, Kimiko looks up at the sky and tells her daughter Takami that she has heard her former school friend call her name.

The moment in *Diebuster* invoking the theme of friendship most dramatically is the scene in which the habitually self-possessed Lal'C breaks down and admits to her yearning to simply be "friends" with Nono. Even the eventual loss of her special powers, she avers, would have been tolerable if that connection had been nurtured. Tycho, who hears Lal'C's cri de coeur through her Buster Machine's remote-control equipment, is taken aback by the mention of the word "friends." At this juncture, it is not clear why Tycho should react the way she does, and whether she is surprised to discover that Lal'C needs friends or is prompted to wonder what friendship could mean in the context of her own life. The epilogue suggests that Lal'C and Tycho have forged a long-lasting friendship capable of defying enormous distances: The lesson learnt by Lal'C in connection with Nono appears to have beneficially impacted on the two ex–Topless' previously adversarial relationship. The most conclusive and deeply touching paean to friendship comes at the very end as Lal'C declares that she has been waiting a long time for the night of Noriko's return and longs to tell her about Nono and her admiration for Nono-Riri's exemplary actions.

The entire saga's handling of scientific (or quasi-scientific) ideas is no less memorably thrown into relief by the compilation. The adventures' dramatic apices are especially noteworthy, in this regard. The plan to escort the *Exelion* into the heart of the alien fleet and to overload the ship's collapsing motor to create a black hole capable of crushing the enemy to a singularity (also seen in Episode 5 of the *Gunbuster* show) is echoed by the Buster Machine # 7's transformation of Jupiter 2's core into a black hole by triggering an ultragravitational collapse (as dramatized in *Gunbuster 2*'s own fifth installment). The relationship between the two enterprises is hinted at by Admiral Dhorasoo's remark that the technology deployed by Nono belongs to the "age of myths," which is entirely logical when one considers the huge time gap separating Noriko's and Kazumi's operation from the sequel's own temporal zone.

In inviting us to juxtapose these interrelated events at the thematic level, the *Gattai* simultaneously prompts us to evaluate the specifically technical resources brought to bear upon their dramatization. The scenes drawn from Episode 5 of Tsurumaki's OVA, in particular, are able to draw an intriguing parallel between its scientific frame of reference and its graphics. As a result, the complexity of the physical theories and hypotheses implicit in the action is matched by that of the mathematical principles invoked in the design of the setting. The depiction of the hordes of Space Monsters eager to follow Nono, specifically, utilizes to maximum effect the tessellation technique, namely, the tiling of a surface through the repeated use of geometric shapes to form a pattern with no gaps and no overlaps. These images also show how tessellation can be effectively accomplished by means of fractals: geometric figures based on the principle of recursive self-division in which features are recapitulated in miniature on incrementally fine scales.

As the two stories near their respective denouements, their scientific strands become increasingly inextricable from ideological and moral issues. *Gunbuster*'s finale (wholly faithful to the OVA's sixth installment) alludes to the thorny ethical issue of whether humanity has the right to annihilate a whole breed of sentient creatures (and an entire galaxy to boot) for the sake of self-preservation. Kazumi's sibylline counsel feasibly reflects Anno's own ambiguity in this respect: "Mankind will be annihilated if we do not do this," she maintains. The alternative would amount to "suicide" and although it is perfectly possible that this option would be preferable, this is "for the historians of the future to judge." *Diebuster* revisits this issue with intensified poignancy in the sequence in which a Council of Elders consults Lal'C about the appropriateness of the *Douze-Mille* operation. (In the series, this occurs in the early part of Episode 6.) The Topless adamantly states: "sacrificing the Earth is the only way to save mankind." When the Chief of Staff Niigo (who, ironically, is an android) asks: "Even if humanity itself evolves into fluctuating gravity wells in order to stay alive?" Lal'C simply ripostes: "Let whoever survives be the judge of that."

The deployment of the Black Hole Bomb in *Gunbuster*'s culmination finds a direct parallel in the plan dramatized by *Diebuster* to strike the Exelio Well with the Earth by means of the portentous *Douze-Mille*. (The Black Hole Bomb's intended detonation device, incidentally, is Jupiter 2's core: the weapon used also in *Diebuster* when Lal'C launches it against the raging Titan Well.) The Black Hole Bomb's failure to detonate is echoed by the thwarting of the *Douze-Mille*'s operation by Nono's Diebuster, which likewise renders the firing of the final piece of ammunition impracticable. Additionally, Noriko's decision to tear back the plating on Gunbuster's chest, expose its collapsing generator and thrust it into the Bomb to allow it to detonate is mirrored by Lal'C's climactic actions. Replicating Noriko's brave gesture, Lal'C pulls back the *Dix-Neuf*'s pectoral armor, this time enabling the *mecha* not to eject but to reappropriate into itself the crucial generator. The fighting machine thus regains its true form. The "Double Lighting Kick" performed by Nono's Diebuster and Lal'C's *Dix-Neuf*— now renamed Buster Machine # 19 — sensationally ensures the Well's cataclysmic termination.

Ultimately, *Gunbuster*, *Gunbuster 2* and their *Gattai* coalescence stand out as enduring monuments in the story not merely of anime but of storytelling at large by virtue of their ethical message. This lesson intimates that self-understanding is the main prerequisite for the ability to advance a cause in a disinterested fashion. When a person is consciously aware of his or her inner core, any obvious reason for acting selfishly falls by the wayside since the self is, quite simply, outside the game. The story further proposes that in the absence of that understanding, human beings are bound to revel complacently in a state of self-delusion that allows them to misconstrue their actions as mindful choices while these actually amount to blindly instinctual means of achieving ego-flattering gratification by the speediest route. This attitude may merely result in a lifelong condition of self-satisfied oblivion. Yet, more often than not, it actually engenders a state of affairs wherein desire is perpetually renewed and fulfillment perpetually deferred. The outcome may consist of dissatisfaction but also, more ominously, of despondency or even despair. The mentality encapsulated by Nono's message is by no means conducive to either lasting happiness or undiluted pleasure. However, by taking nothing for granted, it affectionately fosters both inquisitiveness and creativity, namely, the qualities that enable a person to retain the desire to be moved, to laugh, to go on learning.

Chapter 14

The Anime Magic of Studio Gainax

In the life of an animator there are short and rare moments of true magic. Those moments are the reason I became an animator, and they are the reason I am still one. I'm talking about a moment in which you look at the animation you've just created, and suddenly you believe your own character. Suddenly it's alive, it's there in its own right.

— Doron A. Meir

Harking back to the tradition of the *ukiyo-e* in its alternately affectionate and mocking depiction of the evanescence of life's pleasures, Gainax's works concomitantly echo Japan's graphic arts in their commingling of mythical motifs, monstrous beings and supernatural phenomena with realistic snapshots of everyday life at its least glamorous. Sensational action sequences alternate with ordinary urban scenes peopled by unexceptional personae, as well as placid moments of introspection or intimacy. On occasion, Gainax's artists give their fluent lines free rein in the representation of images so viscerally graphic as to verge on the grotesque, for example, in scenes that dramatize portentous metamorphoses and apocalyptic upheavals. Even in those circumstances, however, the quest for beauty remains paramount, in accordance with an ethos that locates the idea of beauty not in the superficially appealing but in the magic of latent correspondences and analogies among disparate life forms.

Adventurousness, extravagance and even irreverence are words often invoked to describe the peculiar character of Gainax's approach to the art of anime. It could hardly be denied that it is by lending quirky twists to established trends and their customary tropes by recourse to deconstructive gestures that the studio invests its productions with a unique timbre. On numerous occasions, Gainax's formal and generic experiments, underpinned by a hearty appetite for sheer iconoclasm, deliver scenarios wherein the bizarre nimbly translates into comedy. Nevertheless, the studio's oeuvre should not be summed up as a series of anime pieces in which formulaic yarns and personae are routinely transformed into exotic specimens through the infusion of barmy humor into the concoction. In fact, what makes that corpus more memorable still is its commitment to the delineation of an inverse trajectory: the progressive darkening of sunny and familiar situations whereby the most tortuous facets of the human condition come into focus. It is through this ruse that Gainax's "anime magic" asserts itself most sonorously.

It could therefore be argued that the diegetic curve to which the company's directors tend to return is one in which traditional typologies are at first adopted, temporarily sustained and then subverted as the story develops. The transgressive gesture may well consist, initially, of a foray into carnivalesque territory but almost always results in a brave descent into darkness.

Thus, the lightheartedness of the *shoujo* and *moe* modes, of high school romance, of sports comedy and even of farce is wont to give way to somber explorations of the ephemerality of pleasure, beauty and life itself. Likewise, adventure-driven formats such as space opera and the *mecha* genre tend to evolve into pathos-driven psychodramas and journeys into the unknown.

The kind of narrative journey most typically traced by Gainax therefore progresses along two interwinding paths. Along one of these, various anime conventions are unhinged by means of playful displacements of their habitual repertoire. Along the other, a reverse process unfolds whereby accepted trends are redefined with a shift toward gravity. Taken in tandem, the tendency to subvert institutionalized norms through playfulness and the tendency to veer the action toward the dark suggest that Gainax's artists are eager to emphasize that even though the world we inhabit is deeply flawed, we might at least glean some pleasure from this state as long as the imagination is granted unrestricted liberty of action.

The messages disclosed by means of the strategies delineated in the previous paragraphs do not, it must be stressed, amount to abstract philosophical speculation. In fact, their poignance is the result of practical interventions that engage directly with the corporeal properties of the medium in hand. In addition, Gainax's magical flair for stylistic flourishes that are capable of lending seriousness to the mundane derives largely from the animators' physical handling of their tools and techniques. Most remarkable is the meticulous execution of backgrounds capable of blending figure and decoration, patterning and stylization, symbolism and photorealism. The integration of lighting and chromatic effects that rely, by turns, on subtle gradations and lurid contrasts is no less striking. Both the background art and the interaction of light and color are harmonized with methods of characterization that throw into relief the inextricability of the dramatis personae from the worlds they inhabit. However outlandish a character may at first appear to be, his or her personality ends up communicating astounding levels of credibility not only by virtue of sophisticated psychological insights but also by being grounded in a distinctive environment and atmosphere.

If, on the diegetic plane, one of the most abiding aspects of Gainax's signature is the inclination to penetrate the psyche's murkiest recesses, no less noteworthy, stylistically, is the studio's fascination with the intrinsic nature of storytelling. Indeed, Gainax's productions remind us that in spite of technology's impact on narration, this activity remains the art of conveying events through the media of words, images and sounds (jointly or discretely, as the case may be). By integrating manually executed visuals, CGI and legion forms of text, the works call attention to the underlying materiality of storytelling—and indeed its collusion with the physical acts not solely of drawing and writing but also of carving, etching and scratching. When full animation gives way to visuals that appear to have been created by the most primitive means (a proclivity attested to by several Gainax productions over the decades), the most ancestral forms of storytelling are obliquely invoked and celebrated. The irreducible materiality of storytelling is thus underscored.[1]

The physical qualities of sound are simultaneously foregrounded. Rapid dialogical sequences are juxtaposed with drawn-out moments of silence in order to elicit contrasting moods, and both are synthesized with tantalizing soundtracks including both original compositions and classical pieces. Such acoustic effects are so compelling as to fill viewers with rich emotions that enable them to feel as much a part of the story as the characters are.[2]

As argued in Chapter 1, Gainax emplaces textual elements as a key part of its animations. Insofar as these elements are habitually drawn from a pictographic tradition, they aptly underscore the material roots of narration. At the same time, they rise to the status of actors and thus highlight what J. L. Austin terms the "performative" nature of textuality: the power of utterances to function as action. Writing is here posited as an inherently kinetic medium that cannot be restricted to the static space of the page.[3]

The ubiquity of the concept of quest is tirelessly proclaimed across the studio's multifaceted oeuvre through a deft orchestration of the abstract and concrete dimensions of anime. Bolstered by astutely handled animational and cinematographical techniques, Gainax's message gains depth at every turn of the company's lively history as the injunction to embark on the search for self-understanding accrues momentum. Each of the analyses offered in the preceding chapters has endeavored to highlight the quest element with reference to individual plots and characters. The magnitude of the task varies in accordance with the doses of comic relief injected into the action. What remains prominent at all times is the existentialist centrality of exploratory journeys. In these expeditions, various characters learn to take responsibility for creating the meanings of their own lives through ongoing — and always rescindable — choices. Regardless of the particular nature of the task to which a hero or heroine is committed, it is the *concept* of quest as such that is accorded primary significance.

What endows the concept with dramatic power, moreover, is Gainax's ability to demonstrate that it matters deeply to the protagonists themselves. At times, their goals are globally momentous: fathoming the mysteries of outer space, as in *The Wings of Honneamise*; the protection of humankind against alien forces and baleful evolutionary schemes, as in *Gunbuster*, *Gunbuster 2*, *Evangelion*, *Mahoromatic* and *This Ugly Yet Beautiful World*. At others, they are profoundly personal: the exploration of novel emotions and attendant taming of traumatic memories, notably, in *Nadia*, *His and Her Circumstances* and *FLCL*. At others still, they are downright ludic: the accomplishment of a rabid fan's ultimate fantasies (*Otaku no Video*); the construction of playground worlds (*Abenobashi*). To complicate the picture, Gainax frequently combines two or more of those categories within the compass of a single production so as to evoke situations in which the tragic and the clownish meet and merge in mutual suffusion. Ultimately, however, the specific nature of the quest is of relatively scarce importance in comparison with its hold on a character's psyche and, by extension, on the overall rhythm of the typical Gainax plot as a tale of progressive engagement with existential darkness.

Gainax's leaning toward the serious end of the anime spectrum is encapsulated by the fact that not only its explicitly troubled personae but also its cheery and optimistic characters possess cloudy recesses. On several occasions, these consist of uncertainties and anxieties that emanate directly from the imperative to grow up. This manifests itself as an insistent urge to relinquish childhood, on the one hand (e.g., in *FLCL*), and a recalcitrance to do so, on the other (as exemplified by *Abenobashi*). The latter disposition ensues from a recognition of the rampant inadequacy of putative adults. Additionally, Gainax's protagonists are often plagued by disquieting reminiscences and a legacy of abandonment and neglect that intensifies the gloomier facets of their personalities and alternately renders them either listless or fretful. The seminal *Gunbuster* lays the foundations for this typology, whereas *Nadia* consolidates the trend to epic extremes and *Evangelion* takes it into the stratosphere.

The presence of dusky psychological connotations in the portrayal of a character like *Honneamise*'s Shiro cannot possibly come as a surprise, given his presentation as the casualty of a widespread societal malaise and as a pawn in the hands of unscrupulous politicians. Nor is the display of tortured psychologies throughout *Evangelion* and (though to a lesser extent) *His and Her Circumstances*, considering the two series' respective efforts at massive genre-bending on the *mecha* and romance fronts. What *is* surprising is the emergence of shadowy facets from ostensibly upbeat and at first quite uncomplicated characters such as Mahoro (*Mahoromatic*), Yucie (*Petite Princess Yucie*), Hikari (*This Ugly Yet Beautiful World*), Tycho (*Gunbuster 2*) or Kubo (*Otaku no Video*), to mention but a few illustrative instances. Setting out as potentially stereotypical figures fashioned in conformity with the codes of Magical-Girlfriend romantic comedy, fairy tale, gutsy Bildungsroman, or otaku-centered parody, these characters gradually reveal depth and contortions that one would not expect to encounter in any of those forms. Bocca's and Simon's struggles to transcend the boundaries of their cage-like worlds, in *The Melody of Oblivion* and *Making Breakthrough Gurren Lagann*, respectively, also attest to the pervasiveness of the quest motif.

Gainax's philosophical stance is decidedly unsympathetic to the Rationalist world view. Rationalism upholds the notion of an ultimate order founded on metaphysical tenets of universal validity, and its lesson is therefore quite incompatible with the spirit of the quest as an inherently unceasing process. Nor is Gainax's opus amenable to Empiricism, the philosophy that seeks to extrapolate reliable truths from direct observation of the tangible world. In this case, the incompatibility issues from the studio's proverbial refusal to narrow reality down to the experientially observable and attendant determination to maximize the wizardly powers of animation as an art capable of circumventing the laws of both physics and logic. In so doing, the studio repeatedly brings new worlds into existence, bending reality to its own creative will. By summoning those skills within the framework of a medium saturated with pictures of primordial symbolic value, Gainax's works reach toward a very specific understanding of the term "magic."

An evocative description of the notion, provided in an unrelated context and yet applicable to the studio's mission, can be found in the photography website *Equivalence*, where "magic" is posited as the "universe of traditional images, ... a world of eternal recurrence in which everything lends meaning to everything else and everything signifies everything else: a world full of meanings, full of 'gods'" (*Equivalence*). Like the *kami* in the Shinto tradition, these "gods" are not fear-inspiring and vindictive deities of the kind characteristically worshipped by monotheistic religions but rather manifestations of life and energy that pervade the natural domain in its entirety. They are animating forces that find a perfect vehicle in an art form that is itself devoted to instilling life into the inanimate.

While this aspect of Gainax's anime magic is paramount, no less axial is the ethical attitude underpinning its artistic edifice. Beneath the numinous archetypes and esoteric imagery, the ornate cinematography and the technobabble in which the studio's productions periodically revel, there lies a sincere intention to communicate something pressingly real about the human condition. It is, in the final analysis, because the messages underlying an adventure actually meant something to their promoters that they come to mean something to us, as well. It is at this level that Gainax asserts most potently the bond between animation and magic, reminding us that the art of animation finds some of its earliest expression in magic acts associated with, and spawned by, the marvelous universe of optical projection: the Magic Lantern, the Magic Mirror, the Camera Obscura and the Shadow Show. Like the art of stage magic, animation requires a performance ethos capable of directing the audience's attention so that no sleight of hand, coup de théâtre or punch line will be wasted or considered redundant. Thus, animation becomes capable of alternately hypnotizing its viewers and inviting heedful reflection — of nourishing their desire to feel inspired and, most vitally, continue to feel inspired. That's magic.

Filmography

I. Primary Texts: Gainax Case Studies

FLCL (2000). *Original Title: Furi Kuri. Status:* OVA series (6 episodes). *Directors:* Kazuya Tsurumaki, Masahiko Otsuka, Shouji Saeki, Takeshi Ando. *Original Concept:* Tsurumaki. *Screenplay:* Yoji Enokido. *Producers:* Hiroki Sato, Hirotaka Takase, Masanobu Sato, Matoshi Nishizawa, Nishizawa Masatomo. *Production Companies:* FLCL Production Committee, Studio Gainax, Production I.G, Starchild Records. *Music:* Atsuo Ohkubo, Hiroshi Imaizumi, Jun Suzuki, Maki Kamiya, Matarou Misawa, Sawao Yamanaka, Shinichiro Sato, Shinkichi Mitsumune, Takashi Asahi, Takuo Yamamoto, Tatsuya Kashima, The Pillows, Tomohiko Aoki, Yasuharu Nakanishi, Yoshiaki Manabe, Zin Yoshida. *Episode Length:* 30 minutes. *Animation Directors:* Hiroyuki Imaishi, Masahiko Otsuka, Tadashi Hiramatsu. *Art Director:* Hiromasa Ogura. *Character Designer:* Yoshiyuki Sadamoto. *Mechanical Designer:* Yoshitsune Izuna. *Color Designer:* Harumi Takahoshi.

Gunbuster (1988). *Original Title: Top O Nerae! Status:* OVA series (6 episodes). *Director:* Hideaki Anno. *Screenplay:* Anno, Hiroyuki Yamaga, Toshio Okada. *Producers:* Hiroaki Inoue, Minoru Takanashi, Shiro Sasaki. *Production Companies:* Studio Gainax, Bandai Visual, Victor Entertainment, Studio Fantasia. *Music:* Kouhei Tanaka. *Episode Length:* 30 minutes. *Animation Directors:* Toshiyuki Kubooka, Shinji Higuchi, Yoshiyuki Sadamoto, Yuji Moriyama. *Art Directors:* Hiroshi Sasaki, Masanori Kikuchi. *Character Designer:* Haruhiko Mikimoto. *Mechanical Designers:* Kazutaka Miyatake, Koichi Ohata, Mahiro Maeda.

Gunbuster 2 (2004–2006). *Original Title: Top O Nerae! 2. Status:* OVA series (6 episodes). *Director:* Kazuya Tsurumaki. *Screenplay:* Yoji Enokido. *Production Companies:* Studio Gainax, Bandai Visual, Victor Entertainment. *Music:* Kouhei Tanaka. *Episode Length:* 27 minutes. *Animation Directors:* Atsushi Nishikiori, Yoshiyuki Sadamoto, Yuka Shibata. *Art Director:* Hiroshi Kato. *Character Designer:* Sadamoto. *Mechanical Designers:* Bukichi Nadeara, Junya Ishigaki, Shigeto Koyama, Yoshitsune Izuna. *3D Director:* Shinji Nasu. *Digital Director:* Shoichi Masuo. *Sound Director:* Toru Nakano.

Gunbuster vs. Diebuster: Aim for the Top Gattai Movie (2006). *Original Title: Top wo Nerae 2! & Top wo Nerae! Gattai Gekijouban. Status:* Feature Films (x 2). *Director:* Kazuya Tsurumaki. *Production Companies:* Bandai Visual, Studio Gainax, Victor Entertainment. *Music:* Kouhei Tanaka. *Original Character Designers:* Haruhiko Mikimoto (*Gunbuster*), Yoshiyuki Sadamoto (*Diebuster*). *Original Mechanical Designers:* Koichi Ohata (*Gunbuster*), Yoshitsune Izuna (*Diebuster*).

His and Her Circumstances (1998–1999). *Original Title: Kareshi Kanojo no Jijou. Status:* TV series (26 episodes). *Directors:* Hideaki Anno, Kazuya Tsurumaki (episodes 19–26). *Original Story:* Masami Tsuda. *Screenplay:* Anno. *Producers:* Hiroki Sato, Noriko Kobayashi, Takayuki Yanagisawa. *Pro-

duction Companies: Studio Gainax, Gansis, J.C. Staff, SoftX, TV Tokyo. *Music:* Fumiya Fujii, Shiro Sagisu. *Episode Length:* 24 minutes. *Animation Director:* Tadashi Hiramatsu. *Art Director:* Masaru Sato. *Character Designer:* Tadashi Hiramatsu.

Magical Shopping Arcade Abenobashi (2002). *Original Title: Abenobashi Mahou Shotengai. Status:* TV series (13 episodes). *Director:* Hiroyuki Yamaga. *Screenplay:* Hiroyuki Yamaga, Jukki Hanada, Satoru Akahori. *Producers:* Hiroyuki Yamaga, Masafumi Fukui, Taiji Suinou, Toshimichi Ootsuki. *Production Companies:* Abenobashi Project, Dentsu Inc., Studio Gainax, Imagica, Starchild Records. *Music:* Shiro Sagisu. *Episode Length:* 24 minutes. *Animation Directors:* Fumie Mutoi, Hideaki Anno, Hiroshi Kato, Hiroshi Shimizu, Hiroyuki Imaishi, Hiroyuki Ochi, Kim Gi-Du, Masaaki Sakurai, Noriyuki Fukuda, Ryu Kase, Shinji Takeuchi, Tadashi Hiramatsu. *Art Director:* Hiroshi Kato. *Character Designers:* Kazuhiro Takamura, Kenji Tsuruta, Sadafumi Hiramatsu, Tadashi Hiramatsu. *Mechanical Designer:* Takeshi Takakura. *Sound Director:* Kazuya Tanaka.

Mahoromatic — Automatic Maiden (2001–2002). *Original Title: Mahoromatic. Status:* TV series (12 episodes). *Directors:* Hiroyuki Yamaga, Masahiko Otsuka. *Original Story:* Bow Ditama, Bunjuro Nakayama. *Producers:* Hiroki Sato, Mitsutoshi Kubota, Tetsuo Gensho, Yuichi Sekido. *Production Companies:* Studio Gainax, *Mahoromatic* Production Committee, Pioneer LDC, TBS, Wani Books. *Music:* Toshio Masuda. *Episode Length:* 24 minutes. *Animation Directors:* Kazuhiro Takamura, Sushio. *Art Director:* Naoko Kosakabe. *Character Designer:* Kazuhiro Takamura. *Sound Director:* Yoshikazu Iwanami. *Color Designer:* Yoko Mitsuhashi.

Nadia: The Secret of Blue Water (1990–1991). *Original Title: Fushigi no Umi no Nadia. Status:* TV series (39 episodes). *Directors:* Hideaki Anno; Shinji Higuchi (episodes 23–39). *Original Concept:* Hayao Miyazaki. *Producers:* Hiroshi Kubata, Kenichi Maruyama, Kenjiro Kawato, Yasushi Yoritsune. *Production Companies:* Studio Gainax, Korad, Toho. *Music:* Shiro Sagisu. *Episode Length:* 30 minutes. *Animation Directors:* Masahiko Ohta, Nobuaki Nagano, Shunji Suzuki, Tadashi Hiramatsu. *Art Directors:* Hiromasa Ogura, Hiroshi Sasaki, Masanori Kikuchi. *Character Designers:* Shunji Suzuki, Yoshiyuki Sadamoto. *Mechanical Designers:* Anno, Shoichi Masuo. *Sound Director:* Katsunori Shimizu.

Neon Genesis Evangelion (1995–1996). *Original Title: Shinseiki Evangelion. Status:* TV series (26 episodes). *Director:* Hideaki Anno. *Original Story:* Anno. *Screenplay:* Anno, Akio Satsukawa, Mitsuo Iso, Shinji Higuchi, Yoji Enokido, Yoji Enoto. *Producers:* Noriko Kobayashi, Yutaka Sugiyama. *Production Companies:* Studio Gainax, Production I.G, Studio Ghibli (epi. 11). *Music:* Hidetoshi Sato et al. *Original Music Composition:* Ludwig Von Beethoven ("Symphony No. 9 — Ode to Joy"). *Episode Length:* 25 minutes. *Animation Directors:* Kazuya Kise, Nobuhiro Hosoi, Satoshi Shigeta, Shinya Hasegawa, Toshio Kawaguchi, Yuh Honda. *Art Director:* Hiroshi Kato. *Character Designer:* Yoshiyuki Sadamoto. *Mechanical Designers:* Anno, Ikuto Yamashita. *Special Effects Supervisor:* Noriyuki Ohta. *Sound Effects:* Toru Noguchi. *Color Check:* Harumi Takahoshi.

Neon Genesis Evangelion: Death & Rebirth (1997). *Original Title: Shinseiki Evangelion Gekijouban: Shito shinsei. Status:* Feature Film. *Directors:* Hideaki Anno, Masayuki (*Death*), Kazuya Tsurumaki (*Rebirth*). *Original Story:* Akio Satsukawa, Anno. *Screenplay:* Anno. *Producer:* Mitsuhisa Ishikawa. *Production Companies:* Studio Gainax, MOVIC, Production I.G, Sega, Starchild Records, Toei Animation. *Music:* Shiro Sagisu. *Length:* 139 minutes. *Design Directors:* Anno, Masayuki, Yoshiyuki Sadamoto. *3D Animation:* Kaoru Matsumoto. *2D Digital Work:* Yasuhiro Kamimura. *Art Director:* Hiroshi Kato. *Character Designer:* Sadamoto. *Mechanical Designers:* Anno, Ikuto Yamashita. *Special Effects Supervisor:* Noriyuki Ohta. *Sound Director:* Hideyuki Tanaka.

Neon Genesis Evangelion: End of Evangelion (*25': "Air"/26': "My Purest Heart for You"*) (1997). *Original Title: Shinseiki Evangelion Gekijouban: "Air"/"Magokoro wo, kimi ni." Status:* Feature Film.

Directors: Kazuya Tsurumaki (25'), Hideaki Anno (26'). *Original Story:* Anno. *Screenplay:* Anno. *Producer:* Mitsuhisa Ishikawa. *Production Companies:* Production I.G, AIC, *Anime* Spot, Asia-Do, Big Bang, Studio Gainax, Oh Production, Omnibus Japan, Studio Cosmos et al. *Music:* Anno et al. *Original Music Composition:* Johann Sebastian Bach ("Air on G" and "Jesus bliebt Meine Freude"). *Length:* 97 minutes. *Digital Animation Director:* Isao Sato. *Art Director:* Hiroshi Kato. *Character Designer:* Yoshiyuki Sadamoto. *Mechanical Designers:* Anno, Ikuto Yamashita. *Special Effects Supervisor:* Noriyuki Ohta. *Sound Director:* Hideyuki Tanaka.

Otaku no Video (1991). *Original Title: Otaku no Video. Status:* OVA (2 episodes). *Director:* Takeshi Mori. *Screenplay:* Hiroyuki Yamaga, Toshio Okada. *Producers:* Kazuhiko Inomata, Yoshimi Kanda. *Production Company:* Studio Gainax. *Music:* Kouhei Tanaka. *Length:* 50 minutes. *Animation Directors:* Hidenori Matsubara, Takeshi Honda. *Art Director:* Hitoshi Nagao. *Character Designer:* Kenichi Sonoda. *Special Effects:* Rumiko Nagai. *Cultural & Literary Consultant:* Yuuji Watanabe. *Sound Director:* Fusanobu Fujiyama.

Rebuild of Evangelion: 1.0 You Are [Not] Alone (2007). *Original Title: Evangelion Shin Gekijouban: Jo. Status:* Feature Film. *Chief Rebuild Director:* Hideaki Anno. *Movie 1.0 Directors:* Kazuya Tsurumaki, Masayuki. *Original Story:* Anno. *Screenplay:* Anno. *Production Company:* Studio Khara. *Music:* Shiro Sagisu. *Chief Animation Director:* Shunji Suzuki. *Animation Directors:* Atsushi Okuda, Hidenori Matsubara, Kazuchika Kise, Yuji Moriyama. *Mechanical Animation Director:* Takeshi Honda. *Art Directors:* Hiroshi Kato, Tatsuya Kushida. *Character Designer:* Yoshiyuki Sadamoto. *Mechanical Designer:* Ikuto Yamashita. *Special Effects Supervisor:* Shoichi Masuo. *Sound Effects:* Toru Noguchi.

Royal Space Force: The Wings of Honneamise (1987). *Original Title: Ouritsu Uchuugun — Oneamisu no Tsubasa. Status:* Feature Film. *Director:* Hiroyuki Yamaga. *Screenplay:* Yamaga. *Producers:* Hiroaki Inoue, Hirohiko Sueyoshi. *Production Companies:* Studio Gainax, Bandai Visual. *Music:* Ryuichi Sakamoto. *Length:* 125 minutes. *Animation Directors:* Fumio Iida, Hideaki Anno, Yoshiyuki Sadamoto, Yuji Moriyama. *Art Director:* Hiromasa Ogura. *Character Designer:* Yoshiyuki Sadamoto.

This Ugly Yet Beautiful World (2004). *Original Title: Kono Minikuku Mo Utsukushii Sekai. Status:* TV series (12 episodes). *Director:* Shouji Saeki. *Scenario:* Shin Itagaki, Saeki, Sumio Uetake, Tatsuo Sato, Tomoyasu Okubo. *Original Concept:* Hiroyuki Yamaga, Saeki. *Producers:* Tsuyoshi Kamimiyashi, Yuichi Sekido, Yuki Sato. *Production Companies:* Studio Gainax, Geneon Entertainment, Inc., MOVIC, Rondo Robe, Shuubi Committee, TBS. *Music:* Tsuyoshi Watanabe. *Episode Length:* 24 minutes. *Animation Director:* Kazuhiro Takamura. *Art Director:* Satoru Kuwabara. *Character Designer:* Takamura. *Mechanical Designer:* Mei Suzuki. *Monster Designer:* Yoh Yoshinari. *Sound Director:* Yoshikazu Iwanami. *Color Designer:* Hiroshi Hibino.

DVD Releases Used in This Book in the Analysis of the Primary Texts

- *FLCL* (***Fooly Cooly***), volumes 1–3, Broccoli International, 2002–2003.
- ***Gunbuster***, Bandai Visual, 1988.
- ***Gunbuster 2***, volumes 1–3, Bandai Visual USA, 2007.
- ***His and Her Circumstances — TV Series Collection*** (5 discs), Right Stuf, 2006.
- ***Magical Shopping Arcade Abenobashi — Boxed Set*** (3 discs), ADV Films, 2005.
- ***Mahoromatic — Automatic Maiden — Boxed Set*** (4 discs), Geneon (Pioneer), 2005.
- ***Nadia: The Secret of Blue Water, Collection 1*** (volumes 1–5) and *Nadia: The Secret of Blue Water, Collection 2* (volumes 6–10 and motion picture), ADV Films, 2004.
- ***Neon Genesis Evangelion Platinum Edition Complete Collection*** (7 discs), ADV Films, 2006.

- *Neon Genesis Evangelion: Death & Rebirth—The End of Evangelion*, Special Edition, Manga Entertainment, 2004.
- *Otaku no Video*, AnimEigo, 2002.
- *Royal Space Force: The Wings of Honneamise*, Manga Video, 2000.
- *This Ugly Yet Beautiful World*, volumes 1–3, ADV Films, 2006.

II. Supplementary Gainax Productions

Ebichu the Housekeeping Hamster (a.k.a. *Ebichu Minds the House*) (1999). *Original Title:* Oruchuban Ebichu. *Status:* TV series (24 episodes). *Director:* Makoto Moriwaki. *Original Story:* Risa Itou. *Screenplay:* Chinatsou Houjou, Motoki Yoshimura. *Planning:* Hideaki Anno. *Production Companies:* Studio Gainax, Pioneer LDC. *Episode Length:* 9 minutes. *Art Director:* Satoru Miura. *Character Designers:* Jun Yoshida, Mio Tsumoto, Sachiko Oohashi, Takaharu Osumi, Yukiko Oohashi. *Special Effects:* takashi Maekawa. *Color Designer:* Eiko Sekine.

Mahoromatic—Automatic Maiden: Something More Beautiful (2002–2003). *Original Title:* Mahoromatic: Motto Utsukushii Mono. *Status:* TV series (14 episodes). *Director:* Hiroyuki Yamaga. *Scenario:* Yamaga et al. *Original Story:* Bow Ditama, Bunjuro Nakayama. *Production Companies:* Studio Gainax, *Mahoromatic* Production Committee, Pioneer LDC, TBS, Wani Books. *Music:* Toshio Masuda. *Episode Length:* 24 minutes. *Animation Director:* Kazuhiro Takamura. *Art Directors:* Naoko Kosakabe, Yoshinori Hishinuma. *Character Designer:* Kazuhiro Takamura. *Mechanical Designer:* Keiichi Eda. *Sound Director:* Yoshikazu Iwanami. *Color Designer:* Hiroshi Hibino.

Mahoromatic—Automatic Maiden: Summer Special (2003). *Original Title: Mahoromatic: Natsu no TV Special. Status:* TV special (1 episode). *Director:* Shouji Saeki. *Original Story:* Bow Ditama, Bunjuro Nakayama. *Screenplay:* Bunjuro Nakayama. *Production Companies:* Studio Gainax, *Mahoromatic* Production Committee, Geneon Entertainment Ltd., TBS, Wani Books. *Music:* Toshio Masuda. *Episode Length:* 24 minutes. *Animation Director:* Kazuhiro Takamura. *Art Director:* Naoko Kosakabe. *Character Designer:* Kazuhiro Takamura. *Sound Director:* Yoshikazu Iwanami. *Color Designer:* Hiroshi Hibino.

Making Breakthrough Gurren Lagann (2007). *Original Title: Tengen Toppa Gurren-Lagann. Status:* TV series (27 episodes). *Director:* Hiroyuki Imaishi. *Screenplay:* Hiroshi Yamaguchi, Kazuki Nakashima, Masahiko Otsuka, Shouji Saeki. *Producers:* Takami Akai, Yasuhiro Takeda. *Production Companies:* Studio Gainax, Aniplex. Konami. *Music:* Taku Iwasaki. *Episode Length:* 25 minutes. *Animation Directors:* Akira Amemiya et al. *Art Director:* Yuka Hirama. *Character Designer:* Atsushi Nishigori. *Mechanical Designer:* Yoh Yoshinari. *Sound Director:* Toru Nakano *Color Designer:* Harumi Takahoshi.

The Melody of Oblivion (2004). *Original Title: Boukyaku no Senritsu. Status:* TV series (24 episodes). *Directors:* Atsushi Takeyama, Hiroshi Nishikiori. *Screenplay:* Yoji Enokido. *Producers:* Hitoshi Sougawa, Takashi Tachizaki, Tsuyoshi Kamimiyashi, Yuji Matsukura, Yuki Sato. *Production Companies:* Boukyaku no Senritsu Project, Studio Gainax, J.C. Staff, Kadokawa Shoten, Ken Media, TBS. *Music:* Hijiri Kuwano, Yoshikazu Suo. *Episode Length:* 24 minutes. *Animation Directors:* Daisuke Takashima et al. *Art Director:* Shichiro Kobayashi. *Character Designer:* Shinya Hasegawa. *Mechanical Designers:* Yoh Yoshinari, Yoshikazu Miyao. *Monster Designer:* Yutaka Izubuchi. *Sound Director:* Yota Tsuruoka. *Color Designer:* Mayumi Tayahashi.

Petite Princess Yucie (2002–2003). *Original Title: Puchi Puri Yuushi. Status:* TV series (26 episodes). *Director:* Masahiko Otsuka. *Supervising Director:* Hideaki Anno. *Series Composition:*

Hiroyuki Yamaga, Jukki Hanada. *Original Concept:* Takami Akai. *Screenplay:* Jukki Hanada, Takashi Aoshima, Yasunori Yamada. *Production Company:* Studio Gainax. *Music:* Seikou Nagaoka. *Episode Length:* 30 minutes. *Animation Directors:* Atsushi Nishikiori, Atsushi Okuda, Chizuko Kusakabe, Eiji Abiko, Eiji Suganuma, Hiromi Okazaki, Hiroyuki Ochi, Mitsuru Obunai, Naoyuki Onda, Nobuyuki Kitajima, Ryuichi Makino, Yoshiko Nakajima. *Art Director:* Katsufumi Hariu. *Original Character Designer:* Takami Akai. *Character Designer:* Kazuko Tadano. *Monster Designer:* Hiromi Matsushita. *Visual Effects Director:* Yoshifumi Ayuta.

III. Secondary Visual Sources
Titles directly cited in the book are designated by an asterisk.

1. *Ah! My Goddess: Flights of Fancy* (OVA series; dir. Hiroaki Gouda, 2006)*
2. *Aim for the Ace!* (TV series; dir. Osamu Dezaki, 1973–1974)*
3. *Air* (TV series; dir. Tatsuya Ishihara, 2004–2005)
4. *Air Gear* (TV series; dir. Hajime Kamegaki, 2006)*
5. *Akira* (feature film; dir. Katsuhiro Otomo, 1988)
6. *All Purpose Cultural Cat Girl Nuku Nuku* (TV series; dir. Yoshitaka Fujimoto, 1998)*
7. *Angel's Egg* (OVA; dir. Mamoru Oshii, 1985)
8. *The Animatrix* (OVA collection; dirs. Larry and Andy Wachowski et al., 2003)
9. *Appleseed* (OVA; dir. Kazuyoshi Katayama, 1988)
10. *Appleseed* (feature film; dir. Shinji Aramaki, 2004)*
11. *Aquarian Age—Sign for Evolution* (TV series; dir. Yoshimitsu Ohashi, 2002)
12. *Best Student Council* (TV series; dir. Yoshiaki Iwasaki, 2005)*
13. *Blood: The Last Vampire* (feature film; dir. Hiroyuki Kitakubo, 2000)
14. *Blue Seed* (TV series; dir. Jun Kamiya, 1994–1995)*
15. *Blue Seed Beyond* (OVA series; dirs. Jun Kamiya and Kiyoshi Murayama, 1996)*
16. *Boogiepop Phantom* (TV series; dir. Takashi Watanabe, 2000)*
17. *Bubblegum Crisis—Tokyo 2040* (TV series; dir. Hiroki Hayashi, 1998)*
18. *The Cat Returns* (feature film; dir. Hiroyuki Morita, 2002)*
19. *Chance Pop Session* (TV series; dir. Susumu Kudo, 2001)
20. *Le Chevalier D'Eon* (TV series; dir. Kazuhiro Furuhashi, 2006–2007)*
21. *Chobits* (TV series; dir. Morio Asaka, 2002)*
22. *Chrono Crusade* (TV series; dir. Yuu Kou, 2003–2004)*
23. *Claymore* (TV series; dir. Hiroyuki Tanaka, 2007)*
24. *Cowboy Bebop: The Movie* (feature film; dir. Shinichiro Watanabe, 2001)*
25. *Coyote Ragtime Show* (TV series; dir. Takuya Nonaka, 2006)*
26. *Crest of the Stars* (TV series; dir. Yasuchika Nagaoka, 1999)*
27. *Dallos* (OVA; dir. Mamoru Oshii, 1983–1984)*
28. *Disgaea* (TV series; dir. Isako Kiyotaka, 2006)
29. *D.N.Angel* (TV series; dirs. Koji Yoshikawa and Nobuyoshi Habara, 2003)*
30. *Elemental Gelade* (TV series; dir. Shigeru Ueda, 2005)*
31. *Elfen Lied* (TV series; dir. Mamoru Kanbe, 2004)*
32. *Ergo Proxy* (TV series; dir. Shuko Murase, 2005)
33. *Eureka Seven* (TV series; dir. Tomoki Kyouda, 2005–2006)*
34. *Fafner* (TV series; dir. Nobuyoshi Habara, 2004)*
35. *Fate/stay Night* (TV series; dir. Yuji Yamaguchi, 2006)*
36. *Final Fantasy: The Spirits Within* (feature film; dir. Hironobu Sakaguchi, 2001)
37. *Fullmetal Alchemist* (TV series; dir. Seiji Mizushima, 2003–2004)*

38. *Future Boy Conan* (TV series; dir. Hayao Miyazaki, 1978)*
39. *Gasaraki* (TV series; dirs. Ryousuke Takahashi and Goro Taniguchi, 1999)*
40. *Gauche the Cellist* (feature film; dir. Isao Takahata, 1982)*
41. *Genshiken* (TV series; dir. Takashi Ikehata, 2004)*
42. *Get Backers* (TV series; dirs. Kazuhiro Furuhashi and Keitarou Motonaga, 2002–2003)
43. *Ghibli Shorts* (short animations; dirs. Hayao Miyazaki et al., 1992–2002)
44. *Ghiblies 2* (short animations; dir. Yoshiyuki Momose, 2002)
45. *Ghost in the Shell* (feature film; dir. Mamoru Oshii, 1995)*
46. *Ghost in the Shell 2: Innocence* (feature film; dir. Mamoru Oshii, 2004)*
47. *Ghost in the Shell: S.A.C* (TV series; dir. Kenji Kamiyama, 2002–2004)*
48. *Ghost in the Shell: S.A.C 2nd Gig* (TV series; dir. Kenji Kamiyama, 2004–2005)*
49. *Giant Robo* (OVA series; dir. Yasuhiro Imagawa, 1992–1998)
50. *Gilgamesh* (TV series; dir. Masahiko Murata, 2003–2004)*
51. *Girls' High* (TV series; dir. Yoshitaka Fujimoto, 2006)
52. *Gokinjo Monogatari* (TV series; dir. Atsutoshi Unezawa, 1995–1996)*
53. *Grave of the Fireflies* (feature film; dir. Isao Takahata, 1988)
54. *Grenadier* (TV series; dir. Hiroshi Koujina, 2004)*
55. *.hack//Roots* (TV series; dir. Koichi Mashimo, 2006)
56. *Hand Maid May* (TV series; dir. Shinichiro Kimura, 2000)*
57. *Happy Lesson* (TV series; dirs. Akira Suzuki and Takeshi Yamaguchi, 2002)*
58. *Himawari!* (TV series; dir. Shigenori Kageyama, 2006)*
59. *Howl's Moving Castle* (feature film; dir. Hayao Miyazaki, 2004)*
60. *Innocent Venus* (TV series; dir. Jun Kawagoe, 2006)
61. *InuYasha* (TV series; dirs. Masashi Ikeda and Yasunao Aoki, 2000–2004)*
62. *Jin-Roh: The Wolf Brigade* (feature film; dir. Hiroyuki Okiura, 1998)
63. *Kamichu!* (TV series; dir. Koji Masunari, 2005)*
64. *Kashimashi — Girl Meets Girl* (TV series; dir. Nobuaki Nakanishi, 2006)*
65. *Kiki's Delivery Service* (feature film; dir. Hayao Miyazaki, 1989)*
66. *King of Bandit Jing* (TV series; dir. Hiroshi Watanabe, 2002)
67. *K.O. Beast* (OVA series; dir. Hiroshi Negishi, 1992)*
68. *Kurau Phantom Memory* (TV series; dir. Yasuhiro Irie, 2004)
69. *Kyo Kara Maho!* (TV series; dir. Junji Nishimura, 2006)*
70. *Laputa: Castle in the Sky* (feature film; dir. Hayao Miyazaki, 1986)*
71. *Love Hina* (TV series; dir. Yoshiaki Iwasaki, 2000)*
72. *Lucky Star* (TV series; dirs. Yasuhiro Takemoto and Yutaka Yamamoto, 2007)*
73. *Lupin 3: The Castle of Cagliostro* (feature film; dir. Hayao Miyazaki, 1979)*
74. *Macross Plus — The Movie* (feature film; dir. Shouji Kawamori, 1995)*
75. *Maison Ikkoku* (TV series; dir. Kazuo Yamazaki, 1986–1988)*
76. *The Melancholy of Haruhi Suzumiya* (TV series; dir. Tatsuya Ishihara, 2006)*
77. *Memories* (trilogy; dirs. Katsuhiro Otomo, Kouji Morimoto, Tensai Okamura, 1994)
78. *Metropolis* (feature film; dir. Rintaro, 2001)*
79. *Millennium Actress* (feature film; dir. Satoshi Kon, 2001)
80. *Minipato* (short animations; dir. Kenji Kamiyama, 2001)*
81. *Mobile Suit Gundam* (TV series; dir. Yoshiyuki Tomino, 1979–1980)*
82. *Mobile Suit Gundam: Movies* (feature films x 3; dir. Yoshiyuki Tomino, 1981–1982)*
83. *MoonPhase* (TV series; dir. Akiyuki Shinbo, 2004–2005)*
84. *Mushi-Shi* (TV series; dir. Hiroshi Nagahama, 2006)*
85. *My Neighbour Totoro* (feature film; dir. Hayao Miyazaki, 1988)*
86. *My-HiME* (TV series; Masakazu Obara, 2004–2005)*

87. *My-Otome* (TV series; dir. Masakazu Obara, 2005–2006)*
88. *Nadia of the Mysterious Seas* (feature film; dir. Sho Aono, 1992)*
89. *Naruto* (TV series; dir. Hayato Date, 2002–2007)*
90. *Nausicaä of the Valley of the Wind* (feature film; dir. Hayao Miyazaki, 1984)*
91. *Negima!* (TV series; dir. Nagisa Miyazaki, 2005)*
92. *Nerima Daikon Brothers* (TV series; dir. Shinichi Watanabe, 2006)*
93. *Ninja Nonsense* (TV series; dir. Hitoyuki Matsui, 2004)
94. *Ninja Scroll* (feature film; dir. Yoshiaki Kawajiri, 1993)
95. *Noir* (TV series; dir. Koichi Mashimo, 2001)
96. *Ocean Waves* (TV film; dir. Tomomi Mochizuki, 1993)
97. *Oh My Goddess!* (OVA series; dir. Hiroaki Gouda, 1993)*
98. *On Your Mark* (music video; dir. Hayao Miyazaki, 1995)
99. *Only Yesterday* (feature film; dir. Isao Takahata, 1991)
100. *Papuwa* (TV series; dir. Kenichi Nishida, 2006)
101. *Paradise Kiss* (TV series; dir. Osamu Kobayashi, 2005)*
102. *Paranoia Agent* (TV series; dir. Satoshi Kon, 2004)*
103. *Patlabor 1: The Mobile Police* (feature film; dir. Mamoru Oshii, 1989)*
104. *Patlabor 2: The Movie* (feature film; dir. Mamoru Oshii, 1993)*
105. *Patlabor WXIII: Movie 3* (feature film; dir. Fumihiko Takayama, 2002)*
106. *Peach Girl* (TV series; dir. Hiroshi Ishiodori, 2005)*
107. *Perfect Blue* (feature film; dir. Satoshi Kon, 1997)
108. *Piano: The Melody of a Young Girl's Heart* (TV series; dir. Norihiko Sudo, 2002–2003)*
109. *The Place Promised In Our Early Days* (feature film; dir. Makoto Shinkai, 2004)*
110. *Please Teacher!* (TV series; dir. Yasunori Ide, 2002)*
111. *Pom Poko* (feature film; dir. Isao Takahata, 1994)
112. *Porco Rosso* (feature film; dir. Hayao Miyazaki, 1992)
113. *Princess Mononoke* (feature film; dir. Hayao Miyazaki, 1997)*
114. *Ranma 1/2* (TV series; dirs. Tomomitsu Mochizuki et al., 1989–1992)*
115. *R.O.D [Read Or Die]—The TV* (TV series; dir. Koji Masunari, 2004)*
116. *Rose of Versailles* (TV series; dirs. Tadao Nagahama and Osamu Dezaki, 1979–1980)*
117. *Rumbling Hearts* (TV series; dir. Tetsuya Watanabe, 2003–2004)*
118. *Sailor Moon* (TV series; dirs. Junichi Sato et al., 1992–1997)*
119. *Sakura Wars* (TV series; dirs. Ryutaro Nakamura and Takashi Asami, 2000)*
120. *Samurai Champloo* (TV series; dir. Shinichiro Watanabe, 2004–2005)*
121. *Samurai Deeper Kyo* (TV series; dir. Junji Nishimura, 2002)*
122. *Serial Experiments Lain* (TV series; dir. Ryutaro Nakamura, 1998)*
123. *Shingu: Secret of the Interstellar Wars* (TV series; dir. Tatsuo Sato, 2001)
124. *Shounen Onmyouji* (TV series; dir. Kunihiro Mori, 2006–2007)*
125. *Slayers Great* (feature film; dir. Hiroshi Watanabe, 1997)
126. *Solty Rei* (TV series; dir. Yoshimasa Hiraike, 2005–2006)*
127. *Space Battleship Yamato* (TV series; dir. Leiji Matsumoto, 1974)*
128. *Speed Grapher* (TV series; dir. Kunihisa Sugishima, 2005)
129. *Spirited Away* (feature film; dir. Hayao Miyazaki, 2001)
130. *Steamboy* (feature film; dir. Katsuhiro Otomo, 2004)*
131. *Strawberry Marshmallow* (TV series; dir. Takuya Sato, 2005)
132. *Super Dimensional Fortress Macross* (TV series; dir. Noboru Ishiguro, 1982)*
133. *Suzuka* (OVA series; dir. Hiroshi Fukutomi, 2005)
134. *Tales From Earthsea* (feature film; dir. Goro Miyazaki, 2006)*
135. *Teknoman* (TV series; dir. Hiroshi Negishi, 1992–1993)

136. *Tenchi Muyo! Ryououki* (OVA series; dir. Masaki Kajishima, 1992–1993)*
137. *Texhnolyze* (TV series; dir. Hiroshi Hamazaki, 2003)*
138. *The Third: The Girl with the Blue Eye* (TV series; dir. Jun Kamiya, 2006)
139. *To Heart* (TV series; dir. Naohito Takahashi, 1999)
140. *Tokyo Godfathers* (feature film; dir. Satoshi Kon, 2003)
141. *Tokyo Underground* (TV series; dir. Hayato Date, 2002)*
142. *Trinity Blood* (TV series; dir. Tomohiro Hirata, 2005)*
143. *Tsubasa Reservoir Chronicle* (TV series; dir. Koichi Mashimo, 2005–2006)*
144. *Twilight Q2: Labyrinth Objects File 538* (OVA episode; dir. Mamoru Oshii, 1987)
145. *UFO Ultramaiden Valkyrie: Bride of Celestial Souls' Day* (OVA series; dir. Shigeru Ueda, 2004)*
146. *Urusei Yatsura* (TV series and feature films; dirs. Mamoru Oshii et al., 1981–1991)*
147. *Utawarerumono* (TV series; dir. Tomoki Kobayashi, 2006)
148. *Vampire Hunter D — Bloodlust* (feature film; dir. Yoshiaki Kawajiri, 2000)
149. *Vampire Princess Miyu* (TV series; dir. Toshihiro Hirano, 1997–1998)*
150. *Vision of Escaflowne* (TV series; dirs. Kazuki Akane and Shouji Kawamori, 1996)
151. *Voices of a Distant Star* (TV series; dir. Makoto Shinkai, 2003)*
152. *Welcome to the N.H.K.* (TV series; dir. Yusuke Yamamoto, 2006)*
153. *Whisper of the Heart* (feature film; dir. Yoshifumi Kondou, 1995)*
154. *The Wings of Rean* (OVA series; dir. Yoshiyuki Tomino, 2005–2006)*
155. *Wolf's Rain* (TV series; dir. Tensai Okamura, 2003)*
156. *Yumeria* (TV series; dir. Keitaro Motonaga, 2004)*
157. *009-1* (TV series; dir. Naoyuki Konno, 2006)*

Appendix: Anime Productions with Studio Gainax Members

1. ANIMATION

Ai no Wakakusayama Monogatari (TV)
Crimson Wolf (OVA)
Debutante Detective Corps (OVA)
Eternal Family (TV)
Eyeshield 21 (TV)
Fatal Fury 2: The New Battle (OVA)
Honey and Clover (TV)
Koume-chan Ga Iku! (TV)
Mahoromatic — Automatic Maiden (TV)
Mister Ajikko (TV)
Neon Genesis Evangelion (TV)
Neon Genesis Evangelion: The End of Evangelion (feature film)
Oruchuban Ebichu (TV)
Trinity Blood (TV)

2. KEY ANIMATION

F (TV)

3. SECOND KEY ANIMATION

ARIA The NATURAL (TV)
Blood+ (TV)
Eureka 7 (TV)
Honey and Clover II (TV)

4. IN-BETWEEN ANIMATION

Bastard!! (OVA)
Beyond (OVA)
Black Cat (TV)
Blood+ (TV)
Blood: The Last Vampire (feature film)
Casshan: Robot Hunter (OVA)
Cowboy Bebop: The Movie (feature film)
Eureka 7 (TV)
FLCL (OVA)
GUNxSWORD (TV)
Hijikata Toshizo: Shiro no Kiseki (OVA)
Immortal Grand Prix (TV)
Initial D: Fourth Stage (TV)
Mind Game (feature film)
Naruto (TV)
Noein — to your other self (TV)
R.O.D (TV)
Second Renaissance (OVA)
Sol Bianca: The Legacy (OVA)
Sousei no Aquarion (TV)
Strawberry Marshmallow (TV)
Tsubasa Chronicle — Torikago no Kuni no Himegimi (feature film)
XXXHOLiC (TV)

5. SUPPORTING ANIMATION

Spirited Away (feature film)

6. ANIMATION ASSISTANCE

Pokemon Heroes — Latias & Latios (feature film)
Ranma 1/2 (OVA)

7. OPENING ANIMATION

Cutie Honey (live-action feature film)

8. Animation Production

Animé Tenchou (OVA)
FLCL (OVA)
He Is My Master (TV)
His and Her Circumstances (TV)
Magical Shopping Arcade Abenobashi (TV)
Maiking Break-Through Gurren-Lagann (TV)
Neppu Kairiku Bushi Lord (TV)
This Ugly Yet Beautiful World (TV)

9. Animation Cooperation

Murasaki Shikibu Genji Monogatari (feature film)

10. Creation

Abenobashi: Magical Shopping Arcade (manga)
FLCL (manga)
This Ugly and Beautiful World (manga)

11. Original Concept

Comic Gunbusters (manga)
Neon Genesis Evangelion (manga)
Neon Genesis Evangelion: Angelic Days (manga)
Neon Genesis Evangelion (live-action feature film)

12. Original Story

FLCL (OVA)
Magical Shopping Arcade Abenobashi (TV)
Neon Genesis Evangelion (TV)
Neon Genesis Evangelion: Death & Rebirth (feature film)
Neon Genesis Evangelion: The End of Evangelion (feature film)

13. Production Studio

Royal Space Force: The Wings of Honneamise (feature film)

14. Production

Ai no Wakakusayama Monogatari (TV)
Blazing Transfer Student (OVA)

Cutie Honey (live-action feature film)
FLCL (OVA)
Gunbusters (OVA)
His and Her Circumstances (TV)
Komatsu Sakyo Anime Gekijou (TV)
Koume-chan Ga Iku! (TV)
Magical Shopping Arcade Abenobashi (TV)
Mahoromatic—Automatic Maiden (TV)
Mahoromatic: Something More Beautiful (TV)
Mahoromatic: Summer Special (TV)
Maiking Break-Through Gurren-Lagann (TV)
The Melody of Oblivion (TV)
Nadia—Secret of Blue Water (TV)
Nadia of the Mysterious Seas (feature film)
Neon Genesis Evangelion (TV)
Neon Genesis Evangelion: Death & Rebirth (feature film)
Neon Genesis Evangelion: The End of Evangelion (feature film)
Neppu Kairiku Bushi Lord (TV)
Neppuu Kairiku Bushilord (TV)
Oruchuban Ebichu (TV)
Otaku no Video (OVA)
Petite Princess Yucie (TV)
Re: Cutie Honey (OVA)
Top wo Nerae 2! (OVA)
This Ugly Yet Beautiful World (TV)

15. Planning

FLCL (OVA)
His and Her Circumstances (TV)
Magical Shopping Arcade Abenobashi (TV)
The Melody of Oblivion (TV)
Neon Genesis Evangelion (TV)
Neon Genesis Evangelion: Death & Rebirth (feature film)
Neon Genesis Evangelion: The End of Evangelion (feature film)

16. Production Assistance

Urusei Yatsura: The Final Chapter (feature film)

17. Animation Co-production

Re: Cutie Honey (OVA)

18. Production Support
Submarine 707R (OVA)

19. Mechanical Design
Mobile Suit Gundam: Char's Counterattack (feature film)

20. ADR Production
Sky Blue (Korean feature film)

21. Distribution
Restol, The Special Rescue Squad (Korean TV)

Chapter Notes

Chapter 1

1. Justin Sevakis singles out Anno as a classic incarnation of the type: "Otaku-dom has something of a poster child in Hideaki Anno. Scrawny, unkempt, and with self-esteem peaking well below measurable levels, he's become known for his neurotic demeanor as much as for the anime he's directed" (Sevakis).

Chapter 2

1. One of *Wings of Honneamise*'s worthiest successors, where the representation of urban architecture is concerned, is unquestionably Rintaro's film *Metropolis* (2001), in which elements of Art Deco are comparably deployed in the generation of an alternate world of Byzantine intricacy.

Chapter 3

1. Almost contemporaneous with *Gunbuster*, Mamoru Oshii's movie *Patlabor 1: The Mobile Police* (1989) also contributed substantially to the redefinition of the *mecha* genre in the direction of serious sci-fi interspersed with comic elements. The sequels *Patlabor 2: The Movie* (dir. Oshii, 1993) and *Patlabor WXIII: Movie 3* (dir. Fumihiko Takayama, 2002) robustly consolidated this trend.

2. "In *Gunbuster* and *Gunbuster 2*..., heroines Noriko and Nono have close relationships with more experienced female pilots (Kazumi and Lal'C), whom they both call 'Oné-sama.' The term is a respectful form of Japanese *ane* (older sister), but that doesn't mean they're family—in Japan, people often call young adult women *oné-san* to evoke a sense of casual familiarity.... Noriko and Nono employ it to forge closer relationships with Kazumi and Lal'C, but are careful to use *sama* instead of *san* at the end to show their respect for the other girls' higher rank and superior pilot skills" ("Oné-sama," p. 160).

Chapter 4

1. Where generic mixes are concerned, a modality comparable to steampunk is the "pseudo-Western," in which formulae characteristic of typical cowboy movies merge with ingredients drawn from classic science fiction and the martial-arts film. A good example is offered by the TV show *Grenadier* (dir. Hiroshi Koujina, 2004).

2. The plan to deploy old technologies for nefarious purposes, unscrupulously pursued by power-thirsty individuals, also provides a dramatic pivot for the TV show *My-Otome* (dir. Masakazu Obara, 2005–2006). In this series, set in an eminently retrofuturistic world, stringently selected young women are trained to become *otome*— elite bodyguards for the nobility. The heroine Arika Yumemiya, incidentally, recalls *Gunbuster 2*'s Nono (please see chapter 13) by dint of her cheerful idealism and determination to succeed against the odds. *My-Otome* constitutes the second season of *My-HiME* (TV series; dir. Obara, 2004–2005)— a drama-comedy likewise based on a gaggle of girls endowed with magical powers.

3. The Babel topos features prominently in dystopian science fiction of both the live-action and the animated varieties, as attested to by Ridley Scott's *Blade Runner* (1982), Mamoru Oshii's *Patlabor 1: The Mobile Police* (1989) and Rintaro's *Metropolis* (2001).

4. Please note that the movie *Nadia of the Mysterious Seas*, directed by Sho Aono for Seiei Animation and released in 1992, did not involve Gainax in any substantial fashion. The studio's sole contributions to the project were portions of the footage extracted from the TV series.

Chapter 5

1. An endearing example of otaku-based anime casting quintessentially cute characters is provided by the TV series *Lucky Star* (dirs. Yasuhiro Takemoto and Yutaka Yamamoto, 2007)— a show that chronicles the adventures of the obsessive fan Konata Izumi as she and her school friends strive to pursue their all-absorbing interests in the face of problematic adults. The generational tensions that pepper Gainax's own output can here be sensed in a muted tone, abetted by pastelly hues and delicate dynamics.

Chapter 6

1. The prototype for the theme of the reluctant hero entrusted by fate — and exploitative adults — with

mecha-piloting responsibilities is supplied by *Mobile Suit Gundam*, a massive franchise active to this day that originated in a TV series directed by Yoshiyuki Tomino and aired in 1979–1980 and three compilation movies released in 1981–1982. An analogous matrix informs the TV series *Fafner* (dir. Nobuyoshi Habara, 2004), in which teenagers are callously drawn into a war against hostile aliens known as "Festum." The young protagonists' exploitation as sacrificial victims lends *Fafner* a distinctively somber mood often redolent of *Evangelion*.

The topos of children endowed with special powers whose birth takes place after a cataclysmic event, exploited to maximum effect in *Evangelion*, is likewise central to the TV show *Gilgamesh* (dir. Masahiko Murata, 2003–2004) — as is the cloning theme concomitantly deployed in *Evangelion*. Murata's Gothic thriller unfolds in the aftermath of a terrorist attack of momentous scale, responsible for reconfiguring the entire environment and for transforming the sky into a hallucinatory mirror. As two ruthless factions vie for supremacy in a secret and ghastly war, a brother and sister named Tatsuya and Kiyoko are caught in its midst, uncertain about either their allegiances or their destiny.

Another male protagonist who, like *Evangelion*'s Shinji, is transposed from a dull and sheltered existence to a scene of cosmic strife is Renton from the TV series *Eureka Seven* (dir. Tomomi Kyoda, 2005–2006). Renton, too, gradually recognizes the importance of not "running away" as the precondition of both self-understanding and meaningful interaction with others. The female protagonist Eureka, incidentally, is reminiscent of Rei in both her design and her enigmatic nature. Renton's desire to make her "smile" recalls Shinji's wish to elicit that same response from Rei in *Evangelion*'s Episode 6. At the cinematographical level, *Eureka Seven* echoes Anno's saga in its handling of lighting effects, explosions and flashbacks, as well as the visual trope of the biomechanoid's gleaming green eye as it attains awareness.

2. The phrase "Central Dogma" is derived from the field of genetics, in which it designates the law — formulated by Francis Crick in 1958 — whereby once genetic information contained in the RNA and the DNA has been transferred to proteins it cannot flow back to genetic acid.

3. *Evangelion*'s effective employment of pseudo-documentary evidence to lend solidity to its narrative is echoed by the TV series *Gasaraki* (dirs. Ryousuke Takahashi and Goro Taniguchi, 1999), in which the plot is often advanced by recourse to news reports, the style of which closely resembles the coverage of the first Gulf War by CNN.

4. The Shinto religion is also overtly invoked in the TV series *Blue Seed* (dir. Jun Kamiya, 1994–1995) and in its OVA sequel *Blue Seed Beyond* (dirs. Jun Kamiya and Kiyoshi Murayama, 1996). *Blue Seed*'s protagonist, Momiji Fujimiya, is a descendant of the mythical Princess Kushinada and is supposed to offer herself in sacrifice to appease the legendary "Yamata no Orochi" ("Eight-forked Snake") as the "Aragami" ("angry gods") spawned by the monster rampage through Japan and the United States. With the aid of the secret organization TAC and of the human-Aragami hybrid Mamoru Kusanagi, however, Momiji escapes her sacrificial destiny and chooses to fight the invaders instead. Consistent reference is concurrently made to the Shinto god Susanoo, reputed to have rescued the original Princess Kushinada when her own turn to give her life to Orochi had come.

5. In deploying religious symbolism, *Evangelion* has also paved the way for a number of subsequent anime. A recent instance of the medium's unorthodox appropriation of biblical mythology is offered by the TV series *Trinity Blood* (dir. Tomohiro Hirata, 2005). This pivots on the character of Abel Nightrod, a priest working for the Vatican charged with the task of fighting vampires. Neither human nor vampire, Abel is endowed with the nanotechnological power to morph into a demonic creature called a "Kresnick" that is capable of sucking the blood of vampires to nefarious effect. The supporting character of Esther Blanchett, a stylishly plucky nun also employed by the Vatican, provides a further instance of the show's iconoclastic handling of Christianity. (An earlier instance of a demon-fighting nun, sexier and more overtly amusing than Esther, features in *Chrono Crusade*, a TV series directed by Yuu Kou and aired in 2003–2004.)

Evangelion's hearty appetite for occult symbolism is echoed by the TV show *Fullmetal Alchemist* (dir. Seiji Mizushima, 2003–2004). This chronicles the tragic fate of Edward and Alphonse Elric, two boys that roam the world in search of the Philosopher's Stone deemed capable of restoring the limbs (in Edward's case) and entire body (in Alphonse's) they lost in a disastrous attempt to resurrect their mother by alchemical means.

6. The contrast between a subterranean realm and the Earth's surface is likewise central to the TV series *Tokyo Underground* (dir. Hayato Date, 2002). The inhabitants of the world located beneath Tokyo's underground system are people endowed with the magical ability to control various elements (hence their designation as "Elemental Users") and are hell-bent on annihilating the surface people whom they regard as traitors. The show's heroine, the "Priestess of Life" Ruri Sarasa, and her bodyguard and tutor Chelsea Rorec manage to escape to the surface but the Elemental Users are determined to get the girl back at all costs because they need her powers in order to awaken the dragon instrumental to the fulfillment of their mission. The trope of an underground world seemingly devoid of hope wherein a determined, yet vulnerable, youth puts on a heroic performance against all odds is central to the TV show *Texhnolyze* (dir. Hiroshi Hamazaki, 2003). Trapped in the squalor of the subterranean city of Rususku, the professional fighter Ichise lives a life of extreme violence with nihilistic resignation until the psychic Ran ushers him into an alternate vision where the future is not incontrovertibly bleak.

Chapter 7

1. It is also useful to compare the TV show's apportioning of the seventeen Angels to its episodes and *Death*'s own approach to the issue.

TV Episode	Angel	Death Segment	Angel
1	3	1	1
2	3	2	3/17

TV Episode	Angel	Death Segment	Angel
3	4	3	3
4	—	4	3/4
5	5	5	6/7/8/14/15
6	5	6	2/5/14/15/16
7	—	7	—
8	1/6	8	14/17
9	7	9	13
10	8	10	—
11	9	11	2/17
12	1/10		
13	11		
14	—		
15	2		
16	12		
17	—		
18	13		
19	14		
20	—		
21	—		
22	2/15		
23	16		
24	2/17		

1: Adam 5: Ramiel 9: Matariel 13: Bardiel
2: Lilith 6: Gaghiel 10: Sahaquiel 14: Zeruel
3: Sachiel 7: Israfel 11: Iruel 15: Arael
4: Shamshel 8: Sandalphon 12: Leliel 16: Armisael
 17: Tabris

2. Anime's passion for gigantic female figures laden with mythological connotations of the kind seen in the directors' cut of Episode 23 of the *Evangelion* series and in *End* is also borne out by the character of Sharon Apple in *Macross Plus: The Movie* (dir. Shouji Kawamori, 1995) — an idol singer of intergalactic fame that actually happens to be a holographic AI and whose colossal shape fills the screen in the movie's near-apocalyptic climax. In *Bubblegum Crisis—Tokyo 2040* (TV series; dir. Hiroki Hayashi, 1998), the action's crowning moments are likewise dominated by a mammoth synthetic creature known as Galatea who — like the pursuers of Human Instrumentality in *Evangelion*— seeks to assimilate all humans into a single entity. (The series also echoes Anno's saga in its treatment of the themes of parental abuse and political corruption, as well as in its emphasis on the brute materiality of *mecha*.)

3. A project developed in tandem with the new films that offers a radically contrasting take on the *Evangelion* universe is *Petite Eva*— a fun-packed initiative wherein the somber mood of the original anime gives way to both discreet comedy and downright zaniness. The project features adorably bizarre SD versions of the characters executed by manga artist Ryusuke Hamamoto, who belongs to the first generation of *Evangelion* fans. The setting for their adventures is "NERV Academy" and the school-comedy formula accordingly provides a diegetic leading thread. (Unit-01 itself appears as a pupil of indeterminate age named "Evancho." As for Rei, her three incarnations coexist as the "Ayanami sisters.") The first phase in the franchise consists of the release of collectible figurines produced by Bandai Boys Toy Department but is expected to spawn a much wider variety of products as the stories based on these reconfigured characters develop and cross over into other visual media.

Gainax's imaginative approach to ancillary merchandise is also demonstrated by the 2008 calendar tied in with the release of *1.0*. This consists of a minigallery of characters from the saga executed by the artist Youichi Fukano, garbed in costumes that integrate elements of film-noir, Goth and cabaret styles in a classy monochrome. This is succinctly captured by the piece's very title: *Evangelion: 1.0— Black and White*. The figure of the cross — a ubiquitous motif throughout the saga at the levels of both central spectacle and marginal decor — is repeatedly invoked in the characters' accessories. This suggests that religious iconography can serve ornamental purposes, in much the same way as *Evangelion*'s religious and mythological frame of reference is, by and large, candidly deployed for the purpose of entertainment. Moreover, the emblem also alludes to vampire lore, and is therefore perfectly consonant with the costumes' Goth dimension. Fukano's work concurrently shows that in placing the characters in situations alien to the world of the main story and visualizing their feasible attitudes therein, an artist can emulate the ethos of "Method Acting."

Chapter 8

1. Both the TV series and the parent manga are frequently referred to as "*Kare Kano*" (or "*Karekano*"), an abbreviation of the full original title that reflects the tendency, popular among the Japanese, to create new words by combining the opening syllables of existing words. (The English version of the manga, published by Tokyopop, is overtly titled *Kare Kano*.) The original title of the later Gainax show *This Ugly Yet Beautiful World* is, analogously, habitually shortened to "*Kono Mini*" (or "*Konomini*").

2. Significantly, the image placed next to the entry for Hideaki Anno in the "Staff" list presented on the studio's official website, *Gainax Net*, portrays a green-eyed tabby (http://www.gainax.co.jp/staff/index.html). A further feline connection is indicated by the director's curriculum vitae, in which he is said to have played the character of Miyu Miyu in *FLCL* (http://www.animenewsnetwork.com/encyclopedia/people.php?id=15).

3. It is not uncommon for Japanese animation to toy with gender ambiguity, for example, by planting false clues to a character's sexual preferences for dramatic effect, or by using shifts in erotic orientation to illustrate a character's broader psychological development. The TV series *Ranma 1/2* (dirs. Tomomitsu Mochizuki, Tsutomo Shibayama, Koji Sawai and Junji Nishimura, 1989–1992) is a perfect illustration of the deployment of gender-bending for fundamentally comedic purposes. In the show, an ancient curse causes the teenage boy Ranma Saotome to turn into a girl whenever he comes into contact with water, and his father Genma to morph into a giant panda in response to the same stimulus. The two characters' repeated metamorphoses are the trigger of well-sustained hilarity. More recently, *Kashimashi — Girl Meets Girl* (TV series; dir. Nobuaki Nakanishi, 2006) has provided a tantalizing experiment in the field through the complications spawned by Hazumu Osaragi's metamorphosis into a girl when a UFO crashes into him and his body is inadvertently reconstituted by the aliens in female form. Previously

shunned as undesirable, Hazumu ironically becomes popular with ladies in the wake of his transformation.

Chapter 9

1. Young protagonists dissatisfied with the banality of their everyday lives are a recurrent feature in anime. A highly entertaining instance of this trend is offered by the protagonist of the TV show *The Melancholy of Haruhi Suzumiya* (dir. Tatsuya Ishihara, 2006) — an eccentric teenager determined to see mysteries and abnormalities round every corner. Indulging this passion, she founds a school club dedicated to the detection of aliens, time travelers and paranormal activities, thereby plunging her mates into a whirlwind of mind-bending adventures. An explicit homage to Gainax's oeuvre is introduced right from the start in the guise of a "combat waitress from the future," Mikuru Asahina, who is garbed in a Bunny costume, endowed with a bouncing bosom and entrusted with the task of protecting a young man supposed to be an "esper." While explicitly echoing *Daicon 4* and *Mahoromatic*, these elements simultaneously foreshadow *Gunbuster 2*.

2. The show's incorporation of allusions to a fairy tale is quite congruous with its coming-of-age dimension: as Jack Zipes points out, fairy tales indeed play a key part in the socializing process (Zipes). *Puss-In-Boots* is an especially apposite case in which *FLCL* is concerned insofar as the feline figure functions as a potent instigator of both material and emotional growth. Readers with a passion for anime instilled with fairy-tale elements — and especially those who happen to harbor a fascination with felinity — might wish to sample the movie *Whisper of the Heart* (dir. Yoshifumi Kondou, 1995) and its semi-sequel *The Cat Returns* (dir. Hiroyuki Morita, 2002).

3. The image of the Bunny Girl is also used in Episode 15 — "Fortune River" — of *Melody of Oblivion* in the role of one of the protagonist's most lethal enemies.

4. The scene is redolent of the sequence in the TV series *InuYasha* (dirs. Masashi Ikeda and Yasunao Aoki, 2000–2004) in which the protagonist, Kagome, spots the Sacred Tree to which the eponymous hero is sealed with an arrow, asleep, and feels an irresistible longing to stroke his dog-like ears.

5. Readers keen on anime's specifically musical dimension are advised to sample Shinichiro Watanabe's *Cowboy Bebop* (TV series: 1998–1999; movie: 2001), in which the entire action — and most notably the sequences revolving around space battles and martial-arts fights — are set to music explicitly inspired by various jazz and early rock styles, delivering an infectiously funky mood. Director Watanabe's fascination with swish musical accompaniment can again be detected in the TV show *Samurai Champloo* (2004–2005), in which turbulent events drawn from a fictionalized history of feudal Japan unfold against the background of a refreshingly stylish, downtempo soundtrack, infused with a good dose of hip-hop. *Nerima Daikon Brothers* (2006), a TV series directed by Shinichi Watanabe (*not* the same Watanabe, it must be stressed) is likewise worthy of notice as an inspired adaptation of the musical comedy format to the medium of anime. The more classically oriented readers may wish to consider the TV series *Piano: The Melody of a Young Girl's Heart* (dir. Norihiko Sudo, 2002–2003), in which the emotional and psychosexual maturation of the introverted teenager Miu Nomura is consistently tracked with reference to her development as a piano player and, eventually, composer.

Chapter 10

1. Mahoro's relatively immature appearance renders her prowess all the more remarkable, thereby also providing a refreshing alternative to the buxom look typically exhibited by female fighters in sci-fi anime. Notable instances of this trend are the designs for the heroines of the movie *Appleseed* (dir. Shinji Aramaki, 2004), Deunan Knute, of the TV series *009-1* (dir. Naoyuki Konno, 2006), Mylene Hoffman, and — most famously and iconically — of the feature films *Ghost in the Shell* (dir. Mamoru Oshii, 1995) and *Ghost in the Shell 2: Innocence* (dir. Mamoru Oshii, 2004), as well as of the televisual spin-offs *Ghost in the Shell: S.A.C* (dir. Kenji Kamiyama, 2002–2004) and *Ghost in the Shell: S.A.C, 2nd Gig* (dir. Kamiyama, 2004–2005), the incomparable Major Motoko Kusanagi. All of these characters vaunt voluptuous curves and overt sex appeal.

Chapter 11

1. The concept of parallel universes so central to *Abenobashi* (and previously alluded to by *Mahoromatic* in its account of Saint's intergalactic expeditions) has enlisted the creative skills of countless directors. A notable illustration within contemporary anime is supplied by the TV series *Tsubasa Reservoir Chronicle* (dir. Koichi Mashimo, 2005–2006) — the story of Princess Sakura of Clow, whose heart and memories are stolen by an evil sorcerer and scattered in the form of feathers across disparate worlds, and of the young archaeologist Syaoran, who devotes himself heroically to the retrieval of the feathers, although he is aware that Sakura will never remember him or what he had ever meant to her in the occluded past. A further example of anime's fascination with the trope of spatiotemporal displacement can be found in *Kyo Kara Maho!* (TV series; dir. Junji Nishimura, 2006), in which Yuri Shibuya, a perfectly average bloke, ends up in charge of a kingdom of demons as a result of being flushed down a public toilet.

Chapter 12

1. The idea that in order to defeat a monster you have to become one is also elaborated in *Claymore* (TV series; dir. Hiroyuki Tanaka, 2007), in which brain-eating shape-shifters known as "Yoma" can be vanquished only by superhuman warriors (the Claymores) constructed by implanting Yoma flesh and blood into regular humans. Sadly, the latter are deeply suspicious of Claymores and indeed often refer to them as "monsters."

The metamorphosis concept so axial to *This Ugly*

Yet Beautiful World finds one of its most potent realizations with the TV series *Wolf's Rain* (dir. Tensai Okamura, 2003). The story (which additionally shares with Saeki's show a concern with evolution) is set in a post-apocalyptic world seemingly on the verge of termination, in which wolves are believed to have been extinct for two hundred years. It gradually becomes clear, however, that the animals have not been the victims of an irreversible evolutionary warp but have actually managed to survive and learnt how to take on human form when necessary. In the process, the show delivers a captivating string of metamorphoses whose dramatic impact affectively echoes Takeru's own transformations.

The theme of physical mutation is no less prominent in *K.O. Beast* (1992), an OVA series directed by Hiroshi Negishi in which the main characters — shape-shifters capable of alternating between human and bestial incarnations — deploy their powers in pursuit of a legendary treasure. Another anime feat worthy of inspection by any spectator keen on the metamorphosis motif is provided by the TV series *R.O.D* (a.k.a. *Read Or Die*) — *The TV* (dir. Koji Masunari, 2004). In this show, the "Paper Sisters" Michelle, Maggie and Anita utilize their telekinetic powers to manipulate paper so sensationally as to be able to stop bullets by means of mere Post-its, fling index cards as though they were shuriken or even turn flimsy sheets into giant birdlike planes.

2. The schizoid-personality trope is tantalizingly deployed in the TV show *D.N.Angel* (dirs. Koji Yoshikawa and Nobuyoshi Habara, 2003) in which fourteen-year-old Daisuke Niwa, a perfectly ordinary and unpretentious teenager, mutates into the legendary Phantom Thief Dark whenever he thinks about the girl of his dreams. The possession of anomalous DNA is revealed to be the cause of this double personality. Daisuke's mother unscrupulously capitalizes on the boy's metamorphic powers to have him steal treasurable artifacts.

3. The flesh-and-blood Hikari and Akari are merely provisional incarnations of a fundamentally incorporeal force. While this narrative ruse is deployed to memorable effect in Saeki's show, it should be noted that the reverse phenomenon of decorporealization can achieve equally remarkable dramatic results. This is patently borne out by the TV series *Fullmetal Alchemist* (dir. Seiji Mizushima, 2003–2004), in which Alphonse Elric, aided by his brother Edward, tenaciously endeavors to reoccupy the body lost in childhood as a result of their mishandling of magic. The same concept is central to the TV series *Samurai Deeper Kyo* (dir. Junji Nishimura, 2002), in which the protagonist, Demon Eyes Kyo, seeks to regain a material form of his own after his soul has been sealed inside the body of his enemy Kyoshiro Mibu, effectively forcing him to share his corporeality with another being.

4. The butterfly image is similarly deployed to memorable dramatic effect in the TV show *Boogiepop Phantom* (dir. Takashi Watanabe, 2000), in which one of the principal characters, the hyper-evolved Manaka, is able to extract memories from her surroundings and concretize them in the form of butterflies of light. (Importantly, in *Boogiepop Phantom* no less than in Saeki's show, the evolution topos plays an axial part.)

Chapter 13

1. The notion that hard work and guts are vital to the assertion of one's identity at both the personal and the societal levels features prominently in Japanese culture. In the realm of animation, a paradigmatic example is supplied by the sensationally popular TV series *Naruto* (dir. Hayato Date, 2002–2007), in which a young boy who acts as the living container of a nine-tailed demon fox — and should therefore be regarded as an object of respect and even veneration — is actually shunned by all as though he were an evil spirit himself. However, the eponymous hero tenaciously demonstrates his worth through his total and unflinching commitment to *ninjutsu* (a.k.a. *shinobi-jutsu*, the art of the ninja), steadily maturing as the series progresses.

2. As the *Gainax Pages* review of *Gunbuster 2* points out, Tsurumaki has partly harnessed this show to the elaboration of "some of his ideas from *FLCL*." These include:

- Cats are used in both shows to communicate across space.
- Robots pop out of foreheads in *FLCL* through something called N-O Fields, while in *Diebuster* the Busters are controlled somehow through forehead patches.
- There may be a connection between the Fraternity in *Diebuster* and the Fraternity in *FLCL* that Amarao works for.
- Vespa-ish motor scooters ["*Gainax Pages* reviews: *Gunbuster 2*"].

Also worthy of attention are similarities between the character designs for Lal'C and Kitsurubami, and between the *mecha* designs for the *Dix-Neuf* and the coated giant robot presented in *FLCL*'s climax.

3. Of all the anime productions in which Gainax has been involved to date, the one in which adult content is most graphically presented is *Oruchuban Ebichu* (*Ebichu the Housekeeping Hamster*, a.k.a. *Ebichu Minds the House*), a 24-episode series of short animations about a talking hamster, her O.L. ("office lady") owner and the latter's useless boyfriend. Directed by Makoto Moriwaki, the program was first aired in 1999 as one third of the show *Modern Love's Silliness*. The sexual content is here deployed not so much in pursuit of fan service as for the purpose of exuberant comedy. *Ebichu*'s humor might not be to everybody's taste but its artfully simple pictorial style is worthy of notice in its own right.

4. Should the reader wish to sample fictional means of locomotion other than *mecha*, two shows definitely worthy of consideration are the TV series *Eureka Seven* (dir. Tomoki Kyouda, 2005–2006), in which surfing "trapar" (i.e., Transparence Light Particles) waves is a favorite activity, and the TV series *Air Gear* (dir. Hajime Kamegaki, 2006), in which self-propelled inline skates known as "Air Trecks" (or AT for short) enable their wearers to literally ride the air. The aura of playfulness emitted by the Buster Machines in Tsurumaki's show can also be detected in this equipment.

5. The setting of this sequence in a nondescript location tagged "Polydimensional Space, Space-Time Censor Room" is a direct allusion to the "strong cosmic censorship hypothesis" put forward by Roger Penrose

in 1979. This maintains that even though a naked singularity is hypothetically possible, it could never be visible to any observer. It is as though the laws of physics deliberately proscribed that which they cannot account for.

Chapter 14

1. As Haruo Shirane emphasizes, traditional Japanese poetry has likewise attached great significance to a work's corporeal dimension: "Japanese poetry," constitutes "a material object for which calligraphy, paper, and packaging were probably as important as the poem itself.... The type, color, and size of the paper were also important. The poet could also add a sketch, attach a flower or leaf, or add incense or perfume to the poetry sheet. The poem as material object was often a gift for the host, friend, or lover. Matching the poem or paper with the social occasion or season was a key factor in its effectiveness or performativity" (Shirane, pp. 223–224).

2. Richard Williams has usefully commented on the relationship between animation and music: "I think of animation as drawn music. It's very similar; the timing is similar — the passion, the contrast, how you join things together interestingly" (Lennert).

3. Within an educational milieu, Gainax's oeuvre could supply an apposite vehicle for the study of the interpenetration of visual and textual information, as well as a means of stimulating the simultaneous processing of figures and graphemes.

Bibliography

Some of the website addresses provided in this bibliography may not be currently available because of the intrinsically volatile nature of the www. All of the sites were active at some point during the period March 2007–February 2008.

Anime Academy Review: "*Magical Shopping Arcade Abenobashi.*" 2002. http://www.animeacademy.com/finalrevdisplay.php?id=324.
"Anime Meta-Review—*FLCL.*" 2000. http://amr.nextstudio.net/html/furi_kuri.html.
"Anime Meta-Review—*Nadia: The Secret of Blue Water.*" 2002. http://amr.nextstudio.net/html/nadia.html.
AnimeNfo.Com. 2005. "*Otaku no Video* Review." http://www.animenfo.com/animetitle,430,znhlmb,otaku_no_video.html.
"Animonster." 2003. "*FLCL* Review." *AAW—Akemi's Anime World*. http://animeworld.com/readerreviews/flcl.html.
Austin, J. L. 1962. *How to Do Things with Words*. Oxford: Clarendon.
Barthes, R. 1974. *S/Z: An Essay*. Trans. R. Miller. New York: Hill & Wang.
Barthes, R. 1990. *The Pleasure of the Text*. Trans. R. Miller. Oxford: Basil Blackwell Ltd.
Baudelaire, C. 1857. *Les fleurs du mal*. Paris: Garnier [1961].
"Beyond the Review: *Gunbuster* vs. *Diebuster.*" 2006. *vissiOne: an anime and gaming blog*. http://vissione.wordpress.com/2006/12/27/beyond-the-review-gunbuster-vs-diebuster/.
Bollom, B. W. 2002. "*FLCL*: How Gainax Created the First Anime for the 21st Century." http://www.burninghammer.com/misc/FinalFLCL.doc.
Bustard, J. 2003. "*Mahoromatic—Automatic Maiden*: Review." *T.H.E.M. Anime Reviews*. http://www.themanime.org/viewreview.php?id=288.
Clark, M. 2003. "*Mahoromatic: Automatic Maiden—Vols. 1 & 2.*" *Newtype USA* 2, no. 5.
Clements, J., and H. McCarthy. 2006. *The Anime Encyclopaedia: A Guide to Japanese Animation Since 1917*. Revised and Expanded Edition. Berkeley, CA: Stone Bridge Press.
Conrad, K. 2005. "*FLCL.*" *exploded goat*. http://www.explodedgoat.com/animeepguide.php?num=53.
Crandol, M. 2002. "Understanding *Evangelion.*" *Anime News Network*. http://www.animenewsnetwork.com/feature.php?id=14.
Derrida, J. 1982. *Margins of Philosophy*. Trans. A. Bass. Chicago: Chicago University Press.
Drazen, P. 2003. *Anime Explosion: The What? Why? & Wow! of Japanese Animation*. Berkeley, CA: Stone Bridge Press.
Eisenbraun, C. 2003. *Symbols*. "Butterflys." http://www.scootermydaisyheads.com/fine_art/symbol_dictionary/butterfly.html.
"Encyclopaedia of *Gunbuster 2.*" 2007. *Gunbuster 2* DVD, vol. 2 Booklet. Bandai Visual USA.
Eng, L. 2001. "The Politics of Otaku." http://www.cjas.org/~leng/otaku-p.htm.
Eng, L. 2005. "The Fans Who Would Be Kings—A Review of: *The Notenki Memoirs: Studio Gainax and the Men Who Created* Evangelion." *lainspotting—otaku studies, science, technology, and (sub)culture*. http://www.cjas.org/~leng/lainspotting/2005/07/fans-who-would-be-kings.html.
Enokido, Y. 2007a. "Welcome to Outer Space!" *Newtype USA* 6, no. 4.
Enokido, Y. 2007b. "Interview by Y. Izubuchi." *Gunbuster 2* DVD, vol. 2. Bandai Visual USA.
Enokido, Y. 2007c. "Interview." *Gunbuster 2* DVD, vol. 1 Booklet. Bandai Visual USA.

Equivalence. http://www.equivalence.com/labor/lab_vf_glo_e.shtml.
"Fan Service." *Anime News Network.* http://www.animenewsnetwork.com/encyclopedia/lexicon.php?id=54.
"Feline Delight." *Articles Archive. Easy Target: A Fooly Cooly Fan Site.* http://www.nandaba.net/flcl/.
Furuhashi, K. 2007. "Fin de Siècle." *Newtype USA* 6, no. 4.
Gail. 2007. "*Gunbuster 2*, Volume 1 (DVD Review)." *Anime News.* http://www.theotaku.com/news/view/gunbuster_2_vol._1_(dvd_review)/2390.
"*Gainax Pages: Rebuild of Evangelion.*" *Gainax Pages.* http://www.gainaxpages.com/anime/rebuild.php.
"*Gainax Pages* reviews: *FLCL.*" *Gainax Pages.* http://www.gainaxpages.com/anime/flcl.php.
"*Gainax Pages* reviews: *Gunbuster 2.*" *Gainax Pages.* http://www.gainaxpages.com/anime/gunbuster2.php.
"*Gainax Pages* reviews: *Nadia.*" *Gainax Pages.* http://www.gainaxpages.com/anime/nadia.php.
"*Gainax Pages* reviews: *The Notenki Memoirs* by Yasuhiro Takeda." 2005. *Gainax Pages.* http://www.gainaxpages.com/features/notenki.php.
"Gainax turns 20!" 2004. *Newtype USA* 3, no. 9.
Gifford, K. 2007a. "News and *Newtype*: *Gunbuster.*" *Newtype USA* 6, no. 2.
Gifford, K. 2007b. "Royalty Ain't What It Used to Be." *Newtype USA* 6, no. 3.
"Glossary." 2006. Documentary Booklet. *Neon Genesis Evangelion Platinum Edition Complete Collection.* ADV Films.
"Glossary of Terms." 2005. In *The Notenki Memoirs: Studio Gainax and the Men Who Created Evangelion.* New York: ADV Manga.
Grassmuck, V. 1990. "'I'm alone, but not lonely': Japanese Otaku-Kids colonize the Realm of Information and Media. A Tale of Sex and Crime from a faraway Place." http://www.cjas.org/~leng/otaku-e.htm.
Greenfield, M. 2006. "The English Remix Process." *Neon Genesis Evangelion Platinum Edition Complete Collection.* Disc 3. ADV Films.
"*Gunbuster*— The OVA That Defined OVAs." 2006. *Newtype USA* 5, no. 12.
"*Gunbuster*: Series History." 1999. *The Gunbuster Index.* http://www.toponeraegunbuster.com/Gunbuster-History.html.
"*Gunbuster 2* Science Lesson — Chapter 1." 2007. *Gunbuster 2* DVD, vol. 1 Booklet. Bandai Visual USA.
Hairston, M. 1995a. "The 'Lost' *Nadia.*" http://utd500.utdallas.edu/~hairston/lostnadia.html.
Hairston, M. 1995b. "Themes in *Nadia.*" http://utd500.utdallas.edu/~hairston/themes.html.
"Hidden Frames." *FLCL World.* http://www.flclw.com/images-pics/hidden-frames/.
Hikawa, R. 2007a. "The Official Art of *Gunbuster 2.*" *Newtype USA* 6, no. 4.
Hikawa, R. 2007b. "Growing Up Topless." *Newtype USA* 6, no. 5.
"*His and Her Circumstances*—Anime Academy Review." 2002. *Anime Academy.* http://www.animeacademy.com/finalrevdisplay.php?id=246.
"*His and Her Circumstances*—Anime Web Turnpike Review." 2002. *Anime Web Turnpike.* http://magazine.anipike.com/index.php?review=134.
"*His and Her Circumstances*: Producer's Notes." 2002. *His and Her Circumstances* DVD Box Set, disc 1. The Right Stuf International.
Huxley, J. 2004. "*Mahoromatic Vol. 1* Review." *Anime Boredom.* http://www.animeboredom.co.uk/anime-reviews/mahoromatic/416/.
"Ikari Gendo's Ultimate EVA FAQs about the TV Series." http://www.therossman.com/evafaqs1/evatv.html.
Imaishi, H. 2006. "*Tengen Toppa Gurren Lagann.*" *Newtype USA* 6, no. 12.
"[inside] Gainax." *Newtype USA* 2, no. 7.
Izuna, Y. 2007. "Interview." *Gunbuster 2* DVD, vol. 3 Booklet. Bandai Visual USA.
Johnston, C. 2006. "*Genshiken*— Complete Collection." *Newtype USA* 5, no. 6.
Kanoh, A. 2005. "War of the Worlds." *Newtype USA* 4, no. 9.
Kaplan, F. 2004. "Who Is Afraid of the Humanoid? Investigating Cultural Differences in the Acceptance of Robots." *International Journal of Humanoid Robotics* 1, no. 3. World Scientific Publishing Company.
Kawin, B. (1978). *Mindscreen: Bergman, Godard, and First-Person Film.* Princeton, NJ: Princeton University Press.
Kiley, D. 1983. *Peter Pan Syndrome: Men Who Have Never Grown Up.* New York: Dodd Mead.
Kimata, F. 2002. "Everywhere *FLC.*" *Newtype USA* 5, no. 12.
Kimata, F. 2007. "Best of the Best!" *Newtype USA* 6, no. 3.
King, S. 2006. *Lisey's Story.* London: Hodder & Stoughton.
Kovalsky, J. 2004. "*Abenobashi: Magical Shopping Arcade,* Volume 1." *Newtype USA* 3, no. 9.
Lennert, D. K. 2002. "An Interview with Richard Williams." *Animation World Magazine.* http://mag.awn.com/index.php?ltype=search&sval=richard+williams&article_no=1291.
"*Mahoromatic: Automatic Maiden Vol. 03*: Review." 2005. *DVD Times.* http://www.dvdtimes.co.uk/content.php?contentid=56155.

Marc. 2003. "*Wings of Honneamise* Review." *AAW—Akemi's Anime World*. http://animeworld.com/reviews/honneamise.html.
Marc. 2005. "*Gunbuster* Review." *AAW—Akemi's Anime World*. http://animeworld.com/reviews/gunbuster.html.
Martin, T. 2006a. "*This Ugly Yet Beautiful World*— DVD 1: Falling Star." *Anime News Network*. http://www.animenewsnetwork.com/review/this-ugly-yet-beautiful-world/dvd-1.
Martin, T. 2006b. "*This Ugly Yet Beautiful World*— DVD 2: Eye of the Beholder." *Anime News Network*. http://www.animenewsnetwork.com/review/this-ugly-yet-beautiful-world/dvd-2.
Mays, J. 2003. "*FLCL* DVD 2: Review." *Anime News Network*. http://www.animenewsnetwork.com/review/flcl/dvd-2.
Meir, D. A. "Acting and Animation." http://www.cgpark.com.tr/cgpark/animation.htm.
Mikimoto, H. 2007. "A Different Direction." *Newtype USA* 6, no. 1.
Der Mond: The Art of Yoshiyuki Sadamoto. 2001. San Francisco: VIZ Media LLC.
Morikawa, K. "Learning from Akihabara: The Birth of a Personaopolis." http://japattack.com/main/?9=node/108.
Napier, S. 2001. *Anime from Akira to Princess Mononoke: Experiencing Contemporary Japanese Animation.* New York: Palgrave Macmillan.
"*Neon Genesis Evangelion* Review." 2004. *PopCultureShock.* www.popcultureshock.com/reviews.php?id=3024.
okama. 2007. "Interview." *Gunbuster 2* DVD, vol. 3 Booklet. Bandai Visual USA.
"On the Cut-Up." *Social Fiction.* http://www.socialfiction.org/cutup.html.
"Oné-sama." 2007. *Newtype USA* 6, no. 3.
"*Otaku no Video* DVD." *Right Stuf International.* 1997.
"*Otaku no Video*: Liner Notes." 1992. Wilmington, NC: AnimEigo. http://www.rightstuf.com/1-800-338-6827/catalogmgr/6lm9rjuXyDdjeuR31w/browse/item/56298/4/0/0.
Otsuki, T. 2006. "*Evangelion*: Second Impact." *Newtype USA* 5, no. 12.
Otsuki, T. 2007. "Back to Basics." *Newtype USA* 6, no. 2.
Patten, F. 2003. "*Kare Kano*, Volume 2." *Newtype USA* 2, no. 7.
Poitras, G. 2006. "The Word 'otaku' Today." *Newtype USA* 5, no. 12.
Pound, E. 1936. "The Chinese Written Character as a Medium for Poetry." Adapted from Ernest Fenollosa. Extracts from http://www.levity.com/digaland/celestial/fenollosa/fenollosa.html.
Redmond, D. 2003. *The World Is Watching: Video as Multinational Aesthetics 1967–1995.* Carbondale: Southern Illinois University Press.
"The Restoration." 2007. *Newtype USA* 6, no. 3.
Ross, C., and E. Gaede. 2002. "*His and Her Circumstances* Review." *T.H.E.M. Anime Reviews.* http://www.themanime.org/viewreview.php?id=123.
Rubenfeld, J. 2007. *The Interpretation of a Murder.* London: Headline Review.
Sadamoto, Y. 2007. "Interview." *Gunbuster 2* DVD, vol. 3 Booklet. Bandai Visual USA.
Saeki, S. 2006a. "Creator Profile: Shouji Saeki." *Newtype USA* 5, no. 6.
Saeki, S. 2006b. "Interview with *Anikuri*." *This Ugly Yet Beautiful World* DVD, vol. 3: "Red Swarm." ADV Films.
Samuels, D. 2007. "Let's Die Together — Why Is Anonymous Group Suicide So Popular in Japan?" *The Atlantic Monthly.* May.
Sarcasm-hime. 2002. "*Mahoromatic Automatic Maiden* Review." *Anime News Network.* http://www.animenewsnetwork.com/review/mahoromatic-automatic-maiden.
Sarkin, T. 2003. "*Mahoromatic*: Reader Review." *AAW—Akemi's Anime World.* http://animeworld.com/readerreviews/mahoromatic.html.
Sato, H. 2004. Interview in "Gainax turns 20!" *Newtype USA* 3, no. 9.
Sato, H. 2007. "Interview." *Gunbuster 2* DVD, vol. 3 Booklet. Bandai Visual USA.
Schweitzer, A. 1911. *J. S. Bach.* Trans. E. Newman. London: A. & C. Black.
"Scoot." "*The Wings of Honneamise*." *The Nihon Review.* http://www.nihonreview.com/anime/the-wings-of-honneamise/.
Sevakis, J. 2007. "Buried Treasure — Hideaki Anno Talks to Kids." *Anime News Network.* http://www.animenewsnetwork.com/buried-treasure/2007-05-03.
Shirane, H. 2005. "Performance, Visuality, and Textuality: The Case of Japanese Poetry." *Oral Tradition*, 20/2.
Soldano, A. "Time." *Gunbuster Top o Nerae!* http://www.gunbuster.it/.
Sontag, S. 2007. "Pay Attention to the Word." *The Guardian.* 17 March. http://books.guardian.co.uk/print/0,,329748149-99930,00.html.
Die Sterne. 2003. Tokyo: Kadokawa Shoten.

Takamura, K. 2006. "Profile: Kazuhiro Takamura." *This Ugly Yet Beautiful World* DVD, vol. 1 Bonus Insert. ADV Films.

Takeda, Y. 2005. *The Notenki Memoirs: Studio Gainax and the Men Who Created Evangelion*. New York: ADV Manga.

"Tamarro Forever Presents: *The Secret of Blue Water*." 2000. www.thesecretofbluewater.com/.

T.H.E.M. *Anime Reviews*. 2001. "*Nadia: Secret of Blue Water* Review." http://www.themanime.org/viewreview.php?id=221.

Toole, M. "*FLCL*." *anime jump!* http://www.animejump.com/index.php?module=prodreviews&func=showcontent&id=245.

Top 2! Perfect Book. 2007. Tokyo: Media Works.

Tsurumaki, K. 1997. "A Story of Communication." Interview. *The End of Evangelion Theatrical Program Book*. Trans. Bochan_bird. http://www.evaotaku.com/html/rcb-tsurumaki.html.

Tsurumaki, K. 2001. "Amusing Himself to Death." Interview by O. Thomas. *Akadot*. http://www.akadot.com/article.php?a=182.

Tsurumaki, K. 2007a. "Interview by Y. Izubuchi." *Gunbuster 2* DVD, vol. 1. Bandai Visual USA.

Tsurumaki, K. 2007b. "Interview." *Gunbuster 2* DVD, vol. 1 Booklet. Bandai Visual USA.

Tsurumaki, K., and U. Enokido. 2007. "Interview." *Gunbuster 2* DVD, vol. 3 Booklet. Bandai Visual USA.

Ubukata, T. 2007. "What's in a Word." *Newtype USA* 6, no. 2.

Ultimate FLCL: FAQ. 2007. *Ultimate FLCL: A FLCL Fan Site*. http://www.ultimateflcl.com/faq/.

"What's in a Name." 2007. *Newtype USA* 6, no. 8.

Wikipedia, the Free Encyclopaedia—*Otaku no Video*. http://en.wikipedia.org/wiki/Otaku_no_Video.

Wikipedia, the Free Encyclopaedia—*Rebuild of Evangelion*. http://en.wikipedia.org/wiki/Rebuild_of_Evangelion.

Williams, R. 2001. *The Animator's Survival Kit*. London: Faber & Faber.

Wong, A. 2006. "*Moe* Café." *Newtype USA* 5, no. 7.

Wong, A. 2007. "Social Distortion." *Newtype USA* 6, no. 4.

Zipes, J. 1998. *Happily Ever After: Fairy Tales, Children, and the Culture Industry*. London and New York: Routledge.

Index

Ah! My Goddess: Flights of Fancy 149
Aim for the Ace! 36
Air Gear 221
Akai, T. 6
All Purpose Cultural Cat Girl Nuku Nuku 155
Anno, H. 6, 7, 26, 51, 77, 108, 111
Aoki, Y. 220
Aono, S. 217
Appleseed 220
Aramaki, S. 220
Asaka, M. 175
Asami, T. 41
Austin, J.L. 202–203

Bach, J.S. 83, 101, 104
Barthes, R. 6, 36
Baudelaire, C. 19
Best Student Council 175
Blade Runner 36, 217
Blue Seed 218
Blue Seed Beyond 218
Boogiepop Phantom 139, 221
Bubblegum Crisis—Tokyo 2040 12, 219
bushido 54, 152

The Cat Returns 220
Le Chevalier D'Eon 50–52
Chobits 175
Chrono Crusade 218
Claymore 220
Cloth Road 194
Coleridge, S.T. 42
Cowboy Bebop: The Movie 220
Coyote Ragtime Show 146
Crest of the Stars 24

Daicon 3 7–8
Daicon 4 8–9, 57, 155, 220
Date, H. 218, 221
Death & Rebirth 59–60, 72, 78–100, 196
Derrida, J. 11–12
Dezaki, O. 36, 41, 57
The Difference Engine 41
D.N.Angel 221

Ebichu the Housekeeping Hamster 221
Einstein, A. 36, 189–190
Elemental Gelade 41, 175
Elfen Lied 139–40
The End of Evangelion 59–60, 67, 72, 90, 97, 99, 100–108, 219
Eureka Seven 175, 218, 221
Evangelion: 1.0—Black and White 219

Fafner 218
Fantastic Voyage 36
Fate/stay Night 148
FLCL 2, 3, 14, 22, 56, 69, 75, 118, 123–140, 142, 163, 179–180, 181, 203, 220, 221
Fujimoto, Y. 155
Fullmetal Alchemist 41, 218, 221
Furuhashi, K. 50, 52
Future Boy Conan 41, 57

Gasaraki 218
gattai 4, 75, 195–196
Gauche the Cellist 57
Genshiken 56
Ghost in the Shell 220
Ghost in the Shell 2: Innocence 220
Ghost in the Shell: S.A.C 220
Ghost in the Shell: S.A.C 2nd Gig 220
Gibson, W. 41
Gilgamesh 218
Gokinjo Monogatari 113
Godzilla 7
Gouda, H. 149
Grenadier 217
Gunbuster 1, 2, 3, 10, 14, 15, 26–39, 42, 43, 46, 49, 56, 57, 68, 112, 125, 129, 131, 142, 150, 152, 155, 156, 179, 181, 183, 184, 185, 188, 189, 190, 196, 198, 199, 200, 203, 217
Gunbuster 2 1, 2, 4, 13, 32, 22, 131, 151, 152, 165, 178–195, 203, 217, 220
Gunbuster vs. Diebuster: Aim for the Top Gattai Movie 2, 4, 195–200

Habara, N. 218, 221
Hamazaki, H. 218
Hand Maid May 148
Happy Lesson 175
henkei 195–196
Hayashi, H. 12, 219
Heinlein, R.J. 36
hikikomori 58
Himawari! 195
Hiraike, Y. 175
Hirano, T. 33, 150
Hirata, T. 218
His and Her Circumstances 2, 3, 13, 14, 15, 22, 47, 56, 68, 111–122, 128–129, 142, 152, 171, 203, 219
Howl's Moving Castle 41

Ide, Y. 147, 164
Ikeda, M. 220
Ikehata, T. 57
Imaishi, H. 74–75
InuYasha 220
Ishiguro, N. 57
Ishihara, T. 220
Ishiodori, H. 122
Iwasaki, Y. 149, 175

Jaws 155

Kabuki 21
Kageyama, S. 195
Khara 108
Kajishima, M. 175
Kamegaki, H. 221
kami 204
Kamichu! 175, 194
Kamiya, J. 218
Kamiyama, K. 114, 220
Kanbe, M. 139
Kashimashi—Girl Meets Girl 219
Kawamori, S. 24, 219
kawaii 146, 162
Kiki's Delivery Service 42
Kiley, D. 33, 156

227

Kimura, S. 148
K.O. Beast 221
Kobayashi, O. 113
Kon, S. 139
Kondou, Y. 220
Konno, N. 220
Kou, Y. 218
Koujina, H. 217
Kubrick, S. 21
Kyo Kara Maho! 220
Kyouda, T. 175, 218, 221

Laputa: Castle in the Sky 12, 41, 42
lolicon 147
Lost World 41
Love Hina 149
Lucky Star 217
Lupin 3: The Castle of Cagliostro 57, 132

Macross Plus—The Movie 24, 219
Madhouse Studios 5
Magical Shopping Arcade Abenobashi 2, 3, 13, 56, 131, 147, 154–159, 163–164, 203, 220
Mahoromatic—Automatic Maiden 2, 3, 4, 13, 14, 17, 22, 27, 30, 32, 33, 56, 69, 141–153, 156, 164, 174, 203, 220
Mahoromatic—Automatic Maiden: Something More Beautiful 146
Mahoromatic—Automatic Maiden: Summer Special 147
Maison Ikkoku 57
Making Breakthrough Gurren Lagann 1, 2, 74–77, 204
maniakku 16
Mashimo, K. 220
Masunari, K. 175, 194, 221
The Matrix 151
Matsumoto, L. 41, 57, 75
mecha 7, 12, 13, 26, 27, 28, 29, 32, 33, 34, 35, 56, 61, 62, 66–67, 68, 75–76, 125, 127, 128, 132–133, 135, 137, 139, 140, 142, 144, 149, 152, 154–155, 167–168, 170, 171, 180, 182–183, 192, 194, 195, 196, 198, 202, 203, 219, 221
The Melancholy of Haruhi Suzumiya 220
The Melody of Oblivion 2, 151–152, 204, 220
Metropolis (manga) 41
Metropolis (movie) 41, 217
Minipato 114
Miyazaki, G. 169
Miyazaki, H. 5, 12, 41, 43, 131–132
Miyazaki, N. 175
Mizushima, S. 41, 218, 221
Mobile Suit Gundam 12, 57, 126, 218
Mochizuki, T. 219

moe 12, 16–17, 146–147, 148, 152, 162–163, 180–181, 183, 195, 202
MoonPhase 146
Mori, K. 157
Mori, T. 55
Morita, H. 220
Moriwaki, M. 221
Motonaga, K. 175
Murata, M. 218
Murayama, K. 218
Mushi-Shi 193
My-HiME 217
My Neighbour Totoro 36
My-Otome 217

Nadia: The Secret of Blue Water 2, 3, 10, 13, 14, 21, 22, 31, 40–52, 56, 57, 60, 112, 131, 203
Nadia of the Mysterious Seas 217
Nagahama, H. 193
Nagahama, T. 41, 57
Nagaoka, Y. 24
Nakamura, R. 41, 139
Nakanishi, N. 219
Naruto 221
Nausicaä of the Valley of the Wind 36, 192
Negima! 175
Negishi, H. 221
Neon Genesis Evangelion 1, 2, 3, 5, 10, 13, 14, 15, 17, 24, 27, 31, 32, 37, 42, 43, 47, 49, 56, 57, 59–74, 76–110, 112, 113, 116, 118, 121, 127, 128, 129, 131, 134, 140, 142, 144, 145, 155, 156, 163, 167, 183–184, 192, 203, 218–219
Nerima Daikon Brothers 220
Next World 41
ninjutsu 221
Nishikiori, H. 151
Nishimura, J. 219, 220, 221
Noh 21
Nonaka, T. 146

Obara, M. 217
Ogura, H. 22, 138
Oh My Goddess! 149
Okada, T. 6, 8, 55, 57
okama 194
Okamura, T. 221
onmyou 156–157
Osaka 7, 8
Oshii, M. 12, 57, 220
otaku 16–17, 53–58
Otaku no Video 2, 3, 17, 53–58, 68, 126, 152, 155, 203
Otomo, K. 41
Otsuka, M. 150
Otsuki, T. 108–109

Paradise Kiss 113
Paranoia Agent 139
Patlabor 1: The Mobile Police 12, 217
Patlabor 2: The Movie 12, 217

Patlabor WXIII: Movie 3 217
Peach Girl 122
Pessoa, F. 12
Petite Eva 219
Petite Princess Yucie (a.k.a. *Puchi Puri Yucie*) 2, 10, 33, 150–151, 203
Piano: The Melody of a Young Girl's Heart 220
The Place Promised in Our Early Days 24
Please Teacher! 147, 164, 175
Pound, E. 18–19
Princess Mononoke 131
Production I.G 5
Puss-in-Boots 128, 220

Ranma 1/2 219
Rebuild of *Evangelion* 108–110
The Rime of the Ancient Mariner 42
Rintaro 41, 217
R.O.D [Read or Die]—The TV 221
Rose of Versailles 57
Royal Space Force: The Wings of Honneamise 2, 3, 9–19, 14, 15, 20–25, 26, 42, 43, 56, 57, 60, 131, 152, 203
Rumbling Hearts 121–122, 165

Sadamoto, Y. 181
Saeki, S. 162–163, 175–176
Sailor Moon 149, 165
Sakura Wars 41
Samurai Champloo 220
Samurai Deeper Kyo 221
Sato, J. 149, 165
Sawai, K. 219
Scott, R. 36, 217
Serial Experiments Lain 139
Shibayama, T. 219
Shinbo, A. 146
Shinkai, M. 24, 37
shoujo 12, 27, 29, 43, 146, 147, 152, 162–163, 195, 202
Shounen Onmyouji 157
Solty Rei 175
Space Battleship Yamato 7, 36, 41, 57, 75
Star Trek 7–8
Star Wars 7
Starship Troopers 36
Steamboy 41
Sterling, B. 41
Sudo, N. 220
Super Dimensional Fortress Macross 57
Suzuki, A. 175

Takahashi, R. 218
Takahashi, Y. 173
Takahata, I. 57
Takayama, F. 217
Takeda, Y. 6, 7, 8, 9, 10
Takemoto, Y. 217

www.ingramcontent.com/pod-product-compliance
Ingram Content Group UK Ltd.
Pitfield, Milton Keynes, MK11 3LW, UK
UKHW050457150426
5217IPUK00025B/1732